EDMUND SPENSER

Selected Letters and Other Papers

FORTHCOMING FROM OXFORD UNIVERSITY PRESS

The Oxford Edition of the Collected Works of Edmund Spenser

General Editors: Patrick Cheney, Elizabeth Fowler, Joseph Loewenstein, David Lee Miller, Andrew Zurcher

Volume 1: 1569–1590
Volume 2: 1591–1596
Volume 3: 1596–

EDMUND SPENSER

Selected Letters and Other Papers

EDITED BY
CHRISTOPHER BURLINSON
AND
ANDREW ZURCHER

OXFORD
UNIVERSITY PRESS

OXFORD

UNIVERSITY PRESS

Great Clarendon Street, Oxford, OX2 6DP,
United Kingdom

Oxford University Press is a department of the University of Oxford.
It furthers the University's objective of excellence in research, scholarship,
and education by publishing worldwide. Oxford is a registered trade mark of
Oxford University Press in the UK and in certain other countries

First published 2009

Published in the United States of America by Oxford University Press
198 Madison Avenue, New York, NY 10016, United States of America

British Library Cataloguing in Publication Data
Data available

Library of Congress Cataloging in Publication Data
Data available

ISBN 978–0–19–955821–6

Acknowledgements

THIS book could not pass without some saluting of the colleagues, friends, and family who have made that passage possible. Patricia Boulhosa, Amelia Zurcher, Jon Stainsby, and Jane Grogan have, over the years, discharged the parts of tall readers, cheering us as much by their enthusiasm as by their helpful criticisms. Participants at the British and Irish Spenser Seminar courteously tolerated and discussed our work from year to year, for which we owe our respects particularly to Colin Burrow, Richard McCabe, Deana Rankin, Pat Coughlan, and Tom Herron. Dan Wakelin and Richard Beadle supplied manuscript advice, and to Elizabeth Fowler, Joe Loewenstein, David Miller, and Patrick Cheney we are duly grateful for thoughtful shepherding. The Master and Fellows of Emmanuel College, the Master and Fellows of Jesus College, and the President and Fellows of Queens' College, Cambridge, have created the conditions for the labours of all hours, and our colleagues there have our gratitude for their sufferance and support. The staff at the Cambridge University Library, the British Library, the Lambeth Palace Library, the Bodleian Library, and especially the National Archives at Kew have been unfailingly generous to us in all our work on this project. At Oxford University Press we have been conscientiously cajoled and comforted by Jacqueline Baker and Andrew McNeillie, and both Claire Thompson and Mary Worthington have by their expert offices outstripped our means to thank them for them. Una Murphy, an expert in seventeenth-century steganography, produced an excellent first draft of the cipher sheet. We have thanked one another already.

To Patricia Boulhosa and Fionnuala Murphy, upon whose doubled patience this book has proved grossly incumbent in every way, we commit all.

Contents

APPENDICES

List of Illustrations

All photographs appear by kind permission of the National Archives: Public Record Office.

List of Maps

Note on Maps

SOME sixteenth-century features of the landscape (e.g. woods, rivers) and human habitations (e.g. towns, castles) have survived, and their modern positions noted here. The locations of towns, forts, estates, houses, and other places both natural and built have been determined by recourse to several sources:

Sir William Petty, *Hibernia Regnum*, known as the 'Down Survey' of the Baronies of Ireland, 1655–58, facsimile repr. of original papers in the Bibliothèque Nationale (Southampton: Ordnance Survey Office, 1908).

John Speede, *The Invasions of England and Ireland with all their Civill Warrs Since the Conquest* (London, 1600).

Maps of the Escheated Counties in Ireland, 1609, facsimile repr. (Southampton: Ordnance Survey Office, 1861).

In some cases, where cartographic records provide little or no information, the positions indicated here should be treated as provisional; in these cases, the place-name is indicated in italics. We have generally given place-names in the manuscript spellings in which they occur in the present volume's letters; where these spellings differ markedly from modern conventions, we have supplied the conventional Anglicization of the name in parentheses. (The choice of English forms both of place and family names is a practical consequence of the English colonialist nature of this epistolary collection.)

List of Abbreviations

THE following abbreviations are used throughout the text and notes:

BL   British Library
Carew   *Calendar of Carew Manuscripts*
CSPD   *Calendar of State Papers, Domestic*
CSPF   *Calendar of State Papers, Foreign*
CSPI   *Calendar of State Papers, Ireland*
Co.   County
FQ   *The Faerie Queene*
HH   Hatfield House
It.   Italian
Lat.   Latin
LPL   Lambeth Palace Library
NA   The National Archives
ODNB   *Oxford Dictionary of National Biography*
OED   *Oxford English Dictionary*
PRONI   Public Record Office of Northern Ireland
SC   *The Shepheardes Calender*
SP   State Papers
A view   *A view of the present state of Ireland*

For ease of reading, documents from the State Papers collection of the Public Record Office, part of the National Archives of the United Kingdom, are throughout the book cited in their abbreviated form. Thus the document

The National Archives: Public Record Office: State Papers 63/86/83

appears in our references and notes simply as

SP 63/86/83

where the first number indicates the class (here, Ireland: Elizabeth I), the second the volume number, and the third the item number. In the case of enclosures, the reference includes four numbers (e.g. SP 63/90/37/1), where the fourth denotes the enclosure associated with the main item. Documents from other collections in the Public Record Office are cited in the normal way.

Unless otherwise noted, all quotations from Spenser's texts are from *The Works of Edmund Spenser: A Variorum Edition*, ed. Edwin Greenlaw et al., 11 vols. (Baltimore: Johns Hopkins University Press, 1932–57). Passages from *The Faerie Queene* are cited in the form I.ii.33, where the first number is the book, the second the canto, and the third the stanza. Other texts (including *A view of the present state of Ireland*) are cited by poem or line number, as appropriate.

MAP I. Spenser's Ireland, *c.* 1580.

Notes:
Ballinegarragh, Ballinfahnigh, Ballyganim, Rossack, and (in all likelihood) Kilballywerye were all located near to Kilcolman.
Places in italics indicate uncertainty regarding exact location.

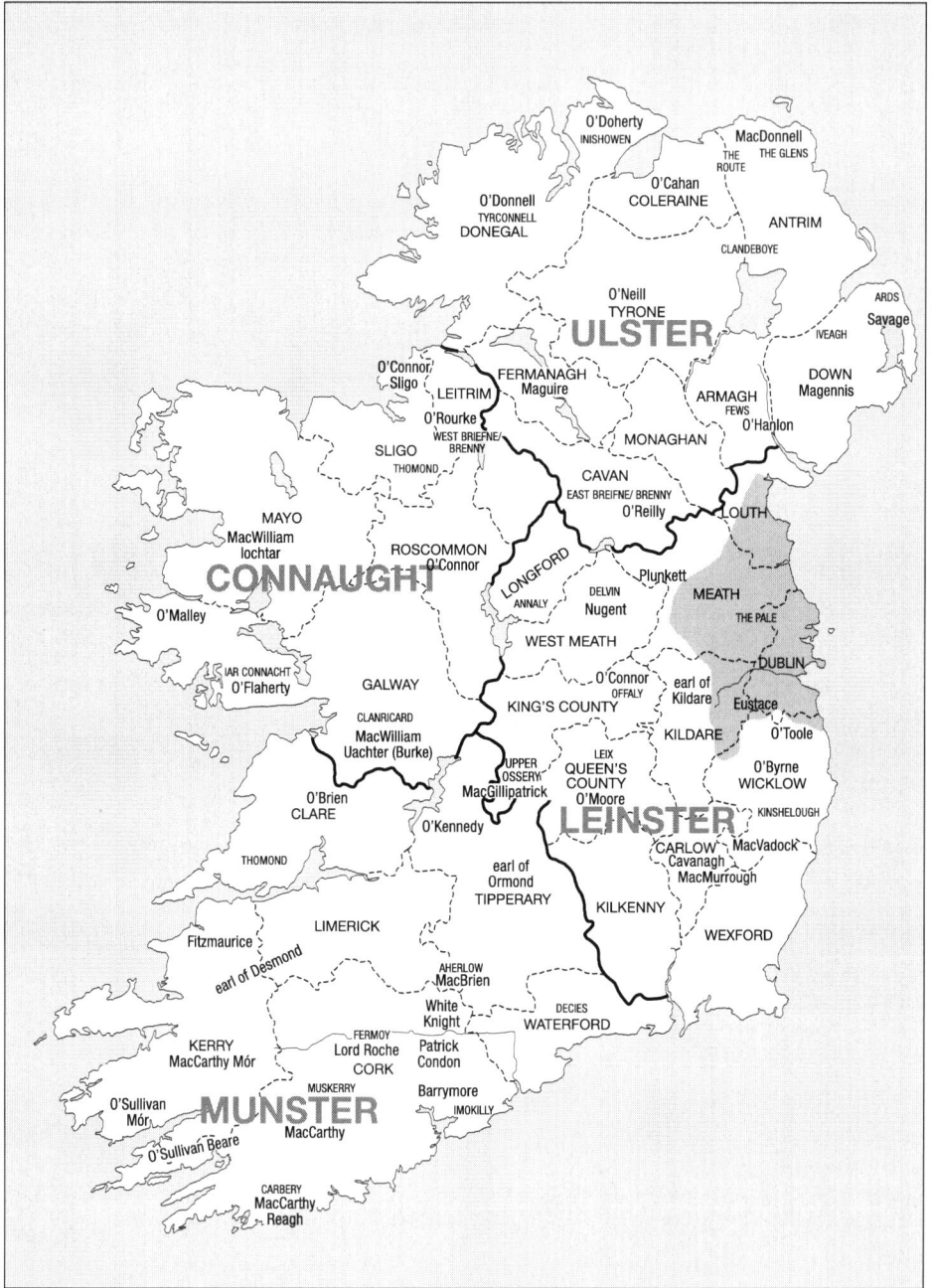

MAP 2. Some lordships and families in Ireland, *c.* 1580.

Introduction

On 13 August 1580, Arthur Lord Grey of Wilton embarked from Chester aboard the *Handmaid*, Queen Elizabeth's stoutest ship in the Irish service, for Ireland. With him probably travelled his new personal secretary, Edmund Spenser. Grey was destined for two years of toil, loss, and disgrace, as he would signally fail in the service expected of him by his mistress, the Queen. Ironically enough, it would be in his commitment to the 'service'—in the sense of 'military service'—that he would most offend her, heaping up expense and acrimony in his determination to force through a military solution to the intransigent problems of social and political reform facing the Elizabethan government of Ireland. But if the *Handmaid* carried on that day in mid-August one hopeful servant whose 'service' would undo him, it also carried another servant whose hand-service would purchase him, at least for a time, a much brighter future. The official letters and other papers that Spenser copied, subscribed, and addressed for Lord Grey, like those he prepared for his later masters the Norris brothers, governors in Munster, record both histories of service at once: that of the soldier-statesman to his queen, and that of the secretary to his master. It is the first purpose of this volume to present these paired histories, telling the story of Elizabeth's Irish governors during the period between 1580 and 1589 as a way of understanding the history of Spenser's own service during the same period—a period that would culminate in one of the most abruptly productive decades of poetic composition ever achieved by an English poet.

The manuscripts documenting Spenser's secretarial service in Ireland, first to the Lord Deputy and then to the Council in Munster, might readily be called ancillary, even marginal texts. At their best, they show Spenser writing on behalf of other men, and for that reason a reader or student of his poetry might initially consider the fact of their existence to be interesting, but not their contents. Grey was preoccupied with waging war, victualling his army, repairing his fortifications, prosecuting traitors, arbitrating disputes, and controlling the crown finances in Ireland. By contrast, the first three books of *The Faerie Queene*, though they must have been completed around 1589, at about the time that this manuscript chronicle of Irish service comes to an end, ostensibly concern holiness, temperance, and chastity. And yet, as we will go on to argue below, this corpus of manuscript remains constitutes a remarkably rich soil for the study not only of Spenser's biography, but of the poetry that would grow from and in it. Many of the concerns dominating modern criticism of Spenser's work—patronage and politics, cultural anthropology and colonialism, allegory and interpretation, moral virtue, authorship, language, violence and power, faith and religion—are similarly shot through the history of his secretarial service in Ireland during the 1580s. These manuscripts help us to chart and date Spenser's movements, and introduce us to the cast of bureaucrats, soldiers, gentlemen, and farmers with whom of necessity he consorted; but they also reveal the landscapes cultural and physical, the ideas, and the arguments to which during this formative period he was exposed. It is the second purpose of this volume to bring into focus the suggestive and fertile correspondences between Spenser's documented Irish experiences and the preoccupations of his poetry.

The history of English colonial government in Ireland during this period proves so apt and persuasive an analogue to the study of Spenser's life and literary career precisely on account of its particularity, its diversity, its activity, and the copiously written character of the records that preserve and constitute it, but these very qualities also give it a forbidding complexity. Even to a student or critic well versed in historical research, the prospect of encountering and attempting to compass the history of Tudor Ireland can appear daunting. This was a land not of a single nation, but of four peoples: the Irish, the Old English (descendants of the Anglo-Norman conquerors of the twelfth century), the New English settlers and administrators of the sixteenth century, and the Scots who flooded seasonally into the country, from year to year leaving a wash of mercenary galloglass in their wake. It was also a land with at least two political and cultural orders: the Irish families and septs, with their customary captains and tanists, as well as the English aristocracy, recently swelled by the addition of newly created baronies and earldoms for submissive Irish lords. Here the Reformation had succeeded far more equivocally than in England, leaving the country deeply polarized between practising adherents of the old Roman faith and the evangelical (and more than lightly armed) new Protestants. Wars and intrigues in sixteenth-century Ireland quickly undid treaties and alliances. Famines and plagues could depopulate whole provinces in a few seasons. In language, dress, means of living, and in countless other ways, the peoples of early modern Ireland offer to the modern reader a dizzying diversity, one that makes the study of Spenser's manuscript remains not a casual but a serious investment. It will be the third and last main purpose of this volume (and chiefly of this introduction) to provide for the reader that contextual historical basis upon which a profitable reading of Spenser's letters and other papers must be constructed.

Before entering into this introductory discussion of sixteenth-century Ireland, it is necessary to observe two special caveats. First, the letters edited for this book are, by definition, English in both language and outlook. Further, because the nature of the surviving written records of sixteenth-century Ireland predominantly favour the English language (over Latin and Irish), and were generally written by English officials, soldiers, clerics, settlers, and tradesmen, nearly all of the sources we have cited in our explication of and annotations to Spenser's letters and papers are similarly English in language and in outlook. Other sources, and other historiographical methods, do exist that would allow readers interested in the history of this period to reconstruct a fuller, more balanced view of the confrontations and cooperations, the antagonisms and affinities between the Elizabethan English and the Irish; our own account is not intended to meet this need, but to give an account of the immediate (that is to say, mostly English) context of Spenser's Irish experiences. This bias in our material has substantial consequences, and it will be worth making a separate brief apology for one of them. The language we have found it expedient to adopt—in fact, almost impossible not to adopt—in our commentary on the people, events, and arguments of the time is the language of the documents we are editing. While we have of course been able to dispense with pejorative terms like 'wild Irish', 'scumme', and 'churls', of almost equal repugnance—because of a consistently colonialist character— is the general register of Grey's diction in its verbs, epithets, metaphors, abbreviations, and so on. Spenser, like Grey and most of the rest of the English administration in Ireland, would have called the Earl of Desmond a rebel, traitor, and outlaw in 1580, nor does he hesitate to use such language on the few occasions on which we see him speaking for himself. The diction of Spenser's colonialist perspective abounds in *A view of the present state of Ireland*, as it does in one of the few personal documents to survive in his hand, the 'Bill against Lord Roche' (No. 45, below, SP 63/147/16), in which he accuses Roche of maintaining 'one Keadagh Okelly a proclaymed Traitour', and of having associations with numerous 'Rebelles'. Where we use such descriptive and nominative terms, inflected as they are by the colonial ideology of Spenser and his fellow New English administrators and planters, we do so instrumentally, to make clear the meaning of the documents and the connections between them; wherever possible, of course, we have attempted to draw our readers' attention to such inflections. We must, as we begin, simply ask our readers to be alert to the ideological skew in the documents themselves, as well as in our commentary, and remember always that, generally speaking, only one side of a very complex story has survived.

'Beinge as nere then as anie': Spenser's Ireland, 1580–1599

Grey served in Ireland for two years, Spenser (in his secretarial capacity) for closer to ten; but most of the officials, both English and Irish, and even many of the soldiers serving under Grey made the Irish service their career, and Ireland was their home. More importantly, perhaps, the policies and broader military history of the period were things Grey inherited, and had little chance to change before his tenure ended. For these reasons, an understanding of the political, military, and social context of the letters and papers in this volume must be based upon at least a loose acquaintance with the broader historical and cultural currents of the period, and upon a considered respect for the extreme conditions of Irish military, political, and social life—so different from his contemporary England that, as Spenser wrote in *A view of the present state of Ireland*, it almost changed his master's nature.[1]

A new English engagement with Ireland was forged and stamped by the tumultuous events of the middle of Henry VIII's reign.[2] In 1534, the rebellion of the Earl of Kildare's brother, 'Silken' Thomas Fitzgerald, led the King to break a hundred years of Geraldine suzerainty in Ireland, and install an English deputy as chief governor in the Earl's place; this adminis-trative revolution was consistent with the accelerating Tudor centralization of state power, but also reflected the Henrician government's exposure after the break with Rome; the Fitzgeralds had consolidated support for their rebellion in 1534 by pleading the cause of religion, and Thomas Cromwell was only too aware of the dangers posed to England by a hostile Ireland still affected to Rome. The Lord Deputies sent over by Henry VIII alternated between military aggression determined to ward the island from Irish rebellion and invasion from the continent, and policies of conciliation aimed at unifying English and Irish cultural, political, and religious prac-tices. Sir William Skeffington and Lord Leonard Grey, the first of Henry's viceroys, led repeated campaigns into Ulster and Connaught, and laid the foundations for the Elizabethan garrisons that would so dominate Grey's military policy in the 1580s. Sir Anthony St Leger, appointed in 1540 after the arrest and execution of Lord Leonard Grey, adopted a much more

---

[1] Answering the charge that Lord Grey was a bloody governor, Irenius defends the natural goodness of one 'whom whoe that well knewe, knewe to be moste gentle affable Lovinge and temperate. But that the necessitye of that presente state of thinges forced him to that violence and allmoste Changed his verye naturall disposicion' (ll. 3327–30).

[2] For a persuasive account of 1534 as a turning point in Irish political and cultural history, see D. B. Quinn and K. W. Nicholls, 'Ireland in 1534', in T. W. Moody, F. X. Martin, and F. J. Byrne, eds., *A New History of Ireland*, vol. iii: *Early Modern Ireland 1534–1691* (Oxford: Clarendon Press, 1978), 1–38.

pacific programme of political and social reform, pushing through legislation in 1541 to redefine Henry VIII as king rather than simply lord of Ireland, and inaugurating a policy of 'surrender and regrant' by which Irish lords, having given up their Irish territories and titles, were recreated peers on the English model and tenants to the King. By war, by statute, and by treaty, these Henrician deputies sought to anglicize Ireland in legal, economic, and cultural terms.[3]

The alternation between martial and political rule continued under Edward VI and Mary, during whose reigns St Leger was twice recalled to make temporary room for the soldiers Sir Edward Bellingham and Sir James Croft, and twice reappointed, to the satisfaction of many Irish and Old English lords. Croft nearly weathered a serious economic crisis, a consequence of the devaluation of the currency that left the Dublin government practically paralysed; St Leger returned under Mary in 1553 to a much more stable situation and departed again (in 1556) before the Irish Parliament's creation of the first in a long series of troubled English plantations, in 1557, based in the newly shired Queen's and King's Counties (Leix and Offaly, respectively), and supported by the fortified towns of Maryborough and Philipstown. Plantations continued to feature in Elizabethan plans for Ireland, and in the strenuous resistance of Irish and Old English magnates—the attempts of Sir Thomas Smith to plant the Ards in 1572–3, and of the Earl of Essex to colonize Antrim in 1574–5, stand out as exemplary later failures of this policy, while the Munster plantation carved out of the Earl of Desmond's lands after 1583 collapsed into the Nine Years' War. St Leger also left Ireland before the most celebrated of his Anglicizations—Conn O'Neill, captain of Ulster and first Earl of Tyrone—saw his lordship broken up by a second-generation fission between old- and new-style claims to title and power. Under the deputyships of the Earl of Sussex (1556–65) and Sir Henry Sidney (1565–71), Ulster was riven by faction as first Shane O'Neill, and then Turlough Luineach, claimed primacy by the ancient Irish custom of tanistry, attempting to exclude Conn O'Neill's designated heir by the English tenure, Matthew Baron of Dungannon, and his son Hugh O'Neill. While Sidney broke the ground for effective new English presidencies in Connaught and Munster, by the time of his recall in 1571 it was clear that Ulster could not be governed by the pacific policies developed by St Leger. New strategies were required.

---

[3] See 28 Hen. 8 cap. 15, which prescribed conformity in language and dress. In exchange for their new English tenures, Irish lords were invariably required to anglicize their lordships in far-reaching and unlikely ways. For the articles and conditions imposed on O'Neill at his creation as first Earl of Tyrone in 1542, see SP 63/10/81 and 63/10/82.

In the years immediately before Grey's and Spenser's arrival in Dublin, two significant developments occurred in the English government of Ireland, which would have far-reaching consequences for Grey's deputy-ship, and Spenser's life in Ireland. Under the Earl of Essex and career soldiers like Sir Humphrey Gilbert, as well as the new provincial presidents Sir William Drury (in Munster) and Sir Nicholas Malby (in Connaught), the English administration returned decisively in the 1570s to the heavy-handed and sometimes brutal militarism that had characterized Lord Leonard Grey's administration. Essex was personally responsible for two barbaric pieces of 'service' that would overshadow anything the comparatively phlegmatic Grey of Wilton would do. In November 1574, having invited the Clandeboye lord Brian MacPhelim O'Neill, along with his wife, brother, and 200 men, to a Christmas celebration at his camp at Belfast, Essex surprised them at the banquet, massacred O'Neill's men, and carted off O'Neill himself, his wife, and his brother to execution in Dublin Castle.[4] Six months later he commanded Sir Francis Drake and Captain John Norris during the infamous Rathlin Island massacre, in which the English forces slaughtered 200 of the guard of the Rathlin castle, and then killed up to 300 men, women, and children of the MacDonnells who had taken refuge in the island's caves.[5] Essex did not hesitate to mingle this brutality with conventional diplomacy,[6] and it was in this period, too, that the English government developed their second new strategy—a political one—for coping with the fractious resurgence of Gaelic and Anglo-Irish resistance to English cultural and political hegemony. The policy was simple: given that the next generation of Irish and Anglo-Irish heirs had fragmented, claiming contesting titles by both Irish and English customs of descent and election, the English governors decided to seize their opportunity by helping families and septs across Ireland to break down and fight within themselves. Under Malby in Connaught, as under Bagenal and Essex in Ulster, the New English administration sought to divide and rule.[7]

[4] See SP 63/48/52/3, 63/48/52/4, 63/48/52/5, and 63/48/57. SP 63/48/57/1 is the copy of a proclamation that Essex apparently disseminated at the time, giving a strongly inflected account of Sir Brian MacPhelim's treasonous actions, and claiming that he had been intending to assassinate Sir Nicholas Malby at a supper.
[5] See SP 63/52/77, 63/52/78, and 63/52/79. Essex's smug commendations of Norris for the slaughter of Sorley Boy MacDonnell's family, while MacDonnell himself looked on impotently from the mainland, are as sickening as they are revealing: this was personal as well as brutal warfare.
[6] In fact, Essex was in negotiations with Sorley Boy MacDonnell just a week before the massacre of his family at Rathlin; see SP 63/52/70, a letter of 23 July 1575 in which Essex reported to Walsingham that he had advised Sorley Boy to travel into England to negotiate directly with the Queen for a grant of land and title.
[7] The celebrated first experiment with this policy was the calculated support of rival claimants for English and Irish titles in Ulster. Both Shane O'Neill and Turlough Luineach O'Neill—O'Neills in

Grey's arrival in Ireland in the summer of 1580 coincided with a sudden upsurge in the intensity, geographical range, and ideological conviction of Irish and Anglo-Irish resistance to the Dublin government. In Munster James Fitzmaurice Fitzgerald, the 'Arch-traitor' of his day, had returned from nearly five years of canvassing for support on the continent, to raise the Pope's banner in the south-west. While his own rebellion was short-lived—he was killed by Tibbot Burke in the late summer of 1579—Sir John of Desmond had since then taken up his mantle, and was attempting to unify a Munster-wide rebellion in the cause of a Catholic Ireland. Desmond's relations with his brother, the Earl of Desmond, had always been cagey, but Lord Justice Pelham (who immediately preceded Grey as English governor of the island) had driven the Earl into rebellion by proclaiming him the year before. By the end of August, the Earl and his brother Sir John would be reinforced by more than 600 Spanish and Italian soldiers, dispatched on a papal commission. In Leinster, only weeks before Grey's arrival, James Eustace, Viscount Baltinglass, had come out for the rebels, joining his forces with the new captain of the O'Byrnes in Wicklow, Feagh MacHugh O'Byrne. To the north Turlough Luineach stirred restively, watching for his advantage, and amassing a considerable power in the Scots mercenaries whose support, by virtue of his marriage to Agnes Campbell, sister of the Earl of Argyle, he enjoyed. As Grey would demonstrate within weeks of his landing, by temperament and conviction he was given to the sharp and definite resolutions promised by military confrontation. He would need to act swiftly, and almost simultaneously, in at least three theatres.

The first of Grey's expeditions went badly: taking the captains Sir Peter Carew, Thomas Audley, and Sir William Stanley south into Leinster, on 25 August Grey attempted to strike decisively at Feagh MacHugh O'Byrne in the soggy fastness of Glenmalure. The attempt failed, Grey losing thirty men including Audley and Carew.[8] Undaunted (Sir Nicholas Malby wrote to Walsingham that Grey was a Hercules in defeat[9]), within two weeks Grey had joined with Sir William Pelham and with Hugh O'Neill, Baron of Dungannon, to ride to Drogheda to confront Turlough Luineach. The Ulster lord, whose main ambition at this point seems to have been to enforce the obedience of his Ulster sub-lords ('urraghs') and thus confirm

Ulster after the death of Conn—claimed the headship by Irish custom; while the English continued to protect the young Hugh O'Neill, potential heir to the earldom of Tyrone, as a counterweight. Malby would follow a similar policy with the Burkes in Connaught, supporting one branch of the family for the Irish title of MacWilliam, and another for the earldom of Clanricard.

[8] See Stanley's account of the expedition, SP 63/75/83.
[9] SP 63/75/82.

himself as O'Neill,[10] retired from the conference with his force of almost 5,000 men, promising to observe the peace. Upon dispatches from Captain Thomas Clinton revealing the arrival of the papal force on the Dingle peninsula in Munster—which Grey disbelieved—the Deputy formed new bands and, in the opening days of October, marched with 800 men deep into Munster. Grey had assigned Admiral Sir William Winter and his deputy, Richard Bingham, to meet him at Dingle, bearing ordnance and victual for the army. Although the ships were initially separated in the same Atlantic storm that made the march to Munster a horrific ordeal, the ordnance secured, Grey's English force entrenched outside the Fort of Gold at Smerwick and besieged the papal troops; within days the invaders had surrendered without conditions, and nearly 600 of them were summarily slaughtered.[11]

The events of the first few crucible weeks of Grey's deputyship bear brief narration because they exemplify the policy and military realities, as well as the ethical and political problems, that would shape Spenser's secretarial experience in Ireland. Perhaps most obviously, they demonstrate the ruthless and almost casual violence on both sides of the conflict in early modern Ireland. This culture of violence was the direct legacy of Skeffington and Lord Leonard Grey, as mediated through the atrocities of Essex, though it was certainly reinforced by the readiness of the Irish to retaliate in kind. Acts of almost unimaginable cruelty were regularly per-formed in calculated ways to create terror and enforce submission. The 'short end' that Grey made of the papal soldiers at Smerwick was in part dictated by the conditions: with a force of only 800, he could hardly march 600 prisoners back to Dublin through inclement autumn weather, surrounded by enemies. But, as Spenser would later attest, his primary concern was to make of the foreign garrison an exemplary and terrifying spectacle—both to the Spanish and Italian soldiers who escaped, and to the Irish who hoped for future continental Catholic support.[12] In a theatre so

---

[10] It was traditional in most of the 'countries' of sixteenth-century Ireland for the captain or *taoiseach* to be known simply by the patronymic: O'Neill, O'Donnell, MacWilliam, etc., were men of the highest authority in their countries.

[11] Grey related the history of the expedition in detail to the Queen in a letter of 12 November; see No. 5, below (SP 63/78/29).

[12] See Spenser's discussion of the negotiations over the fort's surrender in *A view*, ll. 3360–88: it was not thought good, Spenser writes, to show the papal troops mercy, 'bothe for daunger of themselues if beinge saved, they shoulde afterwardes ioyne with the Irishe, and allso for terrour of the Irishe, who weare muche embouldened by those forreine succours, and allso put in hope of more er longe, theare was no other waie but to make that shorte ende of them which was made[.]' Geoffrey Fenton reported from Smerwick to Walsingham that Grey reserved some Spaniards from the slaughter in order that they might report in their countries how they had been betrayed by their Irish allies; see SP 63/78/38.

desensitized to violence, acts of terror had constantly to outdo one another for impact and extent, and the scale of the massacre at Smerwick gives us some indication of the distorted level to which such displays had attained. What is most surprising about this culture of violence, perhaps, is the way it was integrated with an intellectual, humanist outlook. Thomas Churchyard recounts in *A generall rehearsall of warres* (1579) how Sir Humphrey Gilbert had 'pacified' Munster in only six weeks in the autumn of 1569, effortlessly combining an account of Gilbert's tactics with a humanist apology on ethical grounds:

His maner was that the heddes of all those (of what sort soeuer thei were) whiche were killed in the daie, should bee cutte of from their bodies, and brought to the place where he incamped at night: and should there bee laied on the ground, by eche side of the waie leadyng into his owne Tente: so that none could come into his Tente for any cause, but commonly he muste passe through a lane of heddes, whiche he vsed *ad terrorem*, the dedde feelyng nothyng the more paines thereby: and yet did it bryng great terrour to the people, when thei sawe the heddes of their dedde fathers, brothers, children, kinsfolke, and freendes, lye on the grounde before their faces, as thei came to speake with the saied Collonell. Whiche chourse of gouernement maie by some bee thought to cruell, in excuse whereof it is to bee aunswered. That he did but then beginne that order with theim, whiche thei had in effecte euer tofore vsed toward the Englishe. And further he was out of doubte, that the dedde felte no paines by cuttynge of their heddes, accordyng to the example of *Diogenes*, who beyng asked by his freendes, what should be doen with hym when he died, answered in this sorte: Caste me on a dungill quod he, where vnto his freendes replied, saiyng: The Dogges will then eate you, his aunswere thereto was thus why then sette a staffe by me: Wherenvto thei aunswered, you shall not feele them, to whom he again replied with these woordes, what neede I then to care.[13]

Churchyard deliberately and elaborately expends his humanist learning not in defence of Gilbert's crime against the living—surely the nub of his cruelty—but rather in defence of his supposed crime against the dead. The absurdity of Churchyard's ironic, even cynical, apology foregrounds the ruthlessness of Gilbert's retributive violence against the Irish. His acknowledgement of the transactional nature of this terror gives the lie to his subsequent claim that 'by this course of gouernemente . . . there was muche blood saued', and 'through the terrour, whiche the people conceiued therby, it made short warres'.[14]

[13] Thomas Churchyard, *A generall rehearsall of warres, called Churchyardes Choise* (London: Edward White, 1579), sig. Q3ᵛ–Q4ʳ
[14] Ibid., sig. Q4ʳ.

Churchyard's representation of Gilbert's policies may seem extreme, but similar kinds of humanist arguments were adduced to explain and apologize for similar kinds of events—on the English side—throughout Spenser's period in Ireland. Lodowick Bryskett, a Sidney protégé and Spenser's fellow secretary in the Irish service, wrote ingeniously to Walsingham of Ireland as an old cloak too many times patched, that to be worn had to be renewed;[15] his allegory conceals the violent means by which such renewal would have to be effected. At his most lyrical Grey himself was hardly so literary, but his dispatches reveal the constant callousness to suffering to which Spenser must daily have been exposed; in April 1581, for example, Grey wrote to Walsingham in praise of Humphrey Mackworth:

Captayne Mackwoorthe hathe within this moonethe space putt too swoorde & executed very neere a hundrethe of the best of the Omoores, so as the rest of the sept hathe putt in pledge for theyr peacyble & good beehauior; this man certaynely dezerues greate estimation not onely for valure but goouernment, enter hym therfore I praye yow into yowr Cataloge of well deseruers. /
The oother garrisoones heere abowtes arr daylie nybbling vp theyr churles & straggling knaues which beeyng of no greate accounte I lyke not mootche too aduertiss of.[16]

Grey's attitude seems to have been that 'straggling' and loose people—those not 'putt in pledge', or tied by some contractual or social obligation to peaceful and settled living—simply required summary justice, without the need for further explanation or apology. In the same spirit he could report to the Privy Council in July 1581, concerning his return from a journey through Wicklow to Wexford, that he had spent a week 'hunting the Glinnes', putting in 'certein bandes' who:

burned and spoiled, all theire howses, and Cabans, and brought a pray, out of the middest of the fastnes, which was verye desperatly defended by the space of 2. or 3. howers, but not without losse to the rebelles of some of the best of theire horsemen, 10 kearne, and 30 otheres, and with litle hurte to ours or none at all.[17]

As historians have remarked, the tendency on both sides of the conflict during this period to resort to 'scorched earth' campaigning smacks of the brutal policies of General Sherman;[18] Grey's readiness to think of his enemy as quarry, and to treat the 'pray' of a few hundred head of cattle

---

[15] Bryskett to Walsingham, 2 March 1581, SP 63/81/5.
[16] No. 10, below (SP 63/82/6).
[17] SP 63/84/12.
[18] See G. A. Hayes-McCoy, 'The Completion of the Tudor Conquest and the Advance of the Counter-Reformation, 1571–1603', in Moody, Martin, and Byrne, *A New History of Ireland*, iii.94–141.

with more respect than 'churles & straggling knaues [. . .] of no greate accounte', takes this inhumanity a decisive step further.

The constant spectacle of state violence, and the constant threat of violence from Irish and Old English 'enemies'—much of it almost casual—obviously made a significant impression on Spenser during his secretarial service, for it found its way not only into his poetry, but into his analysis of Irish affairs in *A view of the present state of Ireland* (1596).[19] The massacre at Smerwick thus functions as an emblem for one aspect of Spenser's experience in Ireland. The encounter with Turlough Luineach at Drogheda in September 1580 functions as another kind of emblem, in this case for a political rather than a military perspective. The series of letters Spenser was given to copy as one of his first tasks in the Irish service, all of which would shortly be sent to Walsingham, concerned the changing situation in Ulster, where Turlough Luineach was using the general unrest around Ireland to assert his right to the O'Neill's traditional sub-lords, or urraghs.[20] The English policy of the preceding thirteen years, since the assassination of Shane O'Neill, had been to keep Turlough Luineach in check by refusing him the recognition, as well as the rights, of his Irish lordship. With an army of over 4,000 men, however, Turlough Luineach was right to think he could make his own terms. In riding to Drogheda not only with Sir William Pelham, but with Hugh O'Neill, Baron of Dungannon, Grey sought to demonstrate to Turlough Luineach that, despite his success in asserting his control over the Ulster lordship, the English would continue to back the son of Matthew, Baron of Dungannon, and grandson of Conn O'Neill, first Earl of Tyrone. This policy of fomenting factional struggle within Irish families and septs was one Grey's government actively embraced, disregarding the earlier, much more conciliatory policy of St Leger, by which Gaelic and Old English lords were given new grants of title under the English tradition, and expected to be obedient. Instead, Grey's government sponsored rivals for influence and power within families and within countries. Thus the Burkes were regularly goaded against one another, with competing claimants eventually granted political legitimacy according to incompatible power structures: Ulick Burke succeeded to the earldom of Clanricard, Richard Yn Yeren was recognized by the English government as MacWilliam, and his chief rival Richard MacOliverus was given a grant of lands and made

---

[19] The frequent beheadings, dismemberments, and slaughters of Books V and VI of *The Faerie Queene*, from Sanglier (V.i) to the Brigants (VI.xi), are a clear residue of Spenser's experience—unprecedented for their material brutality and almost comic hyperbole in any of Spenser's sources or analogues. These links are further discussed below (pp. lix–lxi).

[20] See Nos. 1 (SP 63/75/75), 2 (63/75/84), 3 (63/76/1), 4 (63/76/9), below, and SP 63/76/10.

sheriff.[21] For the same reason Colonel John Zouche (governor in Munster), in an almost inexplicable volte-face, in May 1582 achieved a devastating raid against David Barry, one of the chief and most ruthless rebels in Munster, and then promptly received his submission and granted him a protection; temporary leniency for Barry, Zouche reasoned, might help to draw support away from the Earl of Desmond.[22] This kind of Machiavellian temporizing was never condemned for its ethical bank-ruptcy, but Spenser himself argued forcefully against it, on practical grounds, in *A view of the present state of Ireland*: Irenius demands, rhetoric-ally, 'And that which is spoken of takinge Shane *Oneales* sonnes from him and settinge them vp againste [Tyrone] is a verie perilous Councell and not by anie meanes to be put in profe / for weare they let forthe and Coulde ouerthrowe him who shall afterwardes ouerthrowe them or what assurance Can be had of them.' He likens the policy to:

the Tale in Aesope of the wilde horse who havinge enmitye againste the stagge came to a man to desyre his ayd against his foe, who yielding therevnto mounted vpon his back and so following the stagge ere longe slue him but then when the horsse woulde haue him alighte, he refused but kepte him ever after in his service and subieccion Suche I doubte woulde be the profe of Shane Oneales sonnes Therefore it is moste daungerous to attempte anie suche plott. ffor even that very manner of plott was the meanes by which this Traytorous Earle is now made so greate, ffor when as the laste Oneale Called Terlagh Lenagh beganne to stande vppon tickle terme this fellowe then Called Baron of Donganon was sett vp a[s] it weare to bearde him, and Countenaunced and strengthened by the Quene so farr as that he is now hable to kepe her selfe playe.[23]

By 1596 Dublin's error in 'setting up' Hugh O'Neill would be manifest— as the second Earl of Tyrone and Arch-Rebel of the Nine Years' War, O'Neill eventually achieved enough power to lead the first truly national revolt against English government in Ireland; but during Grey's deputy-ship, manipulating faction was still perceived as a cutting instrument of Irish policy.

A third almost emblematic event of the first few months of Grey's deputyship is the sudden haste with which he threw over his plans, after the Smerwick massacre, for an expedition to Connaught, and instead raced back to Dublin. The specific piece of intelligence that caused Grey

---

[21] See SP 63/81/42/1, a copy of Malby's report to Grey concerning the wars in Connaught, forwarded to Walsingham.

[22] See SP 63/92/102 and 63/92/103, letters from Sir Warham Sentleger and John Meagh, Justice of Munster, to Walsingham.

[23] *A view*, ll. 3529–45.

so abruptly to alter his intentions has vanished, but it was undoubtedly connected with the subsequent arrest, on charges of treason, of both Sir Christopher Nugent, Baron of Delvin, and the Irish councillor Gerald Fitzgerald, Earl of Kildare.[24] Kildare had been left governor in Dublin in the Lord Deputy's absence, and Grey had repeatedly complained in his letters, while on campaign, that he could get no news of the Pale. He had no doubt been anxious to learn whether O'Neill was keeping the peace, and what was being done by Baltinglass and Feagh MacHugh O'Byrne. In the end, the whole of the subsequent month was discharged in the discovery of an extensive conspiracy to comfort Baltinglass; moreover, the committal of Delvin to prison in Dublin Castle in December led, in turn, to the revolt of his brother William Nugent, which itself spawned a conspiracy throughout the Pale that occupied most of the rest of Grey's deputyship. The consequences for the inner circle of New English and Old English administrators were serious: Sir Nicholas Nugent, Chief Justice of the Common Pleas in Ireland, was hanged at Trim in April 1582 for his alleged part on the periphery of his nephew William's rebellion.[25] Perhaps more importantly, Grey seems not to have appreciated the degree to which his view of the affair was constructed for him by Nugent's enemies in the Pale; the Dillon cousins, Sir Robert and Sir Lucas Dillon, appear to have been particularly anxious to engineer Nicholas Nugent's downfall, and indeed Robert Dillon (who took Nugent's deprived office of Chief Justice) was later investigated for alleged wrongdoing in the matter. Conspiracy and factionalism dogged Grey's deputyship from the moment of his arrival, and the secretary who copied for him not only letters, but judicial examinations, and whose own office of trust (as we shall see) required constant vigilance against spying and interception, could not have failed to observe and negotiate it.

This factionalism and conspiracy did not leave Grey himself untouched, and there is one final element—crucial to an understanding of his period in Ireland, and to an understanding of Spenser's role as his secretary—that emerges clearly from the weeks surrounding Smerwick. Grey wrote to Queen Elizabeth immediately after the taking of the fort that he had preserved about thirty of the best of the prisoners, and bestowed them upon his men. The custody of high-ranking prisoners was a lucrative prize after such a victory, for they could if kept charily be handsomely ransomed

---

[24] Geoffrey Fenton advertised Walsingham at the beginning of December that Grey changed his course 'to remedy the slack service of the Pale' (*CSPI 1575–84*, p. 273); see SP 63/79/3. In the same letter, Fenton noted Kildare's defaults, and urged that, with the Earl of Ormond (also a reputed sluggard in the service), he be recalled to England.

[25] See Grey's report of Nugent's trial and execution, No. 33, below (SP 63/91/22).

back to their homes. Such favours were traditionally in the Lord Deputy's gift, and Grey would later make strenuous representations for his right to engage in 'howse finding'—the practice of bestowing estates and houses upon his loyal servitors or key allies in the military or civil establishment. Spenser himself benefited from Grey's patronage on a number of occasions, not least when he received a 'custodiam' of 'the Newland' in Co. Kildare in 1582, a Eustace estate escheated, or forfeited, to the crown upon the rebellion of its original owner.[26] A subset of the Irish council—Malby, Geoffrey Fenton, and Adam Loftus, the Archbishop of Dublin and from 1581 the Chancellor—reported secretly to William Cecil, Lord Burghley in the late autumn of 1581 concerning the Lord Deputy's allegedly extravagant gifts to 'his men'; this very internecine conspiracy sought to undermine or bring down Grey's deputyship through allegations of faction-building, and the cultivation of personal patronage by corrupt largesse with the crown's resources. Spenser, the occasional beneficiary of Grey's alleged extravagance, was well positioned to observe the delicate distinctions attending Grey's role as both office-holder—a deputy dispensing the Queen's rewards—and lord in his own name—a powerful man seeking to attract a loyal cadre of private servants. This distinction between public and private selves—defined by patronage relations, implicated in complex negotiations between masters and servants, but above all tied to serious opportunities for gain and preferment—was, again, of very manifest importance to Spenser's later writing.

The first few weeks of Grey's deputyship, then, reveal in miniature four key strands that would dominate Spenser's experience of the Irish service during his time as Grey's secretary. In this violent, politic, factionally riven land of opportunity, Spenser observed at the closest possible vantage a succession of military campaigns against the Wicklowmen of Feagh MacHugh O'Byrne (1580), the Munster rebels and their continental allies (1580), the Cavanaghs (1581), Turlough Luineach and his Scots mercenaries (1581), and the O'Connors (1582). 'Beinge as nere then as anie', he took notes when Turlough Luineach's wife, the Scots noblewoman Agnes Campbell, crossed the Blackwater near Benburb to condition with Grey in July 1581;[27] he dispatched the messengers who sailed

---

[26] Spenser's custodiam of the land—a three-year right to enjoy the profits of the estate—is recorded in a book of Grey's gifts prepared as part of the defence he mounted against the Queen's displeasure; see SP 63/88/40/3. Spenser's eventual acquisition—at Whitsuntide in 1589—of the estate of Kilcolman and Rossack was probably also intimately connected with his later secretarial service to the Council of Munster; as we argue below (see pp. 215–16), the contested nature of the Kilcolman estate, which was also claimed by Lord Roche, Viscount Fermoy, made the property unattractive to anyone except a civil servant with powerful connections and a thorough legal knowledge.

[27] See No. 20, below (SP 63/85/5).

to England with the news that the Earl of Kildare had been committed to Dublin Castle on suspicion of treason in December 1580;[28] and, while serving as secretary to Sir Thomas Norris in Munster in 1587, he conspired with his fellow undertakers to seize a prize ship laden with canary wines, and captained it to Cork.[29] 'Beinge as nere then as anie', Spenser witnessed at first hand the relentless fevers that carried off most of the garrisons of Wicklow and of Askeaton in the winter of 1581.[30] He saw, read about, and copied dispatches on the terrible 1581–2 famine caused by the war in Munster—harrowingly recalled in Irenius's infamous account in *A view*.[31] He was there when Grey pitilessly burned the huts and 'cabans' of the Irish living in the glens south of the Pale;[32] he was probably in Dublin castle when Sir Henry Wallop and Adam Loftus, Lords Justice, ordered a trial by combat between Conor MacCormac O'Connor and Teig MacGillipatrick O'Connor, in which the latter killed the former before a crowd of spectators, beheaded his corpse, and offered the head to the governors on the point of his sword.[33] While we know with certainty much less about the places and dates of Spenser's Irish experiences between 1585 and his death in 1599, we can be sure from what does survive—the 1589 bill against Lord Roche, detailing systematic intimidation and harassment,[34] the provision for his tenant of a defensible haven in the bawn of Richardston, in the 'Grant to MacHenry'[35]—that Spenser's career as a gentleman undertaker in Munster required no less steel or cynicism than had his service under Grey. Spenser arrived in Ireland in August 1580 to discharge the office of a secretary; in the course of that employment, and in the offices and estates to which that employment led over the next two decades, he must constantly have been exposed to a series of military,

[28] See SP 63/79/24/1 and 63/79/26.
[29] See TNA: PRO HCA 13/26, fos. 335ʳ–336ʳ, depositions naming Spenser and Sir William Herbert in a complicated case of piracy that took place near Dinglecush in Munster; and BL MS Lansdowne 144, fo. 360ʳ, a letter from Sir Thomas Norris to Sir Julius Caesar, judge of the Admiralty, concerning the affair.
[30] See e.g. Grey's postscript to No. 15, below (SP 63/83/45), a letter to the Privy Council in which Grey reports the 'plauge, or infeccion' ravaging the bands in Wicklow and Wexford in the winter of 1581. In SP 63/84/3, Grey relates to Walsingham that he has had to discharge Captain Hoorde, whose men were nearly all dead of the fever.
[31] Sir Warham Sentleger reported to Burghley in April 1582 the staggering mortality from plague and famine in Cork, a city of a single street not an eighth of a mile long (see SP 63/91/41). Three days later Sentleger wrote to Sir John Perrot that 30,000 people had died in Munster in the preceding six months (SP 63/91/45). For Spenser's account, see *A view*, ll. 3248–70.
[32] See SP 63/84/12, Grey's account of his journey back from Wexford in summer 1581.
[33] These two leading men from their sept of the O'Connors had accused one another of treason. Their combat was held on 12 September 1583 in the castle yard in Dublin. See SP 63/104/69, Wallop's and Loftus's report to Walsingham describing the event.
[34] See No. 45, below (SP 63/147/16).
[35] See No. 46, below (BL Add. MS 19869).

political, social, and economic traumas far more exaggerated and distorted than anything he had known in England. This was life 'as nere then as anie'.

Cabinets, Codes, and Fair Copies: Secretary Spenser

The mode and mindset through which Spenser engaged with these aspects of 1580s Ireland must have been, to a considerable degree, those of his profession of private secretary. A modern reader might easily overlook the fundamentally and pervasively written nature of so much of early modern Irish political life, especially for an administrative officer in Spenser's position. The range of duties required of him—from personal attendance on the Lord Deputy (between 1580 and 1582) and the President or Vice-President of Munster (?1584–9), to the production of fair copies of letters and other documents, the filing and managing of correspondence and papers, and the bookkeeping, financial provisions for carriage and supplies, and other security measures attendant on the post—all turned around the production of written material, and must undoubtedly have kept Spenser constantly busy. Judging by the admittedly scanty and indirect evidence still extant, we can estimate, roughly, that something less than 10 per cent of Spenser's secretarial output survives from his years as secretary to Lord Grey. The bulk of Grey's surviving correspondence, which often contains enclosed copies of other documents, comes from what came to be known as the State Paper Office, a working repository in Westminster that ultimately included the state papers of the Queen, the Privy Council (and some of its members, such as the Earl of Leicester), Sir Francis Walsingham, and William Cecil, Lord Burghley.[36] The surviving manuscripts in Spenser's hand—including letters written, subscribed, addressed, and/or endorsed or annotated by him—were all, without exception, addressed to one of these four recipients. Judging from the evidence of No. 34, below (SP 63/91/26), a record of nine letters recently dispatched to Sir Francis Walsingham of which five now survive, and of SP 63/82/54/1, a similar

---

[36] During Elizabeth's reign, this was probably merely a filing room used and kept by the clerks of the Privy Council. This organized but fundamentally casual repository was subjected to systematic development under the stewardship of Thomas Wilson, one of James VI and I's secretaries, who petitioned for and received the dedicated service of filing clerks to help in the acquisition and classification of documents relating to recent crown business. One of Wilson's major coups was the liberation of a large proportion of the state papers of William Cecil, Lord Burghley, from Hatfield House after the death of Sir Robert Cecil; since Burghley seems himself to have appropriated many of the papers of Sir Francis Walsingham upon his death in 1591, Wilson's timely actions led to the collection and preservation of materials, relating to many departments, that had been addressed or otherwise directed to Walsingham, Burghley, the Privy Council, or the Queen. See M. S. Guiseppi, *Guide to the Contents of the Public Record Office*, 3 vols. (London: HMSO, 1963–8), i. 1–4.

summary of four recent letters to the Queen of which only one survives, we may suppose that something less than half of the documents originally intended for these recipients are now extant. Given the allusions made in a number of surviving letters to inextant enclosures, we can probably consider this figure (of less than half) fairly conservative. Grey's 'official' letters to these court contacts, though, can represent only a fraction of his epistolary business into England; in addition to letters dispatched to victuallers, armourers, and other suppliers, he must have charged Spenser to write and dispatch correspondence to other recipients on both public and private matters. What survives, then, might represent something less than a quarter of the original business trafficked into England; but this figure itself ignores what must have been a considerably greater store of records and epistolary business that remained in Ireland: communications with the presidents of Connaught and Munster, orders and advertisements to captains and to the Old English and Irish nobility, instructions and arbitrations directed to townsmen and merchants, daily communications between Grey and his ministers, and so on. A certain fraction of such papers must have survived into the twentieth century, but nearly all of them perished in the devastating Four Courts fire of 1922, and what we know of them now is only what was copied or extracted by historians or scholars in the late nineteenth and early twentieth centuries.[37] As for Spenser's service to the Norris brothers and the Council of Munster after 1584, it is likely that the extant remains of his employments there represent a much smaller proportion of his original output. These rough but relatively conservative figures—which only relate to the epistolary material Spenser was charged with producing on a daily basis, and not to his other duties, many of which must have been scribal—suggest that he might have produced or supervised the production of as many as 3,500 to 4,000 folios during his service for Grey alone; given the frequency of Grey's campaigns and other inevitable interruptions to Spenser's secretarial work, these figures imply a daily grind in the Dublin secretariat consistent with the considerable sums Spenser was allowed, during these years, for the purchase of ink, parchment, and paper.[38] Between 1580 and 1589 Spenser doubtless participated vigorously in the social and political life of the New English communities of Dublin and Munster, such as in the

---

[37] An example is provided by the Nugent of Farren Connell papers, now held at the Public Record Office of Northern Ireland (D3835), which include twenty-three volumes of papers compiled by Richard Nugent in the second half of the nineteenth century, one of which, the 'Nugent Registry', includes extensive transcriptions of state papers destroyed in 1922.

[38] Spenser seems to have been allowed £15 sterling per year for supplies. SP 63/92/20/1 records that this 'allowaunce' was 'due to him for one whole yere endinge xxiiij⁰ Iunij 1581', which may suggest that Spenser's service with Grey had begun on 25 June 1580.

commissioning of the Musters in Kildare in 1584 and 1585; we can infer, too, his probably tacit presence at many of the key historical events of the period, such as the massacre at Smerwick; but a huge volume of detailed and sensitive information and argument also crossed his desk during these years, and passed through his hands—all of it in writing.

The surviving documents in Spenser's Italian, mixed, and secretary hands—manuscripts that he copied for others, recording their words and experiences, and not his own—record, in a language of inconspicuous pen and fold marks, the evidence of his habits of secretaryship. This evidence suggests that Spenser's place in Grey's secretariat, and likely in the Munster office too, was one of trust, authority, and meticulous oversight, pointing to a strong view of his access to and participation in the central business of the Dublin and Munster administrations. What is more, when read alongside other representations of secretaryship from contemporary literary and other sources, this evidence suggests that the practical, ethical, and epistemological issues attending on a secretary's place, during this period, overlapped substantially with the concerns we have come to consider the staple allegorical and philosophical preoccupations of Spenser's poetry. In other words, not only did Spenser's secretarial position in Ireland bring him into sustained contact, through the medium of written documents, with an immediate, often humanly shocking, and stimulating range of novel experience; but the manner and mode in which he engaged with that experience—as a secretary—itself made important contributions to the nature of his thought, and the forms in which he went on to express it.

In George Gascoigne's story, *The Adventures of Master F.J.* (1573), the love between the book's eponymous hero and Mistress Elinor needs to surmount a number of obstacles, not least of which is a particular third person:

Shee had in the same house a friend, a seruaunt, a Secretary: what should I name him? . . . Hee was in height, the proportion of twoo Pigmeys, in bredth the thicknesse of two bacon hogges, of presumption a Gyant, of power a Gnat, Apishly wytted, Knauishly mannerd, & crabbedly fauord, what was there in him then to drawe a fayre Ladies liking? Marry sir euen all in all, a well lyned pursse, wherwith he could at euery call, prouide such pretie conceytes as pleased hir peeuish fantasie, and by that meanes he had throughly (long before) insinuated him selfe with this amorous dame. This manling, this minion, this slaue, this secretary, was nowe by occasion rydden to London forsothe: and though his absence were vnto hir a disfurnishing of eloquence: it was yet vnto *F.I.* an opertunitie of good aduautage.[39]

---

[39] George Gascoigne, *The Adventures of Master F.J.*, in *A Hundreth Sundrie Flowres* (London: Henry Bynneman and Henry Middleton, 1573), 215–16.

This secretary occupies a prominent position in Elinor's household, and a crucial one in Gascoigne's plot. The affair between Elinor and F.J. is conducted (and narrated) largely through their letters, permitting Gascoigne to explore the erotic possibilities of epistolary communication, as well as the rhetorical codes, at once conventional and intimate, in which love can be expressed and disguised. Indeed, the index to *A Hundreth Sundrie Flowres*, the printed collection in which *The Adventures of Master F.J.* appears, emphasizes the story's interest in letters and other forms of writing: 'conteyning excellent letters, sonets, Lays, Ballets, Rondlets, Verlayes and verses'.[40] Mistress Elinor's secretary is valuable to her as someone who has this eloquence at his fingertips, and it is implied that his letter-writing services also earn him a position of sexual credit (as he 'insinuated him selfe with this amorous dame'). He is very different from the secretary as (s)he is often understood in contemporary culture: a salaried and often subservient office worker.[41] As epistolary intermediary and 'chiefe Chauncellor'—that is to say, as both letter-writer, in a culture in which letter-writing had profound importance, and keeper and legitimator of that correspondence—Gascoigne's secretary prevents F.J. and Elinor from coming into contact with one another (either by letter or by person). Gascoigne's narrator feels the need to denounce the sexual prowess of this 'manling' who seems both to occupy Elinor's desires and to stand in the way of F.J.'s, and it is only when the secretary leaves the house that F.J. can make his move.

What is most curious about Gascoigne's literary representation of the secretary in *The Adventures of Master F.J.* is the way in which the secretary's service makes him the governor of his mistress: by controlling the means of communication between Elinor and those around her, and by making himself the censor and ratifier of her words and actions, the secretary effectively reverses their social position. Gascoigne's paradoxical portrait exploits immemorial tensions in the master–servant relationship, but it is also inflected by the changes that were taking place in the secretarial profession in Gascoigne's England—and in Spenser's Ireland. The position of the Principal Secretary of State was in the process of being transformed, in the hands of men such as William Cecil, Lord Burghley, Sir Francis Walsingham, and Sir Robert Cecil into a role of national political influence.[42] At the same time, a number of writers and political

---

[40] Gascoigne, *A Hundreth Sundrie Flowres*, sig. A1ᵛ.

[41] See Leah Price and Pamela Thurschwell, eds., *Literary Secretaries/Secretarial Culture* (Aldershot: Ashgate, 2005).

[42] For the growth in status and influence of the Principal Secretary during this period, see Florence M. Grier Evans, *The Principal Secretary of State: A Survey of the Office from 1558 to 1680* (Manchester: Manchester University Press, 1923); and Stephen Alford, *The Early Elizabethan Polity: William Cecil and the British Succession Crisis, 1558–1569* (Cambridge: Cambridge University Press, 1998).

administrators attempted to define afresh the responsibilities and the ambiguous social position of the secretary. Some of these men were career secretaries at the highest level, or men closely associated with them—men such as Robert Cecil, John Herbert, Robert Beale, and Nicholas Faunt; their aims in writing about secretaryship were largely professional, and their discourses deal with the everyday material detail of discharging the post. But fresh and formative analyses were also composed by professional men of a lower status, who had a different kind of interest in promoting the accomplishments and dignity of secretaryship, and tended to appeal to the authority of such European humanist models as Erasmus's *De conscribendis epistolis* (1522) and Francesco Sansovino's *Del Secretario* (1565). Both kinds of writer, though, could agree with Faunt that, 'amongst all particuler offices and places of charge in this state, there is none of more necessarie vse, nor subiect to more cumber and variablenes; then is the office of principall Secretarie'.[43] The indispensability of the Elizabethan secretary conferred on the office not only credit, but a kind of social and political—and in Gascoigne's version, sexual—instability.

One popular writer on secretaryship, Angel Day, makes this instability one of the profession's chief honours and enticements. In his 'function and place', according to Day, 'being in one condition a *Seruant*, he is at the pleasure and appoyntment of another to be commaunded: and being in a second respect as a *friend*, hee is charely [i.e. dearly] to haue in estimate, the state, honour, reputation and being, of him whom he serueth'.[44] Like Gascoigne's narrator, who is similarly uncertain about the position occupied by Elinor's secretary ('what should I name him?'), Day calls his secretary both servant and friend, chief courtier and slave, minion and confidant. Day's book, *The English Secretorie*, which was popular enough to go through at least eleven editions in its first fifty years, comprises notes on epistolary practice, a series of model letters, and, in editions from 1592 onwards, an essay entitled 'Of the Parts, Place, and Office of a Secretorie'. Day explains in this essay that whatever mutual affection and love might grow in time between master and secretary, the secretary's position is abidingly one of service; and yet the double 'condition' of his position threatens constantly to entitle him to the same dues of friendship that his master collects from him. As a servant, the secretary satisfies his obligation to his master in the discharge of his master's will, and need go no further; but as the friend—'partaking as he doth with so many causes of

---

[43] Nicholas Faunt, 'Discourse Touching the Office of Principal Secretary of Estate, &c (1592)', ed. Charles Hughes, *English Historical Review*, 20 (1905), 499–508 (pp. 499–500).
[44] Angel Day, *The English Secretorie* (London: Richard Jones, 1592), 111.

importance, & vndiscouered secrets & counsels, standing as he must vpon so neere attendance'[45]—the secretary's obligations are as limitless as his social status is incommensurable with his master's.

But this in turn meant that an Elizabethan secretary needed to be conversant with the social and political skills that governed not only his own ambiguous and sensitive relationship with his master, but also his master's place in the political world of the day: he had to be a man of courtesy. As Robert Beale, brother-in-law and secretary of Francis Walsingham and clerk to the Privy Council, wrote in a document entitled 'Instructions for a Principall Secretary' (dated 1592), the daily business of the Queen's chief secretary involved regular and intimate contact with her, and also, by necessity, a great deal of tact and discretion: 'Learne before your accesse her Majestie's disposicion by some in the Privie Chamber with whom you must keepe creditt, for that will stande you in much steede.'[46] A secretary may have held a position of trust and quasi-friendship with his master or mistress, but still needed to manage that credit by using contacts placed around the court or household; for Beale, the access and credit enjoyed by a secretary was a means to an end, that end being the effective discharge of a place, or even the self-interest of the secretary himself. The secretary's skill at decorum thus becomes the means not to an ethical end (i.e. friendship), but rather to the achievement of the secretary's own desire: 'When her highnes is angrie or not well disposed trouble her not with anie matter which you desire to have done.'[47] Beale's secretary could, by implication, provide or withhold access to the great man or woman whom he served. As in Gascoigne's story, Beale sees the secretary's profession as not only administrative and epistolary, but also intimate and intermediary, bringing forth or holding back business as it suits his purposes.

For those who wrote about the profession at the end of the sixteenth century, the ethical ambiguity of this intermediary role provided an opportunity to reflect on the ideal secretary's virtue, but also upon the power that his epistolary skills purchased him. Day's *English Secretorie* dwells very largely on letter-writing, and Day makes it clear at the beginning of his book that he is presenting his series of model letters as a practical aid in the development of secretaryship: 'the orderly writing of Letters, being a principall part belonging to a Secretorie, is by the Methode hereof deliuered to any Learners capacitie, whereout the Scholler or any

---

[45] Ibid. 119

[46] Robert Beale, 'A Treatise of the Office of a Councellor and Principall Secretarie to her Majestie', in Conyers Read, *Mr Secretary Walsingham and the Policy of Queen Elizabeth*, vol. i (Oxford: Clarendon Press, 1925), 423–43 (p. 437).

[47] Ibid. 438.

other that is vnfurnished of the knowledge thereof, may gather ayde and furtherance, the better by such meanes thereafter [. . .] to become a Secretorie.'[48] But as he begins the final part of the book, his essay on the 'Parts, Place, and Office of a Secretorie', he argues that the responsibilities, and the importance, of the position, are much greater than this. The name of secretary, he writes:

> was not so much at the beginning appropriate vnto him, whose vse and imploiment consisted soly in habilitie to write well, and in neate and fine forme to set foorth his Letters, (albeit also the vse hereof, is not the least part of many other things incident to the same Office) but carying with it selfe a purpose of much weightier effect, was as a deriuatiue from that, which containeth the chiefest title of credite, and place of greatest assurance, in respect of the neerenesse and affinitie they both haue of Trust, Regard & Fidelitie, each with the other, by great conceyte and discretion, vnto him that supplyeth the roome thereof, attributed, and bequeathed, to be called a Secretorie.[49]

As some recent critics have observed,[50] Day's slant on 'conceyte and discretion' emphasizes the etymological and professional association between the secretary, secrets, and secrecy. It is the secretary's task, Day writes, to be the 'keeper or conseruer of the secret vnto him committed'.[51] What allows him to do this, according to Day, is the almost instrumental way in which the secretary serves only the hand of his master: 'The *Secretorie*, as he is a keeper and *conseruer* of *secrets*: so is he by his *Lord* or *Master*, and by none other to be directed. To a *Closet*, there belongeth properly, a *doore*, a *locke* and a *key*: to a *Secretorie*, there appertaineth incidently, *Honesty*, *Troth*, and *Fidelitie*.'[52] As Day implies by the 'as . . . so' construction, a secretary can only be a keeper of secrets—and therefore a secretary—in-so-far as his trust and fidelity remain openable only to his master. But while Day's allegory of the secretary as closet leaves the servant inert to his master's instrumental use, this model does not prevent the danger that someone else will rifle the enclosure. The Elizabethan secretary had special access to, and control over, safe places in the secretariat or household; Robert Beale speaks of 'a speciall cabinett, whereof he is himselfe to keepe the Keye, for his signetts, Ciphers and secret Intelligences'.[53] The codes and ciphers that appear in many of the letters that passed between politicians in

---

[48] Day, *The English Secretorie*, sig. B2^v.

[49] Ibid. 109.

[50] See Jonathan Goldberg, *Writing Matter: From the Hands of the English Renaissance* (Stanford: Stanford University Press, 1990); and Richard Rambuss, *Spenser's Secret Career*, Cambridge Studies in Renaissance Literature and Culture, 3 (Cambridge: Cambridge University Press, 1993).

[51] Day, *The English Secretorie*, 109.

[52] Ibid. 110.

[53] Beale, 'A Treatise', 428.

England and Ireland in the 1580s suggest that this was a very practical, and a day-to-day responsibility of a secretary such as Spenser. And Day also implies that a special, private place in the house would be set aside for the secretary's occupations: 'Thus then by the concurrence of these two parts, it appeareth, that vnto euery Secret there is required a Closet, and the proper vse of that Closet, is onely for the Couertnes, Safety, and Assurance of the Secret.'[54] Secretaries have thus often been seen as key to the negotiation of private spaces in the early modern household, and in particular in the discourse and epistemology of the closet;[55] but whether we construe the secretary as agent of his own interest, or as prone instrument of the interest of his master, all early modern accounts of secretaryship concur that the secretary's 'couertnes' made his position a place of power, constantly under the threat of improper use.

The secretary knew and kept his master's ciphers, could access the written proofs of his master's combinations and ventures, and could influence his master's perceptions and actions. All of this endowed him with a kind of privilege. But if his power lay most obviously in the physical and confidential access he enjoyed to the materials and the information of his master's business, yet as the example of Gascoigne's secretary implies, his custodial office was not the only source of his paradoxical primacy. Because masters and mistresses in a sense alienated themselves from the social, rhetorical, and political skills and sciences necessary to the conduct of their own business, trusting their secretaries to collect the required information and discharge the necessary duties, they came in a real sense to rely on their servants and their epistolary eloquence. Day reminds his reader, as we have seen, that 'the orderly writing of Letters' is 'a principall part belonging to a Secretorie', even if the structure of his book separates this practical business from his discussion of the dignity of the profession. And the titles of many of the epistolary manuals of the seventeenth century make a similar connection between the secretary and the letter-writer: Thomas Gainsford's *The Secretary's Study* (1616), Jean Puget de la Serre's *The Secretary in Fashion* (translated by John Massinger, 1640), and John Hill's *The Young Secretary's Guide* (1687) are all handbooks of the art of

---

[54] Day, *The English Secretorie*, 109.

[55] See Michael McKeon, *The Secret History of Domesticity: Public, Private, and the Division of Knowledge* (Baltimore: Johns Hopkins University Press, 2005); and Alan Stewart, 'Instigating Treason: The Life and Death of Henry Cuffe, Secretary', in Erica Sheen and Lorna Hutson, eds., *Literature, Politics, and Law in Renaissance England* (Basingstoke: Palgrave Macmillan, 2004), 50–70. For Rambuss, *Spenser's Secret Career*, Day's emphasis upon secrecy provides a way to consider the relationship between Edmund Spenser's secretarial and poetic careers: both, as he sees them, concerned with the retaining and selective revelation of secrets, and with the veils and concealments of allegory.

letter-writing. These manuals emphasized the inseparability of epistolary rhetoric and social delicacy—the two parts of a secretary's career, and of the practice of his daily life. Indeed, a secretary like Spenser would have learnt that every aspect of a letter's composition, not only its diction and style, but also its layout, needed to be fashioned according to the relation between the person sending the letter and the person receiving it. William Fulwood's *Enimie of Idlenesse* (1568), for instance, prescribes very clear rules for three parts of a letter: the 'salutation or recommendation' (that is, the address at the top of the letter), the 'subscription' (written after the end of the letter and before the signature), and the 'superscription' or address (written on the back of the letter after it has been folded and sealed). Of the subscription, he writes that it 'must be don according to the estate of the writer, and the qualitie of the person to whome we write: For to our superiors we must write at the right syde in the nether ende of the paper, sayinge: By your most humble and obedient sonne, or seruant, &c. And to our equalles we may write towards the midst of the paper saying: By your faithfull frende for euer etc. To our inferiors we may write on high at the left hand saying: By yours &c.'[56] The master or mistress would rely on the secretary to observe the formal decorum of address.

The practical duties of an Elizabethan secretary, though, went much further than the writing and addressing of letters. He would be expected to digest the information that was contained in letters received by his master, in preparation for presenting them to him; according to Robert Beale, the state secretary had to 'abbreviate on the backside of the lettres, or otherwise in a bie paper, the substantiall and most material points which are to be propounded and answered'.[57] Such receiver-side secretarial notes, listing the important points within letters, are often to be found on the backs of the letters drawn up by Spenser and his fellow servants, as illustrated in Figure 1, a letter from Lord Grey to Lord Burghley (No. 26, below, SP 63/ 88/12); here Burghley's secretary has carefully extracted the heads of all the letter's contents on the back of the paper, either as an aid to Burghley in composing a reply, or to facilitate future use of the letter after filing. In cases where letters were sent to the Privy Council (or, going in the opposite direction, to the Irish Council), the secretary who received the letter would often be responsible for summarizing the letter's main points in a series of marginal annotations, which would help the readers to take up its contents quickly when the paper was circulated; an example of such practice is presented in Figure 2, a letter from Grey to the Privy Council of

[56] William Fulwood, *The Enimie of Idlenesse* (London: Henry Bynneman, 1568), sig. A8[r].
[57] Beale, 'A Treatise', 425.

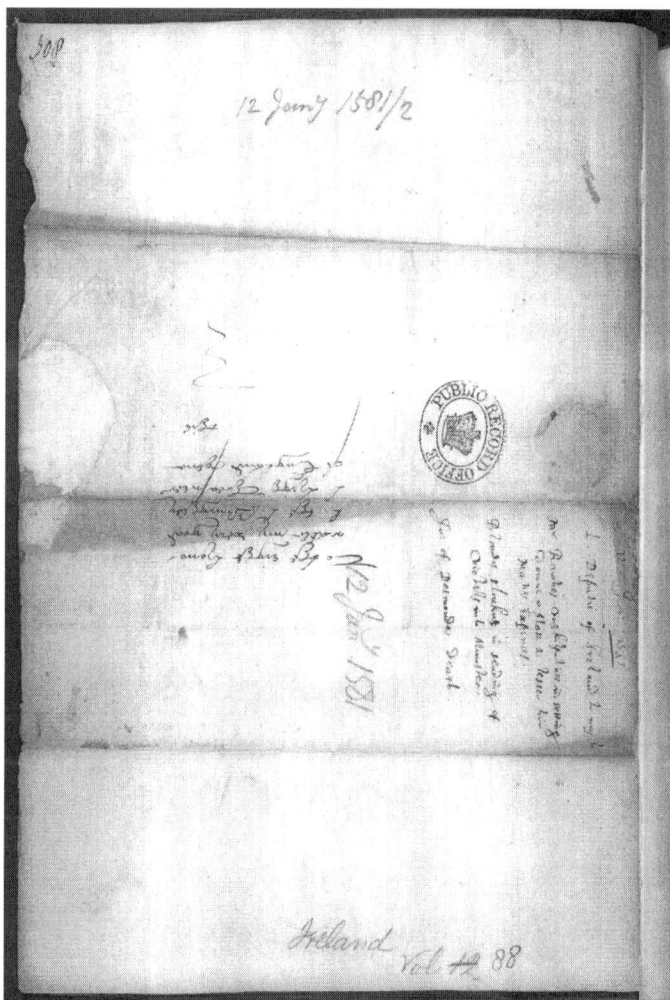

1. Grey to Burghley, 12 January 1581/2, *from* TNA: PRO SP 63/88/12.
Here Burghley's secretary has summarized the letter's contents (called 'docketing')
on the back, adjacent to the original address in Spenser's hand.

6 November 1581 (No. 23, below, SP 63/86/51). Here the secretary, possibly Beale himself, has keyed the marginal annotations to underlined
passages in the text. In other instances, Walsingham's and Burghley's
secretaries extracted minutes from letters received for the Privy Council,
apparently for circulation, or created minutes of letters that would
subsequently be dispatched, presumably for record-keeping. Secretaries
had also to administer the bookkeeping by which they kept secure account

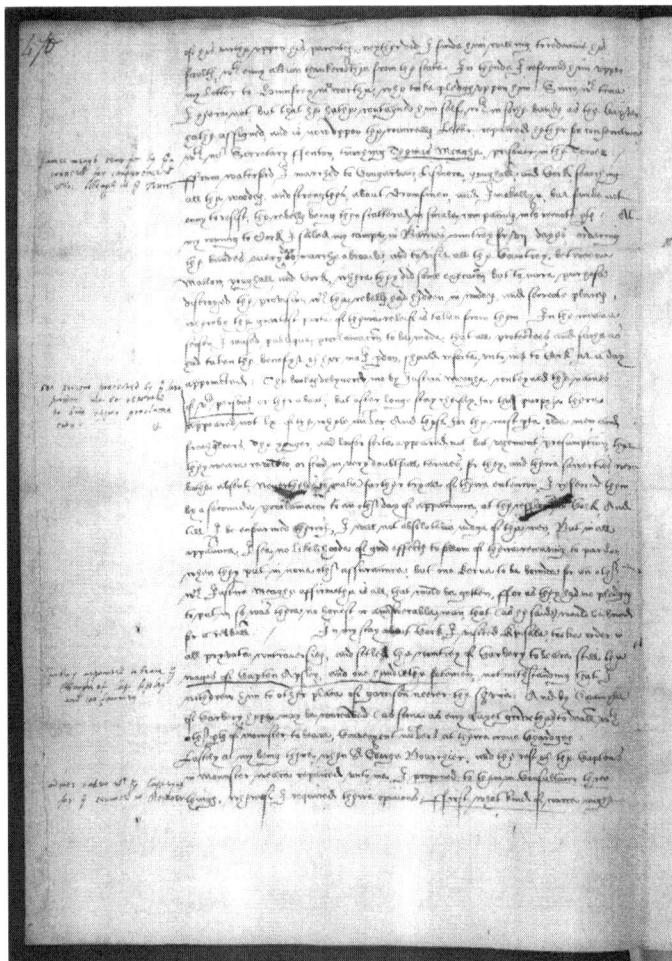

2. Grey to the Privy Council, 6 November 1581, *from* TNA: PRO SP 63/86/51. The secretary who received the letter in London—probably Robert Beale—has here extracted the major heads of the letter's contents, and summarized them in the margins for the ease of the ministers who would peruse and circulate the document.

of the continual receipt and dispatch of letters and other documents.[58] The Principal Secretary, Beale writes, should 'have a care that the Clercks of the Councell keepe a perfect booke of the Lords' sittinges [. . .] also a little note of such as may be committed from the Councell'.[59] Nicholas Faunt adds

---

[58] For an extract from such a book of receipt and dispatch, see No. 34, below (SP 63/91/26), a list Spenser drew up of letters previously sent to Walsingham, itself sent to Walsingham in April 1582. Such lists were probably occasionally sent over for security purposes.

[59] Beale, 'A Treatise', 426.

that he should keep a series of memorial books, noting matters that had been dispatched, as well as a separate 'journall', with details of the dates on which every dispatch was made or received, as well as any ambassadors and other visitors to his master who had arrived. 'And further', Beale goes on:

it wilbee necessarie to haue sundrie bookes of paper for the Regestring of all instruccions and lettres of forraine partes into Ireland or vnto the Sea, and the minutes of lettres of further direccions groweing vpon sundrie accidents and newe occasions sent vnto them beinge materiall and Concerning the seuerall nego-ciations in hand as likewise the answeres and Relacions of their Charges and Commissions with anie other discourse or reporte concerning the same.[60]

Both Faunt and Beale also pay special attention to the books that a secretary ought to equip himself with, in order to furnish himself with readily available intelligence about the lands and subjects that might come under his master's eye: books containing maps, information about matters of religion, geography, munitions, and so on. The secretary was thus charged not only with acquiring full command of the etiquette and decorum appropriate to his master's station, but had also to tutor himself on all the subjects and sciences implicated in his master's affairs. His position of privilege consisted not only in his mediating function, and his control of access and resort to his master, but in the kinds of knowledge and pro-ficiency that, in the course of his duties, he was forced to acquire. The secretary thus served the master as trusty cabinet-custodian, but also as interpreter, translator, and specialist epitomizer of his master's business.

The increasing tendency of masters to rely materially on their servants' skills and knowledge is apparent from what we know of the education and career profile of a range of early modern secretaries. As Edmund Spenser passed through secretarial service to the Bishop of Rochester, to Lord Grey, and possibly, as Richard Rambuss playfully speculates, to other figures in the circle of the Earl of Leicester,[61] he was following a career path that must have appealed to the students of late sixteenth-century Cambridge, thoroughly trained in rhetoric and eager for professional and social advancement. William Cecil employed secretaries almost entirely from the universities and Inns of Court, and Essex chose men with dis-tinguished scholarly backgrounds. Angel Day, too, observes that a secretary needed to be 'furnished with Skill & Knowledge accordingly, whereby the better to be adapted, vnto the ordinary vsage and employment thereof. To this end it behoueth that he be well studied, especially in the Latine tongue.' He had to be:

[60] Ibid. 425.   [61] See Rambuss, *Spenser's Secret Career*, 8.

well languaged [. . .] sufficiently red in Histories and Antiquities of times passed, to haue notice both by reading and conference, or the scituations, customes, manners, and conditions of men, citties, countries, & common weales, to hue familiaritie with straungers, and men of diuers nations, whereby the better to be assertayned of their humors.[62]

When Christopher Marlowe's Edward II elevates Piers Gaveston to the position of 'Cheefe Secretarie to the state and me', among his other new titles, he registers not only the proximity and service that a secretary's position was felt to involve in the sixteenth century, but also the extent to which the secretarial position could be a means of professional advancement, a way for ambitious men to rise in the world. The professional and social mobility of the Elizabethan secretary was the natural consequence of their masters' dependence on their skill and learning; social and economic concessions were purchased by indispensable expertise and skill.

The potential for instrumental dislocation and improper use of the secretary's privilege, though, came under increasing pressure during the bureaucratic transformations of central government in Elizabeth's reign: the professionalization of secretaryship further heightened the secretary's access to and command of the master's confidential business, even as it dislocated him from the social bonds that secured that interest. For the private secretary working in a household, Day's account of the intimate and exclusive relationship between master and devoted servant, a relation based on secrecy, intimacy, and love, probably still held true. Robert Beale and Nicholas Faunt, on the other hand, suggest the ways in which the business of a secretarial office, or secretariat, might have been considerably different: here the secretary did not enjoy an exclusive relationship with his master, but worked alongside other secretaries under a common master or employer. Both Beale and Faunt, writing shortly after the death of Francis Walsingham, use Walsingham's secretariat as an example of the confusion that might arise when too many secretaries were contracted to one master, but both acknowledge that the tasks involved in the administration of a great man's office (or the office of the monarch) were so onerous that they required more than one man. A secretary might well require servants of his own, to carry out the more mechanical record-keeping that his job entailed; or it might have been the case that one secretary within a larger secretariat would be charged with tasks of more responsibility, or even secrecy, and another given less access. Faunt, for example, advocates employing one secretary 'in whome the greatest trust is to bee reposed', and another 'for the dispatch of ordinarie matters, and chiefly for Continuall attendant in

---

[62] Day, *The English Secretorie*, 137.

the Chamber where the papers are whose perticuler charge may bee to indorse them or giue them their due titles'.[63] But if Faunt thus strove to stave off the inevitable changes that professionalization would bring to the master–secretary relationship, his may have been a losing battle: detailed accounts of the secretariats of the Cecils and of the Earl of Essex have shown them to have been large offices, in which secretaries worked together and often in rivalry with one another, in which they were given opportunities to acquire further trust, and promotion, from their masters.[64] The rearguard action that humanist writers and pedagogues had long fought against charges of self-interest and social ambition began to give ground under the new professionalization of the secretariat. Sir Thomas Elyot had given pride of place in his *Boke Named the Gouernour* (1531) to the virtues of friendship and fidelity, and Angel Day had similarly stressed, through exemplary stories, the ethical importance of the secretary's devotion to his master;[65] but in the increasingly bureaucratic secretariats of the 1580s and 1590s, these humanist ideas were openly displaced as the self-interested fictions they had become.

The cynicism of late Elizabethan and of Jacobean literary writers to such ideals exposes the anxieties over interest and power that social and professional changes were provoking. Gentleman stewards like *Twelfth Night*'s Malvolio or *The Duchess of Malfi*'s Antonio are either plainly self-interested, or suspected of being so. The Duchess seeks to use Antonio as an instrument to vex her brothers and, after his supposed death, as an instrument to demonstrate her supposed Stoic superiority to her brothers' torments and the vagaries of fortune; upon the almost posthumous discovery of Bosola's deceit, the cruel irony of her panicked death gives the lie to this superiority, and we cannot help but read her tragedy as one in which the mistress inevitably succumbs to the power of (and worldly love

---

[63] Faunt, 'Discourse', 501–2.

[64] See Alan G. R. Smith, 'The Secretariats of the Cecils, circa 1580–1612', *English Historical Review*, 83 (1968), 481–504; and Paul E. J. Hammer, 'The Uses of Scholarship: The Secretariat of Robert Devereux, Second Earl of Essex, c. 1585–1601', *English Historical Review*, 109 (1994), 16–51.

[65] Day's two main examples both seem to have a curiously Spenserian connection. The first, the narration of the death of the captain Henry Davells at the hand of Sir John of Desmond, in late July 1579, turns on the loyalty of an Irish 'boy' who threw himself between Desmond's sword and Davells' body: 'The Boy [. . .] clasped on his Maisters breast, and with such slender resistaunce as he could, did beare off the blowes, receiued vppon his owne body diuers and sundry wounds, and doe what they could, no one could pull or remoue him from thence, till freating rage kindling in these merciles creatures, made them kill the Boy vppon his Maister, and his Maister vnder the Boy, both at one instant togethers' (Day, *The English Secretorie*, 113). Davells' death was, according to Lord Justice Sir William Drury, the inaugural act of John of Desmond's rebellion in August 1579 (see SP 63/68/6). Day's second exemplary narrative concerns George Castriot, known as Scanderbeg, the Albanian prince whose military career against the Turks was the subject of Spenser's commendatory poem in Z. I., *Historie of George Castriot, surnamed Scanderberg, King of Albanie* (London: William Ponsonby, 1596); see Day, *The English Secretorie*, 114–16.

for) her instrument. More subtle, perhaps, is Middleton's portrait of mistress–servant relationships in *The Changeling*, in which the fates of the servants Diaphanta and De Flores satirize with brutal irony their mistress Beatrice-Joanna's naive attempts to exploit conventional humanist assumptions. Secrecy and instrumentalization are basic to both of these relationships: Alsemero remarks of Diaphanta, 'These women are the ladies' cabinets, | Things of most precious trust are lock'd into 'em',[66] and Beatrice-Joanna hopes to use De Flores (for the murder of Alonzo de Piracquo), making him the alienated instrument of her murderous intent in a bid to keep culpability at arm's length:

> Why, put case I loath'd him
> As much as youth and beauty hates a sepulchre,
> Must I needs show it? Cannot I keep that secret,
> And serve my turn upon him? (II.ii.66–9)

Beatrice-Joanna imagines that her concealed loathing for De Flores will somehow protect her from complicity in Piracquo's murder—as her father Vermandero remarks, insisting on the security of his fortress, 'within are secrets' (I.i.166)—but she is quickly brought, after the murder, to the recognition that, having shared her secret crime with De Flores, she must now 'make [him] master' (III.iv.156). While Middleton's cynical anatomy of self-interest does not deal explicitly, like Gascoigne, with secretaryship, he reveals by his preoccupation with cabinets, ciphers, and secrets where his satire tends. By the 1620s, the quaint humanist ideal of a secretary throwing himself between his master and the point of a sword had been savagely exploded; in the newly bureaucratic, professionalized secretariats of the turn of the century, the master was more likely to find himself fearing exposure than trusting to the protection of his secretary. Contemporary manuals of secretarial and epistolary practice, then, along with early modern literary representations of master–servant relationships, suggest that the office and practice of the secretary was, in Elizabeth's later years, in the process of important transitions, transitions that cut straight to the heart of the humanist ethical ideals of an earlier generation. Secretaries occupied positions of trust and credit, but the new bureaucracy of Tudor government, along with the increasingly accomplished, almost polymathic career profile of Elizabethan secretaries, accorded them unprecedented power and autonomy in an environment increasingly open about the anxiety of interest.

---

[66] Thomas Middleton and William Rowley, *The Changeling*, ed. N. W. Bawcutt (Manchester: Manchester University Press, 1958), II.ii.6–7.

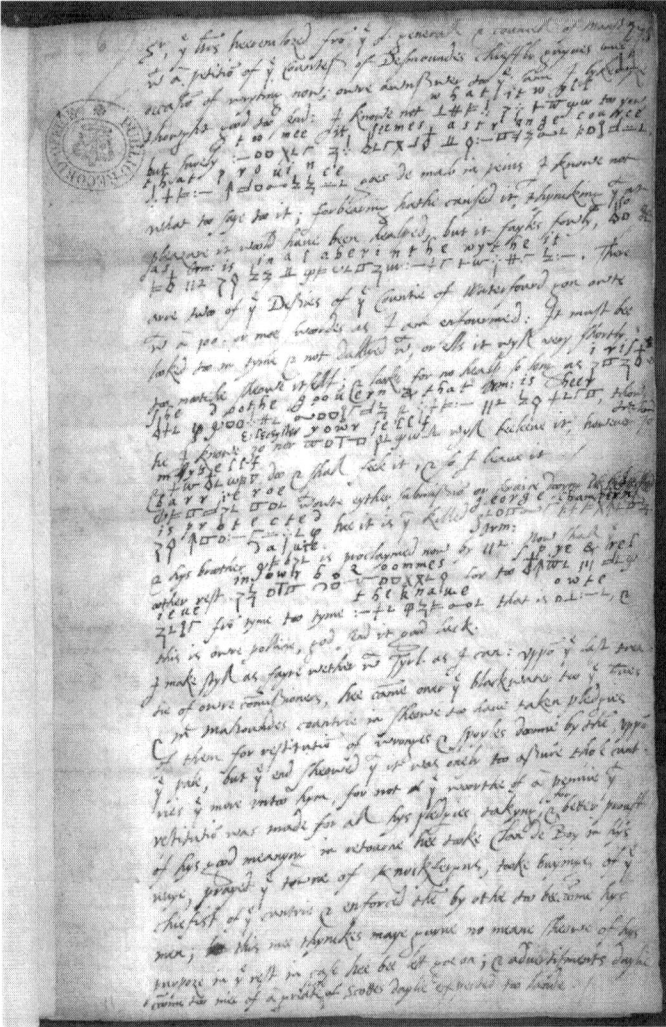

3. Grey to Walsingham, 12 May 1581, *from* TNA: PRO SP 63/83/6, showing
Grey's autograph italic and the usual cipher of his letters to Walsingham.

The evidence of Spenser's secretarial career in Ireland, recorded in the
physical witness of surviving manuscripts, as well as in the comments and
communications of his fellow secretaries and administrators in the Irish
service, reveals a general consistency both with these models of practice,
and with the anxieties attendant on their rapid change in this period; but
the New English government of Ireland—as a result of the extreme violence and politic hypocrisy that defined it during this period—also seems
to have distorted and exaggerated the prescribed practices, the promised

benefits, and the perceived dangers of secretaryship. This manuscript evidence indicates that Spenser enjoyed a considerable trust in Grey's secretariat. Perhaps the most obvious evidence of this confidence in Spenser's 'covertness' is that provided by Grey's Walsingham cipher. Figures 3 and 4 show two letters—one in Grey's autograph, to Walsingham, showing his usual cipher (Figure 3, SP 63/83/6), and one in Spenser's Italian hand, to the Queen, using a different cipher (Figure 4, No. 13, SP 63/82/54). The

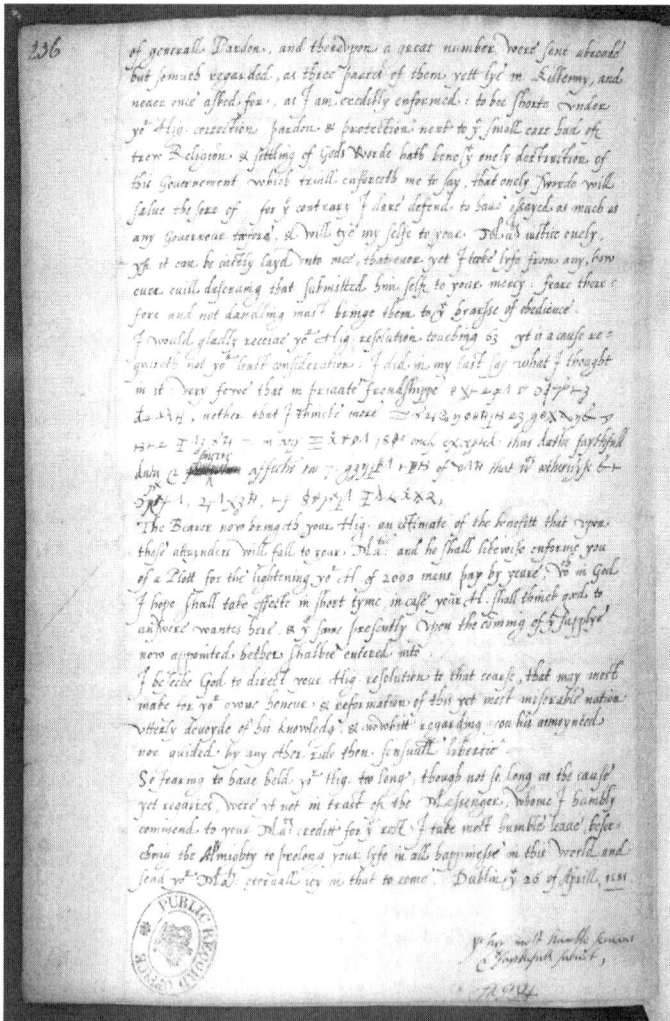

4. Grey to the Queen, 26 April 1581, *from* TNA: PRO SP 63/82/54. This letter, in Spenser's formal italic hand, shows the distinct and more elaborate cipher Grey himself inserted into his letters to the Queen.

simple substitution cipher Grey employed for his communications with Walsingham, like that used by Treasurer Sir Henry Wallop during the same period, represented individual letters of the alphabet with a consistent set of graphs, which might appear in varying orientations but otherwise never varied (for a key to this cipher, see Appendix 3). This cipher was certainly adequate to prevent casual chance perusals of a letter, though because of its simplicity it could not have stood up to a determined effort at decoding. Grey seems never to have used the cipher except in his autograph letters— that is, the cipher never appears in 'fair copies' produced by Spenser from Grey's original—which may bespeak a certain amount of distance between the Deputy and his personal secretary. Similarly, in the one surviving instance of cipher in a letter prepared in Spenser's Italian hand, Grey's letter to the Queen of 26 April 1581 (Figure 4), the pattern of the cipher in its relation to Spenser's hand and, further into the passage, Grey's own effort at a clean Italian script, demonstrates conclusively that Grey had not shared this cipher with his secretary, either. Here Spenser left a blank for the first, short section in cipher, continuing on with his own hand in the phrase 'nether that I thincke more'; thereafter, the rest of the paragraph is a mix of cipher and Grey's interspersed Italian script. The pattern of hands and cipher here suggests that the original copy from which Spenser was working (presumably in Grey's italic hand) probably also included the cipher, as Spenser seems to have been fairly confident about the amount of space Grey would require for the first ciphered passage, but thereafter to have left the unciphered words, too, for Grey to complete; clearly he became nervous about whether he would judge the spacing correctly on a page that needed to remain clean and presentable. (In the event, Grey anyway spoiled Spenser's carefulness by changing his mind, deleting one of his words, and inserting another supralineally.)

On the other hand, another kind of manuscript evidence may suggest that Spenser enjoyed more intimate access even to Grey's personal communications. As we have demonstrated elsewhere, Spenser seems to have had the general responsibility for receiving and dispatching Grey's post, and probably much of the post of Dublin Castle, a duty that required him to keep Grey's seal.[67] Other secretaries sometimes copied and even addressed letters for Grey, but the preponderance of the addresses on letters to Walsingham, Burghley, and the Queen are in Spenser's secretary or Italian hands, indicating that he held a kind of supervisory role in the secretariat. Significantly, while Spenser often addressed letters copied by

---

[67] See our full discussion of folding and sealing in Burlinson and Zurcher, '"Secretary to the Lord Grey Lord Deputie here": Edmund Spenser's Irish Papers', *The Library*, 7th series, 6 (2005), 30–75 (pp. 62–3).

others, there is not a single surviving instance where another secretary
addressed a letter that Spenser himself had copied. As the last one to handle
a letter before its dispatch, Spenser must therefore have been at least poten-
tially privy to the contents of almost every letter Grey sent during his
deputyship. Even in cases where Spenser did not produce fair copies of
Grey's autograph letter drafts, he usually folded, often addressed, and always
sealed these letters. The frequent incidence among the letters of 'addressee
notes'—marginal or dorsal annotations on a letter, indicating to whom the
letter ought to be addressed—demonstrate that Grey and his secretaries
often completed letter drafts and then left them, probably in a locked cabinet,
for Spenser to dispatch. The positioning of these addressee notes is important for our understanding of Grey's habits: the notes sometimes appear on
the recto of the first page of the letter, indicating that the letters were left for
Spenser in a flat, open state, but at other times (as in Figure 5, from SP 63/
84/3) the notes appear on the verso of the letter, adjacent to where the
address would subsequently be written—indicating that they were written
after the letter had been folded. Indeed, the position of some of these notes
directly along what was one of the original folds of the letter indicates
without doubt that, at least in some cases, Grey took the precaution of
folding his letter before leaving it for Spenser, even if he did not (i.e. could
not) address and dispatch it himself. What is perhaps most interesting about
Grey's variable practice in the positioning of these addressee notes is that the
pattern of placement does not seem to correspond to the sensitivity of the
letter; that is, apparently sensitive letters, including passages in cipher, were
at least on some occasions left flat for Spenser to fold, apparently demon-
strating Grey's unconcern about Spenser's access to their contents.

A third type of evidence—that of certain subscriptions—also tends to
support the idea of a close working relationship between Grey and Spenser,
and a high level of access for the secretary. Spenser's usual practice,
especially after he had passed through the first few novice months of his
service to the Lord Deputy, was to add the subscription to his copied
letters, leaving Grey only the need to add his signature. This was not the
practice of Grey's other secretaries, who left the important formal decorum
of the subscription for Grey himself to complete.[68] This tends to confirm

---

[68] Grey seems to have had a junior secretary in service under Spenser from at least July 1581, whom
we have elsewhere identified as Timothy Reynoldes, based on his appearance in the list of concorda-
tums in SP 63/92/20/1 (see Burlinson and Zurcher, 'Edmund Spenser's Irish Papers', 51–2). A number
of other clerks and secretaries also seem to have done occasional work for Grey—Nathaniel Dillon,
clerk to the Council, occasionally drafted documents for Grey's personal signature, and there were
probably other copyists working in various capacities in Dublin Castle whose services were available
when the need arose. Even Edward Waterhouse, the Receiver General for Ireland and a member of the
Irish Council, on one occasion drew up a hasty letter for Grey's signature (No. 7, below, SP 63/81/1).

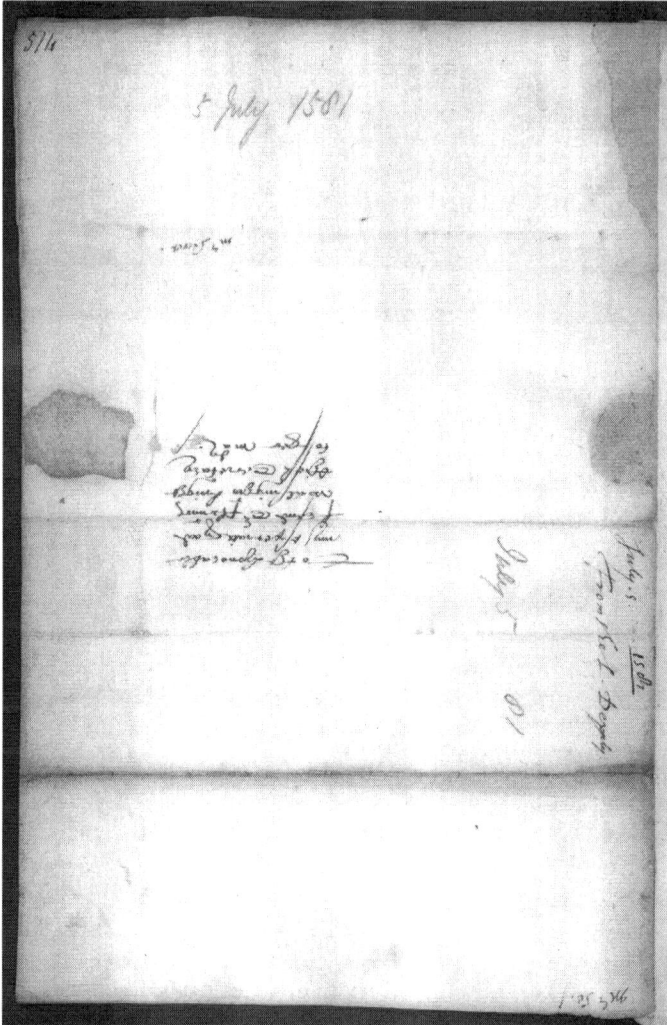

5. Grey to the Queen, 5 July 1581, *from* TNA: PRO SP 63/84/3. Grey's addition of an 'addressee note' along the fold of the letter's verso indicated that he folded the letter ready for dispatch before leaving it for Spenser to address and seal.

for Spenser what Day and Beale suggested of secretarial practice—that the secretary needed to have a good sense of his master's relationships, and had to be skilled enough in courtly graces to know the formulae and diction appropriate to different modes of address. But there are also a few extant examples where Spenser added the subscription to a letter prepared in the hand of another secretary, such as that illustrated in Figure 6, a letter of

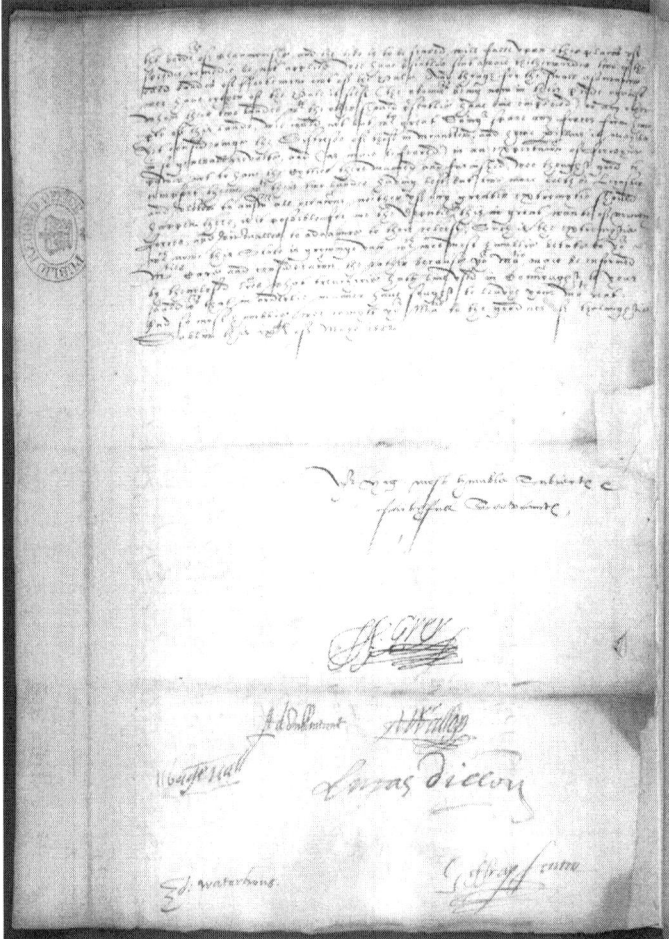

6. Irish Council to the Queen, 9 May 1582, *from* TNA: PRO SP 63/92/20. Spenser has
here added the subscription to a corporate letter to the Queen drafted by another
secretary, suggesting that he may well have been present at council meetings; at the
very least, this kind of activity establishes his supervisory role with respect not only to
Grey's personal correspondence, but to that of the Castle administration as a whole.

9 May 1582 from the Irish Council to the Queen.[69] In this case (as in the
case of SP 63/87/32), Spenser's addition of the subscription, between
the production of the fair copy by another secretary and the addition of the
council's signatures, suggests that he was present at the council's meeting.
This picture of Spenser as a secretary increasingly working at the centre of

---

[69] The other extant examples are SP 63/87/32, 63/89/55, and 63/92/86.

the activity of the Dublin castle administration is also supported by what we know of the general arrangements for the receipt and dispatch of post. The Lord Deputy's dispatches to the Queen and her chief officers were accorded, during this period, a special status that allowed them an expedited passage, often at the charge of the cities through which they passed. Other letters of official business could be grouped together with this post into a 'packet', which was bound together and addressed with the conventional label, 'For her majesty's special affairs', and sometimes 'Haste post haste for life'. These labels were applied to an outer wrapping, probably of paper, that went around the bundle; most if not all of these wrappings have, of course, vanished. But there is one letter extant in this collection that appears to represent a special instance in which the 'express delivery' for-mulae were applied directly to the letter, and not to an outer bundle; in this instance, from SP 63/84/14 (No. 18), the label appears in Spenser's mixed hand, adjacent to his secretary-hand address (see Figure 7). Given the costs and the political sensitivities involved, the right to label packets with this special formula must have been sparely granted; that Spenser applied the label here suggests that he regularly did so—which is only natural, given that he was charged with dispatching the Lord Deputy's post, and was heavily reimbursed at various points during his secretaryship for 'rewardes payed to messengers'. But given that other ministers would naturally have sought to have their own letters empacketed with the Lord Deputy's, in order to take advantage of the efficient and reliable service the Lord Deputy could command, Spenser would probably have acted, at least to some degree, as a general point of contact for the receipt and dispatch of all kinds of official correspondence.

In itself, this may seem a comparatively trivial observation; but in the factionally divided and often plainly backstabbing environment of the Dublin government, the regular handling of other people's post could provide valuable information. Strong evidence exists that Grey actively sought to place gentlemen, soldiers, and secretaries loyal to him into positions of authority during his administration. When the Secretary of State for Ireland, John Chaloner, died in May 1581, Grey promised his place to Lodowick Bryskett, whom he preferred (as a Sidney client) to Geoffrey Fenton; nothing came of Grey's support, as Fenton shortly returned from an errand to court, bearing instructions from the Queen herself that he was to take the place. Similarly, Grey sought on several occasions to establish John Zouche as Chief Colonel or President in Munster after the Earl of Ormond was discharged from the Munster service in 1581, but the Queen overruled him by summoning Sir Warham Sentleger to court, and then returning him to Ireland with personal

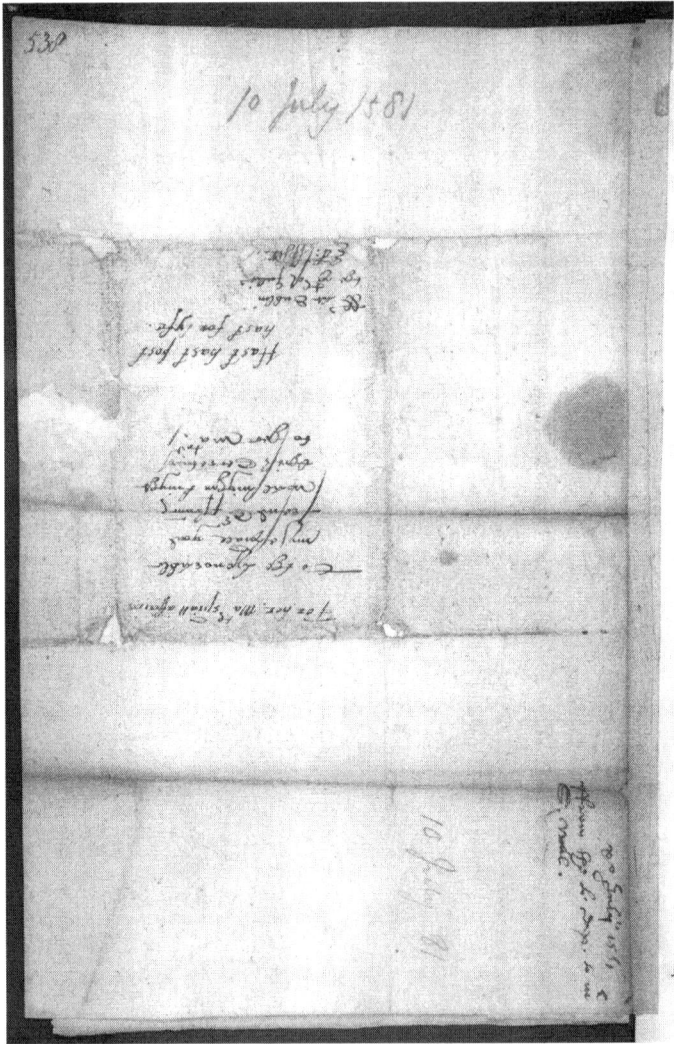

7. Grey to Walsingham, 10 July 1581, *from* TNA: PRO SP 63/84/14.
Spenser's addition of the official label of the Irish 'packett' indicates, again,
the considerable authority he held in the administration of Dublin Castle.

instructions for his appointment. Grey's attempts to place his clients—or,
perhaps, to create clients of these men by placing them—in positions of
authority reflects his anxieties about the plain dealing of others of his
colleagues in the Irish military and political establishment. He had good
cause to be worried: auditor Thomas Jenyson was regularly informing on
Grey to Burghley from 1581 onwards, and even Sir Nicholas Malby, who
was in strong sympathy with Grey's military policy in Ireland, was induced

to conspire—with Fenton and Adam Loftus, the Chancellor—against Grey after the Deputy distributed custodiams of escheated lands to 'his men' (including Spenser) in the autumn of 1581. Perhaps the only minister who remained loyal to the Lord Deputy was Sir Henry Wallop, who wrote to Burghley in protest in the spring of 1582, after Burghley had clearly asked him to report on Grey's activities. In such an environment, it is not surprising to find secretaries like Lodowick Bryskett offering to act as intelligencers to Burghley in return for patronage,[70] nor to discover that Wallop and Loftus, anxious that their covert practices were being betrayed to Burghley, hatched a plan in 1582 to 'turn' one of his secretaries, in order to find out who it was, in Dublin, who was reporting on them to the Lord Treasurer.[71]

In this kind of environment, it was prudent for the Lord Deputy to secure his communications in every way he could. The liberal use of ciphers was one way of guarding his intelligence, but, following the standard secretarial practices of the day, Spenser also used meticulous note-keeping to keep track of his master's letters. Grey occasionally intercepted letters being sent from England into Ireland, probably by using agents like Spenser to keep a close eye on who was travelling on the post-boat, and what letters had been committed for private delivery to its passengers.[72] Grey may also have used more aggressive tactics; Hugh Brady, the Bishop of Meath, complained to Walsingham in late 1581 that it was becoming almost impossible to send any letters at all, so frequently were carriers stopped and searched, and anything suspect confiscated.[73] To avoid similar kinds of interceptions, or at least to be aware when or if they had occurred, Spenser occasionally produced for Grey extracts from his notebook, recording letters and copies recently dispatched; as we have noted above, one such list (No. 34, SP 63/91/26) survives among the State Papers. Grey also made it a habit to acknowledge by date the letters he had received from the Privy Council and from his chief contacts; not only was it important for

---

[70] During the period in which Bryskett was actively seeking preferment as the new Secretary of State for Ireland, he wrote several times to Burghley offering information if Burghley would support his appointment. See SP 63/82/19, 63/82/53, and 63/83/27.

[71] Burghley's informant was probably Thomas Jenyson, the auditor, though he may also have been receiving sensitive information from Geoffrey Fenton. It was Jenyson who reported to Burghley the plan to question his secretary; see SP 63/95/12.

[72] This seems to be how Grey intercepted No. 38, below (SP 63/93/64/1), a letter from Thomas Meagh, then in the Tower, to his brother James Meagh, alias MacKedagh O'More, of 17 May 1582. The Mayor of Chester and Chancellor Gerrarde, similarly, seized a suspicious trunk belonging to one Edward Bulger, a Dublin merchant, in February 1581; the trunk contained seven letters from London recusants to their families and friends in Ireland, which Gerrarde forwarded to the Earl of Leicester, after committing Bulger to prison; see SP 63/81/60 and 63/81/60/1–7.

[73] See SP 63/87/6.

security for his correspondents to know what he had received, but it was crucial to their business to know when it had been received.

Another key way in which Grey sought to create security for the conduct of his business, of course, was to bind his clients and servants to him by the use of liberal rewards. If the remote and factional nature of the Dublin government exaggerated the dangers attending secretarial work, early modern Ireland was also a place in which faithful servants could rise very quickly to wealth and status through their master's gifts. As Spenser's dedicatory sonnet to *The Faerie Queene* attests, and as his faithful memorial of Grey's character and government in *A view of the present state of Ireland* also suggests, Grey seems to have rewarded Spenser handsomely for his loyalty and trust. Spenser acquired title to a manor in Enniscorthy, near Wexford, only weeks after Grey's expedition to Carlow and Wexford in the spring of 1581; this likely reflects Grey's help in securing favours for his secretary there. Similarly, Spenser was awarded a custodiam of Eustace lands out of the escheats occasioned by the Baltinglass rebellion, joining several of Grey's preferred captains and his household gentlemen (significantly, no other secretary was honoured with such a gift).[74] Grey considered this 'howse fynding'[75] to be such a natural and inalienable aspect of his necessary business in Ireland that he responded with grief and disbelief when Burghley and, after him, the Queen charged him with disloyal extravagance with crown possessions.

Spenser's years as Grey's personal secretary in Dublin were thus dominated not only by the violent and politic immediacy of the Irish service, but by the detail, the espionage, the courtesy, and the complex ethics of obligation and reward typical of the early modern secretariat, and, if anything exaggerated in Ireland. The duties of his office must have been constant and completely absorbing, and it is probably no surprise that Spenser seems to have produced no poetry during these years. His 'service', though, hardly went unrewarded: in addition to the grants of land, the sinecure posts, and other favours that he received at Grey's hands, Spenser had managed by 1589 to secure title to one of the least valuable and most contested estates in the Munster plantation—poor and tenuous as his claim would prove, it was a claim. In the 'Bill against Lord Roche' (see Figure 8), a document of 1589 in which Spenser—along with a fellow undertaker, Hugh Cuffe, and some men who appear to have been Spenser's

---

[74] See SP 63/88/40/3, a book of Grey's grants from the escheated lands.

[75] See No. 12, below (SP 63/82/48), which includes one of Grey's typical professions of uprightness and integrity: 'her maiesties paye & ryght of the office for howse fynding shall onely bee my share, for any oother benefitt or takyng, all chardgies I defie & pardoon refuse, how euer deerely it cost mee, as I fynde it doothe,/ & onely God I hoape on, for the world, I feare wyll fayle mee.'

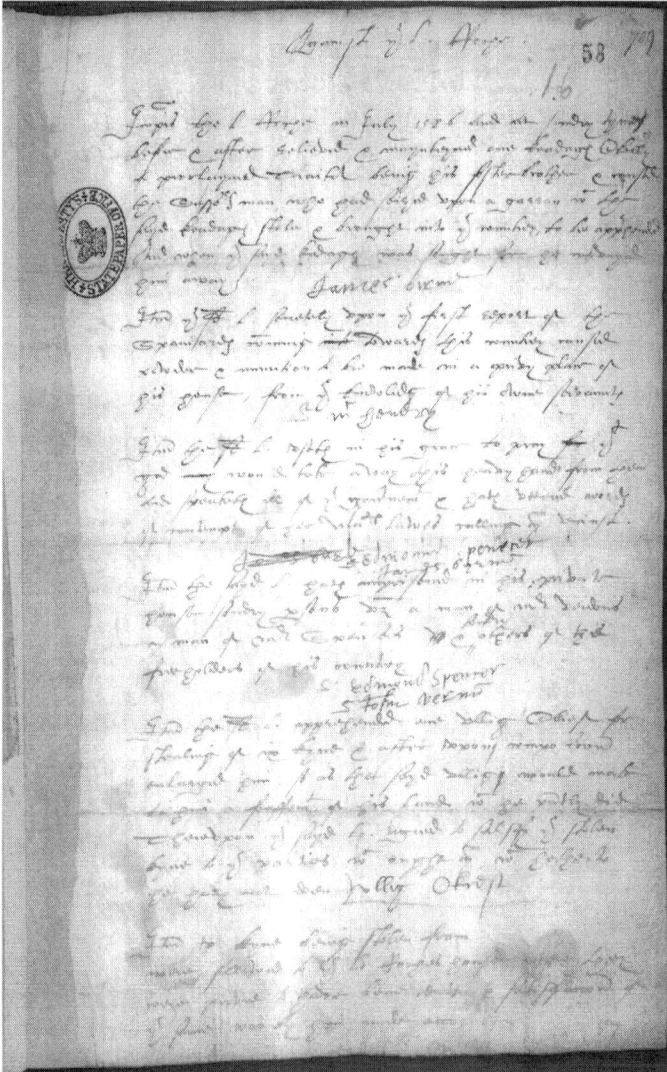

8. Bill against Lord Roche, 12 October 1589, *from* TNA: PRO SP 63/147/16. It is
likely that the 'signatures' to the claims against Roche, pictured here, are not
autograph, but someone has gone to the trouble to change the spelling
of 'Mr Edmound Spenser' to 'Spencer'.

tenants—made representations to the Council of Munster, or possibly to
Walsingham, about the abuse and harassment they had suffered at Roche's
hands, Spenser gives us a fascinating insight into the political instability of
Munster, the violence of his dealings with Roche, and the demographics

of the animosity between New English planters and Old English landlords. But the very fact that this document survives tells us something else, too— not only that Spenser had secured a title to the estate of Kilcolman and Rossack, but that in the attempt to make good his claim, he used New English connections either in the Council of Munster (which he served as clerk), or by writing directly to Walsingham, trading on connections and patronage he had formed in the preceding decade. This paper could not have survived had Spenser not learned well the lessons of political access taught him in Dublin Castle. The document also preserves one other, curious detail: at the end of the passage in Spenser's secretary hand, in the signature applied to one of the claims made against Roche, someone (possibly the poet himself) has corrected the spelling of his name from an original 'Spenser' to a form more favoured in court, 'Spencer'. Perhaps in 1589 Spenser judged that the years he had spent in Ireland copying, certifying, addressing, and sealing; dispatching and receiving messengers; and attending his lords in their campaigns and judicial sittings had finally given him cause.

Diplomatic Readings: Spenser's Letters, Poetry, and Prose

The selected letters and papers published in this volume, like the others that make up the archive of Spenser's manuscript writings as a whole, are of a historical and biographical interest in their own right: they afford a detailed, intimate picture of the political, military, and secretarial spheres in which Spenser, and many men like him, moved in late Elizabethan Ireland. These manuscripts shed light on New English attitudes to the Irish, on the colonial military and political history of the period, on early modern assumptions about patronage and clientage, on the ethical and political problems besetting the relation of masters and servants, and on early modern secretarial and administrative practice. But beyond this considerable historical interest, these papers have a particular importance for students and scholars of Spenser's poetry and prose. They supply otherwise vanished evidence of Spenser's movements during an obscure period in his life, and give us some indication of how he spent his time between 1580 and 1589. Perhaps most interesting, of course, is the way in which the concerns of these documents with war, with treason and conspiracy, with duty, with reform—concerns to which Spenser must daily and unremittingly have been exposed—influenced the writing that, in the late 1580s, began again to occupy his time. Brief sketches of some of the critical connections between the letters and Spenser's other writings will demonstrate how interesting these manuscript documents are.

Probably the most obvious links between Spenser's secretarial work and his later writings are those with *A view of the present state of Ireland*, and, indeed, many of the critical interpretations of *A view* developed in recent years might be easily and profitably extended to take account of the letters. Explicit and very direct connections are legion. For example, Grey reported to Walsingham on 6 April 1581 the Irish Council's frustration at the prospect of charging 'the late endyghted pryzoners heere'—men who had been arrested in connection with the Pale conspiracies around Viscount Baltinglass, the Earl of Kildare, and the Baron of Delvin. Grey identifies to Walsingham two particular 'extreamities' that made it difficult to proceed with conventional legal trials:

The one is the generall linck of kinred & alliance. the whoale sheere, whence these tryalls must bee retourned, hathe with the parties too bee tryed, & beesydes hardly acquyted of fauoure too the cause of theyr offence, what sounde verditt maye bee then hoaped of at sutche Iuries waye yowr sellf; a lawe or custome lykewyze is heere that euerie one is allowed xxxv challendgies, which makes, that if vpryghtnes myght bee looked for, I see not, as the tyme serues, how the number for the guestes woold bee supplyed: The oother is, that admitting theyr casting & condemnation, her Maiesties ryght & benefitt by theyr goods, landes & possessions, is cleane wyped awaye by deedes of guyft & oother conueyancies[.][76]

Ireland, Grey claims, lacks the requisite density of substantial men to make a fair jury trial feasible; most of the men in any given county are related by blood or marriage, and those who are not nonetheless sympathize with the crime—treason—for which the accused were standing trial. This problem was compounded by the common law custom of allowing every defendant thirty-five 'peremptory challenges' during the selection of a jury, which would quickly allow the accused to dismiss any impartial or adverse jurors—if indeed any such could be found. In addition, the whole exercise of the trial was a pointless one from the crown's financial perspective, Grey claimed; normally the Queen would stand to benefit substantially from a treason trial through the escheat (or forfeiture) of the attainted man's goods or lands, but because the Irish were so practised in rebellion, they had invariably devised 'deedes of guyft & oother conueyancies' to rid themselves of their possessions before going into revolt. The Queen thus stood, Grey claimed, to gain neither a conviction, nor any benefit by it. It may be no surprise to find that these two issues both come up in Irenius's discussion of legal abuses in *A view*; but it is perhaps surprising to find them coming up in nearly direct succession, as if Spenser were working from a copy of

---

[76] No. 10, SP 63/82/6.

the letter that, years before, he had sent to Walsingham. Of the jury trial, he writes:

By rehearesall of this I remember me allsoe of another like which I haue often obserued in trialls to haue wroughte great hurte and hinderaunce And that is the Excepcions which the Comon lawe alloweth to a felon in his triall, for he maye haue as youe knowe xxxvj excepcions peremtorye againste the Iurours of which he shall shewe no Cause and as manye as he will of suche as he Cane shewe Cawse, By which shifte theare beinge as I haue shewed youe suche small store of honest Iurymen he will either put of his triall or drive it to suche men as perhaps are not of the soundest sorte, By whose meanes if he Canne acquite himselfe of the Crime as he is likely then will he plague suche as weare broughte to be firste of his Iurye and all suche as made anye partie againste him and when he Coms forthe, will make theire Cowes and garrons to walke if he doe no other mischief to theire persons[.][77]

This discussion leads in *A view* to a brief consideration of the fraudulent conveyances made by felons, who in order to evade conviction regularly exploited an Irish law requiring principals to be tried before accessories in any crime; which Irenius follows with similarly brief comments on the corruption of Irish Parliaments. The discussion then immediately gives way to a long passage on rebellion and corrupt conveyances of traitors' estates, by which 'the Quene is defrauded of the intente of the lawe which laied that grevous punishement vppon Traytours to forfeite all theire Landes to the Prince to the ende that men mighte be the rather terrefyed from Comittinge Treasons'.[78] In the context of Grey's April 1581 letter to Walsingham, Irenius's claim to 'have often observed' these abuses 'in try-alls' not only rings true, but suggests the closely documented, closely observed nature of Spenser's careful arguments in his reform tract.

This kind of direct link might easily be extended from the letters, through other parallel passages in *A view*, to Spenser's legal, political, and ethical concerns in *The Faerie Queene*. An important preoccupation in Grey's letters to the Queen, for example, is his effort to convince her that force, and neither leniency nor laws, must be the means to a reformation of Ireland and a settlement of peace. This was a point of policy that, as we have noted above, Grey shared with other New English soldiers and governors of this period, from Sir Henry Sidney and Sir William Drury to the first Earl of Essex and Sir Nicholas Malby. A typical passage from such letters is Grey's strenuous argument against the general pardon and the reduction of the army in a letter of 6 November 1581 (SP 63/86/50), in

---

[77] *A view*, ll. 759–71.   [78] *A view*, ll. 825–8.

which he recites the general state of unrest to which the kingdom has again fallen as a result of the pardon, and assures the Queen that 'the stay and bitt to all which is onely your force, & not duety nor good will your Highnes can accoumpt of'; further, he claims that 'Madam to make you an honorable & sownd peace some tyme yt will aske, & your warre the onely meanes'.[79] Spenser's interlocutors in *A view* concur without debate on the New English policy of which Grey was so forceful an exponent, noting of the Irish and Old English that:

when soe they make heade no lawes no penalties Cane restraine but that they doe in the violence of that furye treade downe and trample vnderfoote all bothe divine and hvmaine thinges and the lawes themselues they doe speciallye rage at and rend in peces as moste repugnaunte to theire libertye and naturall fredome which in theire madnes they affecte./
Eudox. It is then a verye vnseasonable time to pleade lawe when swordes are in the handes of the vulgare or to thinke to retayne them with feare of punishmentes when they loke after libertye and shake of all gouernement/
Iren: Then soe it is with Irelande Continvallye/ *Eudoxus.* for the sworde was neuer yeat out of theire hand but when they are wearye with warrs and broughte downe to extreame wretchednes then they Creepe a little perhaps and sue for grace till they haue gotten newe breathe. and recouered theire strength againe So as it is in vaine to speake of plantinge of lawes and plottinge pollicies till they be alltogeather subdued[.][80]

The possibility of bringing civility by law without force is constantly raised in Books V and VI of *The Faerie Queene*, and constantly rejected—not only in the summary dispatch, by Talus, of the giant with scales (V.ii.29–54), or in Artegall's and Britomart's crucially opposed responses to Radigund's attempts to propound 'conditions' before her battles (V.iv.48–9 and V.vii.28); but also in the restraint of Mirabella, the 'Ladie of her libertie', by force and power in *FQ* VI.vii–viii, and in Calidore's recognition that, when it comes to villains as illimitable as the prey-taking, border-crossing brigants of Book VI, canto xi, the martial law of a Malby, or Sir Richard Bingham, is the only solution. It might even comfortably be argued that the New English approach to military purgation, a constant theme in *A view*, provides the structure underpinning not only the general relation of Talus to Artegall, but of justice to courtesy.

The conditions and practices of Spenser's secretarial experience, too, likely found their way into his poetry of the late 1580s and 1590s. Even C. S. Lewis was willing to suppose that Spenser's Irish experiences had corrupted his imagination;[81] but rather than read this influence as a negative

---

[79] SP 63/86/50. [80] *A view*, ll. 355–69.
[81] See C. S. Lewis, *The Allegory of Love* (Oxford: Clarendon Press, 1936), 349.

and enervating pressure on Spenser's verse, we might consider the importance of physical violence not only to Spenser's allegories (and not only in the later parts of *The Faerie Queene*, but as early as the first canto of the first book), but to his allegoresis. Violence and *enargeia* enjoy a long association dating back to at least the *Rhetorica ad Herennium*, and Spenser might well have intended to exploit graphic death, corpses, dismemberment, ravishment, and other kinds of violent spectacle had he never been to Ireland.[82] But while this rhetorical and mnemotechnic set of associations between violence, attention, memory, and value is undeniably important to reading *The Faerie Queene*, the conspicuously funny element of much of Spenser's violence, in his allegorical epic, seems to play in another direction. The comic gluing of Corflambo's head back onto his trunk (IV.ix.4–7), the readiness with which Sanglier agrees to Artegall's Solomonic offer to cut his lady in two (V.i.26), even the heavy-handedly allegorical humour of Pollente's death, as his severed head finds a way, having fallen to the ground, to bite the earth (V.ii.18)—all of these scenes of violence or offered violence seem not to provoke pathos, but rather delight. The desensitization to violence, and to what are probably innate animal fears for our corporeal integrity, might be thought necessary steps towards a Christian stoicism, or even Platonist contempt for the insubstantiality of the phenomenal world. The experience of violence in Spenser's letters— Grey's hunting in the glens of Carlow and Wicklow,[83] John Zouche's glib joke in sending John of Desmond's head to Grey for 'a new-yeeres guyfte'[84]—stresses exactly this absurd or even playful aspect to a violence that has gone past the pathos of the human, and surrendered entirely to the divine. Nor is the absurd quality of Spenser's violence in much of *The Faerie Queene* incompatible with experiences of awe and reverence— indeed, the two approaches to suffering are necessarily linked, as in Grey's account of the death of John Cheke at Smerwick:

vnhappely good Iohn Cheeke too carelessely advauncing him selfe, to looke ouer the Trenche, stricken on the head tombled downe at my feete, dead I tooke him & for so I caused him to bee carried away, yet yt pleased God to send him spright

---

[82] As Frances Yates noted in *The Art of Memory* (London: Routledge and Kegan Paul, 1966), the *Rhetorica ad Herennium* makes a strong link between what might be called impact—a striking, 'flashbulb' effect—and the accuracy and durability of the memory. This leads the author of the *Rhetorica ad Herennium* to recommend violent and disgusting images, above all, in the construction of visual mnemonics; see *Rhetorica ad Herennium*, III.30–40. Aristotle also notes the innate human fascination with the violent and the disgusting in the *Poetics*, cap. 4. See also Gordon Teskey, *Allegory and Violence* (Ithaca, NY: Cornell University Press, 1996).

[83] See SP 63/84/12.

[84] See No. 27, below (SP 63/88/15).

agayne & yet doth liue in speache & greatest memory, that euer was seene with
such a wounde, & truly Madam so disposed to God, & made so diuine a Confession of his faith, as all Diuines in either of your Maiesties realmes could not haue
passed, yf matched, yt; so wrought in him Gods spirite, playnely declaring him a
Childe of his elected, to the no lesse comfort of his good and godly frendes, then
great instruction & manifest motion of euery other hearer that stood by, of whome
there was a good troupe.[85]

Cheke's death receives a paragraph of hagiographic veneration, complete
with an apology to the Queen for the tedious digression; to the papal
troops slaughtered the next day, by contrast, Grey gives four words: 'There
were 600 slayne.' The only scenes of violence that matter to Spenser in
The Faerie Queene—for example, Redcrosse's torment in the House of
Holinesse (I.x.24–8), Ruddymane's imbruing of his hands in his dead
mother's blood (II.i.39–61)—are those tied to a godly purpose.

Probably the other most consistent and important aspect of the Irish
experience described in Spenser's letters is the constant state of suspicion
in which Grey held his fellow governors, the Palesmen, the Old English
aristocracy, and of course his Irish allies as well as enemies. Politic dis-
simulation characterized most of the behaviour (both civil and military)
of the main actors on the early modern Irish stage. Spenser coped with
this culture of suspicion, as a secretary, by discharging faithfully and
meticulously the full range of bookkeeping and other security measures
that protected his master's correspondence, from ciphers to seals. Grey
coped with it by gathering more information. The translation of a March
1581 Latin letter from Miler Magrath, Archbishop of Cashel, to Sir Lucas
Dillon, Chief Baron of the Exchequer in Ireland, gives a good portrait of
the cynicism and anxiety that this culture of suspicion produced, and of the
diction that the government used to describe it:

I am by Lettres of late aduertised as of a truth that they of Munster which hitherto
cloked themselues vnder the name of subiectes, and did in truth but desemble it
haue now ioyned themselues to the trayterous *Geraldins* . . . *Cormach Mac Teig* is
holden as suspect and a great nomber of others emongest them of great name &
creat do make open profession of adherency to the Rebelles. And now theire eyes
are wholly bent vppon the sea: God turne the hope of theire Ioy into mourning;
Many of them that do yet coler the name of subiectes dissemble the matter
loking what successe the enemies shall haue. They are allmost all fallen away to
wickednes they are all become vnprofitable there is scarse one emongest vs that doth
good, and such as youe put great trust in, there some do I feare as much as the
other.[86]

[85] SP 63/78/29 (No. 5, below).   [86] SP 63/81/21.

In this climate of fear and cynicism, Dublin officials and their allies not only suspected everyone around them of duplicity, but expected it of them; Magrath goes so far as to suggest that the extension of trust itself constitutes grounds for fear, as if Dillon were exposing himself simply by expecting one or two of the Munster lords to remain dutiful. The radical fear and epistemological insecurity of this environment almost certainly left its mark on Spenser's poetry in the 1590s, as in sonnet 6 of the *Amoretti*:

> Be nought dismayd that her vnmoued mind
>   doth still persist in her rebellious pride:
>   such loue not lyke to lusts of baser kynd,
>   the harder wonne, the firmer will abide.
> The durefull Oake, whose sap is not yet dride,
>   is long ere it conceiue the kindling fyre:
>   but when it once doth burne, it doth diuide
>   great heat, and makes his flames to heauen aspire.
> So hard it is to kindle new desire,
>   in gentle brest that shall endure for euer:
>   deepe is the wound, that dints the parts entire
>   with chast affects, that naught but death can seuer.
> Then thinke not long in taking litle paine,
>   to knit the knot, that euer shall remaine.

'The intollerable pride and insolencye of Turloughe', Grey wrote in August 1581, 'is soche, as Cannot be contynued within the bondes of duetye to hir maiestye',[87] but, as we have seen, Zouche and Gilbert would have argued the line taken by Spenser's first quatrain: great hearts, though 'harder wonne, the firmer will abide'. This sonnet (like Gilbert's policy) reaches after an epistemological certainty that it should regard as absurd. What makes the beloved's reformation a possibility, to the lover's mind, is the fact that she has, so far, demonstrated the resolve of an 'vnmoued mind'; but once she cracks, or catches, her mind no longer constant will no longer support the trust the lover claims she now deserves. This paradox— a central one for the *Amoretti* as a whole, only perhaps resolved by the intervention of a divine power in sonnet 68—by its diction and argument leads us inexorably back to the politic dissimulations and 'rebellious pride' of the Irish and Old English enemies to the Pale government. The very cause of trust, as for Magrath, becomes a cause for distrust.

Spenser wrote about 'suspition' in another letter in the late 1580s, this time to Walter Ralegh. The fear of misconstruction he rehearses in that

---

[87] Grey to the Privy Council, 12 August 1581, SP 63/85/13 (No. 21, below).

letter might at first seem very distant from the 'doubtfulness', the 'coler', the cloaking of the Dublin drudgery he had, by 1589, left behind. Richard Rambuss has, however, rightly drawn our attention to the ways in which the secrecy and suspicion of the Dublin secretariat provides an important hermeneutical model for Spenser's allegorical poetics in *The Faerie Queene*. And yet, rather than construing the impact of Spenser's secretarial career on his poetic praxis simply as a fondness and facility for husbanding secrets, we ought rather to recognize the importance to secretaries not only of concealment, but of communication—albeit managed, authorized communication. Codes, ciphers, subscriptions, seals, and rewards all bespeak an epistemological approach to literary authorship far less cynical and pessimistic than the critical demystification of secretary Spenser as a secret-monger. Instead of privileging words, these material aspects of Spenser's implication in and access to the Deputy's privy business between 1580 and 1582 struggle to privilege trust, faith, and security. It is thus not surprising to find Redcrosse, in his epistemologically fraught encounter with that most literal and unfaithful of readers, Despayre, in Book I of *The Faerie Queene*, suffering from a surfeit of secretaryship. Una intervenes at the moment that Redcrosse has given in to the reading of the post:

> his hand did quake,
> And tremble like a leafe of Aspin greene,
> And troubled bloud through his pale face was seene
> To come, and goe with tydings from the hart,
> As it a running messenger had beene.   (I.ix.51)

Redcrosse stands knife in hand, ready to break the seal on his heart's 'tydings'. In attempting to get him away from the 'running messenger' of his misleading, mortal blood, Una makes an appeal to Redcrosse to transcend what is written for that which lies beyond, and perhaps above, strict justice—the 'grace' one letter-crazed man, a decade before, had lost:

> In heauenly mercies hast thou not a part?
> Why shouldst thou then despeire, that chosen art?
> Where iustice growes, there grows eke greater grace,
> The which doth quench the brond of hellish smart,
> And that accurst hand-writing doth deface.   (I.ix.53)

Spenser puts into Una's mouth an argument that, in conspicuously recruiting the secretary's preoccupation with 'hand-writing', continues the loose sense that Redcrosse is being overwhelmed by bad letters. What implicates this passage even more eerily in the tensions between reading, suspicion, trust, and security that had dominated Spenser's secretarial career is Una's resort to a familiar grammatical ambiguity, one that modern readers would have no cause to recognize. When she asks, 'What meanest thou by this reprochfull strife?' (I.ix.52), her question can be read two ways: either, conventionally, 'what do you mean by this reproachful strife?', or, as validly to a sixteenth-century ear, 'what does this reproachful strife mean (for you)?' The difference may seem slight at first, but it lies in the fact that, in the first case, the words or action are figured as the expression of an intent, whereas in the second, the words or the action define the self. Implicitly Una asks Redcrosse: are you the meaner of your letters, or are your letters the definer of you? If the secretary's place is simply to learn the art of secrecy, there can be no faith; but if the secretary's place is to practise faith, then the letters—so many books and papers—may be defaced. In the material relation of the secretary to his ink and parchment inheres, for Spenser's imagination, the mystery of faith and grace. 'Arise, Sir knight arise, and leaue this cursed place.'

Note on the Texts

THIS selected edition of Spenser's letters and other papers has been designed with the student and scholar foremost in mind. We have adopted a very light editorial touch, in order to preserve not only the impression of the original manuscripts, but as much as possible of their various kinds of textual evidence—crucial to an understanding of Spenser's role in the Dublin and Munster secretariats, and thus to any estimate of the impact upon his literary writing of his secretarial career. We hope that more casual readers will not be put off by the idiosyncratic spellings of Grey and, to a lesser degree, Spenser himself; and have chosen to gloss the more syntactically complex passages, rather than housetrain them by the uniform application of modern punctuation conventions. What these texts may lose in simplicity, though, they gain by fidelity: readers curious about secrecy, secretarial practice, patronage, and courtesy should find useful the preserved evidence of codes and ciphers, addresses and subscriptions, deletions and insertions, and many other elements, both in the letter-texts themselves, and in the headnotes, textual notes, and annotations.

The policy we have followed can be briefly summarized as follows. We have preserved all original spelling, punctuation, and other accidentals not obstructive to the sense (majuscules/minuscules, certain abbreviations), along with some basic aspects of formatting (e.g. indentation, paragraph divisions). Lineation we have generally not preserved (though see below), nor have we attempted to replicate the exact layout of postscripts (which are often found scrawled in any available space, in any orientation) or marginal annotations, though both postscripts and marginalia have been given their appropriate places at the foot and to the sides of the documents, respectively. Most contractions and brevigraphs have been expanded (including the terminal '-es' graph, and instances of p̲ for 'per', 'pro', etc.), and superscripts lowered, in a manner suited to the usual spelling habits in the hand of the writer (thus Grey's contracted 'y^r' becomes 'yowr', but Spenser's 'your'); important exceptions include 'Mr' for 'Master', ordinal numbers (e.g. 'vjth'), and the superscript unit abbreviations li (*libri*, pounds), s (*solidi*, shillings), and d (*denarii*, pence), which we like Spenser and Grey have represented as superscripts (e.g. 'xxvj^{li} vj^s'). Following Spenser's and contemporary practice, we have generally represented the Irish patronymic as 'Mac' rather than 'Mc', though the latter spelling does occur in a couple of isolated instances in the letter texts. The use of Roman numerals for numbers (dates, quantities, etc.) we have throughout retained.

All original underscoring and annotation, whether added by sender in Ireland or recipient in England, we have preserved. Where due to damage to the manuscript or some other impediment we have been left with a partial word, an obscured word, or an absence where a word clearly should be, we have where possible sought to supply in the text or textual notes the appropriate letters, word, or words, again in a manner appropriate to the spelling habits in the hand of a writer; these additions always appear in {curly brackets}. Where such passages have resisted reconstruction, we have included a mark of omission, { . . . }, to indicate the gap. Distinctions between hands (secretary, mixed, italic) and the style of hands (set, cursive, rough) we have described in the headnote to each document and, where further discussion seemed necessary, at the appropriate places in the textual notes.

Coded passages and the use of ciphers present special problems, particularly because Walsingham (or one of his clerks) tended to transliterate supralineally Grey's simple substitution code in most but by no means all instances. In order to preserve as much as possible of the original presentation of the manuscripts, we have retained the (Arabic) numerical ciphers, supplying identifications (where known) in the textual notes. Passages in the Walsingham code have been fully transliterated according to the key presented in the appendix, which itself was compiled from routine observation of existing transliterations in the manuscripts themselves. (Our correct transliterations sometimes disagree with the less scrupulous transliterations provided in the manuscripts themselves.) The shorter and more infrequent passages in code sent to the Queen have not been transliterated, simply because we cannot be certain, based on the small sample, exactly what the symbols mean.

In four special cases we have regularly preserved lineation and indentation. Because the layout of addresses, endorsements, and subscriptions (including signatures) can carry valuably suggestive evidence about the composition, receipt, and decorum of a letter, we have preserved lineation and indentation for these three elements of the letters. We have occasionally also preserved within-line indentations and other unusual blanks, generally in cases where this white space was apparently intended to serve as a form of punctuation, or was inserted to mark a space to be completed later (e.g. when a scribe lacked a piece of information, or access to a code, subsequently left incomplete). The decision not to preserve lineation or pagination in the letter-texts more generally has inevitably resulted in a few unfortunate consequences. Chief among these is the occasional circumstance where a paratextual mark not proper to any particular passage of the document but to the page or the document itself—e.g. an addressee note, a kind of endorsement recording the letter's intended recipient, often appearing on the first page of the letter—no longer has a natural place in the edited text. In these cases we have removed the word or words from the edited text, but preserved it or them in the headnote. Some other para-textual marks (for example, catchwords, or the hyphens used in words broken across the line) we have silently excised. Other paratextual marks— addresses, endorsements of various kinds, and marginal annotations—we have included if and only if there is good reason to think they were added at the document's composition, or at its receipt or original filing; this naturally excludes the notes made on the manuscripts by nineteenth-century archivists and calendarists. In most cases this kind of distinction is clear and easy to make, but in others—where the paratextual mark consists of some underscoring, or the insertion of obscure symbols—we have been forced to exercise our best judgement. Original addresses and endorse-ments appear in a separate section at the front of each letter-text.

The textual notes supplied at the foot of each letter-text provide a detailed account of insertions, deletions, and any damage or other salient feature of the manuscript original. The annotations to each letter provide information on the historical context, supply paraphrases of difficult passages, and suggest routes for further reading. Readers should note that unfamiliar Irish terms, proper names, and Irish place names may not be glossed in these annotations; see the glossary and at the end of the book for Irish terms and proper names, and the maps on pp. xiii–xiv for Irish place names.

Letters and Other Papers

1. *Copy of Hugh Magennis to Grey, 29 August 1580*

TNA: PRO SP 63/75/75

In his first weeks in Ireland, one of the duties in which Spenser seems to have been most involved was the copying of letters received by Grey, presumably for conveyance to England. A number of such letters survive, and a selection are printed here (see also e.g. Nos. 2, 3, and 4, below, SP 63/75/84, 63/76/1, 63/76/9). It is not inconceivable that the limited responsibility associated with such a task is a sign that Spenser was, at the time, an inexperienced or as yet untrusted secretary: certainly, as he gained experience and trust in Grey's service, his role appears to have shifted to a more diverse portfolio of duties, many bespeaking a higher level of access in the secretariat. However, it is equally the case that the task of copying made Spenser privy to important political and military information, much of it concerning Turlough Luineach O'Neill's threats to his neighbouring landowners in Ulster. Sir Hugh Magennis's appeal for Grey's assistance, after Turlough Luineach's attack on his lands and property in Co. Down, provides an account of the tactics typically used in such raids, and an indication of Turlough Luineach's strength at this time. His quarrel with Magennis is also described in Sir Nicholas Bagenal's letter (No. 3, below, SP 63/76/1). Turlough Luineach well knew that Magennis was a proxy for the Dublin government, and his spoil of Magennis's lands a dare; it was English policy in Elizabethan Ireland that the Queen's loyal subjects had to be defended from predations by their neighbouring lords, and Grey knew that many Irish eyes would be watching Magennis's fortunes to see whether the English forces or the prince of Ulster were the more powerful.

The text of this copied letter, including the original letter's address at its foot, is written in Spenser's characteristic secretary hand, here particularly hasty and cursive. The second line of the endorsement, 'To the L. Deputie', is in Spenser's compact secretary hand, while the first and third lines were added later in an italic hand, presumably during the filing process.

ENDORSEMENT

Hugh Magenesse
To the Lord Deputie /
29 August.

TEXT

The Copy of hugh Magenesse his lettre. /

My most humble Duetie promised vnto your honour yt is so right Honorable that the xxvij^th of this present Moneth some of Terlagh Lennagh his men toke from me by pray iiij^C kyne iij^xx mares ij^C swyne iij^C shepe & killed xvj of my poore followeres and also that within this iij wekes past the said malefactores came vnto the borderes of my Countrey with Certein laboreres & hookes & Cutt all the greene corne that they fownd there beseeching your honour to Considre the same and to license me to be revenged and to compell Mr Marshall to ayde & assiste me Terlagh Meanes no goodnes & he is of great force. The Scottes are at Lough foyle with their shippes, beseeching thAlmight &c.

Narrow water the xxix^th of August 1580

> To the right honorable
> & my very good Lord the
> Lord Deputie yeue this

COMMENTARY

Hugh Magenesse] an Irish lord of Ulster, and traditionally a vassal of the O'Neill; see biographies.

Terlagh Lennagh] Turlough Luineach O'Neill; see biographies.

pray . . . kyne] see glossary. O'Neill's attack on Magennis was clearly designed to be financially crippling: 400 cattle, 200 pigs, and 300 sheep must have represented a substantial part, if not the whole, of Magennis's livestock, and the loss of 60 (breeding) mares would dealt him a serious blow in an age when the horse was essential to transport and communication.

Mr Marshall] Sir Nicholas Bagenal, Knight Marshal of Ireland; see biographies.

The Scottes . . . their shippes] Lough Foyle is the estuary at the mouth of the River Foyle, directly north of O'Neill's lordship of Tyrone. Turlough Luineach had strengthened his alliance with the Scots by marrying Agnes Campbell, the widow of James MacDonnell and sister to the Earl of Argyle, in 1569. Mercenaries from Scotland tended to appear in Ireland in the summer every year, supporting Turlough in some of his endeavours and establishing a colony of their own in the eastern land of the Ards. The English government had long found it impossible to intercept or impede communication between the Northern Irish lords and the Scots, and the fear of a Scots–Irish attempt on the English throne persisted until Mary Queen of Scots was executed in 1587.

Narrow water] Narrow Water Keep, held by Magennis, lies near the present-day town of Warrenpoint, on the Co. Down bank of the Newry River, which enters Carlingford Lough a mile to the south.

2. *Copy of Hugh O'Neill to Grey, 31 August 1580*
TNA: PRO SP 63/75/84

On the dispute between Hugh O'Neill, Baron of Dungannon, and Turlough Luineach O'Neill, see note below. This is not Dungannon's only petition to the Lord Deputy for military support, nor his only protestation of beleaguered loyalty: see also his letter to Lord Justice Pelham of 24 November 1579 (SP 63/70/22). As in Magennis's carefully crafted appeal in No. 1, above (SP 63/75/75)—where he uses all his available leverage to enlist the Lord Deputy upon his behalf in what was essentially a regional power struggle—Hugh O'Neill here exploits the English government's fear of Turlough Luineach as a means to building his own power base in Ulster. He advertises his own access to Turlough Luineach's counsels ('my secrete frendes'), offers Grey military advice, and rehearses the loyalty of his lineage, before making a very detailed plea for the control of English military resources. The ethical complexity of Hugh O'Neill's parting offer, to make his private revenge the instrument of the state's justice, resurfaces continually in this collection of documents, as it also does in the uneasy marriage of chivalric quest to ethical and political instruction in *The Faerie Queene*.

The text of the letter, including the original address at the foot of the manuscript's second page, is largely in Spenser's characteristic secretary hand, here fairly rushed; the only exception comes in the words 'Baron of Dungannons' in the letter's title, which are in Spenser's mixed hand. The letter has a composite endorsement: the first and third lines are in Spenser's mixed hand, but the middle line ('To the Lord Deputie') is written in a distinct secretary hand, which was presumably added upon receipt and filing of the letter in Westminster.

ENDORSEMENT

Baron Dunganon
To the Lord Deputie.
Vltimo Augusti

TEXT

The copie of the Baron of Dunganons lettre

Right honorable. Tirlagh Lennagh is repayering to these bordres with a great army of men who pretendeth to invade the pale, as I am credibly given to vnderstand by my secrete frendes about him, notwithstanding his promise of peace lately made to your Lordship

which this his euill pretence I have sundry tymes revealed to her
Maiesties Counsell in England & in Ireland all this yeare past &
forasmuch as he is presently to repaire for executing his pretended
mischief that yt would please your honour to send downe hether
some such force for the defence of the pale & vs her Maiesties
subiectes as your Lordship may well spare. for yf now vpon the first
you shall give him head he will grow so prowde thereof as you will
have more adoe with him then with all the rest her Maiesties enemies
in Ireland which now you may prevent & have what peace you will at
his handes yf you seeme at the first to withstand him which a smaller
force will now doe then hereafter. And forasmuch as my grandfather
my father & my brother hath both bestowed their goodes & lives in
her Maiesties service And also I my self hath ventered the same euer
sence I was hable to beare sword and so will contynew by godes grace
during my life And also vnderstanding from her Maiesties Counsell
in England by lettre ready to be showen by this Bearer my servaunt
her gratious pleasure that I should° have some such enterteynement
for the better mayntenance of my self my kinsmen & followeres (now
ready for want thereof to depart from mee) as your Lordship & my
Lord Chauncellour shall thinck meete for mee I have thought yt good
most humbly to crave the same now in my great extremitie having
already at my late Lord Iustice handes xxv horsemen in pay doe
beseeche them to be made vppe to some such company as thereby I
may be able to doe the better service. And yf your Lordship shall fynd
that there may be any good° ordre taken with Tirlagh Lennagh that
you may stand assured of him, then will I not onely with that force I
have in her Maiesties pay but all other forces that I am hable to make
as skottes shott and galloglasses to repaire to your Lordship and serve
vpon the rest her Maiesties enemies there both dutifully and truly
which hath killed of late some of my frendes whose deaths I would
gladly revenge Thus not omitting my duety &c   Bally scanlin The
Last of August 1580

> To the right honorable
> my very good Lord the
> Lord Deputie of Ireland. /

---

should] inserted above the line.   good] inserted above the line.

COMMENTARY

Baron Dunganon] Hugh O'Neill; see biographies.

Tirlagh Lennagh] Turlough Luineach O'Neill; see biographies.

pretendeth] intends or presumes; not 'simulates'.

the pale] see glossary.

his promise ... your Lordship] See SP 63/73/54, 63/75/20, 63/75/40, 63/75/58. Turlough Luineach had assembled over 7,000 Scots and his 'risings out', and expected further reinforcements with the arrival of his wife. Nonetheless, in August 1580, he made proclamation through his camp that none of his followers harm Elizabeth's English subjects, upon pain of death.

I have ... this year past] see, for example, his letters of 22 December 1578 and 24 November 1579: SP 63/65/4/2 and 63/70/22.

give him head] as with a horse, 'not to check or hold him in with the bridle; to give him freedom, let him go freely' (*OED*, 'Head', *n.*[1] 64).

my grandfather my father & my brother] Hugh O'Neill's grandfather was Conn O'Neill (d.1559), Earl of Tyrone. Matthew (d.1558), Hugh's father, had been nominated by Conn as his eldest son, and had accordingly been created Baron of Dungannon in the expectation that he would succeed to the earldom at Conn's death. However, a younger son, Shane (who also appears to have been the O'Neill tanist), alleged Matthew's illegitimacy and claimed succession to the earldom as well as to the captaincy in 1559, blocking the succession of Matthew's sons Brian (d.1562) and Hugh. In remembering the service of Conn, of Matthew, and of Brian his brother, Hugh implicitly opposes his own house against the rebellious line of Shane, his sons, and Turlough Luineach.

skottes shott and galloglasses] Hugh O'Neill, like most Ulster lords, had a number of Scots mercenaries among his forces. On **galloglasses**, see glossary.

3. *Copy of Sir Nicholas Bagenal to Grey, 2 September 1580*

TNA: PRO SP 63/76/1

Upon news of the landing of Spanish and papal forces near Dingle, one of Grey's immediate concerns was to determine the extent of Irish support for their arrival. Of particular importance was the greatest and most proximate threat to English interests in the Pale, Turlough Luineach O'Neill, whose potential combination with the invaders and the Munster rebels had the potential to pinch and possibly defeat English forces in the east of the island. Bagenal is hardly being rhetorical in his characterization of the developing military situation as a crucible moment in the history of English interests in Ireland, which may help to explain the savagery of subsequent events, and the jubilation in both Ireland and England after the 'victory' at Smerwick (see No. 5, below, SP 63/78/29). On Magennis's quarrel with Turlough Luineach O'Neill, see also No. 1, above (SP 63/75/75).

The text of the letter, including the original address at the foot of the second page, is in Spenser's characteristic secretary hand; the only exception comes in the words 'Baron of Dungannons' in the header, which are in Spenser's italic. The second line of the endorsement, 'To the L Dep.', written in Spenser's compact secretary hand, is the original endorsement. The first and third lines were added in a later italic hand, presumably when the letter was being filed in Westminster.

ENDORSEMENT

Sir Nicholas Bagnoll
To the Lord Deputy
2 September

TEXT

The copie of Sir Nicholas Bagnoles lettre

This very instant my messenger retourned from Turlough Lennogh with another of his by whome he sent thinclosd lines which your Lordship may pervse. The partie for whose death he chalengeth Magneisse so hotely of disposicion was so vile as Magneisse could not have in the killing of any such like donne better. A more notorious thief & murtherer reigned not

And although he shadow his approche vpon some grownd expressed in his lettre yett is he not to be trusted for in hearing of my man he vowed that his Vriaghes he would have before he retourned, yf not with your Lordships consent then otherwise His force is iiij^m more neare five & assuredly bent to take thadvauntage. for one of the farinans a Rome runner knave came vnto him within these v daies from Mounster & so persuaded him of the forces there & your Lord-ship in your last voiage how both were weakened & impaired that hath so kindled his rancour as vnlesse your Lordship speedily send downe force, before he ronne vp, the safetie of the pale wilbe hazarded neuer more: Your Lordships owne presense would here be necessarie yf yt might bee but as you fynd the service most needfull (I speake as one that hath not seene further then here presently) so be yt And yf but the forces come I shall doe what in me shall lye (god please° to temper or withstand according to the necessitie of the tyme. I heare he standes the more vpon the Vriaghs, for that Captein Pieres (as he alleadgeth) gave him assuraunce of the enioying them your Lordship

(**god please**] Spenser did not close this parenthesis, apparently because the line break after these words provided punctuation enough.

knoweth yf he had such Commission to performe yt. Lastly as I have said, force & not elles will salue this for truly he dependes of some promise of the baron of Dunganon to come to him. which yf doe° then yf force doe not come how vncertein the rest wilbee I know & all men elles may adiudge. Euen thus the living god &c.

> To the right Honorable my singular
> good Lord the Lord Grey Lord Deputie
> of Ireland /

COMMENTARY

Sir Nicholas Bagnoll] i.e. Bagenal; see biographies.

Turlough Lennogh] Turlough Luineach O'Neill; see biographies.

thinclosed lines] this enclosure has not survived.

Magneisse] Sir Hugh Magennis; see biographies.

shadow his approach vpon some grownd] 'dissemble some false pretext for his approach [to the English Pale]'. Since the letter bearing 'thinclosd lines' is lost, so, unfortunately, is Turlough Luineach's explanation of his advance to the Pale; but it is possible that Turlough Luineach was claiming to seek redress of Magennis's murder of his man.

Vriaghes] i.e. urraghs; see glossary. Turlough Luineach's main complaint against the crown was the Queen's refusal to permit him the O'Neill's traditional Ulster sub-lords: Maguire, O'Cahan, MacMahon, Magennis, MacQuillin, and O'Hanlon.

farinans] Turlough Luineach appears to have had a messenger by the name of Salamon Farnan (or Faranon).

a Rome runner knave] 'Rome runner' was an opprobrious English term, well attested in the medieval period, for clerics or laymen who travelled to Rome to seek for offices, grants, or other favour from the Pope. O'Neill's servant Farnan may have been this cleric, or they may have been two men of the same family. Bagenal certainly sees Farnan's arrival as a hint that Turlough Luineach may be ready to join an incipient papally supported invasion of the island.

your last voiage] Grey's disastrous August defeat at the hands of Feagh MacHugh O'Byrne in the glens of Wicklow; very little correspondence between Dublin and London survives concerning this defeat, which may be because there was not much to begin with—Grey certainly would not have wanted to advertise his inauspicious entry into the government. But see SP 63/75/80 and 63/75/82, reports from Chancellor Gerrarde and Sir Nicholas Malby that touch on the defeat.

Captein Pieres] William Piers; see biographies. A letter from Piers to Walsingham (SP 63/75/58) mentions Turlough Luineach's request that his urraghs be maintained, in exchange for expelling the Scots from Ulster. Piers regularly overstepped his commission and caused Grey other headaches throughout his

---

yf doe] Spenser's omission of the word 'he', which presumably appeared in Bagenal's original letter, is a case of common eyeskip.

deputyship; see e.g. Grey's impatient dismissal of Piers's self-important claims of 'credytt' with Turlough Luineach in August 1581 (No. 21, below, SP 63/85/13).

baron of Dunganon] Hugh O'Neill; see biographies.

which yf doe] presumably Spenser omitted the word 'he' between 'which' and 'yf'; the English feared the combination of Hugh O'Neill and Turlough Luineach, for between them they could muster most of the province of Ulster.

4. *Copy of Viscount Gormanston to Grey, 4 September 1580*
TNA: PRO SP 63/76/9

Like the other letters copied and forwarded to Walsingham in this crucible month of late 1580, this describes Turlough Luineach's advance towards the Blackwater, the boundary of his country. He had issued a set of demands and a summons to his presence to the neighbouring petty lords of Ulster, and in particular to Hugh O'Neill, the Baron of Dunganon, an increasingly anxious succession of letters from whom is preserved in this sequence: 'Oneile is come vnto the black water & myndeth to send for me to come vnto him' (SP 63/76/6, 3 September 1580), he wrote; and, on 4 September, 'he Lay yesternight on this side the black water, & euery howre send for mee to come vnto him' (SP 63/76/7). As Hugh O'Neill took pains to remind Grey in one of his letters of late August (No. 2, above, SP 63/75/84), he was descended directly from the first Earl of Tyrone, Conn O'Neill—one of the celebrity successes of the early Tudor 'surrender and regrant' policy—and could therefore expect the English government's support against the upstart tanist to the O'Neill headship, Turlough Luineach. In Ulster politics, the name was everything: as Gormanston notes here, the O'Neill tanist repined that 'he is called but Terelaghe lenaghe', and sought to be recognized as O'Neill so that he might assert the traditional privileges of his headship—the submission of his 'urraghs' or petty lords, as well as his 'cuttings' or financial rights over the people of his country. It seems that, to this end, Turlough Luineach planned to exploit the political instability caused the New English administration by the Munster rebellion and conspiracies in the Pale; by threatening to break his borders, he probably hoped to compel English support for his election as O'Neill *taoiseach*. This strategy of sword and buckler diplomacy—common to Irish military politics, on both sides, in this age—was one Spenser had learned thoroughly by the time he composed *A view of the present state of Ireland*:

Eudoxus: It is then a verye vnseasonable time to pleade lawe when swordes are in the handes of the vulgare or to thinke to retayne them with feare of punishmentes when they loke after libertye and shake of all gouernement/
Irenius: Then soe it is with Irelande Continvallye/ *Eudoxus*. for the sworde was neuer yeat out of theire hand but when they are wearye with warrs and broughte downe to extreame wretchednes then they Creepe a little perhaps and sue for grace

till they haue gotten newe breathe. and recoucred theire strength againe So as it is in vaine to speake of plantinge of lawes and plottinge pollicies till they be alltogeather subdued[.] (ll. 361–9)

The text of this copied letter is written in a broad secretary hand (not Spenser's), which appears in other copied letters from this period (e.g. SP 63/75/73); the word 'Copia' in the bottom left margin seems to be in the same hand, though it might be a later addition. The first line of the text ('Viscount Gormanston') is in a mixed hand, probably Spenser's. The endorsement conforms to the appearance of that of other letters in this group: the first and third sections are in Spenser's mixed hand, and the second ('To the Lord Deputie')—probably added later, when the letter was being filed in London—in a cramped secretary hand.

ENDORSEMENT

Viscount of
Gormanstone
To the Lord Deputie
4 September./

TEXT

Viscount Gormanston

My duty done, May it please your Lordship to be aduertised that I am credbly enformed that tirelagh leynaghe is bent to invade the pale And hath for certayne combyned with the rebelles & hat given forth openly speches that he wold stand indefence of religion while Life doth Last him And said further that he is & wilbe oneall who so ever thinketh evill of the same / disdayning as I take it, that he is called but Terelaghe lenaghe, the said Terelagh was in campe asaterday Last nere to aplace mvckno° adioyning to Mac mahownes contrey who comanded the said mac mahowne to mett him vppon monday next with all his force at Caricke bradaghe° with xiiij dayes victualles, he sent to orely° to met{t} him ther as then whose dutyfull behavour is not alitle to be dubted (wherof we had good triall in shaen onelles rebellion) for his whole force was with the said shaen as then, which if he refuse to do hath sent him diffyance this inteligence is gev{en}

mvckno] the copyist has here written the 'v' over what may have begun as a 'u'—the abortive series of minims is not surprising, given that the copyist was probably unfamiliar with the place name.   bradaghe] the second 'a' of this word has been written over an 'r'; again, the copyist seems to have been unfamiliar with the name.   to orely] these two words are very closely touching, but appear to have been intended as two separate words.

by one Mac Lawe of aginemollyne° bilonging to the said Mac
Mahown{e} and one whom he maketh (as I am enformed) no smale
accoumpt° of, myn auctour reportes the said tyrelaghe to be of force
at this present in camp with him fyve or six thowsand at the lest
wherfore if it stode with your good Lordships pleasuer I take it not
amys that force were sent to thies borders and to the countey of
loweth with victuall for certayne dayes for° preventing the emenente
daunger It is greatly to be doubted that the rebelles I meane the said
Tirelagh & the rest intend to invade vppon both the sides of the pale
at one instant whose traytours intencions and most wicked attemptes
I beseche god to prevent So with my humble dutie comytting your
good Lordship to the allmyghty who send her maiestie victory with
many yers Raigne in happie helthfull & good state long to contynew
And your Lordships good successe I humbly take leave nobber the
fourth of Septembre 1580

> Your Lordships to comand
> Christopher Gormanyston

Copia

To the right honorable my
very good Lord the Lord deputie

COMMENTARY

Viscount of Gormanstone] Christopher Preston, Viscount Gormanston; see
    biographies.

tirelagh leynaghe] Turlough Luineach O'Neill; see biographies.

bent . . . pale] cf. No. 2, above (SP 63/75/84) 'Tirlagh Lennagh is repayering to
    these bordres with a great army of men who pretendeth to invade the pale'.

he wold . . . of religion] although Turlough Luineach was obviously of a different
    religion from the New English governors, defence of the Catholic faith seems
    rarely to have been one of his explicit complaints at this time. Cf. SP 63/75/77,
    where he demands to have all his urraghs, the keeping of the Blackwater, and 100
    men in pay at English charge.

he is . . . Terelaghe lenaghe] the head of the O'Neill family was given the title of
    (the) O'Neill. As tanist to Shane O'Neill, this is the position that Turlough
    Luineach claimed, partly in resistance to English support for Hugh O'Neill.

aginemollyne] our reading here is as tentative as, no doubt, the copyist's also
was.   **accoumpt**] the secretary has compressed this word (like many others on the right
margin) to make it fit on the page: the terminal 't' here is written above the penultimate
'p'.   *after* **dayes for**] 'the' deleted.

Mac mahownes contrey . . . bradaghe] MacMahon's strength was in the county of Monaghan. The young MacMahon had succeeded to his title on his father's death in 1579 (*CSPI 1574–85*, p. 159); MacMahon was one of the urraghs that Turlough Luineach strove to retain rights over (see No. 3, above, SP 63/76/1). Hugh Conallagh O'Reilly (see below) also reported to Grey and the Council that Turlough Luineach was 'with a great host in Campe within few miles of moynecan Mac Mathons towne' (SP 63/76/5).

he sent to orely] Hugh Conallagh O'Reilly, Irish lord of the East Brenny (or Breifne). O'Reilly had permitted his country to be 'shired', transforming it into Co. Cavan, in the summer of 1579, and Sir Nicholas Malby called him in September 1581 the best (Irish) subject in the land (SP 63/85/51). A letter of O'Reilly's to Grey and Council (SP 63/76/5), dated 3 September, records Turlough Luineach's instruction that O'Reilly go over to him; it sends to Grey 'a lettre that Terlagh Lennagh Onele sent me desyring me [. . .] & the best in my Country to goe where he is otherwise yf I doe not goe to him he will come to my Country'.

shaen onelles rebellion] Shane O'Neill, whom Turlough Luineach succeeded as O'Neill; see biographies. During his rebellion in the 1560s, until his death in 1567, Turlough Luineach gave brief support to the English, but was reconciled with Shane.

myn auctour] i.e. Gormanston's informer (by whom he has been 'credbly enformed').

fyve or six thowsand] cf. 'His force is iiij^m more neare five' (No. 3, above, SP 63/76/1).

loweth] Louth.

emenente] imminent (though perhaps eminent, i.e. great).

doubted] feared.

nobber] a town in Co. Meath, approximately 70 km north-west of Dublin.

5. *Grey to the Queen, 12 November 1580*
TNA: PRO SP 63/78/29

In November 1580, Spenser was present with Lord Grey at Smerwick, in Kerry, where a papal force of several hundred men had landed and occupied the 'arch-rebel' James Fitzmaurice's old fortification on the Dingle coast. After a short siege, the fort surrendered, and 600 soldiers were executed (along with an Irish priest, an Englishman, and a man by the name of Oliver Plunkett, who were tortured and killed). The event was an important success for Grey, who had only recently, and within weeks of landing in Ireland, been routed by Feagh MacHugh O'Byrne at Glenmalure in Co. Wicklow. But although the victory won Grey praise in England, his critics at court claimed he had deceived and then betrayed the largely Spanish force, and sixteen years later Spenser still felt the need to defend his conduct in *A view of the present state of Ireland*. 'If it weare trewe,' says Eudoxus, 'as some reported surelye it was a greate touche to him in Honour. ffor some saie that he promised them lief, others that at least he did put them in hope theareof.' Irenius, who describes himself as being 'my selfe [. . .] then as neare as anye', refutes this: Grey was 'far from either promisinge or puttinge [them] in hope', he claims, and although the Spanish soldiers 'Craved [. . .] mercye', it being 'not thoughte good to shewe them bothe for daunger of themselues if beinge saved, they shoulde afterwardes ioyne with the Irishe, and allso for terrour of the Irishe, who weare muche embouldened by those forreigne succours, and allso put in hope of more er longe, theare was no other waie but to make that shorte ende of them which was made Therefore moste vntrewlye and malitiouslye do these evill tonges backebite and slaunder the sacred ashes of that most iuste and honorable personage, whose leste vertue of manye moste excellente which abounded in his heroicke spirite they weare never able to aspire vnto' (*A view*, ll. 3357–92). Spenser writes in *A view* that 'Complainte was made againste [Grey] that he was a blodye man'; according to Canino ('Reconstructing Lord Grey's Reputation'), *A view* implies that events at Smerwick led to this judgement, but Eudoxus's imputation of dishonour is certainly absent from contemporary English accounts of the siege.

It is easy to see not only why Grey took the extreme course he did, but why he celebrated his 'service' with such signal satisfaction. The preceding events had been the subject of a copious and ominous correspondence. As early as May 1580, Nicholas Lumbard was sending the 'lothsome newes' that the Pope had levied 6,000 Italians at Santander to travel to Ireland, and that the King of Spain was to follow with 40,000 men (SP 63/73/27). Reports throughout the summer were made on Fitzmaurice's works at Smerwick, Edward Fenton, for example, remarking on its 'slightnes', 'much like vnto his rebellion, without matter to worke vpon or grounde to defende it selfe' (Edward Fenton to Walsingham, 11 July 1580, SP 63/74/21). But Spanish ships began to arrive in September (SP 63/76/31), and 500 Spanish troops were said to have arrived by the 18th, and to be rebuilding the fort, 'meaning to place a garryson there for the sure keping of their municion' (Andrew Martin to Warham Sentleger, 18 September 1580, SP 63/76/40). There were successive reports of ever more Spanish ships arriving: some speaking of eight (SP 63/76/43; SP 63/76/53), others of as many as twenty-seven (SP 63/76/58). With Ulster still unstable, the Pale's Catholic gentry threatening open revolt, and Munster at full alarm, a combined Spanish and papal invasion of Ireland might conceivably, upon overrunning English defences, have united the island as a base for subsequent action against England. To a new Lord Deputy in late summer 1580, the reports from Dingle must have seemed horribly grave; such an emphatic victory, by contrast, quashed the hopes of Irish rebels for significant support from Catholic Europe. The utter failure of the Earl of Desmond's men to rescue the besieged fort was not soon forgotten, and when the Armada did return, in 1588, it touched Ireland only when the storm winds wrecked it there.

The text and address of the letter are in Spenser's formal italic hand. A copy of the letter was apparently sent as an enclosure to Francis Walsingham (see SP 63/78/30). Grey has added his own subscription and signature. As noted below, the letter has suffered substantial damage. The letter was also annotated at some point, with portions of the text underlined; these emphases were probably added after the letter was received in Westminster.

ADDRESS AND ENDORSEMENT

To her Maiesty yeue
         this. /

12 Nouember 1580.
To hir° Maiesty from the lord
Gray.

Entred.

TEXT

It may please your Maiesty the vijth of this date I planted Campe before the forte at Smerwick: three causes hindered greatly my marche: provision of victaile, rysing of waters, which very hardly & with no smal{l}° daunger we passed, and lastly staying for the fleete, of which for many d{ayes} space wee could haue no voyce of, & without which the entreprice had bene {in}vayne, no possibilitie being to drawe any ordinaunce with vs, nether hau{ing} any shipping for such conveyaunce by sea; at the last worde came, that Captein Bingham in the Swiftesure was arriued, and had anchored besi{de} the Forte, I then moved campe and beeing come within viij mile of the forte, {I} tooke my Horssmen & rode to the Hauen to haue talke with the said Cap{tein} and learne what was become of the Admirall and the rest: I fownd{e} by him that storme had parted them, and that after he had neuer heard of them, but had well hoped to haue mett them there: entring then into advice for the environing of the place, before the rest came, we fown{d} our selues altogether vnhable, having nether Pioners tooles (a shipp of limb{...} therewith & victailes laden, not yett come about) nor his shipp altogether hable to

---

To hir] the secretary who docketed the letter in Westminster originally wrote 'From my' (as if to carry on, 'From my Lord Grey'), which he then changed to 'To hir'. The massaging of letter-forms in the transition perhaps explains the unusual spelling of 'hir'.   **no smal{l}**] the first, third, fifth, and seventh pages of the manuscript have suffered damage to the right side of the page, cutting off many letters, and sometimes words, in the margin. Where the nature of the missing letters (or in rare cases, words) has appeared likely enough, we have supplied them in the appropriate spellings; in more ambiguous cases, we have simply supplied a mark of omission: {...}.

supply the munition, that the entreprize was lykely to require: soe
better I helde yt, to forbeare approching yt, not hauing to goe through
with yt, then to make a brauery, & then enforced leaue yt, as I fownd
yt. An{d} eight daies I so helde still my Campe in penurie of victells
& great doubt of the becoming of our fleet and victells; such stormy &
raging wether continually for this space had fallen with contrariety of
windes; & nowe almost in despeire the ix Morning newes came vnto
me first that thre{e} bandes which I had appointed to followe mee,
were coming at hand, I was leaping to horss to meete them, when
another Messenger in great has{te} brought worde that Sir William
Winter with the shippes was at the Ven{try} & would next morning
yf winde helde, bee at Smerwick. The next {day} therefore I roade
thether, where I fownd him newly entered,° & fow{nd} the cause of
his stay to haue bene weather & vncerteyne intelligence of my beeing
& the Enemies estate; conference then had & resolucion for the
service, I retourned; & the next day brought forward my Campe &
pit{ched} by the Dingle, caused there to stay for the taking in of
certein victailes. The day following beeing the foresaid vij^th I settled
7. November camp here, in which sp{...} taking Captein Bingham with mee
I went to viewe the Forte & grownd for the carriage of my Trench &
planting of Ordinaunce. To lett vs in this, and to draw oures within
the play of their Counterscarfe and Courteyne, where theyr Musket-
iers lay, x or xij Shott were putt forth, who were answered° by 50 or
60 loose shott that I had with mee, to enterteigne them the whilest;
the leaders of these were Iohn Zouche & Captein Mackworth, who
very gallantly carried themselues. In this skirmish 3 of theires were
slayne, none of oures touched, sauing that Iohn Zouche had the graze
of a bullet on the knee, but not to bee reckoned of. That doen that wee
came for, I retyred: the same afternoone we landed our Artillerie &
munition. In the Euening we fell too worke, caried our trench within
8. xiiij skore of the Piece, & planted 2 Culuerings with which the next
morning anone vpon day we saluted them, & they for an howre or 2 as
freshly requited vs, till twoo of their best pieces at laste taken away,
they had not on that side but Muskett & hackabuse-acroke too answer
vs, which with good heat they plyed vs with. The day so spent, at
night to spade wee fall agayne & by morning brought our trench
within v score of theyr Dytche: this night they made 4 saylies to
haue beaten our laborers from worke, & gaue vs their volleies very
gallantly, but were as gallantly sett in agayne by Ned Denny and his

after **entered,**] illegible single-character deletion.   *after* **anwered**] 'w' deleted.

company who had this night the watch: no sooner day peeped, but they played very hotly vpon vs, yett as god would, for a good tyme without hurt, till vnhappely good Iohn Cheeke too carelessely advauncing him selfe, to looke ouer the Trenche, stricken on the head tombled downe at my feete, dead I tooke him & for so I caused him to bee carried away, yet yt pleased God to send him spright agayne & yet doth liue in speache & greatest memory, that euer was seene with such a wounde, & truly Madam so disposed to God, & made so diuine a Confession of his faith, as all Diuines in either of your Maiesties realmes° could not haue passed, yf matched, yt; so wrought in him Gods spirite, playnely declaring him a Childe of his elected, to the no lesse comfort of his good and godly frendes, then great instruction & manifest motion of euery other hearer that stood by, of whome there was a good troupe.

Pardon mee I beseeche your Highnes in case my Digression bee tœdious; the affection I beare the Gentleman causeth the fault, yf there bee anye. I therefore knitte yt vp thus: if god doe take him, as such is the likelyhode, your Maiestie looseth a servaunt, whose matche for euery good vertue accompanied with {the} most true, duetifull, & zealous hart to your selfe (as his prayers in this {. . .} case notably haue declared) in no great nomber wilbee fownd.

Hee so had away, I stayed in the Trench, and fynding theyr shott mo{re zea}lously to beate at vs, & that oures did litle or nothing anoye them, for {that} wee did not discerne ether by spike hole or smoke on the rampier wher{e they} lay; I endeuored as I might to watche their next volley, & happely did {. . .} yt to come from vnder a certeyn building of Timber, that at the point of the ca{mpe} was sett vp, propped outwardly like a houell, & inwardly slanting like {a} Pentisse. I went streight to the Barricadoase, I willed the Gonners to {. . .} their pieces at that place. Sir William Winter himself made that sho{t. . .} at 2 tyres our gentlemen were displaced & the Trenche at great good {. . .} and by that 2 other tyres were given, in great hast leapes one of the{. . .} to the toppe of their Vauntmure with an 9. Ensigne of a sheete & craues a Parlea: hereof streight was word sent mee by Iohn Zouche, who then had the warde, I willed him & the TrencheMaster (one Captein Piers, a very sufficient & industrious man) to know what they would: yt was retourned vnto mee, that theyr

realmes] inserted above the line.

Coronell would send one out to mee, to treate with mee, in case his
Messenger might safely goe & retourne; vpon aduice yt was
graunted there was presently sent vnto mee one <u>Alexandro their</u>
CampMaster: he tolde me that certeyn Spaniards & Italians were
there arriued vpon fayre speaches & great promises, which altogether
vayne & false they fownd; & {that} yt was no part of their entent to
molest or take any gouernement from y{our} Maiesty for proof, that
they were ready to depart as they cam, & deliuer in{to} my handes
the Forte: myne answere was that for that I perceyved theyr people to
stand of twoo nations Italian & Spanish I would give no a{nswer}
vnlesse a Spaniard were likewise by: he presently went & retourned
{with} a Spanish Captein. I then tolde the Spaniard that I knew their
nation {to} haue an absolute Prince, one that was in good league &
amity with your M{aiesty} which made mee to merveyle that any of
his people should bee fownd associates {with} them, that went about
to maynteyne Rebelles against you & to disturb any your Highnes
gouernements & taking yt that it could not bee his Pri{nces} will, I
was to know by whome & for what cause they were sent his Replye
was that the King had not sent them, but that one Iohn Martines de
Ricaldi Gouenour for the King at Bilbo had willed him to levie a band
& to repaire with yt to St Androes & there to bee directed by this
theyr Coronell here, whome he followed as a blind man not knowing
whether. The other avouched that they were all sent by the Pope for
the defence of the Catholica fede. My answere was that I would not
greatly haue merveyled yf men beeing commaunded by Naturall &
absolute Princes did sometymes take in hand wrong actions; but that
men & that of accoumpt, as some of them made showe of, should be
carried into vniust desperate & wicked actions by one, that nether
from God nor man could clayme any princely powre or empire, but
indeed a detestable shaveling the right Antichriste & generall ambitious Tyrant ouer all right principalities, & patrone of the Diabolica
fede, I could not but greatly reste in wonder; theyr fault therefore
farre to bee aggrauated by the vilenesse of their Commaunder, & that
at my handes no condition of composition they were to expecte, other
then that simply they should render me the forte, & yield theyr selues
to my will for lyfe or death: with this answere he departed; after
which there was one or twoo courses two and fro more to haue gotten
a certeinty for some of their liues, but fynding that yt would not bee,
the Coronell him self about Sunne setting came forth, & requested
respitt with surceasse of armes till the nexte morning, & then he
would giue a resolute answere; fynding that to bee but a gayne of

tyme for them & losse of the same for my self, I definitely answered I
would not graunt yt, & therefore presently either that he tooke my
offer or elles retourne & I would fall to my busines. He then embraced
my knees, simply putting him self to my mercy, onely he prayed that
for that night hee might abyde in the Forte, and that in the morning
all should be putt into my handes: I asked hostages for the per-
formance; they were giuen. Morning come I presented my companies 10.
in battaile before the Forte: the Coronell comes forth with x or xij of
his chiefe ientlemen, trayling theyr ensignes rolled vp, & presented
them vnto mee with theyr liues & the Forte: I sent streight certein
gentlemen in° to see their weapons and armures layed downe & to
gard the munition & victaile there lefte for spoile: Then putt I in
certeyn bandes, who streight fell to execution. There were 600 slayne;
munition & vitteile great store, though much wasted through the
disorder of the Souldier, which in the furie could not bee helped.
Those that I gaue lyfe vnto, I haue bestowed vpon the Capteines &
gentlemen, whose seruice hath well deserued: for though your
Maiesty may, & I doubt not shall haue g{reat} services donne, yet
truly for toyle and misery susteyned in yt, through len{gth} and
hardnesse of wayes, extremity of weather, coldnesse of season,
conty{nuance of} watching, & penury of vittayle, hardly by other
Souldiers will the like aga{ine} bee performed. Your Maiesty at this
service had here but 800; they haue p{utt} out of a Forte well forte-
fied, better victailed, excellently stored with armure {&} munition,
600 whereof 400 were as gallant & goodly personages, as of any {. . .}
I euer beheld. So hath yt pleased the Lord of hostes to deliuer your
enemies into {your} Highnes handes, & so too, as one onely excepted
not one of yours is els lost or hu{rt} I had in this iorney a great <u>iewell</u>
<u>of Captein Bingham, whose restlesse trau{ail} & grownded skill hath</u>
<u>bene no small cause of shortening the same. I mos{t} humbly there-</u>
<u>fore commend him to your Highnes favour and good opinion; which</u>
<u>({with} creditt I dare gage) shall shewe deseruedly to bee bestowed in</u>
<u>euery empr{ise}</u> The Coronell at his coming forth shewed to the
gentlemen, that I had sent in before, a Coffer of his wherein he told
them was all the threasure he had; yt was brought to mee vntouched;
I caused yt by the same Gentlemen to be opened & tolde; yt came to
329^li v^s all in double ryalls of plate. I caused yt streight to bee distributed emongst the bandes that kept the stand in the° fielde & warde
in the Campe that day, & sondry priuate gentlemen, which I learned

---

in] inserted above the line.   the] inserted above the line.

to haue sought for no spoile, I relieued therewith so farre as yt would goe: I trust your Maiesty will allowe of yt. Other particularities about this service to the Bearer hereof I referre; whose forwardnesse I could of right commend to your Highnes but that I fe{ar} you will take yt rather partialitie, then desert: but sure Madam affec{tion} shall neuer draw mee to deliuer vnto you in anyes behalf, what theyr w{orth} shall not beare; I humbly therefore beseeche your Highnes to affoord him your g{ood} countenaunce & fauour: for in this action he hath & will I doubt not m{uch} more dese{rue;}°

If tydings of this event stay yt not, there is a great remaynder of this for{ein} force to bee yet looked for. I haue thought good therefore to stay yet for a {. . .} your Maiesties admirall, & then dismissing him, to reteyne for this winter C{aptein} Bingham the Viceadmirall with the Achates & Merlian. For the defence of {. . .} partes by land, I leaue Iohn Zowtch Coronell of 400° footmen & 50 hors{s} The trauailes & toile of the Souldiers hath bene so excessiue, as they are cle{ane} out of clothes, the country & season so coald, as not possible in such plight to {con}tynewe yt. <u>I most humbly therefore beseech your Maiesty in consideration of</u> your owne service & compassion of the poore, ragged, & naked creatures to affoord them a thorough pay; otherwise sure great lacke to your seruice yt will bring & as little gayne to your threasure by the delay.

What is donne in the English pale I cannot heare. Connagh is greatly troubled by that the Earle of Clanricardes sonnes. I meane therefore with Gods leaue to take the Prouince in my retourne & leaue with Sir Nicholas Malbey some of my force for the tymely quenching of these sparkes. Surely Madam I cannot fynd but a most hard & stiffenecked people of this Nation and farre from the bent of loving obedience vnto you. I feare I shall doe your Highnes litle service emongst them; for certeinly a harde & forcible hand, I too well fynd, must bring them to duety, which I confesse, falles not with my nature. Your Highnes must determyn absolutely with your owne forces to defend & keepe in awe this land; expecte no country ayd, vnlesse you would giue raynes to Poperie, stelth, murdering, & all other insolency of lyfe. This

---

for in . . . more dese{rue}] this phrase appears to have been added after Spenser had begun copying the ensuing paragraph; whether Grey made an addition to the letter, or Spenser only belatedly noticed an omission, the cramped space available forced him to insert the final words 'more dese{rue}', below the line.   **400**] Spenser originally wrote '4000', but deleted the final zero.

wilbee heavy for your Highnes to doe, I know, in this sort that now yt goeth; but in myne opinion the way might bee fownd, that would make yt light vnto you. What part of Ireland is yt, that beareth not the charge of an idle villanous kind of kerne iij tymes tolde aboue the nomber of your Soldiers? & the end they serve to, onely to bee instrumentes of revenges in private quarrels, or els the force & strength of publique rebellions: now half the chardge that this scumme putteth the country vnto, and doth nothing for yt, but maynteigne quarels, committ murders and stealthes, vphold Rebellions; would, I say, fynd a competent nomber of English Souldiers, that should roote out this detestable crewe, whereby the Country should be quieted, causes of quarels & wronges taken away, iustice & redresse onely at your handes sought, factious & rebellious myndes should neuer trouble nor putt to chardg your Maiesty wanting ministers & adherentes to execute, and seeing still forces ready to prevent. Since thus the chardg of the Realme might bee lessened, the quiete and good state greatly advaunced, your Maiesties service and governement furthered & made safer, why should yt not be putt in vre? I leaue yt to your Highnes consideration and good pleasure. Once this I can say, since my coming into this Gouernement could I not see any man of those that in defence or offence of priuate quarell would haue fownd an hundreth swordes at his devotion, that euer yett without pay in this your service would affoord mee a man; and now in this action (to notch the willes of the good people) they that before my coming had beene contynuall ayders of the Strangers with all necessaries, & to theyr workes had holp{. . .} them with an Hundreth churles (of which kind I now stood in great need) the same persons came now into mee, & submitted them selues, which I took imposing onely on them to putt mee in sufficient pledges and to furni{sh} me for money with Beofes, and to gette mee an hundreth Churles to labor{.} I was driven of from day to day, and in the end did fynde that this coming in was onely to play on both sydes, till the euent of this action were knowen; yf one way, a Rebell as before, yf the other, a Subiec{te} and yet° surely so° but in showe, and the other in hart; for not one thing with go{od} will, till to threaten I beganne, could I gett of them, nether yet {to} ouerthrow the Forte, can I emongst 3 or 4 of them gett half{e. . .} that the Enemy by one of them was serued with in the building {. . .}

yet] inserted above the line.   so] inserted above the line.

Thus too tœdiously perchaunce haue I helde your Maiesty with this discourse but hauing thought yt not vnnecessary to acquaint your Maiesty with the duetifulnesse & good mynd, that I fynd the People to carry, did embolden mee to yt. And so submitting all to Your Maiesties iudgment I take m{y} humble leave, beseeching the Almighty god to prolong your lyfe with contynuall health, & to governe you with his spright for your owne avayle & his glory, and mee euer to serve your Maiesty as I desyre. / In campe at Smer{wic}k the xij of November 1580.

> Yowr Hyghnes most & faythefull°
> subiect & seruaunt,
>
> Arthur Grey

COMMENTARY

my marche] Grey must have set off in October; a letter from Chancellor Gerrarde and the Irish Council to the Privy Council in England, dated 3 November, writes that they understand that Grey has written from Waterford of 'his purpose for attempting of the strangers in their newe fortification' (SP 63/78/4); the letter may have passed through Dublin on its way to England. Another letter from Gerrarde and the Irish Council to Burghley (SP 63/78/69) apologizes for Grey's silence on his march, which they explain by the difficulty of dispatching messengers from close to Smerwick. This claim had also been made by Warham Sentleger to Burghley on 9 October: 'The weyes be so beset, as no messenger can passe betweene vs and them, but either they bee hang'd or kild, so as it is a great Chaunce when we can heare eny thing of Thenemyes dooinges' (SP 63/77/24).

staying for the fleete] waiting for the arrival of the ships.

Captein Bingham in the Swiftesure] the *Swiftsure*, under the command of Richard Bingham, was among the English ships (alongside the *Achates*, *Tiger*, *Isaac*, *Merlin*, *Aid*, *Revenge*, and other victualling ships) that supported the siege from the bay. According to Glasgow ('Elizabethan Ships'), it was one of the larger ships, and remained at anchor well out in the bay. Richard Bingham had been separated from Admiral Winter in a storm, and had been in the bay at Smerwick since 17 October (SP 63/77/51), exchanging shots with the Spaniards. He told Francis Walsingham on 18 October that he had information that the papal soldiers were 'a thowsande poore symple Bysswynes verie ragged and a great part of them boyes', that they had made rendezvous with Desmond, and that John of Desmond had come to the Dingle 'and [was] loked for heare at the fortresse' (SP 63/77/42). Bingham, perhaps unsurprisingly, was keen in these letters to speak highly of his own service and to emphasize Winter's absence: Grey was to speak later of Winter's 'greate dislyke' for the much younger captain, who had 'not alyttle sheowed hys skyll & diligence in this seruyce', and would say that Winter 'affectes greatly

---

most & faythefull] judging from other comparable parting salutations (see, for example, the conclusion of No. 13, below, SP 63/82/54), Grey probably intended to write 'most humble & faythefull'.

the gloric of this seruyce; & chyefly for that hee takes the assent too the parlea too bee hys onely aduyce' (Grey to Walsingham, 9 November 1580, SP 63/78/30).

the Forte] a contemporary Spanish plan of the fort, with a map of the surrounding area, is printed by Jones ('Plan of the Golden Fort').

the Admirall and the rest] Admiral Sir William Winter, in the *Revenge*, arrived on 9 November with the remaining ships (including the *Aid*, *Tiger*, *Achates* and *Merlin*). Some of his fleet (the *Lion*, the *Foresight* under Martin Frobisher, and the *Bull*) never arrived, apparently returning to the docks at Chatham after having been separated from the others in a storm. Winter seems to have been particularly involved in Irish military affairs and victualling from the mid-1560s. He was still in service against the Spanish Armada in 1588.

environing] surrounding, and (likely) besieging.

Pioners tooles] i.e. pioneers', or trench-digging tools.

a shipp of limb{. . .}] the word lost by this damage to the manuscript may be 'limber', the fore-part of a gun, including ammunition chests (*OED*, *n.*, 2).

brauery] precipitous act of bravado.

becoming] fate.

ix Morning] i.e. the morning of Grey's ninth day at camp, not the morning of 9 November.

bandes] troops of soldiers.

the Ven{try}] at Ventry, or Ventry Bay, on the southern side of the tip of the Dingle peninsula, at the mouth of Dingle Bay.

intelligence of my beeing] information about my condition or whereabouts.

the Dingle] probably Dingle Bay, to the south of the Dingle peninsula (on the north side of which was the fort at Smerwick).

carriage of my Trench] i.e. the digging of the trench.

lett] hinder.

Counterscarfe and Courteyne] the counterscarp is the frequently fortified external wall of a ditch (i.e. the wall closer to the attackers) used in fortification. The curtain is the main defensive wall of that fortification.

were putt forth] i.e. by the papal forces.

loose shott] scattered marksmen.

Iohn Zouche & Captein Mackworth] John Zouche and Humphrey Mackworth; see biographies.

within xiiij skore of the Piece] a **score** may be 20 paces; Grey's trench is within approximately 280 paces (*c.*250 metres) of the fortress (see *OED*, 'Piece', *n.* 11b).

Culuerings] culverins, light cannons.

Muskett & hackabuse-acroke] a musket is a hand-held, long-barrelled gun, fired from the shoulder. A **hackabuse**, or arquebus, was an older long-barrelled gun: a **hackabuse-acroke** (arquebus à croc) was a heavier type of such a gun mounted upon a wagon.

saylies] sallies.

Ned Denny] see biographies. It was apparently Denny who conveyed this letter to England (see the report of Chancellor Gerrard and the Council to England, SP 63/78/69).

Iohn Cheeke] John Cheke was the second son of Sir John Cheke, humanist and educator. In his biography of the elder Cheke, John Strype describes him as 'a youth of great hopes, Comely and Learned, and of a Gentleman-like, and very obliging Deportment: Of whom also his Unkle, the Lord Treasurer Burghley, took particular care, making him one of his own Family. [. . .] Among his other Qualities he was Courageous and Brave, which Spirit carried him to the Wars in Ireland' (*Life of the Learned Sir John Cheke* (1705), p. 180). His death at Smerwick was lamented by Robert Dudley, Earl of Leicester, who wrote sorrowfully of 'Mr John Cheke, a querry under my rule, a tall valiant gentleman he was' (see *ODNB*).

spright] spirit, i.e. life.

& yet . . . wounde] Cheke, in fact, died of his wound.

either . . . realmes] i.e. England and Ireland.

Childe of his elected] the language here, and the reference to the working of the holy spirit, seems to remember Article 17 of *The Thirty-Nine Articles*: '. . .the godly consideration of Predestination, and our Election in Christ, is full of sweet, pleasant, and unspeakable comfort to godly persons, and such as feel in themselves the working of the Spirit of Christ, mortifying the works of the flesh, and their earthly members, and drawing up their mind to high and heavenly things, as well because it doth greatly establish and confirm their faith of eternal Salvation to be enjoyed through Christ, as because it doth fervently kindle their love towards God.' Cheke reveals himself by his declaration of his faith to be one of the elect, and Grey's narrative of his death prepares him to be something of a Protestant martyr.

knitte . . . vp] conclude.

spike hole] small hole in the wall.

rampier] the ramparts, fortified walls.

Pentisse] or penthouse, at that time meaning an outhouse or annexe built onto the outside of another building.

Barricadoase] barricades, improvised fortifications, in this case protecting the English guns.

at 2 tyres] damage to the manuscript makes the exact course of events unclear, but a **tyre**, or tire, is a volley of ordinance. The English battery forced the fort to surrender.

Vauntmure] a work raised in front of the wall.

an Ensigne of a sheete] a white flag, symbolizing surrender, made out of a sheet.

Parlea] parley, discussion of terms. Grey wrote to Walsingham (SP 63/78/30) that discussions were held about this parley between himself, Winter, Bingham, and Geoffrey Fenton.

TrenchMaster] officer in charge of the construction of trenches.

Captein Piers] probably William Piers; see biographies.

Coronell] Colonel.

treate] negotiate, discuss terms.

in case] as long as, on the condition that.

Alexandro their CampMaster] Alessandro Bertone, or Bartoni, of Faenza, named in SP 63/78/27 and 28. Though see Spenser, in *A view*: 'theire Secretarye Called as I remember *Segnior Ieffrey*, an Italian beinge sente to treate with the Lo deputie for grace was flatlye refused and afterwardes theire Coronell named *Don Sebastian*: Came forthe to entreate that they mighte parte with theire Armours like souldiours, at leaste with theire lives accordinge to the Custome of warr and lawe of nacions' (ll. 3362–7). Spenser's memory may have been playing tricks with the name of the Italian colonel, Sabastian de San Josepi (or Sanioseffi), but Grey also acknowledges that there were 'one or twoo courses two and fro more' after his initial parley.

certeyn Spaniards . . . great promises] the promises may have been Irish or papal. The Spanish forces may have believed that they could rely on reinforcements from the Desmonds: 'if they founde them selves weake & vnhable to heepe the fortes then th' Earle & Sir Iohn promised to be on the mountaines by with xvi^C men & would [. . .] with theyre forces come downe & remove our siege but in conclusion theare was a writte returned *Non fuerunt inuenti* [i.e. They were not found]' (William Smith to Burghley, 28 November 1580, SP 63/78/67). Grey also wrote to Walsingham, on the same date as the present letter, that he had discovered in the fort 'infinite letters & wrytinges with bulles as I take them & Commissions from the Pope': despite only having had time to skim through them, he tells Walsingham that they make 'promyss styll of greater forcies too arryue heere withall expedition' (SP 63/78/30). There is clearly an anxiety in this case that these **promises** were not vain, and that there would be a further Spanish landing in Ireland: the letter goes on to say that the examination of Oliver Plunkett suggested that there was a fleet of twenty-four ships at preparation at Coruna, and twelve at Santander.

an absolute Prince] King Philip II, an **absolute** monarch, is a ruler free of constitutional restraint or restriction, and not subject to any other prince. It is tempting to think that Grey had read Jean Bodin's *Les six livres de la République* (Paris, 1576), which discourses at length on the criteria for absolutism.

his Replye] it was on this basis, that the papal forces held no direct commission of war from the prince of their country, that Spenser, in *A view*, had Irenius justify Grey's refusal to grant mercy: 'they Coulde not ius[t]lye pleade either Custome of war or lawe of nacions, for that they weare not anie lawfull enemyes, and if theye weare [Grey] willed them to shewe by what Commission they Came thither into another Princes dominions to warr whether from the Pope or the kinge of Spaine or any other. The which when they saide they had not but weare onelye adventurours that Came to seke fortune abroade and serve in warrs amongest the Irishe whoe desired to entertaine them, yt was then toulde them that the Irishe themselues as the Earle and Iohn of desmounde with the rest weare no lawfull enemies but Rebells and Traytours and therefore they that Came to succour them no better then Roges and Runnagates speciallye Comminge with no license nor Comission from theire owne kinge, so as it shoulde be dishonorable for him in the name of his Quene to Condicion or make anye termes with suche Rascalls' (ll. 3368–81).

Bilbo] Bilbao, on the north coast of Spain.

repaire . . . St Androes] St Androes (i.e. St Andrews) is Santander, a city on the north coast of Spain. On 24 May 1580, it had been reported that 'doctor Saunders was in a town in the partes of Asturia in spaine called Sainte Anderouse with companye of 6000 Italianes [. . .] which company were sent thether by the pope to com into yrlande' (Nicholas Lumbard to the Master of the Rolls, SP 63/73/27). Santander is in the modern district of Cantabria, not Asturias.

Catholica fede] Catholic faith (It.).

Naturall & absolute Princes] on **absolute** princes, see above. A **naturall** prince was to be distinguished from an elected prince (or, indeed, pope). In the period's popular political discourse of sovereignty, the two words were regularly collocated, for the simple reason that elective monarchies (following the work of Jean Bodin in the 1576 *Six livres de la République*) were considered to be inherently limited or contractual.

shaveling] a contemptuous term for a monk (with shaven head) or any other religious figure: here alongside other anti-Catholic slanders.

ambitious Tyrant] early modern discussions of tyranny used the term to connote either unjust rule or usurpation, and often linked it to questions of the justness of tyrannicide. For the political contexts of the term, see Skinner, *Foundations*. It is doubtful, however, whether Grey meant anything more than that the Pope was evil.

Diabolica fede] Devil's faith (It.). The phrase may be Grey's coinage, even if the idea is commonplace.

no condition of composition they were to expecte] they could not expect to make conditions for a truce.

one or twoo courses] return journeys in and out of the fortress.

either . . . my busines] Grey 'lefte them to theire Choise to yealde and submitte themselues or noe' (*A view*, ll. 3381–2).

certein gentlemen] according to Hooker, the English troops were led by Ralegh and Mackworth.

armures] either armour or, more generally, military equipment.

600 slayne] this number is broadly consistent with figures given in other accounts of the massacre (O'Rahilly, *Massacre*, 22). Some subsequent reports reduced the number (e.g. the Mayor of Cork reported to the Mayor of Waterford that 400 had been 'putt to the sworde', SP 63/78/53/1). It is likely that these were simply mistakes; there seems little reason to question Grey's figure.

bestowed vpon the Capteines & gentlemen] fifteen soldiers were ransomed (for their names, see O'Rahilly, *Massacre*, 11).

grownded skill] thorough proficiency.

329 . . . vˢ] Grey quotes almost exactly the same sum of money in a letter to Walsingham of the same date: 'Three hundrethe twentie nyne powndes & syx shyllynges came too my handes of theyr mooney' (SP 63/78/30).

double ryalls of plate] or 'royalls', a name given to various English and European coins (see *OED*, 'Royal', *n.*, 2).

a great remaynder] a letter dated 15 November 1580, from Thomas Wadding, one of the Earl of Ormond's men, to the Mayor of Waterford, suggests that fears that a contingent of the papal army was still at large, and assisting Irish rebels, were widespread, but in his view unfounded: Desmond, Baltinglas, and John of Desmond are, he writes, 'butt accompanied of Raskall [. . .] And of the forrein Ennemies butt fowr spaynards [. . .] to make men belev that they have a greate nomber of the strangers. Butt in troth they have no more' (SP 63/78/45/3).

I haue thought good . . . Achates & Merlian] damage to the manuscript at this point makes Grey's exact proposal uncertain, though the missing word is likely to have been 'while' or, more likely, 'time'. The *Achates* and *Merlin*, which would stay in Ireland throughout the winter under Bingham's command, were two of the smaller ships in the fleet employed at Smerwick (Glasgow, 'Elizabethan Ships', 163).

affoord . . . pay] such requests are of course commonplace in this correspondence, but this one is backed up in a postscript to Grey's letter to Walsingham of the same date: 'Further earnestly, I praye yow my sute too her Maiestie for a thowrorghe paye./' (SP 63/78/30). This is not the only time that Grey drew Walsingham's attention to points in his other correspondence, and asked for his help in expediting them.

English pale] on the Pale, see glossary.

Connagh . . . sonnes] Wick and John Burke, against whom Malby had supported their rival, Richard yn yeren Burke. See No. 9, below (SP 63/81/39). Fighting among the Burkes had worsened with expectation of the death of John Burke, MacWilliam Eighter (which actually took place on 24 November, just twelve days after the writing of this letter).

stiffenecked] obstinate, stubborn.

a harde . . . to duety] The conviction that the irrationality of Irish will, and the ingrained customs of the Irish people, would make voluntary reform impossible, is expressed in *A view*: according to Bradshaw ('Sword, Word and Strategy'), it was the distinctive position of the Grey circle in Ireland. It is curious, then, that Grey acknowledges himself unfit for the policy.

falles not with my nature] *A view* makes this claim specifically with regard to Grey's actions at Smerwick: 'the necessitye of that presente state of thinges forced him to that violence and allmoste Changed his verye naturall disposicion' (ll. 3328–30).

country ayd] native support.

kerne] see glossary.

revenges in private quarrells] that the Irish were either too busy fighting among themselves to support the English, or that these private quarrels were connected to their rebellion, was a common cause of complaint for Grey. See No. 39, below (SP 63/94/15).

stealthes] stealthy acts of theft.

putt in vre] put into practice.

notch] weaken, impair, undermine; the metaphor is obscure.

churles] fellows, men (though the term can have various pejorative meanings, ranging from 'commoner' to 'bumpkin' to 'villain', any or all of which Grey might be implying).

Beofes] cattle, beef-cows.

6. *Grey to Burghley, 28 November 1580*

BRITISH LIBRARY, ADDITIONAL MS 33924, ff. 6–7

Notes on victualling and (increasingly, as Grey's service went on) complaints about the lack of supplies occupied much of Grey's correspondence with Burghley and the Privy Council; but this particular letter specifically illustrates Grey's plans and logistical arrangements for establishing and victualling garrisons in Munster, in the wake of the siege of Smerwick and of the continued threat presented by Desmond's rebellion. The placement of garrisons was a central aspect of late sixteenth-century English military strategy in Ireland, just as plans for a network of garrisons across the entire country acquired 'an orthodoxy of aspiration', in Ciarán Brady's words ('The Captains' Games', 141), among military captains in the 1590s. Grey's report to Burghley of 6 April 1581 (see No. 11, below, HH Cecil Papers 11/91) acknowledges that the placement of garrisons in Munster required rethinking, due to supply problems, as well as a shift of the foreign threat from Spanish to Scots invasion. Grey's notice and account to the Privy Council of his journey to Munster in the following year (SP 63/86/51, 6 November 1581) also makes provision for a reinforced set of garrisons in Munster (described in detail in an enclosed 'callender', SP 63/86/51/1). See also *A view*, ll. 4231–86.

The text and address of this present letter are in Spenser's usual secretary hand, although slightly more upright than usual. The subscription and signature are Grey's. The marginal annotation is in the same hand as the receiver-side endorsement.

ADDRESS AND ENDORSEMENT

To the right Hono
rable my very good
Lord the Lord Threasurer
 of England yeue
       this./

xxviij^{mo} Novembris 1580
The Lorde Deputie
of Irelande his Lettres
vnto my Lord Treasourer
for the payment vnto Alderman
pullisonne CC iiij^{xx} ^{li} for
iij^{C}l. Barrelles of wheate
and m^{l} m^{l} of Newlande
fisshe and for other
      causes

TEXT

My very good Lord forasmuch as I stande assured that my former advertizementes of my Kerry iorney and of my successe there (which proceeded not of my travell, but of the providence° and mighty powre of god) I therefore leave now to trouble your Honour therewith. And

---

providence] the darkly inked 'v' of this word has apparently been written over an initial 'i'; this is probably a case of scribal anticipation, quickly corrected.

having determined a Iorney too Thomond & Connagh to Curbe short
the Rebelles there, yett vpon intelligence of some occasion of my
present repaire into the pale, Whereof I will wryte to your Lordship
when I shall arrive at Dublin I thought good to send force to Sir
Nicholas Malbey & to garrison some of the Army in this Province for
the better defence thereof, to thend the Traitour Desmond should
have but small Comfort of abyding within the same. I have placed in
Kerry at Dingle Iohn Zouche Captein Case and otheres in all iiij^C
footmen and L horsemen besides the ward in Castlemainge. I have
settled at Asketen CC footemen besides the ward of the Castle in
number iij^{xx}. At Kilmallock Sir George Bouchier with his company &
xxv horsemen vnder George Thorneton & in the Abbey of Aherloa
CC footmen; so as there is no starting Corner lefte in the County of
Limerick for the said Traitour, but one or other of the said garrisons
shalbee at hand to meete with him. I have appointed to remayne at
Corke C, at Youghill C at Lismore CC & at Dongarvan C; and thus
doe this day take my iorney toward Dublin.   Nowe for to vitle
these & for the places apt to staple the vittles which must bee for their
provisions I thought good to signifie vnto your Lordship that for the
garrisons at Corke Youghill Dongarvan & Lismore, Corke is the place
to land their provision for that thence yt may be conveyed safe by
water to euery of the said places.   And for this County of
Limericke & Kerry bycause such ships as come hether must needes
passe nere the Coast of Dingle and nothing out of their way to touche
in them, yt shall doe well that all such ships as shall come hether
with vittle doe first ancre at Dingle & there discharge vittle sufficient
for the said number, & the remayne to bring hether vnto this cittie
to furnish the said garrisons, which is the onely place to vittle
Kilmallock Asketen & Aherloa. But now vnderstanding the small
proporcion of the remayne of vittles here with vs, but of wheat C
quateres; mele C barrelles, malt xx quateres, biskett iiij^m; And
meeting here with a ship loaden with wheat of Alderman Pullisons
goodes, I was driven to buy the same; and for iij^C L barrelles of wheat
have promised that he should bee paid in England by your Lordship
after the rate of xiiij^s sterling the barrell, CCxlv^{li} sterling; and for ij^m
newland fish at xv^{li} the one thousand & xx^{li} the other xxxv^{li} sterling In
all CC iiij^{xxli} sterling. Which Sum I pray your honour to Cause to be
answered and paid vnto him out of the next masse that shalbee made
out for this Realme. And thus praying your Lordship to hasten hether
more store of vitle with speed, (for this will last no tyme to speake of,
and drinck there is none nor other vittle butt bread which I beseech

Deliuered at
Lymericke to
Iames Brincklow
and Iames
plancke.
Victualers there.

your Honour to consider I take my leave; at Limerick this xxviij[th] November 1580

> Yowr Lordships most
> assured,
>
> Arthur Grey

COMMENTARY

Address **Lord Threasurer of England**] William Cecil, Lord Burghley; see biographies.

Endorsement **Alderman pullisonne**] Thomas Pullison; see biographies.

Endorsement **Newlande fisshe**] i.e. Newfoundland fish, fish caught off the Grand Banks of Newfoundland. Robert Hitchcock's *Pollitique Platt* for the development of fisheries (London, 1580) advocates a more active English involvement in this trade, a trade in which, he claims, the French and Dutch were taking a great share. Presumably the fish would have been preserved and dried through salting. See Tawney and Power, *Tudor Economic Documents*, iii. 239–56.

my former . . . successe there] Smerwick, Co. Kerry, was the scene of Grey's victory over (and massacre of) a fortified garrison of several hundred papal (mostly Spanish) troops. For Grey's 'advertizement', written 12 November 1580 from the 'campe at Smerwick', see No. 5, above (SP 63/78/29).

travell] travail.

a Iorney . . . Connagh] Grey's planned journey against the rebels (perhaps the O'Connors) in the western parts of Ireland may have taken place in February (Maley, *Spenser Chronology*, 17).

Curbe short] curb, restrain; this compound verb is not cited in the *OED*.

Sir Nicholas Malbey] Malby; see biographies.

in this Province] Munster (whence Grey was writing this letter). The garrisons that Grey goes on to mention (Dingle, Castlemaine, Askeaton, Killmallock, Aherlow) are all situated in Co. Kerry and Limerick, or western Tipperary. The first three are named as sites for garrisons in 1581 (see No. 23, below, SP 63/86/51, and headnote); Aherlow (or Aherlo, Arlo) was a heavily wooded area that enjoyed a reputation for lawlessness during the 1580s, and which, as Arlo Hill, hidden around with 'faire forrests', found its way into *The Faerie Queene* (Burlinson, *Allegory*, 176–8; Hadfield, 'Spenser, Ireland', 171).

the Traitour Desmond] Gerald Fitzgerald, Earl of Desmond; see biographies.

Iohn Zouche] see biographies.

Captein Case] John Case, stationed in Galway from at least 1579 to 1580, and then in Dinglecush (Dingle) in proximity to John Zouche. His and Zouche's bands were badly affected by sickness (Bingham to Walsingham, 9 January 1581, SP 63/80/2). In September 1581, he bore a letter to Walsingham from Zouche, also containing his commendation, and he was paid for his service in late 1581 or early 1582.

the ward in Castlemainge] Castlemaine, Co. Kerry, bordering on Desmond lands, was the seat of a permanent garrison; see maps.

Sir George Bouchier] or Bourchier; see biographies.

George Thornton] see biographies.

the Abbey of Aherloa] Moore [Moor] Abbey, near Galbally, at the western end of the Glen of Aherlow; see maps.

starting Corner] presumably, a place from which to begin rebellious action.

staple the vittles] receive and store the provisions.

thence yt . . . said places] Youghal and Dungarvan lie to the east of Cork, along the southern coast of Ireland. Lismore lies on the River Blackwater, at the mouth of which Youghal is situated; see maps.

and nothing . . . in them] and not go out of their way in landing there. The Dingle peninsula lies to the south of the mouth of the estuary of the River Shannon, on which Limerick lies.

which . . . onely place] Limerick lies in the centre of this group of towns: Askeaton to the west, Kilmallock to the south, Aherlow to the south-east; see maps.

mele] grain ground to powder, flour; perhaps specifically oatmeal (*OED, n.*[1], 1).

Iames Brincklow] Brinklow held positions with responsibility for victualling in Ireland during the 1570s and 1580. On 3 January 1580, though, Sir Henry Wallop informed Walsingham of Brinklow's bad character (SP 63/70/1), and on 23 December, Burghley was told by John Shereff (SP 63/79/34) that Captain James Vaughan was going to declare Brinklow's abuses to Elizabeth. This declaration does not seem to have survived, but it is the last that we hear of Brinklow.

Iames plancke] no other reference to James Plancke can be found in the Irish State Papers.

newland fish] see note above.

answered . . . masse] deducted from the next consignment of treasure, and paid to Pullison in England.

7. *Grey to Walsingham, 1 March 1580/1*

TNA: PRO SP 63/81/1

This short letter bears witness to the copious and urgent correspondence that passed between Ireland and England throughout 1581 on the subject of the Earl of Kildare's involvement in the rebellion of James Eustace, Viscount Baltinglass. Kildare was suspected as 'a principall comforter of the vice-counte to enter into this action', on the specific charge that 'he certainelie knewe the vicecount woulde breake out, and hadd assured intelligence of diuers his principall Councellors and partakers, and that notwithstanding hauing the vicounte after in his companye, hee rather guarded him from apprehention, then assented or liked to haue apprehendid him' (SP 63/79/26). He was imprisoned in Dublin Castle with Baron Delvin, who was likewise suspected of involvement in the rebellion.

A crucial piece of evidence against Kildare was the testimony of Adam Loftus, Archbishop of Dublin, who had met him during a muster on the Hill of Tara, Co. Meath on 4 July 1580. A record of their exchange, in which Kildare was not only said to have refused, against Loftus's advice, to apprehend the Viscount by means of the soldiers gathered there, but also to have sheltered him and to have been privy to his plans for rebellion, is preserved (in the form of a dialogue) as SP 63/79/26/1. Loftus's information was summarized and repeated in several items of correspondence sent to England, including, for example, a digest made by John Hammond for Walsingham; 'The Erle', writes Hammond, 'went to the hill of Taraghe to meete with the Archbishop of Dublin there and to viewe the musters. The Vicount in that iorney was in the Erles companie, but went not through to the musters, staying with the Erles horsemen at Killilen. The Erle nether required the Vicount to goe forward with him to the hill, nor fownd fault withe his staye [. . .] After the Erles returne from the sayd hill the Vicount accompanied him backe to Killmyllen.' Loftus's testimony, writes Hammond, is 'that at this meetyng at the muster, which was the 4th of Iulye, 1580: and xii dayes before the Vicounts revolt: The Erle tould him that the Vicount and other purposed to rebell, & the B: aduisyng him to take the present oportunitie of Sir Henrie Harrintons horsemen for the apprehension of the Vicount, he tooke tyme to consider thereof vntill wedensday followynge, on that daye he further declared that he knewe the whole conspiracie & the maner of everie mans othe & the chiefe cownsellor Rocheford: but excused him selfe that he could not withowt perpetuall infamie of his howse apprehend the Vicount' (SP 63/81/48/1; see also SP 63/81/47, in which Hammond urges Walsingham that 'the credite thereof might mutche have been encreased (in my simple opinion) by proofe made of the circumstances deposed by the bishopp').

Loftus's conduct in this affair earned him the praise of Grey, who wrote to Elizabeth to say that he 'hath shewed no small trouth and Constancy in this service having not a litle endangered him self by avouching his Charge against the Earle' (SP 63/79/24/1), and also praised Gerrarde's role in prosecuting the case: 'The Lord Chauncellour his great pollicie & intolerable travaile to the great empairing of his health and no lesse perill of his life hath Chiefly yf not onely beaten out this matter. I therefore humbly beseeche your Highnes that he maye have his deserved thanckes.'

The text of the letter is written in the hurried and cursive secretary hand of Edward Waterhouse, Receiver General in Dublin: an unusual and unaccustomed secretary for Grey. As often, Grey has penned his own subscription and signature. The address is in Spenser's usual, bold secretary hand.

ADDRESS AND ENDORSEMENT

To the Honorable
my very loving
frend Sir fraunces
Walsingham° knight Chieff

Address **Walsingham**] inserted above the line.

Secretary to
her Maiestie

1 Marche 1580
From the Lord Deputy

TEXT

Sir, Since the enclosing of my other letters it seemid good to the rest
of the Counsaill that two examinacions shold be sent you, which° in
part concerne therle of kildare and both approve that conference
passid betweene the Archbisshop & therle concerning Iames Eustace,
Sir henry bagnoll allegith that the day after the assembly at Tarragh
where the first Speach passid betwene the lord Keper & therle, the
archbisshop revealid to him some part of their talke, Burnell A man
well knowen to you is the only Counsaillor in lawe to therle and he
doth in sort° witnes that the erle was movid by the Archbisshop
to apprehend him, though not presisely as apperith in the 7 Article /
I leave it to be iudgid by your self thinking neuertheles that you haue
alredy the copy of burnells confession And so I committ you to god.
At Dublin the first of March 1580

Yowres euer assured,

Arthur Grey

COMMENTARY

the enclosing of my other letters] it seems impossible to say to which letters Grey
here refers, and they may not have survived; he was in frequent correspondence
with England, in particular with Walsingham, throughout January and February
1580/1.

two examinacions] examinations are formal records of answers to interrogation.
Neither of these examinations seems to have survived.

therle of kildare] Gerald Fitzgerald, Earl of Kildare; see biographies.

approve] 'Attest (a thing) with some authority, to corroborate, confirm' (*OED*,
v. 1, 2).

the Archbisshop] Adam Loftus; see biographies.

Iames Eustace] James Eustace, Viscount Baltinglas; see biographies.

---

    sent you, which] 'that' deleted *after* **sent you**, and 'w^{ch}' inserted above the line.   *after* **in
sort**] a three- or four-letter deletion appears here, possibly 'conf'. It may be that Waterhouse
was intending to write 'confirm', but changed it to 'witnes' instead, suggesting that the letter
was drafted directly from dictation.

Sir henry bagnoll] son of Sir Nicholas Bagenal, Knight Marshal; see biographies.

the lord Keper] Loftus, who acted as Lord Keeper of the Great Seal between 1573 and 1581.

Burnell] Henry Burnell, Kildare's attorney, later to be Justice of the Common Pleas in Ireland, and in previous years prominent opponent of the cess, a general levy collected throughout the country (see glossary, and Brady, *The Chief Governors*, 235–7). In 1577, he had been taken to England and examined on the matter beside Richard Netterville (see SP 63/52/81), another lawyer and landholder in the Pale; the Privy Council wrote to Lord Deputy Sidney on 14 October to tell him that these men had 'conceyvid a Malitious & obstinat opinion', and had been committed to the Tower. It appears, though, that whatever renewed suspicion is suggested by the present document, Burnell was not irrecoverably tainted by his proximity to Kildare: there survives a letter of recommendation from Loftus himself to Walsingham, dated 15 March 1583, in which he speaks of his 'wisdome gravitie and good behauiour', describes him as 'verie Learned in the Lawes', and points out that 'in theis late seruices he hathe so carried him selfe that he resteth free from any suspicion of vndutiefull entencion' (SP 63/100/16).

in sort . . . 7 Article] 'in sort' might be translated by the modern idiom, 'in a way'; Grey means 'Burnell as good as witnesses this, though perhaps not precisely as it is set down in the seventh article against the Earl of Kildare'.

you haue . . . burnells confession] Walsingham may have had it; unfortunately, we do not.

8. *Copy of Earl of Ormond to Grey, 13 March 1580/1*

TNA: PRO SP 63/81/36/1

Thomas Butler, Earl of Ormond, had been appointed Lord General in Munster in October 1579, charged with suppressing the revolt of the Earl of Desmond. Ormond's allegedly slow prosecution of the service in Munster drew attacks from most of the New English soldiers serving in the area, including Walter Ralegh (see SP 63/80/82) and Captain Thomas Lee, whose tract on the Irish service, the *Discovery and Recovery of Ireland* (*c.*1599), identified Ormond as a kind of traitor to English interest there; the Queen cut off Ormond's funding in the early part of 1581 (SP 63/80/87), but he continued to send reports of his service such as this for some time. For a review of his service from this period, see the 'observations' on his government, SP 63/90/67; and Ormond's note of over 5,000 traitors slain during his service in Munster, SP 63/86/3/1. For Ormond's reaction to his discharge, see No. 15, below (SP 63/83/45).

The text of this copied letter is in Spenser's regular secretary hand. Spenser has also certified the letter at the foot of the page with his usual 'Copia Vera' and signature. The letter's single endorsement is apparently a composite: the first two lines ('Copie of my L. of Ormondes lettres') are in Spenser's usual mixed hand, while the final lines ('to the Lord Deputie' and the date) are in a later mixed hand.

ENDORSEMENT

Copie of my Lord of
Ormondes lettre°
to the Lord Deputie
.13. March. 1580

TEXT

My very good Lord I have thought good to lett your Lordship vnderstand that since the dispatch of my servaunt Iohn Daniell with my
lettres to you Barry Roe brother to Davie Barry playd the gentleman
with me in taking away some of my horses that were at Sesse in his
Countrey (which I have recovered from him). vpon this I marched
with such forces as I had with me to Carbry towardes his countrey
and missing him self have warded his castles for her Maiestie and
after retourned to Corke bringing with mee Sir Owen Macharty with
all the chiefest freeholderes of his countrey to putt in assuraunce for
their loialtie and to doe service against the Rebelles, the rather for
that his Nephew fynin Machartie was held to bee a doubtfull man, I
sent also for all the Galloglas beyond the leape in Carbrie and vpon
their coming to me have taken their othe for their duetifull behaveour
and meane to employ them in her maiesties service. This day by
thadvise of the councell of this province of Mounster yt hath bene
thought good and concluded that David Barrie should be sent for to
bee talked with, and to vnderstand the cause of the breaking of his
castles and the gathering of such forces as he had about him, Who
was content to come to me here, having Sir George Bowchier, the
Sherief Sir Cormock, and Richard Shee for the assuraunce of his safe
retourne at his pleasure and being in that maner brought in, he
seemed to make his quarrell for that he said Commissions were procured by Sir Warham and Capten Rawley for the apprehending &
killing of him self and warding of his fatheres houses, as formerly I
have written to your Lordship by my man Daniell, and for that being
refused proteccion by me he had no assuraunce of his life since the
tyme of Sir William Pelhams gouernement, who gave him proteccion
with promis of pardon and in respect of the premisses stood at his

---

Endorsement **lettre**] 's' deleted at the end of this word. The scribe who added the last two
lines of this endorsement seems to have corrected Spenser's note, deleting the original 's'. If
there were originally two Ormond letters contained in this enclosure, the second was apparently
lost or removed at a very early stage in the archiving of this document.

keeping. Considering the weaken{es}° of the bandes that are here to serve vnder mee and that I have determined to bend my forces in one way intending to meet with the principall Traitoures shortly god willing I have given him my word and assuraunce not to harme him nor his till your Lordships pleasure bee knowen farther touching him, with condicion that he shall keepe her Maiesties peace, and that vpon ij or iij daies warning given him by your Lordship or my self, his assuraunce to bee voide, And being requested by mee to serve her maiestie against the Rebelles during his being vpon my word, would not promis the same, seing he would not purchace him self enemies, before his pardon were graunted him; which being graunted he said he would putt in pledges for his loialtie and doe the best service he could. I pray your Lordship lett me vnderstand your pleasure herein with speed / This day I received advertizement that the traitour Sir Iohn of Desmond and the Brownes of the county of limerick came to take the pray of the towne of kilmallock and having taken some cattell, a fewe horsemen with some footemen of the garrizon there pursued them, reskued the pray and presently slewe Thomas Browne, with one or ij other Horsemen, wounded Vlick Browne very sore, who is said to bee dead since and took iiij horses from them. So having no farther matter to wryte for this tyme I committ your Lordship to the guyding of Almighty god. Corke xiij° March 1580

> Your good Lordships as assured to commaund
> as any may bee, /
>
> Thomas Ormonde ossory
>
> > Copia Vera
> > Edmund Spenser

COMMENTARY

1580] i.e. 1581, new-style.

Iohn Daniell] a John Daniell is mentioned as one of Grey's servants in a summary book of Grey's grants from 1582 (SP 63/88/40/3); if this was the same man, it may suggest that he was an Irish man making his way up, via Ormond's service, in the New English administration. In 1581 he wrote to Walsingham supplying

weaken{es}] damage to the manuscript here has cropped the final letters of this word; the word itself is clear enough from context, and the spelling adapted from instances in others of Spenser's letters.

intelligence of James Eustace, and offering to infiltrate the Old English traitors then in exile in Spain; the insider status implied by this offer may support the idea that this was the same man.

Barry Roe brother to Davie] David Barry, Viscount Barrymore from April 1581, was a powerful Irish lord in Munster, in rebellion with the Earl of Desmond during Grey's deputyship; Barry Roe, his brother, enjoyed Grey's protection after killing the rebel George Champern.

playd the gentleman] been a gentleman (although this phrase is not mentioned in *OED*); Ormond is of course being sarcastic.

at Sesse] for **cess**, see glossary. Horses 'at cess' were thus government animals whose maintenance had been imposed upon local people as part of their contribution in kind to military taxation.

warded his castles] garrisonned his (empty) castles.

Sir Owen Macharty] or MacCarthy; also known as MacCarthy Reagh, of Carbery. He stood out in rebellion with the Earl of Desmond briefly in 1581, but (as is here related) was brought in by the Earl of Ormond and afterwards remained loyal. He petitioned the Queen for relief from government severity in 1583, mentioning two sons then at Oxford (SP 63/105/2/1).

chiefest freeholderes] the most substantial men of the country.

assuraunce for their loialtie] Irish landowners of doubtful loyalty were required to put in pledges for their loyalty, which would be forfeit upon their 'coming out' in rebellion. These pledges might be sons or other kin.

service] military service.

fynin Machartie] or MacCarthy. Also known as Florence MacCarthy; see biographies. He may have joined Desmond's rebellion at the end of 1579 (see SP 63/70/42).

doubtfull] to be feared.

Galloglas] see glossary.

beyond the leape in Carbrie] Leap is a small village south-west of Cork, near Carbery.

breaking of his castles] in February 1581 Ralegh reported to Walsingham that David Barry had burned all his own castles before going into rebellion. Cf. Turlough Luineach's action, mentioned in No. 20, below (SP 63/85/5), carried out to prevent Grey's assault upon him: 'he merueiled why I should make such præparation as he heard of to take his Castelles, which to præuent he signified that he had broken & in maner razed, as indeed he had.'

Sir George Bowchier] or Bourchier; see biographies.

Sherief Sir Cormock] Sir Cormac MacTeige MacCarthy, Lord of Muskerry, and Sheriff of Corke, reputed the best-disposed Irish lord in Munster.

Richard Shee] Shee, of Kilkenny, was accused of harbouring Catholics (SP 63/74/69) and of various treasons and felonies (SP 63/115/9–10); he was pardoned at least once (SP 63/107/79–80).

Commissions] formal licences from the Lord Deputy.

Sir Warham] Sir Warham Sentleger; see biographies.

Capten Rawley] Sir Walter Ralegh; see biographies.

as formerly . . . man Daniell] this letter appears to be lost.

proteccion] a formal guarantee of safety from the military government; see glossary.

the tyme of Sir William Pelhams gouernement] Pelham served as Lord Chief Justice of Ireland between October 1579 and September 1580.

in respect . . . his keeping] permitted him to retain his castle provided that he kept it garrisonned.

pledges for his loialtie] it was common practice in Ireland at the time for Irish lords to surrender hostages for their good behaviour.

Sir Iohn . . . county of limerick] for John of Desmond, see biographies; the Browne family of Limerick, with their adherents, stood out in rebellion against the Queen until at least June 1583; see Ormond's letter to the Queen, SP 63/102/86.

take the pray of . . . kilmallock] to 'take the prey' of a town was to sack, loot, and in some cases burn it.

Thomas Browne . . . Vlick Browne] two of the leading men of the Browne sept; little is known of them.

Copia vera] 'a true copy': one of the standard forms of secretarial certification added to copied documents.

9. *Copy of submission of MacWilliam Eighter to Sir Nicholas Malby, 1580/1*

TNA: PRO SP 63/81/39

This document gives an account of a political victory in the west of Ireland as significant as any of Grey's military campaigns: the submission of Richard Yn Yeren Burke, a powerful rebel of long standing, and his official recognition as MacWilliam Eighter (or Eughter, Ewghter, or Iochtar), traditional leader of the Burkes. The event is also described in another document copied in Spenser's hand, the set of legal articles drawn up between Burke and Sir Nicholas Malby (Governor of Connaught) in the Tower of Co. Mayo on 7 March 1580/1 (SP 63/81/15). At that meeting, Burke agreed to submit himself to Queen Elizabeth, to give over his son, Tibbot Burke, to Malby as a pledge of his good behaviour and fidelity, to pay Elizabeth all the rents and duties that he would acquire from his lands, and to promise not to support any Scottish or foreign troops. In return, Malby agreed to recognize Burke as MacWilliam Eighter, '& to give him the stile preheminens and title of mac William by her Maiesties Authoritie'.

The submission reflects a significant policy shift in the New English administrations of Elizabeth's reign. Henrician engagements with Irish septs and families had been dominated by a process known as 'surrender and regrant', whereby great Irish magnates were persuaded to 'surrender' their Irish titles, with all their concomitant customary tenures and rights ('cuttings', or traditional exactions or taxes levyable on their people), in favour of the 'regrant' of an English title, by which they would afterwards hold their estates by fealty to the King as tenants *in capite*. This policy was introduced as part of a general anglicization of Ireland after Henry was declared constitutional King in Ireland in 1540, forsaking his identity and rights as *dominus* or lord, inherited from Henry II by right of conquest. The problems that the policy of surrender and regrant was introduced to solve, however, did not go away; Irish lords continued to wield unfettered power in their local fiefdoms—power that was, if anything, confirmed and strengthened by the new grants—and the Dublin administration found that, due to the uninherited and co-elective nature of the traditional Irish form of sept or family headship, known as 'tanistry', new generations of Irish magnates considered themselves anyway free of feudal obligations to the crown. Elizabethan governors, and particularly Sir Nicholas Malby in Connaught, recognized that the failure of surrender and regrant had, however, created a very functional ambiguity in Irish politics, and that the two forms of legitimate political and social authority—Irish tanistry and English nobility—might be exploited in a new policy of 'divide and rule'. By encouraging great families like the O'Neills in Ulster and the Burkes in Connaught to divide, assigning the earldom to one young hopeful, while recognizing another man as the Irish tanist or even *taoiseach*, Malby, Sidney, and Grey hoped the great families would become riven by faction, weakened, and eventually manageable. This policy led to the carefully orchestrated antagonism between Turlough Luineach O'Neill and Hugh O'Neill, Baron of Dungannon, in Ulster; and, in April 1581, the official recognition of Richard Yn Yeren Burke as MacWilliam Eighter.

Malby's tactics were straightforward: he ruthlessly harried Richard Yn Yeren with overwhelming military force until he submitted, and then offered him the Queen's recognition as the new MacWilliam tanist (see SP 63/73/8). Burke's capture and surrender in April 1580 are described in a long document entitled 'A discourse of Sir Nycholas Malbies service & procedinges' (SP 63/72/39: see notes below, and Brady, *The Chief Governors*, 282–3); this was followed by Richard Yn Yeren's formal document of submission, in which he petitioned for his local, quasi-feudal powers of rentgathering in Mayo, in return for his obedience to the English administration, and further requested the Queen's protection (SP 63/72/62). All seemed to be going according to plan until, upon Sir John Burke's death in November 1580, Richard Yn Yeren Burke had himself installed as the new MacWilliam and, far from dividing the power of the Burkes, joined with the sons of the Earl in rebellion against the crown. Another merciless military campaign followed, in which Malby again crushed Richard Yn Yeren Burke into the present submission, and earned the government the opportunity to do the startlingly strange work of the present document: to make an Irish tanist sue for letters patent from the Queen for recognition not of his English title, but his Irish headship. This lesson in the unscrupulous (and sometimes bizarre) manipulation of prestige and power relations was hardly lost on Spenser; one of Irenius's primary preoccupations in *A view* is the careful fostering of mutual and debilitating antagonisms within Irish septs: 'The Lordes and Captaines of Countries the principalles and heades of septes are made stronger whom it shoulde be a moste speciall care in policye to weaken and to set vpp and strengthen diuerse of his vnderlinges againste which whensoeuer he shall Offer to swarve from duetye maye be hable to bearde him; ffor it is verye daungerous to leave the Commaund of soe manye as some septes are, beinge v or vj thowsand persones to the will of one man whoe maye leade them to what he will as hee him selfe shalbe inclyned' (ll. 1102–10; see also the discussion of the O'Neill headship at ll. 3529–48, and Zurcher, *Spenser's Legal Language*, 191–8).

This copied document (including the reproduced signatures), written on successive sides of a single sheet of paper, is entirely in the characteristic secretary hand of Spenser. The endorsement was affixed to the letter at some later date, and is written in an italic hand; most of this attachment has been lost. Although it is dated by *CSPI 1574–85* to 20 March 1580/1, no evidence of such a date appears on the letter; it may be that the editors of the *Calendar* believe that the copy was made to accompany Nicholas Malby's letter to Walsingham of that date (SP 63/81/38), in which he mentions the submission. It may be more likely, though, given his status as Grey's secretary and servant, that Spenser's services as copyist, perhaps producing this document and SP 63/81/15 at the same time, were called upon by Grey when writing to Leicester (about Malby and MacWilliam) on 23 March 1580/1 (SP 63/81/41).

ENDORSEMENT

{. . .}4.
Copie of mac Williams
Sub{mission to} Sir {. . .}°

TEXT

To the right worshipfull Sir Nicholas° Malbey Knight Gouernour of Connagh and Thomond

In most humble wise sheweth vnto your worship Richard Inyren Burke alias mac William: Whereas vpon the Death of Sir Iohn Burke Knight late mac William the name & lorship of mac William Ewghter ought to descend & remayne vnto your Suppliaunt° as the best and eldest of his sept according the Custome of the countrie, which the

---

Endorsement **Sir** {. . .}] most of the endorsement, on a separate slip once affixed to the copied letter, has been lost.   **Nicholas**] the name is abbreviated here, as in a few other places in this letter, 'Nichas'. We have expanded it, throughout, to the usual form.   **Suppliaunt**] a terminal 'es' brevigraph has been deleted at the end of this word.

said Richard by the persuasion and Counsell of the Clandonelles & other vnduetifull persones tooke vpon him, and entred into the possession of the lordship rentes and revennue thereof without her Maiesties authoritie or your Worships license And also by the like advice & persuasion of the said euill disposed persones reteyned a nomber of Scottes and Galloglas and ioyned with therle of Clanricardes sonnes in warre and rebellion against her Maiesty And perceiving how much he hath bene hetherto seduced and deceived by his said euill Counselloures and how farre he hath offended her Maiesty & incurred her displeasure & indignacion through his said vnduetifulnes & lewde disobedience, and that he is in no sort hable to withstand or resist her Maiesties forces, and that also by your worships travell he is driven & compelled to come in & yield him self vnto you at her Highnes pleasure, he therefore confesseth and acknowledgeth his said offences & ill behaveour & is very penitent for the same and doth simply submitt him self vnto her Maiesties mercy and to you her Chief officer in this Province, by whome in her highnes behalf he is content & willing to be ordered ruled gouerned & directed in all thinges, acknowledging further° that without her Maiesties further favour & mercy he is not worthy to live vpon the earthe He therefore most humbly besecheth your Worship to receive him into her Maiesties favour and to accept this his most humble Submission, and bee a meane for him to her Maiesty & the Lord Deputie to graunt him her Highnes gratious pardon, and that the said lordship may be confirmed vnto him by her Maiesties lettres Patentes as the late mac William had yt; for without her Maiesties allowaunce & graunt thereof he will not take yt vpon him, nor presume more therein then he hath doen already for the which he is hartely sory. And he will not onely yield and answere vnto her Maiesty all suche rentes composicions dueties and services as the said late mac William did yield to her maiesty but also will stand to Your Worships ordre for all thinges touching thadvauncement of her Maiesties service & quietnes of the Country and putt away & expell the Scottes & enterteyne none hereafter nor suffer none to come within his countrey And during his life shall contynue her Maiesties faithfull Subiect & servaunt And will daylie pray for your Worship.

Richard Burkes alias
mac Williams marke. /

<hr>

after **further**] 'w¹⁾' deleted.

Being present when Richard Inyren made this
Submission & deliuered the same to the aboue named
Sir Nicholas Malbey in her Maiesties behalf, we whose
names are subscribed . /

                              Edmond Athenry
Merbury   Richard Burke
                              Anthony Brabazon
Teig mac William Okelly   Edward White
                              Huberd boy mac Davie Chief &c
Robert Fowle
                              Richard og mac Iohnnes
William Martin   William Cotton
                              Thomas Correres

COMMENTARY

Gouvernour . . . Thomond] Malby had held this post since 1576. Thomond is the
region that covers the south of Connaught and north of Munster.

Richard Inyren Burke alias mac William] see biographies.

the name & lorship of mac William Ewghtcr] on this title, see headnote.

the best and eldest . . . Custome of the countrie] a **sept** is a clan. 'It is a
Custome amongst all the Irisherie that presentelye after the deathe of anie theire
Chief Lordes or Captaines they doe presentlye asemble themselues to a place
generallie appointed and knowne vnto them to Choose another in his steade,
wheare they doe nominate and electe for the moste parte not the eldest soonne
nor anie of the Children of theire Lorde deceased but the next to him of bloode,
that is the eldest and worthiest as Comonlye the nexte brother vnto him if he haue
anye or the nexte Cozen germaine or soe forthe as any is elder In that kindred or
sept, And then nexte to him do they Chose the nexte of blood to be Tanist, whoe
shall nexte succede him in the saide Captenrye if he liue thearevnto' (*A view*,
ll. 191–201).

Clandonelles] Malby writes in his 'Discourse' that Richard Yn Yeren had 'perswaded the Clandonells in the County of Mayo to ioyne with hym in rebellyon
against the state' (SP 63/72/39).

took vpon him] assumed; i.e. he took the title of Mac William Eighter without due
permission from the English crown.

rentes and revennue thereof] in SP 63/81/15, Malby promises to procure 'the
profittes rentes revenues & lorships' of the title, by authority of 'her Maiesties
lettres Patentes'. Among the benefits that Richard Yn Yeren is accused of falsely
obtaining are the feudal duties from his title, which he now signs over to the
English.

without her . . . Worships license] the authority of Elizabeth's majesty, and of
Malby's regional governance, supersede Burke's feudal claims.

a number of Scottes and Galloglas] on galloglas, see glossary, and Hayes-McCoy, *Scots Mercenary Forces*. Richard Yn Yeren had procured Scottish troops to assist him in his rebellion. The Clandonnells, Malby writes in his 'Discourse', were 'accompted alwayes an invincible people, and the most strongest sept of Galloglasse in Ireland'; as well as their support, Richard Yn Yeren had petitioned the 'owt ylles [isles]' of Scotland for aid, and 'gathered for hym aboute ahoundrethe bowes in the province of Vlster', where there was a continued Scottish presence (SP 63/72/39).

therle of Clanricardes sonnes] Malby's 'Discourse' suggests that Richard Yn Yeren was joined by other Burkes in his rebellion: he was initially supported by 'Vllyke Boorkes sept', and also apparently by one Thomas Roe Burke, who quickly submitted himself to Malby 'without protection' (SP 63/72/39).

travell] efforts.

her Chief . . . this Province] see above. Malby had effectively held this post in Connaught since 1576.

the said lordship] on surrender and regrant, see headnote.

composicions] payments of debts. The wording is again here close to SP 63/81/15, where Richard Yn Yeren promises to pay Elizabeth all 'rentes services customes dueties compositions and rysing out' that were paid by his successor.

Edmond Athenry] Edmond Bermingham, tenth Lord Athenry (1540–1614). Athenry lies approximately 25 km east of Galway. Also signatory to Richard Yn Yeren's document of submission (SP 63/72/62: see headnote). Present at the signing of the articles (SP 63/81/15).

Merbury] probably John Merbury, gentleman of Connaught (see SP 63/110/21), also present at the signing of the articles (SP 63/81/15).

Richard Burke] Richard MacOliverus, brother of John (alias Shane) MacOliverus, late MacWilliam.

Anthony Brabazon] deputy governor of Connaught (see No. 31, below, SP 63/90/1), and Malby's son-in-law. Present at the signing of the articles (SP 63/81/15).

Teig mac William Okelly] Also present at the signing of the articles, when Richard Yn Yeren promised to pay 'vnto the said Sir Nicholas the fine agreed vpon betwixt them for his nominacion [. . .] ether in ready money or good in calf kyne' (SP 63/81/15).

Edward White] Clerk of the Council in Connaught between April 1579 and April 1582, he was present at the signing of the articles (SP 63/81/15).

Huberd boy mac Davie] listed as paying rent in Connaught in 1577 (SP 63/59/71) and 1581 (SP 63/87/37).

Robert Fowle] Captain and Provost Marshall of Connaught in 1581 (appointed by Grey on Malby's recommendation: see SP 63/87/19, Grey to Privy Council, 9 December 1581, where Grey describes Fowle's 'sufficiencie in service, and his well deserving of longe tyme').

Richard og mac Iohnnes] perhaps the Richard MacJonyn, MacJoyne or MacJones, who was examined in February and March 1577 (see SP 63/57/39/26, 63/57/39/30, 63/57/39/31, apparently on the charge of having taken part in Clanricard's rebellion, claimed that he had been compelled to do so by Clanricard, and that he had sent the heads of three or four rebels to Galway as a token of his wish to be obedient.

William Martin] perhaps the William Oge Martyn who had served as Bailiff of Galway in 1566–7, High Sheriff of County Galway and Jailer of Athlone Castle in the 1570s and 1580s, in which capacity he had hanged William Burke, third son of the second Earl of Clanricard in 1580. He would be Mayor of Galway in 1586–7, and was present at the signing of the articles (SP 63/81/15).

William Cotton] unknown. Present at the signing of the articles (SP 63/81/15).

Thomas Correres] unidentified.

10. *Grey to Walsingham, 6 April 1581*

TNA: PRO SP 63/82/6

One of the most interesting things about this letter is the considerable overlap between Grey's points on procedural problems in common law trial process and Irenius's account of Irish law in *A view of the present state of Ireland* (1596); like Grey, Spenser spends considerable time on the thirty-five challenges afforded to prisoners, and on the means by which those of the Irish nobility accused of treason managed to alienate and convey away their titles in land, in order to avoid the escheats that would disinherit their children. See *A view*, ll. 759–74, 818–74.

The text of the letter is in Grey's usual italic hand, including several phrases in the customary code. The letter has been annotated in the left margin throughout, probably by Walsingham, and the code transliterated above the line. The address is in Spenser's characteristic secretary, the later endorsement—probably added during the filing process—in a different hand. An addressee note ('Mr Secretary') appears at the left foot of the first page of the manuscript.

ENDORSEMENT

To the Honorable
my very Loving frend
Sir Fraunces Walsingham
Knight Chief Secre-
tarie to her Maiestie

6 Aprill. 1581
From the Lord Gray.

TEXT

Sir, vppon aduyce taken with the choyce of my companions in
Twoe councell heere & adding vntoo them certayne of her Maiesties learned
extreamities in councell best too bee trusted, wee fynde twoo extremities too ryze in
proceadynge the ordinarie proceeding too tryall of the late endyghted pryzoners
agaynst the
prisoners heere, too goe on wherin the late letters from my Lords there & her

Maiestie directed mee. The one is the generall linck of kinred & alliance the whoale sheere, whence these tryalls must bee retourned, hathe with the parties too bee tryed, & beesydes hardly acquyted of fauoure too the cause of theyr offence, what sounde verditt maye bee then hoaped of at sutche Iuries waye yowr sellf; a lawe or custome lykewyze is heere that euerie one is allowed xxxv challendgies, which makes, that if vpryghtnes myght bee looked for, I see not, as the tyme serues, how the number for the guestes woold bee supplyed: The oother is, that admitting theyr casting & condemnation, her Maiesties ryght & benefitt by theyr° goods, landes & possessions, is cleane wyped awaye by deedes of guyft & oother conueyancies, as this bearar Iustice Dillon more particularly shall enfourme yow, whowse aduyce hathe not alyttle auayled in this cause, & for his trust, endeuoure & lernyng I haue now made choyce of hym for the followyng of this buzines, lett hym therfore I praye yow haue yowr fauorable° hearyng, furtherance & countnance. Well Sir, for these inconueniencies no healp that wee can see but onely a parlament, which if, vppon my sundrie former letters had bee harckened vntoo, the matter ere this tyme had been in good dispatche too her Maiesties greate proffitt, no less honor, & more terror too these & all oother the lyke deseruers; & therfore lett it now bee well considered, & harckned vntoo,° for els the contraries of these wyll assuredly fall owte. Lett not the obiection of the vnfittnes of the tyme stagger the assentyng too it, for, God wyllyng, it shall bee° so dealt in as no preiudice too oother seruyce shall growe by it, neyther shall the vnquyettnes any whytt empeatche the repayre of the best & dutiefullst sorte° that in former tymes the assemblie hathe moast stoode on. I haue allso wrytten now abowte this same too her Maiestie, & too my Lords a generall letter from the° table heere, which, if yow shall not thynck amiss, I could wysshe 6o° first acquaynted with, that sum choyce of yee myght bee made too consider of it beecause you arre nott all one mans chyldren.° Remember I praye yow the° callyng of those too bee Lords that in my former I wrytte for: it wyll bee moast requysite for this action the onely weakenes & dowght° restyng in our temporall lordes,° as a note

Marginal notes (right column):

.1. Alliance between the prisoners & Iurours.

.35. chalenges.

.2. Fraudulent conueyghances

Mr Dillon a man trustie &c. whome he employeth therfore in this iorney & cawse.

A parlament the only healpe of those extreamities.

which shall be so heald as no preiudice of this tyme shall therby grow to other seruice.

lettres to hir Maiestie & my Lords for this parlament

twoe to be created Barons A note of the Lords spirituall & temporall

---

theyr] the 'e' in this word has been inserted above the line.   *after* **fauorable**] '&' deleted.   *after* **harckned vntoo**] 'yᵉ contr' deleted.   *after* **shall bee**] 'no' deleted.   *after* **sorte**] '&' deleted.   *after* **from the**] 'tak' deleted.   6o] Queen Elizabeth.   **choyce of . . . mans chyldren**] much of this passage, from '6o' onwards, is in cipher ('choyce of yee myght', 'consider of it because you arre', 'all one mans children'), all of which is transliterated above the line.   *after* **praye yow the**] 'adua' deleted.   **dowght**] the 'w' in this word has been inserted above the line.   **in our. . .lordes**] in cipher, transliterated above the line.

heerencloazed wyll sheowe. Sir Nycholas Mallbie hathe commended

Request for three
to be Bushops.

vntoo mee° Steeuen Kerroan° bysshop° of Kilmacdoock too bee translated to the Bysshopprick of Clomfartea° in the cuntrie of Clanriccarde, I praye yow sir gett hym confirmed, & allso the oother twoo which by° Mr Fenton I recommended too yow. / Sir Wylliam Standley & Captayne Russell twoo nyghtes past made a roade intoo

Sir William
Stanley & Mr
Russell spoyl
Feaghes Contrie

Coalerannell in hoape too haue° surpryzed Phyagh Mc Hugh, but the fourdes & passes they were too pass were so well kept as they crye roaze beefore they coulld reatche hys howse, wherby hyssellf had gotten owte & assembled his force too the number of 200 kerne & xx or 30 horss, yet dyd hee guyue them leaue too burne hys towne & howse called Ballinacore & kyll certayne of hys kerne & churles, withowte the loss or hurtt of any of owres.

Commendation
of Captain
Mackworth & his
seruice against
the Omores

Captayne Mackwoorthe hathe within this moonethe space putt too swoorde & executed very neere a hundrethe of the best of the Omoores, so as the rest of the sept hathe putt in pledge for° theyr peacyble & good beehauior; this man certaynely dezerues greate estimation not onely for valure but goouernment, enter hym therfore I praye yow into yowr Cataloge of well deseruers. /

The oother garrisoones heere abowtes arr daylie nybbling vp theyr churles & straggling knaues which beeyng of no greate accounte I lyke not mootche too aduertiss of.

I haue dispatched twoo Ientlemen too Chester & Bristowe for conducting ouer of the 1000. men yow last wrote for the supplies.

The letters by mr Fenton now is the onely woorde that euer I hard thence of all the packetts that I haue sent since my retourne from my last ioorneye, I praye yow sir haue vs mynde in deedes there how sieldoome so euer wee bee thowght of by letters.

To hasten the
dispatch of Mr
Dillon : & to
fauour him in his
priuate businesse.

So crauyng yowr earnest furtherance for the good & speedie dispatche of this bringer & lykewyze that yow wyll affourde hym° yowr

---

after **vntoo mee**] 'one' deleted.   after **Steeuen Kerroan**] 'for the' inserted above the line, and subsequently deleted.   **bysshop**] 'pᵣck' deleted at the end of this word.   **too bee ... Clomfartea**] inserted above the line.   **by**] inserted above the line.   after **too haue**] 'tak' deleted.   after **pledge for**] 'yᵉ' deleted.   **affourde hym**] inserted above the line.

good fauoure in his owanc priuatc rezonable buzyness, I take leaue & beeseetche the Allmyghtie euer too keepe direct & prosper yow. Dublin this vj^th of Aprill Anno 1581. /

Yowres euer most assured,

Arthur Grey

Sir at the ending heerof Mr Threasurer came too mee & sheowed a warrant from her Maiestie for my entertaynement browght now by mr Fenton, therin I am allowed but 50 footmen, & agayne but 1500^li Irisshe for my diett: Yow knowe sir that I was promyzed as lardge a dyett as euer any heertoofore had, I was allso promyzed 100. footmen: Vppon this & hauyng more care of the seruyce then priuate estate, I sowght not° too staye too capitulate but relying mysellf vppon yowr woord & care for mee came as inconsiderately for myne owane beehouff as myght bee; I praye yow therfor Sir see mee better dealt with, or els presently wythedrawen, for surely as hauyng that that I accounted of I shall farre cum shortt of sauyng, so in beeyng thus scantled I shall noot saue mysellf in shortt tyme from vtter vndooyng; whytche I trust is not her Maiesties wyll, moutche less yowr wysshe I knowe: but sir it is no small grieff too mee in the meane, the world beeyng able too testifie with mee & myne° owane conscience how farre from gayne my purpoze is° in this seruyce, that so small consideration is had of it as enforced I am too craue my due or els by peace hollding encurre a harder meazure: too conclude, I praye yow Sir, eyther procure mee the allowance according too the warrant drawen by Mr Waterhowse, as yowrsellf appoynted,° wherin my diett is no more then the new establisshement allowethe,° & my bandes of 100 foot. & 50. horss as was promyzed mee at my sending awaye, or els good Sir, as beefore I sayed, procure mee my leaue, which shall bee farre wellcoomer vntoo mee then three sutche entertaynements the appendices considered; & her Hyghnes pleazure heerin with sutche conuenient speede as yow maye I beeseetche yow procure mee.

(Marginal notes:) The warrant° sent ouer abbridgeth his allowance.

To procure the warrant a draught of which now sent.

COMMENTARY

the choyce of my companions ... too be trusted] to Walsingham Grey could admit—even advertise—his care in managing the factional nature of the Irish Privy Council. It is curious that he makes a distinction between his 'companions' and the members of the Irish Council; Grey seems to have relied—at least to some degree—for policy advice on his own gentlemen servitors.

twoo extremities] an 'extremity' is literally a 'severity' of some kind; Grey is pointing out that the legal proceedings against the conspirators are threatened by two problems inherent to the customary mode of legal process itself.

the late letters] no minutes or drafts of these letters appear to have survived.

generall linck of kinred & alliance] blood and marriage bonds.

sheere, whence these tryalls must bee retourned] under English common law (which ran in Ireland after the Irish Parliament acknowledged Henry VIII King of the country in 1540), felony trials had to take place in ('be returned to') the defendant's home county or district, with a jury comprising local peers.

hardly acquyted of fauoure too the cause of theyr offence] Grey suggests that, if the whole shire were tried for their sympathy to the conspirators' rebellion, they would be acquitted, if at all, with great difficulty.

xxxv challendgies] it was a custom of the common law of England to allow defendants thirty-five 'peremptory challenges' in the selection of jurors; nearly three full panels of proposed jurors could thus be eliminated by the defendant in advance of the trial, making it difficult for the court, which was drawing from a limited population of potential jurors, to choose men who would not be biased.

casting & condemnation] prosecution and sentencing.

ryght & benefitt by theyr goods, landes & possessions] felons (including traitors) upon conviction forfeited ('escheated') their estates and possessions to the crown.

deedes of guyft & oother conueyancies] in order to avoid the disinheriting of their children or collateral descendants, defendants thus sought legal means ('deeds of gift' and other 'conveyances', or property transactions) to give or sell their estates or possessions as quickly as possible, upon the fact or even the likelihood of an appeal of felony or treason.

Iustice Dillon] Robert Dillon, second justice of the Common Pleas (Ireland); see biographies.

inconueniencies] i.e. the 'extremities' rehearsed above, touching the difficulty of securing a fair trial, and of ensuring that the Queen benefit from the prisoners' escheated lands and goods.

sundrie former letters] see for example Grey to the Earl of Leicester, SP 63/81/25; other letters advocating a Parliament have not, it seems, survived.

stagger] delay or impede.

the vnquyettnes] the stir or trouble caused by the Pale rebellion.

empeatche the repayre of the best & dutiefullst sorte] frustrate the assembling of loyal subjects (in the Parliament, when summoned).

wrytten now ... too her Maiestie] it seems that this letter has not survived.

too my Lords ... table heere] Grey advertises to Walsingham that, with the rest of the Irish Council, he has written separately to the Privy Council on the same matters; this letter does not appear to have survived, but the extant extract dated 2

April (SP 63/82/1)—though it only includes material on Turlough Luineach O'Neill—may have come from this lost original.

sum choyce of yee] some subset of the Privy Council, only, should be consulted on the present matter.

you arre nott all one mans chyldren] a dark phrase, apparently meaning that Walsingham cannot count on the 'brotherhood' (or common purpose) of the whole of the Council, some of whom might well be affected to the rebel Irish lords.

a note heerencloazed] this note has apparently been lost; but Grey seems to suggest that the Parliament will only go the government's way if it can 'stack' the upper house with new-created lords favourable to its cause.

Steeuen Kerroan] Bishop of Kilmacduagh.

Kilmacdoock] Kilmacduagh, a diocese founded around the monastery of St Colman Macduagh, is located about 35 km south-east of Galway.

Clomfartea in the cuntrie of Clanriccarde] Clonfert is located about 60 km due east of Galway.

Sir Wylliam Standley] i.e. Stanley; see biographies.

Captayne Russell] William Russell, who would eventually become Lord Deputy in 1595, at this point commanded one of the Pale garrisons under Grey; see biographies.

Coalerannell] modern Coolanearl, close to Glenmalure, where Feagh's fortress of Ballinecor was located; see maps.

Phyagh Mc Hugh] on Feagh MacHugh O'Byrne, see biographies.

they crye roaze] i.e. the cry (or alarm) was raised upon the detection of the attacking English force.

hys towne & howse called Ballinacore] Ballinecor was situated at the opening to Glenmalure; Feagh MacHugh would go on to re-edify it and live there securely for another decade or more.

kerne] see glossary.

Captayne Mackwoothe] Captain Humphrey Mackworth; see biographies.

Omoores] one of the two powerful Irish septs in Leix.

putt in pledge for theyr peacyble & good beehauior] it was standard practice for the government to require the heads of rebel Irish families to 'put in pledges', or surrender hostages, to guarantee their 'good behaviour'.

yowr Cataloge of well deseruers] Walsingham's House of Fame.

daylie nybbling vp theyr churles & straggling knaues] Grey paraliptically passes over the small fry captured or killed by the Pale garrisons.

letters by mr Fenton] no record of these letters survives. Fenton had been sent to England by the Irish Council on 23 December, bearing news of the imprisonment of the Earl of Kildare and the Baron of Delvin (SP 63/79/26); Grey had been calling for his return since at least 19 January 1581 (SP 63/80/15).

Mr Threasurer] Sir Henry Wallop; see biographies.

too capitulate] to draw up a formal schedule (under headings) of his 'entertainment' (the number of footmen and horsemen allowed him) and his 'diet' (his personal allowance for expenditure).

yowr woord & care for mee] Grey's appeal to Walsingham's brotherly love is typical of his private letters during these years, and helps to indicate the degree to which government policy and practice were dependent upon personal relations.

scantled] scanted.

procure mee the allowance . . . as yowrsellf appoynted] Grey seems to have enclosed a draft warrant for his entertainment and diet, prepared by Edward Water-house, and here reminds Walsingham that it conforms exactly to Walsingham's own original direction upon Grey's first sailing for Ireland.

new establisshement] Grey seems here to refer to new orders laid down by the Queen and Privy Council for the Lord Deputy's living in Ireland.

the appendices considered] given what will befall afterwards—i.e. the painfulness of the service—though Grey may also be alluding to the royal displeasure he knows will follow upon his due remuneration; Elizabeth was famous for her petulant parsimony.

11. *Grey to Burghley, 6 April 1581*

Hatfield House, Cecil Papers 11/91

Grey's letter to Burghley bears the marks of (and bears witness to) an uneasy relationship, and shows the instrumentality of such personal epistles in repairing offence. In fact, one of its primary purposes seems to be to repeat an apology made after an indiscretion by Edward Denny—which reveals, in turn, how essential it was for a politician in Grey's position to select the bearers of his letters wisely, from men whom he could trust not to overstep their commissions or to speak out of turn. As the letter makes clear, though (with probably deliberate irony), and despite its emphatic assurance that Grey trusts Burghley's care for the victualling of Ireland, the Lord Deputy was still waiting for a shipment of supplies from England: such shortages, which Grey here claims were caused by the abuse of Burghley's associates and officers, formed a common subject of correspondence throughout Grey's deputyship.

    The text and postscript of the letter are in Grey's characteristic italic, subscribed and signed with his usual autograph. The address is in Spenser's secretary hand.

ADDRESS AND ENDORSEMENT

To the right Ho-
norable my very
good Lord the Lord
Threasurer of
England. /

6. April 1581.
The Lord Deputie of Ireland
to my Lord by Mr Dillon /

TEXT

I render yowr good Lordship many humble thanckes for yowr letter
by Mr Fenton; it gladding mee very mootche too fynde styll the
contynewance of yowr Lordships good° wyll & fauoure toowardes
mee which truly my Lord I wyll euer cheerisshe what in mee lyethe,
& hathe alwayes been esteemed of mee far beeyonde the sheowe.

As tootchyng Ned Dennys reporte, I meruayle what came in his head
too deale any waye in a° matter which in no sorte any hys instructioons tootched, & so mootche the more It woonders mee that in a
thyng concernyng yowr Lordship his ouershootte shulld happen,
Whowme greatly too honor & reuerence I allwayes; that yowr Lordship is satisfyed with my assertion therin it contents mee mootche,
& surely but ryght yow yeeld mee in it, which yet very thanckfully
I take.

Yowr Lordships care for owre relieff with vittayles can neyther bee
denyed nor goethe vnacknowleged°, & I woolld too God that vnder
officers had been as carefull yn the executyng as yowr Lordship hathe
euer been fownde in the directyng.

Of the later proportions appoynted too coome hyther wee haue not
as yet receaued any, but contrarietie of wynde wee fynde too bee the
cause; & I praye God, whan it doothe coome, too send vs honest
ministers for the issuyng of it, which is no small trowble & grieff
vntoo vs heere, whow see daylie the nawghtiness & abuse of the
officers & yet can not redress it. /

The little seruyce in Mounster I can not alltoogeathe excuse, &
yet my Lord there hathe been more doonne then I perceaue is
conceaued: for my parte withowte it bee of sum importance I take no°
delyght too aduertiss of euerie common persons head that is taken of,
ootherwyze I could haue° certyfyed of a hundrethe or twoo of theyr

after **good**] 'f' deleted.   **a**] the word 'any' has been reduced to 'a'.   **vnacknowleged**]
the letter 'n' inserted above the line, above a deleted 'w'.   *after* **no**] 'ly' deleted.   *after*
haue] one or two (illegible) characters deleted.

lyues ended since my coomyng from those partes, but in deede sum
hinderance it browght too the greater seruice that the garrisoones
could not remayne in sum of the places appoynted fyrst of by reazoon
that theyr vittayles coulld not bee so readily conueyed too them as was
hoaped of.

As tootchyng the imperfections of the bandes surely my Lord it
hathe not fallen so mootche° by the Captaynes defawlt as by the
eeuyll choyce of men sent hyther whowse lazie dispositions &
vnable bodies guyue ouer beefore they feele trauayle or at the least
vppon the first prooff, but beesydes an esspecyall cause hathe
happened this wynter eeuen from the beeginnyng heere amongst all
owre garrisoons, a generall feruent or rather pestilent ague which in
deede° not pulld downe but allmost hathe spoyled the bandes,
Gods sufferance it is, & hys good pleazure I trust wyll bee agayne
too cease it; but onece thowrogly with a good choyce supplyed, as I
perceaue yowr Lordships there haue allreadie guyuen direction
for it, I hoape in God, too see them heere after in better state
mayntayned.

Where yowr Lordship thynckethe the perill of this State too lye
moast in forrayne aydes, I no whytt varie from yowr Lordships
mynde; but yet dowght I not so mootche any forenar that westward
shulld attempt, as Northe warde, in case the Scottes maye bee
accounted forenares, for heere sure{ly} hathe, doothe & wyll daylie
more & more growe the disquyett & mischieff of this lande, if
speedely it bee not looked vntoo & preuen{ted} as often I haue certyfyed thyther; Too° force the rebell from the sea syde° wee neede not
for the inwarde cuntrie is° hys owane see{k}yng, fynding there all his
relieff & sustenance, & all owre trauayle is too dryue hym too the
coastes where neyther fastnes for hymsel{f} nor succoor for his create
but sielldoome is fownde: the garrisoon of the Dingle was not layed
so mootche for the annoyance of the rebell as the° empeatchyng of
forayne landing, &° for the auayle of the cuntrie seruice is thowght
now meete too bee drawen too Castle Magne there beeyng the verie
Isthmus that deuydes Kerrie from° Clanmorr{ice} Connalaghe &

<hr>

after **mootche**] single-character (illegible) deletion.   **deede**] inserted above the
line.   *after* **Too**] 'seeke' deleted.   *after* **syde**] 'to' deleted.   **is**] 'for' deleted and 'is'
inserted above the line.   *after* **as the**] 'awnssw' deleted.   *after* **landing, &**] two-
character (illegible) deletion.   *after* **from**] 'yᵉ' deleted.

Desmonde, wheraboutes the rebell Earl hathe moast parte this wynter wallcked; & so mootche in the better rest, for that Ihon Zowtche hyssellf was with sicknes browght too deathes doore, & the whoale garrisoone beesydes so vizited as there were not left among them xl. able bodies, but eare summer goe, I hoape in God; yow shall heare that ennemie ootherwyze too bee layed vntoo, if yowr Lordship with the rest hoald on yowr fauourable care in supplying owre lackes & esspecyally of vittayle.

Tootchyng remoouyng of Collman heetherto I haue hard nothyng, but it so fall owte, in that or any oother thyng, yow shall fynde at yowr Lordships direction.

The reazonable good estate of Connaghe throwghe Sir Nycholas Mallbies late good seruice I dowght not but yowr Lordships is acquaynted with by my late aduertisments too yowr Lordship there of the same; & so mootche in awnsswer of yowr Lordships letter.

The occasion of this bearar, Iustice Dillon, hys sending ouer is this: I was wylled by yowr Lordships of the Councell in a letter receaued now by Mr Fenton too proceede too the tryall of the meaner pryzoners heere that stande endyghted: Wheruppon considering with sum of my associates & too them adding the learned councell; of whowme in trowthe I fynde this the very sufficientiest & no less honest withall, wee fownde twoo greate inconueniencies in the cause of ordinarie tryall; the one that no sownde iurie could bee hoaped of; the oother, that thowghe they were cast, yet all benefitt that therby was too fall too her Maiestie of goods, landes, or possessions, by deedes of guyftes & former conueyancies is cleene wyped awaye; these extremities hathe stayed my executyng of yowr direction, tyll I had aduertised therof; & the onely healp that wee see in it is a parlament, for the solicityng wherof & further instructing & resolluyng° of her Maiestie & my Lord in any scruple that therabowtes maye ryze I haue sent this Ientleman, whowme, I earnestly praye yowr Lordship too further, countenance & fauour, not dowghtyng but yow shall° fynde hym woorthie of it. Waye well, I beeseetche yowr Lordship° the loss not deuoyed of dishonor too her

---

& **resolluyng**] inserted above the line.   *after* **shall**] 'to' deleted.   *after* **Lordship**] 'y^t' deleted.

maiestie, &° greate preiudice too the whoale cause, if these me{n}
{. . .}ff° or lyuyng shulld goe acquyted by vniust bearinges & {. . .}
dealinges, & therafter forwarde the healp with a speedie {. . .} So
commending the rest too the bearares creditt, & mysellf in an{. . .}
I maye assured too yowr Lordships deuotion, I take leaue for this
tyme, prayeng the Allmyghtie God euer too keepe direct & prosper
yowr Lordship. / Dublin this vjth of Aprill Anno 1581 /

> Yowr Lordships vnfaynedly too
> commaunde,
>
> Arthur Grey

Good my Lord beare with mee if not so often as mysellf woold &
yowr Lordship maye° expect, I doo visitt yow with letters of myne
owane, that infinitenes of my toyle passethe my ableness too
perfourme my dezyre therin; dutie acknowleged. /

COMMENTARY

the Lord . . . England] William Cecil, Lord Burghley; see biographies.

Mr Dillon] Justice Robert Dillon; see biographies.

yowr letter . . . Fenton] Geoffrey Fenton, secretary of state for Ireland; see
biographies. Fenton had borne letters to the Queen and Privy Council in late
December 1580 (see SP 63/79/26); in early March, he seems to have been in or
near to Chester, awaiting transport back to Ireland (SP 63/81/9 and 63/81/19),
possibly bearing Burghley's letter to Grey. This letter has not survived.

far beeyonde the sheowe] far beyond the gratitude and esteem that I have shown;
though Grey may also be making a wry point, in this patently formal passage,
about the difference between real trust and politic courtesy.

Ned Dennys reporte] on Sir Edward Denny, see biographies. Grey had already
written to Burghley on 29 January (SP 63/80/41), to say that 'I am geven to
vnderstand that your Lordship receyved a sharpe Message by Ned Dennye from
her Maiesty for the defalte of vitualls here, for the which I am righte hartelye
sorrye and so muche the rather lest your Lordship shoulde deme the same to haue
proceeded of some intelligence vnto her Maiestie from mee'. Denny's role in
this transaction is uncertain: Grey goes on to mention 'my lettre [to Elizabeth],
sent at that tyme by Ned Dennye', in which he had humbly requested more
funding for the victualling of his troops; we may assume that Denny was acting as
Grey's bearer, but it seems also that Elizabeth used him to bear a critical message
of her own to Burghley, one suggesting to Burghley that Grey had gone 'over
his head' to the Queen about a matter pertaining directly to his office. If it is
the same incident that Grey is writing about here, the reference to Denny's

---

after **maiestie, &**] 'y^e' deleted.   **me{n} {. . .}ff**] damage to the manuscript, covering this
and subsequent lines, has obscured the readings.   **maye**] inserted above the line.

oucrshoottc (i.e. the exceeding of his orders) suggests that Grey was attempting to distance himself from his bearer's (and, by marriage, his kinsman's) mismanagement of what should have been a delicate transaction with the Queen. At some level Grey must have known that this defence would not wash, for he was as answerable for his bearer's (and his client's) actions as Burghley was for his victuallers' corrupt dealings—it is no accident that Grey immediately tries to teach Burghley a lesson by disassociating the Lord Treasurer's provident stewardship from his victuallers' disorders, then going on to cite this very disorder as the cause of those deficiencies in the service for which Burghley had, apparently, chastised him. Indeed, one question raised by the opening part of this letter might be said to be the complex problem of the accountability of masters for their servants.

too deale . . . tootched] Denny was a captain in the army, and held no administrative position (for example on the Council). He appears to have traded on his family and court connections (with Grey, the Sidneys, and the Queen herself) where he ought to have observed the politic decorum of his position in the Irish service.

Whowme greatly . . . allwayes] the syntax is strange here, but the sense clear: whom I always greatly honour and revere.

ryght yow yeeld mee] you give me my due. One of the important tensions in this anatomy of duty and responsibility is that between merit/culpability and thanks/ blame; Grey is anxious here to assert his right to be cleared of blame, while at the same time professing thanks for it, which (as his emphasis demonstrates) he knows to be a logical nonsense. Similarly, Grey goes on to imply, Burghley is to thank the Lord Deputy for not criticizing him for the 'nawghtiness & abuse' of his officers. For more on these transactions of credit and blame, see the postscript to No. 37, below (SP 63/93/64).

vnder officers] administrative officers responsible for distributing the money and victuals sent from England.

later proportions] Grey clearly means 'more (or most) recent allotted amounts (of victuals)', perhaps close to *OED*, 'Proportion', *n*. 6(b), 'An allotted portion (of land, etc.)', though the earliest cited usage is 1616.

little seruyce in Mounster] Grey was also concerned with the state of Munster, writing to Walsingham on 12 May 1581 that it goes 'de malo in peius I knowe not what too saye too it' (SP 63/83/6). He made an expedition to the province in September and October of 1581.

I take . . . taken of] Grey made a similar claim, that he had merely been quiet about numerous services performed, in his letter to Elizabeth of 26 April 1581 (No. 13, below, SP 63/82/54), in which he enclosed a 'Colleccion' of such services.

imperfections . . . ague] Grey had told Leicester on 13 March that 'a certayne raging feeuer is heere merueylus rieff' (SP 63/81/25), and complained elsewhere to Walsingham that the plague had depleted his bands: on 18 July 1581 he would report that 'Gods hand is styll heauely vppon vs with sicknes, the most parte of owre men newly supplyed fallyng dayly sick in theyr garrisoons' (No. 19, below, SP 63/84/26); and on 9 December 1580 (SP 63/79/5) he was still drawing Walsingham's attention to 'the weaknes of the bandes heere [. . .] by continuall vizitation of sicknes, as often I haue aduertyzed' (SP 63/87/18).

forrayne aydes] i.e. from Spanish or papal forces, or, as Grey points out, from Scotland.

yet dowght . . . Northe warde] 'I don't fear an attack on the western shore, as much as from the North.'

fastnes] a defensible hiding-place, such as a cave.

the Dingle] the location of the landing of papal forces at Smerwick.

empeatchyng] hindering, impeding.

Castle Magne] Castlemaine, in Munster; see maps.

the rebell Earl] i.e. Gerald Fitzgerald, Earl of Desmond; see biographies.

Collman] presumably Richard Colman, chief Remembrancer and responsible for the issuing of money in Ireland, who had been the subject of correspondence between Burghley and Wallop in 1580, in which he was accused of making false declarations about the money he had issued (see SP 63/72/5). This may explain Grey's remarks about corrupt 'vnder officers'. Grey's rhetorical delay in mentioning the business of Colman—another instance of corruption by one of Burghley's men—allows him to drag up and emphasize again the problem of a master's or patron's accountability.

Connaghe] i.e. Connaught.

the meaner . . . endyghted] meaner (less noble, or less significant) than the Earl of Kildare and the Baron of Delvin, who had been arrested in December 1580 and were being held in Dublin Castle. 'Their be many prisoners in this castell', wrote Henry Wallop to Walsingham on 20 March 1581 (SP 63/81/37).

thowghe . . . cast] 'even if they were to be condemned'.

parlament] a frequent preoccupation of the time. Grey wrote to Leicester on 13 March 1580/1, to say 'forgett not I pray yowr Lordship a parlament heere for the proceeding agaiynst these noble men', including Kildare (SP 63/81/25), a passage almost entirely in code, transliterated above the line. Edward Waterhouse wrote to Walsingham seven days later, to advise him that 'It were verie good in my opinion that as maynie apt men as might be founden might be pleasid to make the vpper house in parlement'; 'without a parlament', he writes, 'it will be hard to make triall' of those people 'whose faultes be very manifest' (SP 63/81/37).

12. *Grey to Walsingham, 24 April 1581*

TNA: PRO SP 63/82/48

This letter, following close on the heels of the Queen's resolution for a general pardon for nearly all of the Irish rebels (see SP 63/82/42 and 63/82/43), reveals Grey at his most caustic and disappointed: frustrated by a lack of support for his hard-handed policies and his militant Protestantism, the Lord Deputy rails against his court enemies—Burghley and the Countess of Lincoln above all—in very thinly veiled terms.

The text of the letter is written throughout in Grey's usual italic hand, with his autograph signature. Spenser has added the address in his usual flowing secretary hand. The endorsement, in a later hand, was probably added during the filing of the letter in London. The mixed hand of the

marginal annotations is probably Walsingham's. The addressee note added
to the right foot of the last recto of the letter (reading 'mr Secretary') is in
Grey's distinctive hand, and was added to remind Spenser, upon dispatching
the letter, to whom it should be addressed—hardly unimportant, given the
incendiary nature of Grey's sarcastic complaint.

ADDRESS AND ENDORSEMENT

To the Honorable
my very Loving
frend Sir Fraunces
Walsingham Knight
Chief Secretary
to her Maiesty /

1581.
Aprill. 24.
From the Lord Deputye.

TEXT

Sir, the xvjth & xviijth of this moonethe I receaued from yow twoo
packetts the one by Moumperson a seruant of myne owane whow in
deede seemed° too make but slowe haste, the oother by the° poste
which made as greate speede & came vnto mee beefore that° of the far
elder date: The contents of them, with the aduertisments now from
the Northe agayne haue caused not onely these my letters too her
Maiestie, my Lords, yowrsellf, & oothers, but allso the sending of this
bearar for the more perfitt enfoormyng, earnest soliciting, & speedie
dispatche of the cause. I haue sett downe as playnely as I maye with
reuerence, the peryll & dishonor that is lyke too coome of it if it bee
not gon thowroghe with; & certaynely Sir if shee eyther wyll not, or
bee not able too beare the chardge of it, I see so farre into the condition & disposition° of the peeople that shee wyll not long beare rule
heere; That shee maye see how a good parte of her chardgies wyll bee
requyted, I haue by the bearar sent her a valew of those landes which
wyll fall vntoo her, & the same rather vnder then ouer estimated;
neyther arre these in my conscience the hallf of them that wyll coome
into the same predicament, in case her Maiestie hoald owte: but if the

if hir maiestie
will not beare the
charges of a
suffecient force
to bridle the
rebels she is not
lyke to rule long
there.

A great part of
the charge will be
borne by the
rebels lands.

---

after **deede seemed**] 'but' deleted.   *after* **oother by the**] two-character deletion,
possibly 'pe'.   *after* **beefore that**] 'f' deleted.   **condition & disposition**] these words
were probably underlined by the same reader responsible for the marginal annotations.

proclamation, & general pardon yow wryte of coome ouer,° & now
therbie bring them in blood whowse harttes the swoorde hathe in
manner burst, as if it bee followed, in God I rest assured, wyll very
shortly appeere, fare well all, & lett her hyghnes accounte of no oother
amendes then that allreadie shee hathe & doothe feele;° vnless shee
take one waye, wherby in deede her chardgies maye bee saued hence-
fourthe, & a good rent perchaunce too bee° rayzed beesydes, for so
long as it wyll last; 76.° I woolld haue enlardged & Leinster comitted
too his goouernment with a good rent imposed,° in lyke sorte 120° too
112,° Vllster, too 4.° & Connaghe too 40.° & all Inglisshe men called
awaye,° this were a moast ccrtayne waye too putt them owte of dowght
that 60° meanes no inuasion, whereas yowr proclamations, theyr
consciencies condemnyng themsellues,° wyll eyther breede dowght in
them, or els bee as greatly esteemed of them as former° experience
hathe fownde, wherof I° haue putt her hyghnes allso in mynde: & in
good earnest Sir,° I meruayle mootche that yow arre caried in it so
farre as too thynck it canne doo no hurt: wyll it not thynck° yow
encourage & harten a° rebell too haue pardon offered where noane
was sowght, can that doo no harme, wyll it not bee a good reazoon
for the chieffes too perswade by that her Maiestie is wearie of the
warre, wyll that doo no harme, wyll it not discouradge & putt in feare
the true & good subiect that boathe in action vppon them,° & in
beewrayeng theyr offencies haue harmed them, can that doo no
harme, wyll it not thynck yow stoppe oothers mouthes that arre in
openyng too discoouer the rest, & can this doo no harme, iudge now
yowrsellf, beesydes the dishonor it woold turne 60. too, in case it
shulld fall owte as lightly regarded, as° oother beefore haue doonne./

The bearar lykewyze shall enfourme her Hyghnes of the plott
that is entended presently too bee putt in vre vppon coomyng ouer
of the supplie for the defrayeng of her Hyghnes sum chardge in paye
of bandes, & in greate coomforte I am too bryng it eare a yeare more°
goe abowte° too a good recknyng if greate ones cross it not mootche,

the pardon will doe more hurt then good.

sendeth a plotte for the defraying of some part of the charge.

after coome ouer,] 'fare' deleted.   *after* feele;] 'sauyng' deleted.   bee] inserted above the line.   76.] the Earl of Kildare.   *after* imposed,] single-character illegible deletion.   120] possibly a cipher for Munster.   112] the Earl of Ormond.   4.] unknown cipher.   40] unknown cipher.   awaye,] inserted above the line.   60] the Queen.   themsellues,] inserted above the line.   *after* former] 'ep' deleted.   *after* wherof I] 'hu' deleted.   Sir,] inserted above the line.   no hurt . . . not thynck] 'can it doo no harme' deleted *after* no hurt:, and 'wyll it not thynck' inserted above the line.   a] inserted above the line.   them,] inserted above the line.   *after* regarded, as] single-character deletion, possibly 'p'.   more] inserted above the line.   *after* goe abowte] 'too bryng it' deleted.

or that 60 with sudden pintchyng mar not all: which, if bcc fowndc to moue hir
vncurabe, I praye yow vppon all professed freendshyp, earnestly too maiestie for his
further my dezyre concurring with yowr owane wysshe, that I bee reuocation if
called hoame. sufficient assistance be denyed him

The remoouyng of 112 that yow wysshe mee too press, I doo as
mootche as I maye in, that respected that I can not bee careless of;° it The remouing of
goes neere mee on eyther syde, ease mee therfore I praye & lett not 112.
the whoale burden swaye on mee: but yet I see not why 30.° & yowr
self° shulld conceaue that 112 shulld harme more° beeing yn° 65° then
70.° in° 65 onely woordes can harme & yet not so but that awnsswers
of greater reazoon & more creditt arre there readie too fruntt hym:,°
& heere° deedes hurt, beesydes perswasion with the greate credit that
presence° daylie encreasethe, & therin beesydes reazoon, experto
crede Roberto; & in shortt the wownde of that parte wyll neuer bee
perfectly cloazed, tyll the prowde flesshe bee withdrawen, deale in it
therfore as yow shall thynck good; but if neyther this nor encrease of
force wyll bee harckned too, remember the foote of my song, awaye
with mee for Gods sake in tyme that trust of yowr frendshyp beecoome not my ouerthrowe. Beecause° her Maiestie, I vnderstoode,
thynckes very small seruice doonne heere for her greate chardge, I
haue by° this brynger sent a collection of sutche seruicies as since° my sendeth a
chardge hathe been doonne, wherby I trust shall appeere that the collection of such
bandes haue neyther been idle, nor theyr trauayle vainely employed, seruices as haue
been don since
& surely sir thynges arre throwghe Gods good blessing browght now his coming
too that issewe that were it not for 40 bearing one waye, & 112. thither.
forbearing an oother, 65 shulld rest no quyeter then 70 shulld beecoome; but that the fawlt manifestly seene maye not bee harckned
too,° mootche less redressed is certaynely this, that the wrong eend
is beegoonne at, rebellioon & oother disobediencies too the Prince
warde arre chieffly regarded & reformation sowght of, but Gods cause The cause why
is made a seconde or nothyng at all, & bee yowr sellf the wittness, for the reformacion

---

careless of] 'in' deleted *after* careless, and 'of' inserted above the line.   30.] the Earl of
Leicester.   yowr self] in cipher, transliterated above the line.   *after* harme more]
single-character deletion.   beeing yn] in cipher.   65] unknown cipher, possibly
Ireland.   70.] unknown cipher, possibly England.   in] in cipher.   hym] in
cipher.   heere] in cipher.   credit, presence] in cipher.   ouerthrowe. Beecause]
'that' deleted *after* ouerthrowe, and 'Because' inserted above the line.   *after* haue by] four
letters, possibly 'thys', deleted.   since] illegible single-character deletion between the letters
'n' and 'c'.   too,] inserted above the line.   *Marginal note* sough] not only has the secretary
omitted the terminal 't' here, but the word includes an extra pen stroke, which we have ignored.

intended taketh
no better effect is
because outward
obedience only is
sough° and
relligion left
alone.

the manie challendgies & instructioons that I haue receaued for the
ciuill & politick goouernment & care taking too the husbandrie of
worldly treazure, where is there one article that concernes the looking
too Gods due seruice, seeyng of hys churtche fed with true food, &
repressyng of superstition & idolatrie, wherwith the groues of
Canaan were surely no° more filled nor infected then this lamentable
Ilande is, naye rather haue I not been watchewoorded that I shulld not
bee too eeyfull therin, & I confess my sinne, I haue followed man too
mootche in it, &° this the cause that neyther the chyeff can harcken
too that that concernes boathe honor &° saftie most, nor yow that
perswade the truthe bee beeleeued, nor I that dezyre the ryght can
bee satisfyed, but Balls prophetts & councelors shall preuayle: I see it
is so, I see it is iust, I see it past healp, I rest dispayred, healp mee
awaye agayne for Gods sake. /

By one of yowr letters it seemes enfoormed yow that I had° lett the
countrolershyp of the impostes too oother & depryued Brisckett,
truly sir, neyther lett nor guyuen haue I it too any then too hymsellf &
therfore the information° was hastier then trew: & amongst oother
good opinions I hope yow carie of mee lett this bee settled, that
Arthur Grey, wyll neuer by anye office, lease or warde in this lande
bee euer the woorthe of° a pennie the better; her maiesties paye &
ryght of the office for° howse fynding shall onely bee my share, for
any oother benefitt or takyng, all chardgies I defie & pardoon refuse,
how euer deerely it cost mee, as I fynde it doothe,° / & onely God I
hoape on, for the world, I feare wyll fayle mee. /

How 76. syster dealethe° with mee by ootherwyze I allso partly heare,
well, I had rather it were her° wrong then my dezertt, & dowght
not but in end faythe shall decypher fynes.   So for this tyme
wyll I leaue trooblyng yow any further, repoasing the rest of the
bearares sufficiencie whowme too creditt, countenance & procure
speedie dispatche I earnestly praye yow. /° God increase all his

no] inserted above the line.   *after* **in it, &**] 'not' deleted.   *after* **honor &**] single-character deletion, possibly 's'.   *after* **I had**] 'too' deleted.   *after* **information**] single-character deletion, possibly 'n'.   of] inserted above the line.   *after* **office for**] illegible two-letter deletion.   **doothe**] the last three letters of this word, 'the', inserted above the line.   **syster dealethe**] in cipher.   her] in cipher.   yow. /] inserted above the line.

vertewes in yow, keepe & direct yow euer. / Dublin this xxiiijth of Aprill Anno 1581. /

Euer vnfaynedly

yowres,

Arthur Grey

It greeuethe mee° too see good sir Nycholas Mallbie so thancklessly vzed, & breedes no less coomforte in oothers of lyke rewarde: greate wrong hee hathe for if any hathe deserued well in this lande hee surely it is. /

COMMENTARY

Moumperson a seruant of myne owane] Richard Mompesson is named in SP 63/88/40/3 (a list of the Lord Deputy's grants of lands and other benefits to his followers) as one of Grey's gentlemen ushers; Grey would write to Walsingham on 18 July 1581 in behalf of Mompesson, who had suffered a loss of the promise of financial gain upon the escape of his Spanish prisoner (presumably another benefit bestowed by his master); see SP 63/84/28, a document in Spenser's own hand.

aduertisments now from the Northe agayne] it is not clear whether or not Grey is here referring to some specific news; he must have been receiving regular reports of the disposition of Turlough Luineach O'Neill during these months, and would in the next few days learn from Sir Nicholas Bagenal of a serious seasonal influx of Scots galloglass (SP 63/82/52).

this bearar] unidentified.

the cause] i.e. the new 'aduertisments now from the Northe'.

her chardgies] Elizabeth's expenses in the war.

sent her a valew of those landes] see the enclosure to his letter to Elizabeth of the following day, SP 63/82/54/2, where he values the known traitors' lands at £5,030; the copy now catalogued as 63/82/49 may have been prepared for Walsingham.

the same predicament] i.e. those lands that will be escheated by as yet undetected traitors.

in case her Maiestie hoald owte] in case the Queen should remain firm, without issuing a general pardon.

the proclamation ... yow wryte of] for extant drafts of the proclamation see SP 63/82/42 and 43, both annotated by Burghley. Grey complained of the pardon to Walsingham on 14 May (see SP 63/83/16), and to the Privy Council on 10 June (No. 15, above, SP 63/83/45), by which time it must have been promulgated.

bring them in blood ... burst] give them courage whom a strict military policy has subdued.

---

mee] inserted above the line.

76. I woolld . . . in mynde] Grey's transparent sarcasm here exposes his funda-
mental incomprehension of Elizabeth's mistrust of her own governors: as he
writes, her pardon merely served to suggest her own guilt for his policies ('con-
sciences condemnying themsellues'). It seems obvious from his wording here that
Walsingham must have argued, in a now lost letter, that Elizabeth pursued the
pardon to make it clear to her Irish subjects that she meant no large-scale campaign in or 'invasion' of Ireland.

the chieffes] a chief (*taoiseach*) was the head of an Irish sept, or family.

stoppe oothers mouthes . . . the rest] serve to gag them that were about to come
forward (out of fear) to expose further conspiracies and treasons.

in vre] i.e. in use.

the supplie . . . of bandes] Grey had inherited from previous governors some
serious deficits, including the pay of some English soldiers in Ireland. Auditor
Thomas Jenyson reported to Burghley on 14 May that he was still paying off the
debts of Sir Edward Fitton, but had paid all the Leinster captains through the end
of March (SP 63/83/19); on 20 July he reported to Walsingham that he had
finished Fyton's account (SP 63/84/39), but on the other hand Treasurer Sir
Henry Wallop wrote to Walsingham on 15 May that he had disbursed all of
that month's treasure without having discharged a full debt to any single man (SP
63/83/23). Grey seems here to be referring to a new scheme by which he would
cashier some forces and schedule money for the rest, in order to bring the situation
under control.

eare] ere, i.e. 'before'.

with sudden pintchyng] Elizabeth and her Privy Council were notorious—at least
in the eyes of the Dublin administration—for their capricious fits of economy.

that respected . . . eyther syde] Grey reminds Walsingham that, while he suffers
from Ormond's abuse of his office in Ireland, he fears to push for his removal
because of Ormond's close relation to the Queen.

with the greate . . . encreasethe] Grey insists that Ormond is more of a danger in
Ireland than in England, for in Ireland his presence acts as a great spur to his credit
with the local lords and gentry.

experto crede Roberto] Lat. 'Trust in the experienced Robert' (i.e. Dudley, Earl of
Leicester). Grey suggests that Leicester has had some experience of Ormond that
will make it obvious why he should be removed.

foote of my song] 'my refrain'.

collection . . . been doonne] see SP 63/82/54/1, Grey's first enclosure to the
Queen of 26 April.

repressyng of superstition & idolatrie] like Spenser in *A view*, Grey sees the real
threat to true religion in Ireland to come not exclusively from Roman religion, but
from ignorance and paganism.

watchewoorded] warned.

Balls prophetts & councelors] this passage alludes repeatedly to 1 Kings 18, in
which the prophet Elijah overcomes the prophets and counsellors of the pagan idol
Baal, and persuades King Ahab to return Israel to the worship of God. Grey seems
to be imagining himself as a latter-day Elijah, but one doomed not to success but
failure.

countrolershyp of the impostes] a valuable monpolistic commodity eventually
granted to Bryskett by letters patent from the Queen; in return for his labour in
governing the collection of imposts (mercantile taxes), the holder was allowed to

retain a percentage of the crown revenues. Bryskett complained to Walsingham about Grey's dealing with the controllership in a letter of 2 March 1581 (SP 63/81/5); he finally lost the commodity in 1583, when the Lords Justice Wallop and Loftus let individual imposts out to farm; see SP 63/99/67 for Bryskett's complaint to Walsingham.

Brisckett] Lodowick Bryskett; see biographies.

ryght . . . for howse fynding] Grey seems to be referring to what he undoubtedly considered the most inalienable perquisite of his position as Lord Deputy, the ability to reward good service by the disposal of lands and manors that came into his hands.

How 76. . . . with mee] Elizabeth Fiennes de Clinton (née Fitzgerald), Surrey's Geraldine, the widow of Sir Anthony Browne and, after her second husband's creation as Earl of Lincoln in 1572, Countess of Lincoln; see biographies.

faythe shall decypher fynes] Grey holds out a vain hope that constancy and truth will prevail over courtly subtlety (finesse); the spelling of 'fynes' is clearly a joke on the Countess of Lincoln's married name.

13. *Grey to the Queen, 26 April 1581*

TNA: PRO SP 63/82/54

This letter sees Grey adopting a surprisingly forthright tone to Elizabeth ('marry now. . .'), as he attempts to defend himself against charges of expensive and unsuccessful service, and indeed conscious that he may be exceeding the limits of decorum: 'pardon likewise humbly I craue, if herein I exceede any thing the limits of becoming.' He also attempts, within these limits of becoming, to argue against the general pardon that Elizabeth is about to issue for all but the most prominent rebels: on the grounds that it may simply not be taken up by most rebels, that those who do take it up may throw it back in the face of the English, and that in any case it will force Grey into a disadvantageous position in his dealings with rebels such as Turlough Luineach O'Neill, in the struggle with whom he had recently been denied extra soldiers.

The text of the letter is in Spenser's formal italic hand, typical of formal reports from Grey to the Queen. Grey has added the subscription and his signature in his own hand. A long passage on the final page of the manuscript, inserted in Grey's hand, includes a cipher distinct from that which Grey normally used in sensitive letters to Walsingham; this probably represents a system designed specially for letters to the Queen.

ADDRESS AND ENDORSEMENT

To her most excellent
Maiestie

26 Aprill 1581
To hir Maiestie from the Lord
Grey.

Entred

TEXT

It may please your Highnes The course of thinges here willeth me
agayne to trouble your Maiesty with former causes and besides to
sende this Bearer for solliciting of the same fynding resolutions there
not to answere that which the necessitie here requireth. I haue often
tymes advertised to my Lords and lately to your Highnes selfe the
tickle hoalde or rather rebellious disposition that Tirlagh contynually
resteth in, & dayly more and more makes shewe of, as the Marschalls
lettres to mee herewith sent to your Highnes will nowhitt darkly
display, besides a generall holownes of hartes here to your Maiesty
The contentes whereof falling out true & the mammering condition
of all the other provinces weighed, howe necessary yt is for your
Maiestie to haue care of it, & in the meane how nerely yt toucheth
me importunately to putt you in mynde of the same your Highnes
selfe bee the decerner: To prouide for the worst hath neuer bene
faulty, nor gone without commendation, though shewe haue not
brought forth the effecte; to bee secure, and that in manifest
warninges, besides great losse & late repentaunce, neuer with the wise
escaped condemnation; If then no doubtfull signes of the perill
appeare vnto you, & the looking to yt is to you ether the safetie or
losse of this state, I most humbly beseeche your Maiestie in your own°
honours behalf & especially in gods respect, who hauing betaken vnto
you the interest & gouernement of this land with nolesse duety of
care and charge, then of the same wherein you abyde, will doubtles
challenge nolesse accoumpt at your handes for the one then for the
other, most humbly, I say, I beseche your Highnes to haue earnest
regard in tyme of it & pardon likewise humbly I craue, if herein I
exceede any thing the limits of becoming, the Lord is my witness true
& earnest zeale to your honour and service is the onely cause of the
miscarriage, yf any there bee. Vnlesse your Maiesty will affoord
the encrease of force I late wrote for, I see not but one of these°
inconveniences will light, ether a most dishonorable composition with
Tirlagh contayned in one Article or rather worde, namely his owne

own] inserted above the line.   of these] inserted above the line.

will, & the same to stand on no better certenty then his owne liking; or els hazard yf not losse of the whole; the numbers already here not being hable both to front him and leaue sufficient force to answere the Rebelles of the other provinces, as but now they are, which weakenes in vs once fownde, & that your Highnes will not goe through with what you haue begonne, for one that is out now accoumpt then of tenne, & setled they will growe in their already commune boast, that for the chardge they will enforce your Highnes to giue them ouer. Your Highnes charge indeed is very great, I cannot denye & to God I would, that I might as well, as willing I am to helpe yt; but your Maiestie in this case is not to looke onely vpon the chardge, but vpon the cause as well, and then I doubt not but the cause shall appeare as rare as the charge vnwonted: That any needlesse or without good grownd hath bene raised or lenger contynued then the cause required, with your Maiesties indifferent favour I dare take vpon me to answere; & where I beare some fault to be fownd at the number of Colonells that should be here, truly Madam there are in all but twoo, Sir George Bourchier for the Garrisons in the County of Limerick & Connelagh, which is very necessary the Lord Generall not being alwaies in the Prouince, and Iohn Zowche in Kerry a farre remoued place from all other companies, where necessitie nolesse required the like Officer I am also giuen to vnderstand that your Highnes is the more grieued at your charges for that you find the same very sclenderly answered in seruice; indeed so great seruices as such cost might seeme to craue, I will not affirme to bee doen nether doo I hope will your Maiestie measure accidentall euentes by such a continuall certein grownd, but if endeuour haue bene ouerslipped or trauaile & aduenture spared, then lett your threasure be accoumpted vaynely wasted & the burden on me layd. I haue not euer certefied of euery seruice doen, because I expected still as I desyred such a one, as worthely might haue come to your Highnes eares but yf taking of Cowes, killing of their Kerne & churles had bene thought worth the aduertising I could haue had euery day to haue troubled your Highnes the which seruices in totall yett not beeing to goe vnaccounted of, would in particular report haue brought but meane delight; marry now seing that by saying nothing, nothing is thought to be doen I thought good too commend to your Highnes by this Bearer a Colleccion of all the services doen here since my gouernement, so farre as may be remembred, which though not so great as ether your Highnes may expect or my self would wish, yet doubt I not but it shall appeare, God to haue fauored your Highnes

forces as much in this tyme, as in any other heretofore I tarry not
so long in this theme, that I would carry your Highnes to the con-
tynuaunce or encrease of charges or proceding in the Action further
then apparent reason holde with me for your owne honour & safety of
state here; yf any other shall bring better reason to the contrary &
shall thinck with lesse charge & yett safety this gouernement may be
carried, which I confesse to goe far beyond my reach ether in conceipt
or execution, I most humbly craue for furtheraunce of your Highnes
service to be called home and such a one to haue the place: yett is it
not vnknowen to me, that thinges might be patched vp, and a face of
peace & quietnes made to appeare, but then the gouernement or
rather Confusion must be this; that no vice, disobedience or insolencie should ether be punished, or brideled, your Highnes lawes
answered by none, but by a handfull of the English pale murder,
stealth, rapes & all other insolencies to haue free allowaunce, otherwise the maske of this quiete would soone be throwen of, as daylie
experience shewes; for he that to day semes a duetifull Subiect, lett
him for any of these or other lesse crimes be to morrow called vpon to
come & answere, streight a proteccion is demaunded & in the meane
he wilbee vpon his keeping, as here they terme yt, which in plaine
English is none other, then a Traitour that forcibly will defend his
cause & not answere to iustice: I know the great feare, due reverence
& sownd knowledg your Highnes hath of god, besides the naturall
regard to your honour & place cannot suffer you to like or rather not
to detest such kynde of gouernement: your wisedome then cannot
but see the great vnsurety of the same, & as touching the sparing
thereby lett the forepast charges of so many yeares caused onely by
this irresolute proceeding in the action, shewe the gayne & whether in
reason one eight or tenne of these yeares charges bestowed at once
vpon a thorough reformation had not bene a farre more sparing way,
besides other good, then to suffer yt to runne into this continuall
consumption of threasure which neuer wilbee helped vnlesse the
plott bee altered. A peaceable gouernement were the easiest &
quietest trade for me or whosoeuer should supply this place, &
travaile enough well entended too, shall any Gouernour here finde of
ciuile & politique causes, what reason should then induce me, to that
labour to adde care, toile, & hazard of warre° causes, yf with duety &
conscience to God & Prince saued I might eschewe yt. Your Maiestie
I heare, is in purpose° bestowe a generall pardon vpon this nation

<hr>

warre] 's' deleted at the end of this word.   *after* **purpose**] 'to' deleted.

with some exceptions; I beseche your Highnes to consider well of it: of myne owne tyme this proofe I haue; in the proclayming of these mountayne Traytours a generall pardon was graunted to all, certayn of the chief exempted, that would leaue the rest, & reward withall sett downe, to whomesoeuer should bring in aliue {or}° dead any of the Archknaues; since agayne infinite secrete offers of pardon and hire haue I made to the chiefest for seruice vpon other chieffs: nay further haue I aduentured my self vpon your grace in maner against one of my Instructions from your self at my coming away; I offerd to Desmond him selfe pardon, in case he would quick or dead deliuer into mee his brother Iohn & Doctor Saunders; which most easely I knew he might haue doen, being hourely & forcelesse in his hand: what of all these offers is hearkned to, what thancks is giuen, what submission is made, what grace accepted? nay in trouth Madam I neuer fownd but these mercifull dealinges haue euer lifted them vp to greater insolencies, nether holdes this my experience by the tyme of their most prosperitie, but in their most ebbe and misery hath lenitie fownd this effect: after the Fortes wynning passed my offer to Desmond since my coming into these partes very lately after many spoiles &° slaughters executed vpon Pheagh and his followers, so that his self demaunded the Parley; sondry tymes like grace hath bene graunted, but in end Beggers fall to pride, raile at your Maiestie leaue god, & onely relye vpon the Pope, & that charges shall in end free them: herevnto laye for the good that pardons here worke, that in Sir William fitz Williams tyme there was like to this now entended a graunt of generall Pardon, and therevpon a great number were sent abroade, but somuch regarded, as three partes of them yett lye in Kilkenny, and neuer once asked for, as I am credibly enformed: to bee shorte vnder your Highnes correction pardon & protection next to the small care had of trew Religion & settling of Gods Worde hath bene the onely destruction of this Gouernement which triall enforceth me to say, that onely sworde will salue the sore of. for the contrary I dare defend to haue essayed as much as any Gouernour toofore, & will tye my selfe to your Maiesties iustice onely, yf it can be iustly layd vnto mee, that euer yet I tooke lyfe from any, how euer euill deseruing that submitted him self to your mercy: feare therefore and not dandling must bringe them to the byarsse of obedience.

{or}] a large inkblot has obscured this word, but the reading is obvious from the context.   **spoiles &**] inserted above the line.

I would gladly receiue your Highnes resolution touching 63.° yt is a cause requireth not your least consideration: I did in my last say what I thought in it: very fewe that in priuate frendshippe {······ · ····· ····}, nether that I thincke more {··········· ·· ······· ··· ·····} 7.° in any {····· ····} onely excepted: thus doothe faythfull dutie & sincere° affection too 7. {······ ···} of {···} that which ootherwyse {·· ····, ·····, ·· ····· ······},°

The Bearer now bringeth your Highnes an estimate of the benefitt that vpon these attaynders will fall to your Maiestie and he shall likewise enforme you of a Plott for the lightening your Highnes of 2000 mens pay by yeare, which in God I hope shall take effecte in short tyme, in case your Highnes shall thinck good to answere wantes here, & the same presently vpon the coming of the supplye now appointed hether shalbee entered into. /

I beseche God to direct your Highnes resolution to that course, that may most make for your owne honour & reformation of this yet most miserable nation vtterly deuoyde of his knowledg, & nowhitt regarding you his annoynted nor guided by any other rule then sensuall libertie.

So fearing to haue held your Highnes too long, though not so long as the cause yet requires, were yt not in trust of the Messenger, whome I humbly commend to your Maiesties creditt for the rest I take most humble leaue, beseeching the Almighty to prolong your lyfe in all happinesse in this world, and send your Maiesty eternall ioy in that to come. Dublin the 26 of Aprill, 1581.

> Yowr hyghnes most humble seruant
> & faythefull subiect,
> Arthur Grey

COMMENTARY

this Bearer] very possibly Rowland Cowick, formerly Clerk of the Council, who attended the Privy Council bearing a commendatory letter from the Irish Council (SP 63/82/55), also dated 26 April, and a petition (SP 63/82/55/1), describing

---

63.] unknown cipher.   7.] unknown cipher.   **dutie & sincere**] a deletion of about eight illegible characters appears *after* **dutie &**; 'sincere' has been inserted above the line.   {······ ... ······}] this long passage includes several sections in an illegible cipher, distinct from that used in Grey's letters to Walsingham.

his loss of cattle and sheep at the hands of the 'mountayne Rebells' in an attack on his farm in September 1580.

lately to your Highnes selfe] it is not clear to which letter to the Queen Grey here refers. He had recently written letters to Leicester (SP 63/81/25, 12 March) on 'the arrogant traytor Tyrlowghe' and his 'dishonorable & most danegerous temporisinges', and also to Burghley (SP 63/81/27, 13 March).

tickle hoalde] i.e. the precarious control exercised over Turlough Luineach. Cf. 'your onely losse is the fyne, which surely the tickle hold & vse of land here, as dayes now are, & the generall extreme pouerty with all weighed, can growe to no great accoumpt' (Grey to Queen Elizabeth, 25 January 1581/2, SP 63/88/39).

Tirlagh] in his recent letter to Leicester (SP 63/81/25), Grey had spoken of Turlough Luineach's continued reinforcement with Scottish galloglas, with whom, he says, 'hee sustaynethe the rebells of Connaught'. He repeats here his point, recently made to the Privy Council, that 'want of force' leads them to settle for a 'trustless peace' with Turlough Luineach, and asks for greater supply of money and men.

the Marschalls ... Highnes] the **Marschall** is Sir Nicholas Bagenal, Knight Marshall (see biographies). This letter does not seem to be enclosed, but may be catalogued elsewhere.

nowhitt darkly display] clearly reveal.

mammering] 'hesitating' (*OED*), either in the sense that they are in a precarious state (cf. 'tickle hoalde'), or that their affection for Elizabeth is hesitant.

how nerely yt toucheth me] how particularly it concerns me.

though shewe haue not brought forth the effecte] 'even if, in the course of things, the worst-imagined scenarios did not come to pass'.

if ... I exceed any thing the limits of becoming] if I am being at all improper.

miscarriage] misconduct.

the encrease ... for] there seems to survive no 'late' (recent) letter from Grey to Elizabeth requesting such an increase in troops. In SP 63/82/41 (19 April), the Privy Council had communicated Elizabeth's refusal to give Grey more than the thousand troops promised, though when Grey speaks here (see below) of Elizabeth's *intention* to issue a general pardon, it suggests that these letters had perhaps not yet reached him.

composition] agreement.

contayned ... his owne will] i.e. any composition with Turlough will amount to his drawing up conditions according to his own will, and with only his personal inclination to determine whether he will abide by the agreement.

front] confront.

out] out in rebellion, in open rebellion.

that I might ... helpe yt] i.e. I wish my capacity to reduce the charge was as great as my desire to do so.

the charge vnwonted] i.e. the unusually high charge arising from the Irish service comes from a uniquely precarious situation.

the Lord Generall] the Lord General of Munster was Thomas Butler, Earl of Ormond; see biographies.

Kerry a farre remoued place] Kerry is one of the furthermost south-westerly counties of Ireland, remote from Dublin and from Turlough Luineach's movements in the North.

grieued at your charges] cf. Privy Council to Grey, 19 April 1581 (SP 63/82/41): 'her Maiestie lookyng narrowly into the present charges she is at in that realme and findyng the same so exceading great as in deed they are.'

sclenderly answered in seruice] slenderly, or slightly, repaid, by Grey's services and successes.

nether doo . . . certein grownd] i.e. I hope that you will not judge our fortunate successes or defaults—which are out of our control—by such a rigid standard. Grey encourages the Queen, rather, to judge his, and his officers', 'endeuour . . . trauaile & aduenture'.

ouerslipped] omitted.

I haue not euer certefied of] I have not always accounted for, written about.

Kerne] see glossary.

churles] base men and servants.

a Colleccion] SP 63/82/54/1, enclosed with this letter. This note lists the following services done by Grey, and points out the letters in which they are described: 'Twentie rebell slaine and two hurte by their owne report but lx supposed to be slaine and some hurte' (in a letter from Grey to Elizabeth, 28 August 1580); 'Threscore rebelles wherof some greate harme doers to the pale slaine by our horsemen' (in a letter from the Council of Ireland to the Privy Council, 18 September 1580); 'The forte at smerwick yelded simply, 600 slaine there' (in a letter from Grey to Elizabeth, 12 November 1580); 'Sir Nicholas Malby followeth the E. of Clan. sonnes hottlie and hath hanged the pledges of Vlick burk in gallowey', and 'Sir William Stanley toke a praie from the rebell in Leinster and after slew Feagh mac Hughes brother and divers of the rebelles' (in a letter from Grey to the Privy Council, 14 January 1580/1). Only the third of these letters (No. 5, above, SP 63/78/29) seems to survive among the Irish State Papers. This collection of services suggests that the volume of correspondence from Ireland to England was substantially higher than that preserved in the extant records, and also indicates that Grey's secretaries kept detailed letter-books, listing and describing the letters sent not only by Grey but also by the Council.

carried] conducted.

ether in conceipt or execution] either in that I can imagine such a thing, or bring it about.

to be called home] these requests for revocation become ever more frequent in subsequent correspondence.

brideled] restrained; as a horse is by its bridle.

stealth] secret theft.

rapes] violent acts of theft. The word had its contemporary meaning by that time, too (*OED*, *n.*²).

a proteccion is demaunded] Grey means that anybody called in on such a charge will demand a document or assurance ('proteccion') that they will not be arrested.

he wilbee . . . terme yt] to be **upon one's keeping** is to be on one's guard, in this case ready to defend oneself, and one's case ('cause') by force.

forepast charges] previous expenditures and costs.

plott] design, plan.

& travaile enough well entended too] and work enough in itself, if well attended to.

shall any ... warre causes] the syntax here is knotty, but Grey's sense is clear enough: I would have work enough in civil and political government; why should I add military travails, if it were not necessary?

a generall pardon] on 19 April 1581, Elizabeth had issued a general pardon to all Irish rebels apart from Desmond, John of Desmond, Dr Sanders, Viscount Baltinglass, and the Seneschal of Imokilly (the latter on Grey's discretion). A draft of the pardon (with corrections by Burghley) exists in the Irish State Papers (SP 63/82/42), as does a draft of a letter from the Privy Council explaining the pardon, and telling Grey that 'in case you resolue to enter into anie action of warre agaynst Tirlaghe, wee then thincke it verie meete that you should fyrst offer vnto him confirmation of suche thinges as by your Lordship weare thought meet to be allowed vnto him' (SP 63/82/41).

these mountayne Traytours] such as the Cavanaghs and Birnes (O'Byrnes), against whom he would shortly make a campaign (see No. 15, below, SP 63/83/45). Cf. 'It is now x dayes since owre happie generall pardoon was proclaymed, & yet no one offer from any of the Mountayne rebells' (No. 19, below, SP 63/84/26).

for seruice vpon other chieffs] evidence of the English administration's desire to take (and sponsor) sides in local, factional disputes, as a way of purchasing obedience from certain rebels.

I aduentured ... your grace] on Grey's initial departure for Ireland, a number of memoranda were drawn up to give him directions for his service, or to direct discussion among the Privy Council about those directions (see SP 63/74/37–40: Burghley's hand is evident in the drafting and correcting of these memoranda). No notes concerning Desmond survive, but one might extrapolate from Grey's remark that he was instructed to pursue Desmond without offer of pardon.

Desmond him selfe] no record of this pardon seems to exist.

quick or dead] alive or dead.

his brother Iohn & Doctor Saunders] John of Desmond (Sir John Fitzgerald) and Dr Nicholas Sanders; see biographies.

hourely & forcelesse in his hand] since they were in his power, continually and with no need for any force.

in their most ebbe] in their greatest misfortune (the **ebbe** is the flowing of tidal water back to the sea).

the Parley] a meeting to discuss a truce.

Beggers fall to pride] this sounds proverbial, and the association of beggary and pride is certainly conventional (e.g. 'Behold I come, to let you see the Pride | With which Exalted Beggars always Ride', Daniel Defoe, *The True-Born Englishman*, ll. 608–9), though no contemporary usages can be found.

& that charges shall in end free them] this seems to repeat the earlier boast: that the English will be forced to leave Ireland, or to stop prosecuting the rebels, because of the cost.

Sir William fitz Williams tyme] William Fitzwilliam was Lord Deputy between December 1571 and September 1575 (and would be appointed again between 1588 and 1594).

three partes of them] uncertain. Perhaps three quarters of them.

the small care had] an unusually explicit voicing of concern for the religious failings of reform.

onely sworde will salue the sore] Grey's commonly expressed opinion, that the obedience of the Irish can only be achieved through compulsion, not voluntarily. See Bradshaw, 'Sword, Word and Strategy'.

dandling] pampering.

byarsse] perhaps the bias, or leaning, towards obedience.

attaynders] indictments for treason; traitors forfeited their goods and lands to the crown upon attainder, and their blood was said to be corrupted, so that neither title nor possession might pass to the heir.

sensuall libertie] cf. the 'libertie and ill example' of the Anglo-Irish that Spenser describes in *A view* (ll. 1951–2133) and the sensual government of Ireland that Grey describes to Walsingham in May 1581 (SP 63/83/16).

14. *Grey to Walsingham, 9 June 1581*
TNA: PRO SP 63/83/43

Grey had been advertised over the course of winter and spring 1581 of the increasing disorder of the O'Byrnes and Cavanaghs, in the counties south of Dublin; he set out on a journey against them in the middle of May, in an attempt to assert the Pale's authority in territories formerly kept in awe by the (now imprisoned) Earl of Kildare. From Wexford he dispatched this typically harried and slightly outraged letter, protesting against the Queen's policy on the proclamation of pardon and reporting his position on Turlough Luineach O'Neill. The letter is interesting for its careful negotiation of the distinction between Grey's public responsibilities and his private cares and duties, especially as expressed here in his friendship for Sir Francis Walsingham. Spenser's presence with Grey on this journey to Wexford may be tied to his acquisition of the twenty-one-year lease of the house of friars, manor, lands, and a weir in Enniscorthy, issued on 15 July 1581.

The text of the letter, including the subscription, signature, and several passages in cipher, is in Grey's usual italic hand. The address is in Spenser's characteristic secretary, and the endorsement—presumably added during the process of filing the letter in Westminster, in a later italic. An addressee note ('{Mr Sec}retary') appears at the left foot of the first page of the manuscript.

ADDRESS AND ENDORSEMENT

To the right
Honorable my
very good frend
Sir Fraunces
Walsingham
Knight Chief
Secretary to
her Maiestie ./

1581
June .9.
From the Lord Deputye.

TEXT

Sir, the xxvij^{th} of the last I receaued a packett from yow beeyng in Camp then in the Birnes countrie, which causethe that sooner I could neyther awnsswer them, nor as yet execute the direction for the proclamations: well I see that lyke or dislyke of goouernment heere is alltoogeather° settled vppon encrease or decrease of the chardge, no honor, no saftie of the State, no obedience too Prince or God, no pollicie & quyett of the Common Wealthe at all respected or regarded; in conscience too Godward & dutie too my Prince that it greeues mee not I maye not surely denye, thowghe in myne owane pryuate beehallf° too thynck God moste good vntoo mee that° this contrarie cource too myne aduyce & dezyre is taken greate cause I conceaue. I wyll God wyllyng with best endeuoure followe what is directed mee, & esspecyally yowr owane moast freendly aduyce, too patche vp thynges as I maye, since I maye not as I woolld. I acknow-ledge sir yowr greate trauayle & endeuoure for too haue had the best waye taken wherin thowghe I know the cause itsellf was yowr princi-pall inducement, yet hauyng° fownde my priuate in creditt & good euer cared for & fauoured by yow I can not but moast thanckfully take yowr moast freendly or rather° brootherly cariadge toowardes mee euer since my beetakyng too this place, wherin so long as hoape remayned too doo God, prince & cuntrie seruice, toyle & care were the both lyghter burdens vntoo mee, but those endes now dispayred of all encouragement is depryued, beesydes tootche of conscience that this cource must bring too see & suffre all insolencie & wicked-nes: I vrdge not this that I woold requyre any further laboor too allter the direction now sent, it is far from my meanyng, onely & lastly, I trust in God, tendes it too craue yowr woonted earnest trauayle too gett mee ryd° of° the office, good Sir fauoure mee in this sute, the which, beefore God I protest, with more earnestnes & dezyre too obtayne I make, & with opinion of more bonde vntoo yow for I woolld receaue, then any that euer yet I had vntoo yow; press it° therfore I beeseetche yow.

after **alltoogeather**] two-letter deletion, possibly 'es'.   *after* **beehallf**] 'it' deleted.   *after* **mee that**] single-letter illegible deletion.   *after* **yet hauyng**] 'euer' deleted.   **rather**] 'ly' deleted at the end of this word.   *after* **mee ryd**] 'fro^{m}' deleted.   *after* **mee ryd . . . of**] 'fr' deleted.   **it**] inserted above the line.

I haue signified too my Lord of Ormond her Maiesties pleazure for hys dischardge as yow directed mee; The care of that prouince now, waying the loase condition that itsellf & oothers now stande in & no goouernor too remayne in it doothe not a lyttle trooble mee, & sure presently order & direction from the table there must° coome or els it is lyke in a moonethe too growe too that that perchaunce in a yeare wyll not bee recoouered, & vnder correction, great ouersyght it was withowte an oothers placyng too displace hym & so I euer aduyced. For the tyme how there in I meane to deale, as of this my Ioorney hythertoo, & oother thynges concernyng this state at sum lengthe I haue written too my Lords in generall, crauyng awnsswer therof with sum conuenient speede, & prezent dispatche of Mr Fenton & amongst the rest lett not yowr resolutions for Tyrlogh Lennough bee forgotten, ootherwyze if too mee it bee referred, truly I hoald it best, as this purpose hoaldes, to grawnte hym all, for ootherwyze the offre of pardon wyll bee as mootche of hym regarded, as one from the Pope of mee. I vnderstande by mr Fenton that the certificate of the check° yow woolld not haue emparted beecaused of the smallnes therof, I can not tell sir what it maye seeme or what° is expected, but I am sure that as strayght oreders for true dealyng in it & oftener viewes, where they myght bee, haue been taken then euer toofore were, & if former checkes for x yccares space bee compared with this scarce of one since my tyme, I durst wager that the one shall matche the x., & if yet it content not, for my lyeff I knowe not how too healp it.   As tootchyng my opinion for renewyng of the inhabitantes charter of Dublin, I can not saye any thyng too it hauyng neuer as yet seene the same, & therfore must requyre too bee borne with tyll my retourne thyther.

Thus hauyng enfoormed yow° of all that at this tyme is needefull I wyll take leaue beeseetchyng the Allmyghtie God too bee with yow contynually & sende yow all happynes in this & the lyeff too coomme. / Waxford the 9th of Iune Anno 1581.

Yowrs most assuredly euer,

Arthur Grey

---

after **there must**] 'p^rsently' deleted.   *after* **the check**] 'it' deleted.   *after* **or what**] 'it' deleted.   **yow**] inserted above the line.

112° I thynck eare long° wyll repayre ouer. hee seemes too dislyke wythe this coorce of pardons greatly & proteste{t}he that hee was neuer acquainted withe the adui{c}e. hee gueeues° owte° speatchies that 10° dealest not the firmeliest wythe hym.

For that no poste lyethe the waye that these arre too pass I thowght conuenient too beetake the packett too a° specyall messenger, the rather too that hee was of hys owane buzynes to repayre ouer / , I sett downe the for feae of blame for the chardge. /

COMMENTARY

the Birnes countrie] Wicklow, the seat of the Irish family of the O'Byrnes. Grey undertook a journey south from Dublin in mid-May, primarily against the Cavanaghs of Co. Carlow (Catherloughe), reaching Wexford at the beginning of June. Wallop had reported the Cavanaghs in rebellion, in a letter to Walsingham of 1 March (SP 63/81/2), in which he had also spoken of a dissension between Thomas Maisterson, Seneschal of Wexford, and Anthony Colclogh, of Tintern, Wexford. Grey's journey seems to have been directed at both problems: he wrote to George Carew on 28 April licensing him to open negotiations with the Cavanaghs in advance of the journey (LPL Carew MS 488), and Wallop reported to Walsingham on 8 June that Maisterson had been discharged from office (SP 63/83/41). Grey provides an account of his expedition in his letter to the Privy Council of 10 June (again, from Wexford), SP 63/83/45 (No. 15, below).

the proclamations] Walsingham's order for the promulgation of a general pardon, often alluded to in the letters of the previous months, reached Grey on 26 May; because he was on campaign, he did not 'execute' the proclamation of pardon until returning to Dublin, possibly not until the end of June.

the chardge] the expense of the Irish service.

thowghe in myne owane . . . I conceaue] Grey takes solace from the fact that, this course of proceeding being so antipathetic to his own policies, he will undoubtedly now be recalled from service.

this cource . . . insolencie & wickednes] as often, Grey insists that the extension of a general pardon throughout Ireland will only embolden the rebellious Irish and Old English, who hitherto under his rule had begun to quail.

fauoure mee in this sute] i.e. to be recalled.

press it] take it up with the Queen.

my Lord of Ormond] Thomas Butler, Earl of Ormond; see biographies.

112] the Earl of Ormond. This paragraph ('112 I thynck' . . . wythe hym') is largely in cipher.   *after* **eare long**] four characters appear in an unknown cipher. These unfamiliar symbols (as in the two following cases, below) may simply be fillers, included to put an unwelcome eye off the track.   *after* **gueeues**] four characters in an unknown (perhaps dummy) cipher appear here.   *after* **owte**] three characters in an unknown (perhaps dummy) cipher appear here.   10] the identity of '10' remains uncertain; it is possibly the Queen herself.   a] inserted above the line.

her Maiesties pleazure . . . directed mee] in a letter of February 1581, the Queen had ordered Grey to deprive Ormond of his office, citing his ineffectuality despite huge resources (see the extant draft letter, SP 63/80/87).

that prouince] Munster, the Lord Presidency of which Ormond had just been deprived.

I haue . . . in generall] see No. 15, below, SP 63/83/45, a letter of the following day.

Mr Fenton] Geoffrey Fenton; see biographies.

yowr resolutions for Tyrlogh Lennough] the Privy Council had sent Grey directions on dealing with Turlough Luineach O'Neill in a letter of 19 April (see draft, SP 63/82/41), but the circumstances in the North had been changing rapidly, not least because of the promised seasonal influx of Scots mercenaries (which often created summer chaos). Edward Waterhouse reported to Walsingham on 10 June (SP 63/83/51) that Grey intended to confront O'Neill in person and with force.

certificate of the check] the Privy Council had written to Grey requesting a certificate of the check (an account of all servants and dependents in royal pay in Ireland) in the middle of April (for the draft letter, see SP 63/82/41). Treasurer Wallop forwarded a 'certificate of the checks set upon the captains of the army from 1 April 1580, to 31 March 1581' on 13 May (see SP 63/83/12/1); this seems to be the matter of Walsingham's complaint and Grey's defence; though see also the 'total of the certificate of the Clerk of the Check', SP 63/80/25/1 (24 January 1581).

former checkes . . . space] the certificates of the check over the preceding ten years.

the inhabitantes . . . Dublin] the Irish Council heard and approved the petitions of the citizens of Dublin by 18 July, when Grey signified as much to Walsingham (see No. 19, below, SP 63/84/26); the Privy Council instructed the Attorney General to prepare the charter for the new Corporation of Dublin on 13 August (SP 63/85/16).

this coorce of pardons] again, referring to the proclamation of general pardon. Sir Henry Wallop reported to Walsingham on the following day that the Earl of Ormond was indignant at being deprived of his charge in Munster; Grey's sensitive handling of the matter here—reporting Ormond's obedience in the main body of the letter, but his disgruntlement at a related matter in the postscript—may reflect his anxiety about Ormond's privileged connections, as rehearsed in other letters.

a specyall messenger] unidentified.

I sett downe . . . chardge. /] this phrase seems to have been written carelessly, probably in haste. Grey probably intended 'feare' for 'feae', and perhaps 'this' for 'the'. Grey's apology for his apology seems to mean: 'I have explained my use of a special messenger, which is costly, because I suspect I will be blamed for the extra expense.'

15. *Grey to the Privy Council, 10 June 1581*

TNA: PRO SP 63/83/45

This is one of a pair of letters detailing a campaign Grey made into south Leinster in May-June 1581 against the O'Byrnes and Cavanaghs (often described elsewhere as the 'mountain rebels'). He was evidently accompanied by Spenser and at least one other secretary (working, as the sequence of copy and address makes clear, in a position below Spenser). In SP 63/84/12, Grey would continue the narrative, recounting 'the rest whiche hathe fallen out in my retorne towerdes this cyttie [i.e. Dublin]'. The National Archives also holds a summary of this present letter ('Extracts out of the Lord Deputyes lettres of the 10. of Iune 1581', SP 63/83/46), presumably made by a secretary in Westminster, which suggests that it was of more interest to the Privy Council for Grey's incidental comments extraneous to his account of his journey: the secretary summarized points on the dishonour and danger of the general pardon, Grey's desire for revocation, his plans for a president in Munster, his intention to bring to trial all freeholders of Wexford who favoured the rebels, and the 300 Scots whom Grey meant to 'entertain', or put into military service.

The text of the letter is written throughout in a compact secretary hand (not Spenser's). Grey's subscription and signature are in his own hand, while the marginal annotations are in a distinct rough italic, probably Walsingham's. Grey's careful review of the letter, after the fair copy had been produced by the secretary, is attested by two insertions in his hand (see below). The address is in Spenser's characteristic secretary hand, while the endorsement is in at least two different hands, one of which ('From the l. Deputye') is undoubtedly that responsible for the annotations within.

ADDRESS AND ENDORSEMENT

To the right
Honorable my
very good Lords &
otheres of her Maiesties
privie C{ouncell}

1581 Lordes
Iune .10.
From the Lord Deputye

Entred.°

TEXT

It may please your Lordships   In my last letters, I declared vnto you
my purpose to bestowe some time, in Leinster vppon the Birnes, and   The Birnes and
Cavenaughes, and vppon suche loose people, as they had drawen vnto   Cauenaghes

---

Endorsement] a small amount of what appears to be secretarial doodling, added at some later date, appears adjacent to the endorsement; we have not reproduced it here.

notwithstandinge the garrisons planted about them to bridle them did still remayne in strength to annoy the pale.

His iournye against them

leauyeth 300 labourers in the pale for the seruice at the chardges of the Countrye

Repayreth Castell Comin and Castell Keuan and bestoweth wardes in them to annoy the rebells

His exploytes against the said rebells

They dare not abide him

them, who albeyt: they had bene muche deminished, by the garrison° planted vppon them, this last winter, namely by those, that weare placed at Wicklowe, and Artlowe, vppon the Este parte, and at Fernes, Clonmore, castle Dermote, and Ballemore vppon the Southe, and west partes, yet they remained so vnited, as they weare able to annoy greatly the good Subiectes bothe of the pale, and of this countrey of Wexforde:

And therefore, as soone as there was enny hope of grasse to bee founde for the feeding of horses, I did set forwarde from Dublin the 16 of May with purpose to seuer the Cavenaughes, and the Birnes, and to searche theire fastenes, and to plante in places of most comoditye, for theire annoyance other garrisons, that should offende the Birnes more neerely, then those whiche weare before planted vppon the Sea, at Wicklowe, and Artelow: According to whiche determinacion, hauing leuied in the pale at the chardges of the counteyes 300 laborers, I came to Castle Kevan, the 17 day, whiche together with castle Comin, (3 miles from yt southwarde) weare the ruins of old fortificacions, made (as yt seemeth) by the Englishe, at the conqueste, to disseuer the Birnes, and the Raniloughes, the one from the other, and are bothe so situated, as ether from Wicklowe, or Artlow the one or the other place might be victeled by horsemen, without passinge enny woode, or paas: / Thes places (as before I had conceaued) seemed vppon the viewe to bee most apt for garrisons, and therefore I bestowed in eache of thes fortes .4. or 5. daies, in whiche time I made them Wardable, and by the worke of masons, and carpenters, comodious for the Soldiours to lodge in, And also entrenched strongly large bawnes, by the labour of the Pioners, easye to be defended, the rather to allure the countrey people (if they weare well affected) to inhabyt, and liue vnder the proteccion of the garrisons: While the worke was in finishing I searched all the mounteines, and fastnes adioyning, and tooke from the rebelles, stoare of their leane, and weake cattell, and slew diuers in those roades, and burned theire villages, and places of releif as Clande-loughe, and suche like:

The Substaunce of the men of warre in those mounteines vnder the leadinge of Feaghe, and Garret did sometime shew them selues, vppon the Toppes of the clifes, and in the edges of their strongest

---

after **garrison**] an inkblot or a single-character deletion appears here.

woodes, To whiche as soone as enny offerr was made, they woulde
retire themselues, without shew in manner of enny resistaunce
Neuerthelesse, in my passage throughe a longe paas strongely
plasshed, betweene castle Kevan, and castle Comen, they sett vppon
my cariages, and slew some of the garrans, and 3. or 4. poore leaders.
In whiche paas Bryan Fitzwilliams was hurte, with a shott in the
arme, but with no daunger of Deathe, three other Soldiors weare
slaine, and one of mine owne cariage horses drawen into the woode,
and the Basquettes rifled, wherein they did light vppon some litle
plate of mine, whiche before I slept, was fownde° deare bought, on
theire partes, if I may beleaue soche of them selues as weare after
taken, and executed:

Receaueth some smaull losse at their handes which afterwardes is reuenged

In thes two fortes I left 400 footemen, and 100 horsse, vnder the
charge of Sir Henry Harrington, because both places, weare within
his office and rule of the Birnes countrey, And taking order for theire
victualling, and for the retorne of the laborers into the pale, I prescribed to Sir Henry what cours of prosecucion of the rebelles should
be taken in mine absence, And so departed towardes the Cauenaughes
the 28 of the laste.

The chardge of the 2. fortes committed vnto Sir Henry Harrington with 400 footmen and 100 horse.

After my coming into this county of Wexford, in my first daies
martche neere vnto Fernes, I tooke a greate praye belonging to the
cheif of the best sept of the Cauenaughes, called Crephin mac
Moroughe, and burned some parte of mac Vadockes countrey.
because he had lincked himself to the rebelles, and become as yt
weare a followcr of Chrephin before named: vppon which pray and
burning, bothe Crephin, and mac Vadock, and all the freeholders of
that parte of the Kinsheloughe made meane to bee receaved to mercye
alleaging priuate iniuries betweene them and the Seneshall, to be the
causes of theire declining from theire duetye: Wherevppon suffring
Chrephen to repaier vnto me I was contented bothe to heere his
complainte, and vppon this condicion to accept him, that he should
presente him self and all these freeholders at Wexforde within v.
daies, and that vppon pledges to bee receaued both of him, and them,
I would bestowe hir maiesties grace vppon them, and not otherwise,
For accomplishmente whereof they are now with mee heere to deliuer
theire pledges for theire good behauiour heereafter. / . It is like that
the other Cauenaughes of Simolin, and of Arte Boyes sept will frame

Taketh a great pray from Crephin Cauenagh. And burneth mac Vadocs Countrye.

They both excuse their vnduty-fulnes and desier to be receauid to mercye with a great number of the freehoulders of Kingsheloughe

He receaueth them vppon pledges.

---

fownde] inserted above the line. Both the spelling of the word, and the characteristic hand, indicate that this is Grey's own insertion.

Hopeth of the submission of other Cauenaghes.

them selues to the like Submission, For which I vse the Soldiours as Instrumentes who hath alreadye made a pray vppon those of Simolin and shall vse all violence to the other in my retorne homeward, the rather to bringe them to suche a conclucion as may promisse theire better obedience heereafter.

Corrupcion of the gentlemen and free- houlders of the Countye of Wexford.

Houldeth a session amongst them. there the cheefest of them are appeached for fauoringe the rebells.

meaneth to put them to their triall.

Walter Galto Cauenagh and others executed.

The vnduetifull Dealinges whiche I haue founde many waies in the gentlemenn and freeholders of this countye, by deadly hatred emong- ste them selues, and by secrett supporting of the rebells, the rather to revenge priuate quarrells one vppon an other, did geue me occacion to leaue my campe, And with assistaunce of Mr Threasorour, Mr cheif Baron, and Mr Waterhous, to repaier hether to houlde a Ses- sions, for the discerning of all those differences, and secrett confedra- cies with the Traytoures, In whiche sessions this falleth out, that the best of the countrey are appeached, and cannot excuse them of ouer- muche favour to the rebelles, And therefore I haue imprisoned soche, as are accused meaninge to put them to theire tryall, and haue exe- cuted other malefactoures, Whereof Walter Gallte Cauenaughe was one, the most infamous of all the rebells of his name, and that hath comytted most murders, and Spoiles vppon this county of Wexford by the space of 20 yeares past: From hence I purpose to hould my cours towerdes Rosse, and so to retorne to the garrisons, I planted emonges the Birnes: /

The new supplye of 700 men deffectyue in number, persons and furniture

Dischardgeth Capten Cecill and Horde, and taketh their brooken bandes

In my marche hether I receaued lettres from Dublin by whiche I vnderstoode the ariuall of the supplies of the 700 men appoincted to land there, emonges whiche there is not only defect in the number, but many of them old, and impotente and diuers very badly fur- nished, (as the Lord Keeper aduertisethe) And albeyt I preuented thes wantes, as muche as might be, by sending Capten Sentleger to conduct them, and to make choice of apt men, and conuenient furniture (of whose iudgement, and carefulnes I nothing doubt)° yet I perceaue he could not be his owne choser, but must either bring those, or none, And therefore to help those imperfeccions, both in number and furniture, is one cause that Drawethe mee towerdes Dublin, and to take with mee the broken bandes of Capten Cicill, and capten Owrde, whome I do dischardge, to keep the Supplies: A seconde cause and most of emportaunce is, that I haue receaued other

---

of whose . . . I nothing doubt] this phrase was originally enclosed by commas; the secretary later changed these commas to parentheses.

lettres from your Lordships signefieng hir maiesties pleasur for a to helpe the said
generall pardon to be published by proclamacion for all offenders new supplye
within this realme very few excepted: Thes proclamacions I perceaue
be ariued thoughe not yet come to my handes, but are enclosed in
a casquet, remaining in the castle of Dublin: To this by way of
preuention, I haue saied my opinion in my former lettres, touching The offer of
the offer of pardon, to suche, as must be entreated to receaue yt, and generall pardon
being offred perhappes will not accept yt, whereunto I add this: that I daungerous and
dishonorable.
cannot but iudge, the honour of the state someway touched, and hir
maiesties best Subiect{es}° that haue opposed them selues to rebells,
and (as yt weare set vpp there ref {. . .}° for hir maiesty) vtterly
vndoon: For I see the sequeall of this cours cariethe euidente perill to
the good Subiecte, whiche now vppon this reconsiliacion must liue at
the deuocion of his outragious neighboures, who vndoubtedly will
take theire times, to reuenge all good seruices done, vppon them and
theirs, so as yt is likely that the good wilbe weeded out by the euell, or
if they be not yet,° in our age yt wilbe hard, for enny gouernour to
draw them againe to hazard them selues, and theire posterity, for Desyreth to be
theire Soueraigne, And for mine owne parte I must confesse, I haue reuoked as vnfitt
to gouerne any
so constauntly affirmed° in hir maiesties behalf the prosecucion, and longer there now
extirpacion, of the ill affected and the Defence of the good, as this that theis
contrary cours being now taken (whiche puttethe litle difference pardons are
betweene the one, and the other) I finde how vtterly vnapt I am to bee offered, having
waaded so farre
continued heere, hauing broken with the best sort, in a cace that so as he hath don
muche concerneth theire liues, and whole estates, And therefore I into a contrary
hope I shall not wante your Lordshipes furtherances for my spedy coorse.
reuocacion, Neuertheles submitting my opinion to your Lordshipes
better iudgementes, and obeieng in euery thinge to hir maiesties Will publishe the
direccion, I will make the more hast to Dublin, to veiw and publish proclamacions
for the said
the proclamacions, and will also follow the cours prescribed mee in pardons with
offringe the pardon to Turloughe Lennoughe, with whome yt had speede /
bene to be wisshed, that suche a treatye might haue bene made, as Yt had ben fitter
that I might haue bene able to haue shewed force in the feild, so to haue reduced
prepared to haue annoied him if° he had bene obstinate as he might Tirlough to
suche termes that
rather haue sued for, and thankefully embraced the pardon, and put he might haue
in his pledges, then that it should haue bene sent so nakedly, as by the sued for pardon,

---

Subiect{es}] damage to the right margin of the manuscript has truncated this word; context demands the plural, and spacing considerations make it likely that this was an 'es' brevigraph.   **ref** {. . .}] damage to the right margin of the manuscript here has cropped the end of this word, making it illegible.   *after* **not yet,**] two characters deleted.   *after* **affirmed**] 'the' deleted.   *after* **annoied him if**] a clumsy 'he' deleted after **annoied him if** and a second inserted above the line.

then to offer yt
him so nackedly treaty of comissioners it must needes seeme, for this cause principally
I required the 1000 men out of England. But since that cours stand-
eth not with hir maiesties liking, I will frame my self wholy to the
direccion geuen mee, and set as good a collour vppon yt as I may,
Dischardgeth him Wisshing that yt may take successe, aboue mine expectacion, and to
self of the blame fall out to hir maiesties honour and benifit, And if the contrary should
that may light happen, ether there, or els where, vppon this platte of generall par-
vppon him for any don, then I must needes craue to wasshe my handes of yt, as a matter,
inconvenience lykely wherein I was oueruled, and not standing with the reasons whiche I
to ensue of this offer had conceaued for the seruice. /
of pardon.

I haue Declared to my Lord of Ormounde, (who is heere now
with me) hir highnes pleasure, for the ceasing of his aucthority in
Mounster, according to the direccion sent from° hir maiesty in mr
Secretaries Lettres, wherevnto he seemeth contentedly to submitt
him self, but very sorye, that he should stand in hir highnes disgrace,
Thearle of° and desirous to satisfye hir maiesty touching the causes of hir dis-
Ormonds pleasure, wherein he imputeth somewhat to his owne forgetfulnes,
excuses, and in not aduertising of suche seruices, as hathe bene done within his
meaninge to charge, A matter (as he saiethe) omitted by him, because, he lighted
satisfye her not vppon the slaughter, or apprehencion of therle of Desmounde, or
maiesty tow- of his brother Iohn, or of the Seneshall, whome he thought the only
chinge his seruice personnes, for whose Deathe he might haue deserued thankes;/ but
lest yt might seeme, that litle or nothing hathe bene done vnder him,
within that prouince he meanethe to collecte the seuerall seruices,
with the names of soche of the rebells, as the warres in Mounster
haue consumed, to thende, that the same might bee knowen to hir
maiesty, before whome he saiethe he doubtethe not, but to aunswere
to all obieccions that may be made against his Creddyt, and honour,
Lastely he saied, that this discharge came the more vnseasonably,
vnto him, because he hath lost muche of his reuencwc, by the wasting
of his landes in this rebellion, whiche in troath I did partly finde in
Dammages his lordship, or landes of Artlow, and know the like at Clonmore,
susteyned by where an english garrison was planted: /
{the}° said earle

But now I truste your Lordshipes will deapely looke into this
broken state, and how I am distracted into seuerall partes: Leinster

after sent from] the beginning strokes of 'Sr' deleted here.   Marginal note after Thearle
of] 'Desmou' deleted.   Marginal note {the}] here, and below, damage to the manuscript
(perhaps in the process of binding the manuscripts into volumes) has obscured part of the
annotations; the nature of the missing words, however, is obvious from context.

requiereth my attendaunce, for prosecution of this warre against
the confederates whiche is the more perilous, because this parte,
is the harte as yt weare, and the other provinces but members; It
weare reason I should looke also vnto the northen border, or els
I doubt comissioners will make but a dishonourable conclucion with
Turloughe, who will not muche respect a pardon, if he haue not also
the rest of his demaundes: / The brooken
state of the
realme is suche
that dyuers
places requier his
presence at once /

Mounster being now without a comaunder would haue requiered my
presence there till some setled gouerment, had bene sent from hir
maiesty, but because all places cannot be supplied by me in person, at
one instaunte, I must leaue Mounster to the captens, euery one to
defend the partes about theire garrisons till ether I may resorte
thether, or els till your Lordshipes procuer a presidente to be sente, The necessity of
placinge {a}
president in
mounster
that may direct the whole, whiche in mine owne opinion, and my
assosiates heere is most necessary bothe for warre, and peace: The
prouince is lardge the people many, and the rebells in suche force, and
the state so generally euell, as if they haue not a gouernour to rule
them by hir maiesties lawes and aucthority, they will vndoubtedly
depende vppon those now in rebellion, and so in shorte time make
the secounde errour worse then the first: And therefore I leaue this
principally to your Lordshipes consideracions.

In Connought Sir Nicholas Malbey by diligente following of the All Connaught
quiet Orworck
only excepted
rebells is entered into some calme of the stormes there, only Orwark
yeldeth not to conformity, bearing him self very stoute vppon the
strengthe of his Scottes, whereof he had° 300 in pay or neere that Sir Nicholas
Malby wynneth
300 Scotts from
Orworke /
number: Thes Scottes haue bene allured by Mr Malbey to leaue
Orwark, and to serue hir maiesty, vppon whose perswacion, I heere
they haue taken a pray from Orwark, and are repaired to Sir Nicholas,
withe the whole company, And because I cannot heere entertaine He meaneth to
enterteyne the
said Scotts in
steede of kerne as
more seruiceable,
and to geue them
the pay allowed
for the now
cashed bands of
Capten Cecill
and Horde /
enny kerne whome I may trust, and that in all seruices yt is necessary,
to haue some soche light men, to driue and take cattell, and that the
Scottes are more seruiceable, and more feared emongst the irrish then
the kerne are, I am resolued for a while to entertaine them in steade of
kerne, thereby aswell to strenghten hir maiesties parte, as to weaken
the rebells either orwarke, or enny other withe whome they shoulde
happen to be entertained, And if the warre consume them, the losse is
tollerable ynoughe, for in a matter so indifferentlye made, betweene

had] inserted above the line. The familiar hand indicates that this is Grey's own insertion.

them, and the Irrish rebells, I care not greatly whether I loose, or winne. Theire charges shalbe borne by the pay of the two casshed bandes before named vnder Mr Cicell, and Thomas Owrde, whose

infection amonge
the souldiors

companies weare consumed at Fernes, withe a kinde of plauge, or infeccion; that hathe likewise taken away diuers vnder the leading of Sir William Standley, Capten Denny, and capten Scopham while they remained in the garrison at Wicklow.

Lastely I haue not to presse your Lordshipes further withe my requeste solicited by mr Fenton for the 1000 men requiered for

meaneth not to
prosecute the warre
against the Vlster
rebells vntill he see
how they frame
themselues after
the proclamacion

Vlster, for since hir maiestye meaneth to make proof of the conformity, of hir badde Subiectes by the lenitye of hir generall pardon, I will not attempt muche warre vntill the proclamacions be published, and till I see that they reiect peace, And yet I hope the proclamacion is so tempered withe assurraunce of obedience heereafter, as whosoeuer will take benefytt by yt muste putte in pledges by a day for his good

Condicion that
they shall delyuer
pledges.

behauiour to come, And withe that condicion I will not take exceptions to ennye, but to suche as alreadye (as I heere) are set downe to bee excepted by hir maiesties owne order: And therefore desiring your Lordshipes, to retorne Mr Fenton, to execute his place heere, I comytt you to the Lord: At Wexford the 10th of Iune 1581

Yowr Lordshipes most assured to
Commaunde,

Arthur Grey

COMMENTARY

In my last letters] we cannot be sure which letters these are, or indeed whether they survive; there is reference to Grey's intention to go on campaign against the **Birnes** and **Cavenaughes**, though, in the correspondence passing from Ireland at the time. See SP 63/83/24 (Wallop to Walsingham, 15 May 1581).

the garrison . . . Ballemore] these garrisons form a circle around the eastern counties, around the north of Meath and down to Ferns and Artlow in the south-east; see maps.

this countrey of Wexforde] at the very south-east of Ireland, south of the Pale and of the ring of garrisons described above.

fastenes] fastnesses, fortified and often concealed hideouts (e.g. in mountainous or wooded country).

plante] not in the sense of plantation-building, but Grey's choice of this word certainly reminds us of that aspect of English policy in Ireland.

the counteyes] the counties of the Pale: Louth, Meath, Dublin, and Kildare.

Castle Kevan ... castle Comin] approximately 50 km south of Dublin, in Co. Wicklow. Grey remained at Castle Kevyn until at least 22 May, when he wrote a letter from there: 63/83/31. Comin Grey used as a base on his return: he 'came to the border of the Glinnes the xxth day of Iune, encamping neere to the forte, which I before builded at Castle Commin, In that place or neere vnto yt, I continued my campe till the xxvijth, euery day hunting the Glinnes' (SP 63/84/12).

the ruins of old fortificacions] *A view* also comments upon the presence of ruins in the Irish landscape: 'Theare weare thoroughe all places of the Countrie Convenient, manye good Townes seatd which thoroughe that invndacion of the Irishe which I firste tould youe of weare vtterlye wasted and defaced of which the ruines are yeat in manye places to be sene and of some no signe at all remayninge saue onelye theire bare names but theire seates are not to be founde' (ll. 5196–201).

Raniloughes] the Ranelaghs (Gabhal Raghnaill), a branch of the O'Byrnes. Hugh MacShane O'Byrne was their chief until his death in 1579, after which time their chief was Feagh MacHugh.

without passinge ... or paas] it was a commonplace in contemporary accounts of Ireland that such woods, and the passes through them, were used by the rebels to ambush English troops; there were many attempts, motivated partly by this, to clear safe passages through the woods along which the English could travel. Safe transit and traffic through these places is an important focus of Irenius's and Eudoxus's discussion in *A view* (see ll. 2585–99, and especially ll. 5120–44).

Wardable] defensible with a guard, or ward.

entrenched strongly large bawnes] a **bawn** is an Irish term referring either to a fortification, or to a fortified house and cattlefold. Spenser refers to Irish bawnes (also 'stronglie trenched') in *A view*: 'But these rounde hills and square bawnes which youe see soe strongelye trenched and throwne vp weare (they saie) at firste ordeyned for the same purpose that people mighte assemble themselves theareon' (ll. 2405–7). Spenser also came into possession of one—the bawn at Richardston—when he gained title to Kilcolman in 1589.

Pioners] pioneers, soldiers responsible for the digging of trenches, fortifications, and mines.

places of releif] cf. the description of bollies in *A view*, where criminals 'finde reliefe': 'But by this Custome of Bolloyinge theare growe in the meane time manye greate enormityes vnto that Comon wealthe for firste if theare be any outlawes or loose people (as they are never without some) which live vppon stealthes and spoile, they are evermore succored and finde reliefe onelye in those Bollies beinge vppon the waste places, wheares els they shoulde be driven shortelye to sterve or to Come downe to the townes to steale reliefe wheare by one meanes or other they woulde sone be Caughte' (ll. 1532–9).

Clandeloughe] the vale of Glendalough is located about 20 km west of Wicklow. Its inaccessible, mountainous terrain would have offered mobile Irish kern considerable safety from English military forces.

The Substaunce of the men of warre] see *OED*, 'Substance', *n.*, 15a: 'The greater number or part, the majority, mass, or bulk'. Grey means, presumably, that it was only on those occasions that the soldiers showed themselves in any numbers.

Feaghe ... Garret] on Feagh MacHugh O'Byrne, see biographies. Captain Garrett, alias Garrett Jones, had 'gone over' to Baltinglass with fifty horsemen in August 1580, just as Lord Grey arrived in Ireland. In March 1581 Garrett offered to come in if he might be assured of a pardon (SP 63/81/28); news of this offer may have reached the Earl of Kildare in prison, for in December 1581 he sent to Feagh

MacHugh to have Garrett executed, apparently because Garrett had information that might inculpate him (see SP 63/87/53).

a longe paas strongely plasshed] to **plash** is to bend down and interweave branches into a fence: apparently the pass has been cleared and defended on either side by this plashing.

garrans] small horses bred in Scotland and Ireland.

Bryan Fitzwilliams] leader of a band of horsemen in Leinster (and discharged later that year, see SP 63/88/40/1), who travelled to England in July 1581, bearing letters of recommendation from Grey and the Irish Council, speaking of his long service and the money he had lost.

deare bought, on theire partes] i.e. they paid for the capture of the plate with the lives of some of their soldiers.

Henry Harrington] Harrington was apparently still stationed there on 23 July, when Edward Waterhouse wrote that Grey had instructed him to accept Feagh MacHugh's offers (Waterhouse to Walsingham, SP 63/84/44).

Fernes] Ferns, seat of one of the garrisons mentioned above.

best sept of the Cauenaughes] a **sept** is a division of a family or clan.

Crephin mac Moroughe] unidentified.

mac Vadockes countrey] unidentified.

freeholders … Kinsheloughe] Grey would receive pledges of obedience from these freeholders on his return journey: 'At my passing by Fearnes, I receaued pledges of the freeholders of the Kinsheloughe' (SP 63/84/12).

made meane … to mercye] made advances to plead that they be granted mercy.

the Seneshall] Sir Henry Harrington, Seneschal of the O'Byrne country; see biographies.

Simolin] see SP 63/84/12: 'The ix^th of Iune, I departed from Wexforde, towerdes Rosse, and came thether the xj^th day, leauing my campe, vppon the skirtes of the baronye of Simolins, a countrey possessed by Oceon mac Caier Cauenaughe a confederate with the rest in this rebellion, thoughe not so malitious, as other of his surname.'

Arte Boyes sept] a sept of the Cavanaghs from Wicklow: they would indeed offer their submission later in Grey's journey: 'the remaine of the Cauenaughes of the septe of Arteboye, offred submission vnto me in my campe' (SP 63/84/12). As Grey implies here ('shall vse all violence'), they were under considerable military pressure at the time.

priuate quarrells] in No. 39, below (SP 63/94/15), Grey also notes the 'pryvat quarrells' that support rebellion in Ulster.

Mr Threasorour, Mr cheif Baron, and Mr Waterhous] Henry Wallop, Treasurer; Lucas Dillon, Chief Baron of the Exchequer; and Edward Waterhouse, General Receiver; see biographies.

to houlde a Sessions] to convene a county court (generally for the purpose of hearing civil cases and 'light' pleas of the crown; but Grey's presence made it possible to hear and decide even the most outright treasons).

appeached] impeached.

Walter Gallte Cauenaughe] unidentified.

Rosse] a small town (now known as New Ross) in south-west Co. Wexford, whence Wallop addressed a letter on 14 June (SP 63/83/54).

lettres from Dublin] these letters (including one, apparently, by Adam Loftus: see below) do not survive among the State Papers Ireland.

impotente] weak, decrepit.

badly furnished] Poorly equipped.

Lord Keeper] Adam Loftus, Archbishop of Dublin and Lord Keeper of the Great Seal; see biographies.

Capten Sentleger] Warham Sentleger; see biographies.

conuenient furniture] suitable equipment.

broken bandes ... capten Owrde] On Captains Cecil and Hoorde, see SP 63/83/47 (No. 16, below) and 63/84/26 (No. 19, below).

to keep the Supplies] Grey used the men surviving from these discharged bands to compensate for those who had arrived in Ireland, unfit to fight.

I haue ... pardon] on 19 April 1581, Elizabeth issued a general pardon to all Irish rebels apart from Desmond, John of Desmond, Dr Sanders, Viscount Baltinglass, and the Seneschal of Imokilly (the last on Grey's discretion). A draft of the pardon (with corrections by Burghley) exists in the Irish State Papers (SP 63/82/42), as does a draft of a letter from the Privy Council explaining the pardon, and telling Grey that 'in case you resolue to enter into anie action of warre agaynst Tirlaghe, wee then thincke it verie meete that you should fyrst offer vnto him confirmation of suche thinges as by your Lordship weare thought meet to be allowed vnto him' (SP 63/82/41).

enclosed ... Dublin] presumably copies of the letter and proclamation described above, with accompanying letters, arrived after Grey's departure in May. Dublin Castle, it is clear, was used as a repository and a stronghold for documents and valuables coming from England.

To this ... of preuention] in an attempt to prevent this (pardon).

in my former lettres] see, for example, No. 13, above (SP 63/82/54): 'Your Maiestie I heare, is in purpose [to] bestowe a generall pardon vpon this nation with some exceptions; I beseche your Highnes to consider well of it.'

someway] to some degree.

the sequeall of this cours] these events, as they will turn out.

vtterly vnapt ... continued heere] Grey here continues to appeal for revocation, an appeal that was being noted by the Privy Council (see headnote).

hauing broken ... best sort] Grey believed that in making no distinction between obedient subjects and rebels, the general pardon constituted an act of treachery, and was perilous, to the former.

offringe the ... Turloughe Lennoughe] as the marginal annotation makes clear, Grey was dismayed at having to offer pardon to Turlough Luineach, and would have preferred to have compelled him, through military pressure, to sue for pardon on less advantageous terms.

annoied] attacked in battle.

so nakedly] so unconditionally.

set as good a colour vppon yt as I may] make it seem as good as I can.

vppon this platte] as part of this scheme (*OED*, 'Plat', *n.*³).

Lord of Ormounde] Thomas Butler, Earl of Ormond; see biographies.

hir ... Mounster] Ormond had until this point served as Lord General of Munster; the Queen insisted on his discharge because of accusations that he had killed or apprehended very few prominent rebels.

mr Secretaries Lettres] these letters from Walsingham to Grey have not survived.

not aduertising of suche seruices] Ormond quickly complained to Burghley that he had been the victim of slanders (SP 63/84/19), and wrote again on 1 October 1581, to provide a list of the rebels whom he had slain (SP 63/86/3/1): over 5,000 in two years. He was quickly reinstated, not only as Lord General, but as Governor of Munster.

this broken state] of Ireland (as the marginal annotation makes clear). Cf. BL MS Titus B.XIII, fo. 345, Chancellor Gerrarde's notes on the broken state of Ireland.

confederates] allies, i.e. rebels allied to one another: presumably families such as the Cavanaghs and O'Byrnes against whom he was then engaged.

the harte] perhaps because of its geographical centrality in Ireland, or because of its proximity to the government in Dublin, or because of its status as the scene of such rebellion.

Mounster . . . comaunder] since Ormond had been deposed from his command. In his letter to Francis Walsingham of 9 June (No. 14, above, SP 63/83/43), Grey had been much more forthright about the authority vacuum in Munster, created by Ormond's discharge: 'greate ouersyght it was withowte an oothers placyng too displace hym & so I euer aduyced'.

the captens] the captains of the bands garrisoned there.

presidente] no President of Munster was appointed until 1584, when the title was granted to Sir John Norris, but the idea that such an appointment was necessary for the government of the region appears in a good deal of correspondence from mid-1581 (see e.g. *CSPI 1574–85*, pp. 315, 316, 325).

make the . . . the first] make their rebellion in an ungoverned state worse than that when Ormond was in charge.

Orwark] Brian O'Rourke (see biographies), of whose disobedience (and the comparative quiet of Connaught) Malby reported to Walsingham on 30 June 1581 (SP 63/83/63) and to Burghley on 6 July (SP 63/84/7).

yeldeth not to conformity] also mentioned by Malby, who writes that 'William Nugent has established O'Rourke in the roomishe religion which rule he holdethe for his only quarell' (SP 63/83/63).

vppon the strengthe of his Scottes] O'Rourke employed a substantial number of galloglas, Scottish mercenaries: see glossary and Hayes-McCoy, *Scots Mercenary Forces*, 131–4, 138. The English administration frequently attempted to prohibit the keeping of such mercenaries, but as can be seen here (below), and as Hayes-McCoy argues, they frequently sought to hire them for themselves.

kerne] see glossary.

light men] lightly armed men, light infantry.

the Scottes . . . entertaine them] on English willingness to contract the services of Scots galloglas, see Hayes-McCoy, *Scots Mercenary Forces*.

a kinde of plauge, or infeccion] the decimation of Cecil and Hoorde's bands through sickness is also mentioned by Edward Waterhouse (Waterhouse to Walsingham, 10 June 1581, SP 63/83/51); **Captain Scopham**, in fact, died of the plague very shortly after this letter was written (see No. 19, below, SP 63/84/26). On **William Stanley** and **Ned Denny**, see biographies.

my requeste . . . mr Fenton] a request for soldiers to attack Turlough Luineach if he 'stand resolute to ronne the course of warre' is made in a letter from Fenton to Walsingham of 16 April (SP 63/82/30): 'for this seruice, your honnor cannot perswade to send ouer les then a thousand men with their victuells for two monethes.' Fenton writes this letter 'in haste at Dublin'; it seems that he may have been on his way to England to solicit Irish causes (see SP 63/82/47; 63/83/3 is a letter written from Fenton to Leicester when both men were in London).

16. *Grey to Walsingham, 10 June 1581*
TNA: PRO SP 63/83/47

This typical letter of recommendation, on behalf of a gentleman from the band of Captain William Cecil (and not on Cecil's behalf, as the endorsement suggests), is the more typical for its trust in Grey's special relationship with Sir Francis Walsingham. Little information survives of Cecil's career in Ireland: on 3 October 1580, he is recorded as leading footmen into Ireland (SP 63/77/7); on 18 November 1580, it is said that he has gone to Ross (perhaps the town of New Ross, *Ros Mhic Thriúin*, in Co. Wexford) with 100 men (SP 63/78/45); a letter of 10 June 1581 (No. 15, above, SP 63/83/45), the same date as this, refers to the depletion of his band by sickness, and its consequent discharge, which may explain the need for a letter of recommendation for this particular soldier at this time; and a note of September 1581 records a payment of £300 to him (SP 63/85/70).

The text of the letter, including the address and subscription, is in Spenser's characteristic secretary hand; the signature is Grey's usual. The endorsement is the unremarkable mix of italic and secretary forms common to these letters, filed and refiled over several years.

ADDRESS AND ENDORSEMENT

To the Honorable
my very good
frend Sir Fraunces
Walsingham Knight
Chief Secretary
to her Maiesty.

10 Iune 1581
From the Lord Gray
on the behalfe of Cap
ten Cecill

TEXT

Sir, this gentleman the bearer hereof having served lately vnder Captein Cecill, and being presently to repaire into England hath requested my lettres of favour in his behalf; which I could not but reasonably doe, knowing him by his good service here to have well deserved the same. Wherefore I desire you to affoord him such favour and furtheraunce in his reasonable causes there, as he may perceive these my lettres to have bene effectuall in his behalf; for the which I will account my self behoulding vnto you, and will rest alwaies ready to requite the same. Wexford, the xth of Iune. 1581.

Youres most assured,

Arthur Grey

COMMENTARY

behoulding] i.e. beholden, obliged.

17. *Grey to the Privy Council, 10 July 1581*
TNA: PRO SP 63/84/13

It is difficult to tell whether Grey was deeply alarmed by the report of a war between Turlough Luineach O'Neill and Hugh O'Donnell in Tirconnell or whether, by contrast, he was using it to generate a plausible case for further supply from England. Malby certainly seems not to have left Dublin in any great hurry; as late as 18 July he was writing to Walsingham to ask him to favour him with alterations to his title of Roscommon, and was collecting a concordatum from the Irish Council for reimbursement of his expenses in Connaught. In any case, this letter gives a vivid picture not only of the mutability of Irish affairs, but of the substantial hardship suffered by the soldiers on both sides.

The text of the letter, along with the postscript and the address, is in Spenser's characteristic secretary hand, here bold and hasty. Grey has added the subscription and signature in his own hand. The endorsement, probably added later when the letter was being filed in London, is entirely in a broad-nibbed and inelegant secretary hand.

ADDRESS AND ENDORSEMENT

To the right
Honorable the
Lords & other of
her Maiesties
privie councell. /

Lordes. 1581
Dublyn the xth of Iuly
From the Lord Deputie

TEXT

My very good Lords; since my last aduertizementes sent vnto your Lordships I have received knowledge of a certein bickering which was lately betwene Tirlagh, & ODonell in the which there were certein of Odonelles chief capteins taken & slayne, besides many other of his men. which quarell now by them begonne yt is here by vs thought good to mainteigne, least yf happely otherwise then well should happen to the said Odonell, besides the great discoragement, which yt would generally strike into the hartes of such the Irishrie (how euer fewe) as have carried them selues well & duetifully towardes her Maiestie to see them selues in most distresse lefte aidlesse yt would moreouer adde great stomach & haughtines to thenemy to oppresse the true Subiect, seeing him so destitute. For such occasion my self with the advice of the rest of the councell here, have thought yt expedient presently to make a iorney into those partes, which being of so great importaunce, as yt is, & fynding that not onely her Maiesties threasure here is clene emptied but also all this Cittie so bare & needy as no money is here to be borrowed for the necessary furnishing & provision of all such thinges as to this or any other iorney apperteyne, I am earnestly to crave of your Lordships that requisite consideracion may hereof bee had for present supply of this extremitie, vpon which all the successe of this entreprice & generall service here besides dependeth, not knowing otherwise how to take the same in hand, by reason that bakeres & breweres cannot be sett on worke, nor conveyaunce by sea had for vittailes, beside infinite occasions of present paymentes that such expeditions will of necessitie require together with the daylie charge of carriage for vittelles to the places of garrizons here aboutes with the contynuall cry of the soldier for his private pay

All which referring to your Lordships gravest consideracion and earnestly praying that such speedy care hereof may bee had as the weightines of the cause requireth I humbly take leave.   Dublin the xth of Iulie 1581

Yowr Lordships most assured
to Commaund,
Arthur Grey

Since the wryting hereof I heare that Odonelles losse hath bene more extreme then the first report & that his whole force is in maner ouerthrowen & that Tirlagh remayneth yett in Tirconell spoiling & slaying at his pleasure. /

I have appointed Sir Nicholas Malbey with thenglish forces in Connagh and such Irish as he can vppon the soddein levy within his Rules to repaire to Odonell to his assistaunce And if the cause so require to meet me at Liffer at a day appointed.

COMMENTARY

bickering] cf. the wording of No. 18, below (SP 63/84/14).

Tirlagh] Turlough Luineach O'Neill; see biographies.

ODonell] Sir Hugh O'Donnell, Lord of Tirconnell; see biographies.

mainteigne] to support O'Donnell against O'Neill, 'maintaining' his right against him.

stomach] boldness of spirit.

those partes] Tirconnell, which lies to the west of O'Neill's country in Ulster, in what is now Donegal.

the contynuall cry of the soldier for his private pay] the Dublin government found itself permanently in arrears in the pay of its soldiers; because the life expectancy of a soldier in Ireland was short, behindhandedness proved an astute policy.

I heare ... the first report] none of the dispatches reaching Grey from Tirconnell were forwarded; none survive. But this note is interesting because it clearly demonstrates the fast pace of changing information and the degree to which responsive government had to be capable of mobilizing quickly.

in maner] almost entirely (*OED*, 'Manner', *n.* 13).

spoiling] destroying (by burning and looting) the local towns and fields.

Connagh] Malby was the English governor of the province of Connaught and Thomond, but he was often in Dublin; see biographies. On this occasion he appears to have marched to Lifford from Athlone, where he raised his forces (see 63/85/47, his report to Burghley after the journey into Tirconnell). He claimed to Burghley that, following O'Neill's peace with Grey, he camped with 500 men before O'Neill's 2,500, for five days. He was back in Dublin by 20 September.

within his Rules] it is not clear whether Grey means 'within the province' (i.e. of Connaught), or 'within the limits of his licence to do so'.

at Liffer] Lifford, on the opposite bank of the Mourne from Strabane, in Tirconnell.

18. *Grey to Walsingham, 10 July 1581*

TNA: PRO SP 63/84/14

This brief letter provides little more than an appendix to Grey's description of the fighting between Sir Hugh O'Donnell and Turlough Luineach O'Neill in his letter to the Privy Council, No. 17, above (SP 63/84/13). But it shows very clearly that Grey considered Walsingham to be his most sympathetic contact on the Council, and the member of the Council most likely to support his requests. It shows, furthermore, that he saw the shortage of funds ('whereof wee are here vtterly destitute') as the most urgent point to be emphasized from the other letter, in which he writes that 'not onely her Maiesties threasure here is clene emptied but also all this Cittie so bare & needy as no money is here to be borrowed for the necessary furnishing & provision of all such thinges as to this or any other iorney apperteyne', and adds that 'I am earnestly to crave of your lordships that requisite consideracion may hereof bee had for present supply of this extremitie'. What is perhaps most interesting, then, about this letter is the way it implicates Grey, his ministers, and his secretaries in a carefully complementary traffic in official and personal correspondence, each distinguished by its own rhetorical modes (e.g. information and argument for the Privy Council, brevity and pathos for Walsingham).

The main part of the letter, with its address, is in Spenser's usual secretary hand, the only exceptions being the phrases 'For her Maiesties speciall affaires', and 'Hast hast post hast for lyfe' (on which see notes, below), which are in Spenser's italic hand, and of course his certificatory signature, which is in the usual ornate italic form. Grey has added the subscription, signature, and postscript in his own hand. The endorsement is in the same chunky secretary hand as that of No. 17, above (SP 63/84/13).

ADDRESS AND ENDORSEMENTS

For her Maiesties speciall affaires

To the Honorable
my especiall good
frend Sir Fraunces
Walsingham Knight
Chief Secretary
to her Maiestie. /

Hast hast post
hast for lyfe.

Deditum at Dublin°
the xth of Iulie
Edmund Spenser. /

x° Iulij 1581
From the Lord Deputie to mr
Secretary Walsingham

TEXT

Sir, vpon occasion of certein aduertizementes lately received concerning a bickering betwene Tirlagh and Odonell I have written vnto my
Lords for the present supplying of vs with money, whereof wee are
here vtterly destitute, without the which all the service here is like to
fall to grownd. Wherefore praying you very instantly to vrge their
Lordships with the due consideracion of the present extremitie, and
withall to hasten the expedicion thereof, what in you lyeth I committ
you to the goodnes of the Highest. Dublin. / the xth of Iulie. 1581 . /

Yowrs most assuredly
Arthur Grey

By my next yow shall haue awnsswer° of the letters receaued° from
yow with examynacyons & oother Instructions tootchyng the erl
of Killdare & oother prisoners heere: I receaued that packet the viijth
of this present.

COMMENTARY

For her Maiesties speciall affaires] this is the only letter among those addressed
by Spenser in which this extra endorsement appears; it was the standard superscription added to a sealed bundle of letters to be sent as a packet (see Crofts,
Packhorse, Waggon and Post, 73–4).

Hast hast post hast for lyfe] versions of this urgent supplementary endorsement
are not uncommon in early modern letters. See the inscription 'post hast hast hast
post hast for lief' in one of Burghley's letters, illustrated in Stewart and Woolf
(*Letterwriting*, 138). On this inscription, see also Crofts (*Packhorse, Waggon and
Post*, 76–7).

    Deditum at Dublin] the application of the Lord Deputy's special label for the Irish service,
which gave his packets of letters special priority on the route from Dublin to London, required
the authentication of his secretary. These special packets were subject to frequent logging
during their passage, and it seems that 'deditum' (Lat. 'applied', or perhaps simply 'sent') was
the accepted formula for the initial declaration; later handlers might be expected to record the
places through which the packet passed, along with the dates of passage, though no such
evidence survives in this case.   **awnsswer**] inserted above the line.   *after* **receaued**] 'of'
deleted and 'from' inserted above the line.

certein aduertizementes ... bickering ... Odonell] in No. 17, above (SP 63/84/13), Grey writes that he has 'received knowledge of a certein bickering' between O'Donnell and Turlough Luineach O'Neill, in which several of O'Donnell's chief men had already been killed. The original **aduertizementes** seem not to have been copied or forwarded to Westminster, and so have not survived.

I have written] clearly No. 17, above (SP 63/84/13).

By my next] this letter apparently does not survive, though it is possible that Grey's intended answer to Walsingham's letters was overtaken by the urgency of developments in Tirconnell: Grey had left on his hastily coordinated journey against Turlough Luineach O'Neill by 19 July.

packet] small parcel of letters.

19. *Grey to Walsingham, 18 July 1581*

TNA: PRO SP 63/84/26

This strange and pleading letter should be paired with No. 21, below (SP 63/85/13), Grey's report to the Privy Council of 12 August, concerning his journey into Ulster against Turlough Luineach O'Neill. The present letter—apparently the last he wrote before the journey—makes a point of insisting on three things above all: the miserable condition of the Irish service, the uprightness of the Dublin government, and the lack of direction from Westminster concerning negotiations with Turlough Luineach. In short, the letter seems designed as a proleptic apology for what Grey was about to do: make head into Ulster on his own authority, to conclude terms with Turlough Luineach without the Queen's warrant. The dispatch of Hoorde to Walsingham, in this context, performed a symbolic function, reminding Walsingham of the personal costs of the Irish service (Hoorde's band had been destroyed in Wexford by sickness) and of the patronage relationships upon which Grey would depend, if his journey against Turlough Luineach proved to anger the Queen.

The text of this letter, including the subscription and postscript, is written in Grey's characteristic italic hand. The signature is Grey's own. The address is written in Spenser's characteristic secretary hand, and the endorsement, probably added upon receipt of the letter in London, is written in a distinct mixed hand. The 'addressee note' (reading 'Mr Secretary') is in Grey's usual hand, and appears against the top edge of the verso of the letter.

ADDRESS AND ENDORSEMENTS

To the Honorable
my especiall good
frend Sir Fraunces

Walsingham Knight
Chief Secretary
to her Maiestie./

.18. Iuly. 1581
From the Lord Deputie
of Ireland.

TEXT

Sir this bearar Captayne Howrde myght not pass withowte sum my salutyng of yow: I haue now aduertysed my Lords there of the accidents that since my last haue happened heere: which° I knowe wyll styll bee thowght as nothyng neyther for any greate thyng doo I certyfie it, onely this with the rest maye° well wittness that wee arre styll dooyng, which in deede is all that of owre sellues maye bee perfourmed or in ryght of yow can bee expected, the success well or yll, greate or small beeyng onely Gods; & if for that which onely rests in hym, wee yet° shall rest dislyked & condemned, owre healp onely is pacience too attend boathe hys good pleazure, & beare yowr displeazure so mootche the better that owre conssciencies doo cleere vs of the dezert.   But how lyttle so euer owre seruyce hathe heethertoo been, or at the least seemed, I dare assure yow, it wyll bee less if thus hardly° yee deale with vs for mooney,° earnestly therfore I beeseetche yow too lett her Maiestie & the rest of my Lords bee enformed of it, that° boathe treazure & vittayle maye° with all speede bee supplyed ootherwyze that neyther too doo seruyce nor yet too hoald the garrizones wee haue planted shall wee° bee able; which hauyng aduertyzed & beeyng there neglected & so the eeuyll happenyng, lett mee I beeseetche bee cleered.

Gods hand is styll heauely vppon vs with sicknes, the most parte of owre men newly supplyed fallyng dayly sick in theyr garrisoons, Captayne Scopam this nyght dyed.

I woold too God, Sir yow had but the true feelyng of the miserable condition that I heere stande in, the decayeng of the Coompanies by sicknes on the one syde, the Continuall haytyng & crying owte for

---

after **heere: which**] one word, possibly 'thowghe', deleted.   *after* **rest maye**] 'maye' deleted.   *after* **wee yet**] two or three letters have been deleted.   *after* **hardly**] 'wee' deleted.   *after* **mooney,**] two or three letters deleted.   *after* **it, that**] 'if' deleted. **maye**] inserted above the line; the caret mark deletes an indecipherable character or pen-stroke.   **wee**] inserted above the line.

mooney & vittayle on the oother syde, with the generall lamentable estate of the cuntrie the peeple staruyng as they goe for want of sustenance, & too make vp all the hard disposition there too doo any thyng for the healpes heerof & small thanckes for my trauayle, in hell on earthe yow could not but thynck mee too lyue, & loouyng mee, as I knowe yow doo, no reazoon woold carie yow but too procure my release.

It is now x dayes since owre happie generall pardoon was proclaymed, & yet no one offer from any of the Mountayne rebells, afewoe° free-hollders vnable too guyue any assurance for° theyr loallties excepted, which flattly sheowes too bee a pollecie, theyr coomyng in tendyng onely to the gathering in of theyr haruiest, which doonne they° wyll beecoome as they were, with° sutche relieff too the rest as afloate the cause wyll goe agayne: this is manyfestly seene, yet arre they not refused, least then the fauourares of this good courss woold aleage that the cause of the small effect (if so it prooue) of the politick aduyce. More at thys tyme I haue not too trowble yow with; but too commend this Ientleman too yowr former good care &° fauoure, which, I fynde hathe° not, nor wyll bee amyss employed: So too owre good God I beetake yow, whow euer bee with yow, & ryd mee from this graceless office, which as hys greatiest earthely blyss I woold accounte. Dublin this xviij^tie of Iuly. Anno 1581.

Yowrs most assured euer/

Arthur Grey

This dispatche was so sudden as I could not for my lyeff make any more letters: lett my good Lord of Leaster therfore accept too bee a partener heerof at this tyme with my most Zelus dutie, & hoald mee excused for not wryghtyng too hymsellf, constraynt causyng the defawlte. I heare my Lord of Bedford & my Lady arre gon Westwarde./

I haue sent yow heerwith the° petitions of this towne considered by vs according too yowr° direction, by the postilles wheron yow maye knowe owre opinions./

---

afewoe] the sense here is as obvious as the spelling is unusual.   *after* **assurance for**] 'y^e' deleted.   *after* **doonne they**] 'we' deleted.   *after* **were, with**] one or two indecipherable letters deleted.   *after* **care &**] one or two indecipherable letters deleted.   **I fynde hathe**] 'is' deleted *after* **fynde**, and 'hathe' inserted above the line.   *after* **heerwith the**] one letter, possibly 'a', deleted.   *after* **too yowr**] two letters, possibly 'to', deleted.

Her Maiesties pleazure tootchyng Tirlagh Lenoghes petitions is forgotten yet too bee sent mee; in the last letter from my Lords there it was mencioned but noane came: I shall therfore if wee meete now goe by ayme; but the best is that so a peace bee made I shall not neede (as° I thync{ke)} too° feare what I grawnte; yet I praye yow procure mee a direction in it with all possyble speede./

COMMENTARY

Captayne Howrde] Grey had stationed Thomas Hoorde in Wexford in December 1580, in a bid to pacify the Cavanaghs; Hoorde's band, decimated by sickness, had been cashed upon Grey's May journey to Wexford, at Hoorde's own request (see No. 15, above, SP 63/83/45).

pass] cross over into England from Ireland.

wee arre styll dooyng . . . onely Gods] a typically Greyan Calvinist sentiment.

in ryght of yow can bee expected] that you can (have right to) expect.

if thus . . . for mooney] like most Lord Deputies before and after him, Grey struggled with a lack of funding for his military and administrative activities. While the letters that occasioned this reply are lost, it is clear from much of the correspondence during this period, going in both directions, that Westminster was as anxious to resist spending as Dublin was eager to increase it; see e.g. SP 63/86/22.

treazure & vittayle] money and provisions.

planted] disposed, in forts around the Pale and elsewhere.

haytyng] obscure; possibly just 'hating'.

It is now . . . was proclaymed] Grey received direction for the proclamation of the pardon toward the end of May; because of his journey to Wexford against the Cavanaghs, he was not able to proclaim it until 8 July. His repeated criticism of the pardon gives his description of it as **happie** a measure of irony.

freehollders] landed yeoman or farmers.

vnable . . . assurance] rebels seeking pardon were expected to commit some form of pledge or hostage into the hands of the governor or Deputy for the safe keeping of their loyalty.

pollecie] stratagem.

with sutche . . . goe agayne] the taking in of their harvest will allow these farmers to lay up provisions to support further insurrection.

least then . . . politick aduyce] Grey is complaining that he cannot refuse professions of loyalty from hypocritical landowners who seek only to take in their harvest and then 'come out' into rebellion again, because he fears the criticism that such a course would provoke from those who—against his counsel—sponsored the general pardon.

---

neede (as] two or three letters—probably the beginning of 'too'—deleted *after* **neede** (, and 'as' inserted above the line. The parenthesis mark is very close to the word 'neede', and so may have been added at the same time as the deletion.   **too**] inserted above the line.

This dispatche was so sudden] weather and tidal conditions could sometimes force a sudden departure of the post-ship.

Lord of Leaster] Robert Dudley, Earl of Leicester, then in London; see biographies.

the petitions . . . yowr direction] see the enclosure, SP 63/84/26/1. Walsingham had written to Grey in early June requesting his opinion on the petition of the Dublin citizens to incorporate the city; Grey responded from Wexford on 9 June (see No. 14, above, SP 63/83/43) that he had not yet seen the paper.

postilles] Grey's own annotations.

Tirlagh Lenoghes petitions] the Queen's reply to Turlough Luineach's petitions did not, Grey later claimed (see No. 21, below, SP 63/85/13), reach him until after he returned from his sudden journey later in the month to confront Turlough Luineach at the Blackwater; this gave him the opportunity to negotiate with Turlough Luineach on his own authority.

goe by ayme] act to achieve the desired outcome, without limiting his negotiating conditions.

that so a peace . . . I grawnte] Grey's pessimism about Turlough Luineach O'Neill's ability to keep the peace is so strong that he does not fear overstepping his mandate in the forthcoming negotiations; no matter what he promises, he implies, O'Neill's inevitable violation of the agreement will mean he will not be forced to deliver.

20. *Grey to the Queen, 10 August 1581*

TNA: PRO SP 63/85/5

This letter's main business is to present an official and formal account of Grey's recent meeting with Turlough Luineach O'Neill at the Blackwater, with his attempts to resolve O'Neill's recent war with Sir Hugh O'Donnell (also described, as a 'bickering', in Nos. 17 and 18, above, SP 63/84/13 and 63/84/14). Grey had requested more troops from England to guard against Turlough Luineach's threat to the Pale, but his requests had been denied; furthermore, when sending over information about the proclamation for general pardon in April 1581, the Privy Council had specifically urged Grey to offer reconciliation and pardon to Turlough Luineach: 'in case you resolue to enter into anie action of warre agaynst Tirlaghe, wee then thincke it verie meete that you should fyrst offer vnto him confirmation of suche thinges as by your Lordship weare thought meet to be allowed vnto him' (SP 63/82/41). What we see in this letter is Grey's attempt, once again, to criticize this 'temporizing' course of action: he repeats that it has been ordered by 'your Highnes councell', not by himself, he anticipates the failure of the composition that he had predicted in earlier letters ('in case he shall refuse to stand to the order'), and he claims to be vindicated in his prediction (cf. No. 13, above, SP 63/82/54) that few rebels would accept the terms of the pardon: 'I heare of very few & none indeed of accoumpt that make any reckoning of the pardons your Highnes wonted great mercy vnworthely, as it shewes, hath vouchsafed'. Finally, he returns (cf. No. 15, above, SP 63/83/45) to Ormond's dismissal as Lord General of Munster, and gives the impression that the vacancy provides an opportunity for him to forward the claims of Colonel John Zouche.

One of the most fascinating aspects of this letter is its account of Grey's negotiations with Turlough Luineach's wife, the Scots noblewoman Agnes Campbell (see biographies). In complete contrast to Grey's account of Turlough Luineach himself, whom he presents as fickle, emotional, and neurotic, Campbell comes across in Grey's account as shrewd and serious, an able negotiator and someone whose word (almost despite himself) Grey seems to respect. Unlike Turlough Luineach, who admits to certain dealings with the rebels at one time, and denies them at another, Grey's brief report of Agnes Campbell reveals an adversary who neither temporizes nor lies, neither boasts nor defies. It is unusual for Grey to report his dealings with an Irish rebel (or, for that matter, Palesman) without offering some incidental insult or expression of contempt, but Agnes Campbell receives neither.

The other interesting aspect of this letter is Grey's approach to his other female interlocutor, the Queen. Grey had made it clear in the letters sent to Walsingham before his departure for the Blackwater that he planned to take the matter of Turlough Luineach's petitions into his own hands, despite the fact that Captain Piers was still in transit on a direct embassy between O'Neill and the Queen. Grey seems also to have played false with the Queen's instructions, claiming before his departure that he had not received them, but, upon his return, that he had discovered them after the fact; at the very least, Grey exploited his opportunity in mid-July to race northward against Turlough Luineach without the burden of the Queen's direction. The treaty he then concluded was designed, as he patiently recounts here, to capitulate to O'Neill on all points—Grey conceded all his demands and established the peace without requiring pledges or other security. Grey's gamble was that O'Neill would break his own agreement and, having had ground given him on all points, would have no further defence against the charge of faithlessness and ambition. Crucial to this project was Grey's pretence in this letter of absolute submission to the Queen's pacific policy; his politic attempts to satisfy and defy what he took to be her capricious ignorance leave him looking distinctly less noble than Agnes Campbell, who seems to have served an equally difficult master with perhaps greater integrity.

The text of the letter, with the address, is in Spenser's formal Italian hand, the norm for official letters from the Lord Deputy to the Queen. Grey has decorously added his own subscription and signature at the right foot of the final page. The endorsement, in a later hand, was probably added by a clerk handling the letter during the filing process.

ADDRESS AND ENDORSEMENT

To the Queenes
most excellent
Maiesty./

10.° Augusti 1581
From the Lord Deputy of Irelande
to the Quenes Maiesty

Entred./.

TEXT

It may please your Highnes vpon the contention betwixt Tirlagh &
Odonell and an ouerthrow therein fallen to Odonell (as formerly I
aduertized thether) yt was by your Highnes councell here thought
necessary, that I with some parte of your forces here should make
to Tirlogh ward, both for the saving of Odonelles vtter spoile &
suppressing, (who since my coming, hath euer most duetifully carried
him self) as also to stay the sayd Tirloghs further attemptes against
the Pale, which reason gaue greatly to bee mistrusted, or rather
certeinly looked for. The order & purpose of my expedition was this;
Liffer is a Riuer, that parteth Tyrone & Tirconell: vpon yt are twoo
castelles, the one called the Liffer the other Strabane; these Castelles
are the onely keyes of Odonnelles countrey towardes Tirloghs: Sir
Nicholas Malbey I directed with fowre Companies that he had in
Connagh and his horssmen to ioyne that way with Odonell & so
drawe downe to the Liffer. My self with eight Companies of Foot. &
300 Horss. to marche by the black water, & to meete them at the sayd
Castle: the purpose was to haue taken these Castelles & deliuered the
one into Odonelles handes, namely the Liffer, & into Strabanc to hauc
putt an English warde; in case Tirlogh came not vnto me to the black
water. This plott layde; a day or two before I entred on my iorney,
I dispatched lettres to° Tirlogh signifying vnto him that bycause
I heard of a great stirre betwene him & Odonell, & the same to haue
gone further then I liked, or ought on their sydes, in case theyr
dueties° to your Highnes had rightly bene weighed, I could not but
put them both in mynd of them selues, & for theyr owne behoofes &
quiett of their Countreys take the traueill to repaire into those partes,
for the appeasing of the quarrell, and therefore willed him to surcease

after **lettres to**] 'him' deleted.   *after* **dueties**] 'doen' deleted.

from further forceable dealing against Odonnell, & with all convenient speed to repaire vnto mee to the Black water, where I would endeuour to compownd the cause betwixt Odonell & him, & besydes empart somewhat vnto him of your Highnes pleasure concerning parte of his Petitions: which though I had not then receiued, yett knowing that the same would be no small cause to draw him to talk, & hauing besydes former direction from my Lords of your Councell to vse myne owne discretion in yt, for the holding of quietnes with him, I tooke the boldenes to giue him that knowledg. On my way now° at Dundalk lettres from Tirlogh mett mee that he would meete me, as I had appointed him, & that he had vpon my warning surceassed from further invading of Odonell; marry that he merueiled why I should make such præparation as he heard of to take his Castelles, which to præuent he signified that he had broken & in maner razed, as indeed he had. In my answere to these I did comfort him to the meeting, I willed him not lightly to creditt rumors, I doubted not but he should bee well satisfied in all thinges at our meeting, wherevnto I referred the rest.

So I came to the Black water, where I stayed twoo or three dayes before I heard any thing of him, in no small lacke both of Beoffe & grasse; yet to auoyd all causes of quarrell on his part (farre against nature I confesse) I would nether remoue to the farsyde being his Countrey, nor yett take a Cowe of the Galloglasses, whose creat lyeth all on this syde vpon your Maiesties owne grownd without answering you any rent, nor yett owing you, at least affoording you any trowth or alleageaunce, but in good or euill holde to him & bend against you. At the last he comes, & first he sendes his wyfe vnto me both for the appointing of the place for the Parlea, as also to impart vnto mee some of his griefes: the place he desyred migt bee vpon the Riuer, hee on the one syde, and I on the other: his griefes were partly for iniuries doen him by the Baron of Dunganon, & agayne that his Messenger (so he termed him) Captein Piers was so long stayed with his Petitions: I answered that the Place was very vnfitt, for the Riuer beeing betwixt, causes of such weight could nether bee well debated, nether was yt convenient that euery stander by should bee priuie to the thinges that therein were to passe, which in this sorte could not bee eschewed; I wished therefore that either he would come to my Campe vpon sufficient Saufconduct or Protection, or els that wee

might meete° in the playne field, equall numbers on eyther syde
appointed. As touching his griefes, I sayde that whatsoeuer iustly
could bee challenged by him not onely of the Baron, but any other
Subiect, he should bee assured of all iustice that was in mee to helpe
him too, & that hisself knewe, how I had purposely appointed
Commissioners for the taking of order in those causes. Concerning
Captein Piers his stay, that I looked euery howre for his retourne, &
that I tooke his stay now rather to growe vpon his owne particulare
businesse, then that he was not dispatched by your Highnes neuerthelesse that I had receiued some notice of your pleasure in some of
his Petitions, which I was to emparte vnto him, in case I found his
dealings to answere the office of a good & duetifull Subiect; I added to
this that as he seemed to fynd him self grieued with the forereckened
causes, I was no lesse but more iustly to complayne of his carriage,
first that he had often made shew of armes against the state, espetially
at such tymes, as he fownd me bent to iorneyes against your Maiesties
open Rebelles, that he demaunded iustice still by force, that he was a
dayly receauer of Traitours messengers, & by their owne reportes
a Combiner with them, that contrary to his peace late made and
sworne with the late Earle of Essex, namely that he should apprehend
& deliuer any Traitour, that should come vnto him, & bee demaunded
of him, he of late flatly refused it to the Knight Marschall, who
hauing knowledg that William Nugent was with him, did earnestly
demaunde him of him, lastly that before any complaint exhibited &
redresse required at your Maiesties handes, he had invaded & fought
with Odonnell one of your Highnes good & duetifull subiects. In her
reply to this, the best shee could say, was, that the dislike her husband
had taken agaynst the Baron, had carried him into farther shewes of
offence, then he indeed euer meant, neither that messengers from the
Traitours had bene with her Husband could she denye, but that he
euer combined with them, that she withstood, nether could she
excuse the charge for William Nugent, Odonolles matter shee
defended, in that Odonell had first broken truce, & sett vpon her
husband: finally whether her Husband would come into my Camp,
or haue talke any otherwise, then that the Riuer might part vs, she
doubted, but the next morning early that I should haue knowledg: so
shee departed. His answere the next day was, that onely vpon the
riuer he would speake with me: as force was, I agreed, thincking that
yt might yet bee an enteraunce to further talke by Commissioners, to

meete] inserted above the line.

how small purpose soeuer yt otherwise were: as I meant yt, so by his owne request occasion fell out; for after a very litle talke with him, hisself required, that bycause of the vnaptnes of the place, & inconuenience it might bring to the cause, to haue so many hearers, I would send ouer some Commissioners to treat with him of the affaires, the choice I tolde him was his owne fault, yet since I was content in the worse to assent to him, I wold not refuse it in the better, & so I presently sent ouer Iustice Dowdhall & Lodouick Briskett our Clerk of the Councell here with Instructions; in summe these, that the Peaces heretofore taken & covenanted by him with Sir Henry Sidney late Gouernour & the Earle of Essex should stand & bee performed by him; next that the cause now betwixt him & Odonell should bee heard & determined by such Commissioners as I should appoint; lastly that for performaunce hereof he should putt in° such Ostages as I should require or lyke of; To stand to the former peaces he vtterly refused; marry to holde the Composition that with me he tooke this last yeare, he was content till Captein Piers his retourne with your Highnes resolution to his demaundes. To putt the cause betwixt him & Odonell to Commissioners, with much adoe he was thus farre brought, that by my Commissioners yt should be heard but adiudged onely by my self. Pledges for performaunce of these, he in maner disdayned to heare of, to bee sworne to the keeping of these Conditions, was all the surety that could be wonne of him; the conditions of his part consisted onely to haue former orders (by the Commissioners therefore appointed) against the Baron of Dunganon & others for iniuries towards him & his executed by a day, as he likewise was to answere right, for such as were on his peace by the same orders, & that all wronges hereafter to happen, should likewise be tyed to the Commissioners order.

Thus is there a peace with him concluded, which though nether for the surety of yt, nor honour I can greatly commend, yet weighing the dislike your Highnes carryeth to enter into force with him, & besides hauing by your Highnes Lords of Councell there bene giuen to vnderstand, that by any meanes to holde him in, & temporize with him should bee accepted for no small good seruice, I haue endeuored in all that I might to frame the course to your Maiesties lyking & their Lordships direction; in discourse whereof though I haue bene the longer & perchaunce tœdious, I am to craue humble pardon, & withall

in] inserted above the line.

to say for iust excuse therein, that fynding hard taking and diuersly construing of all my doings here hath willed me to lay before your Highnes the whole circunstance of the action, submitting the same to the censure your Highnes shall thinck yt to deserue.

And now I am humbly to craue your Highnes direction, how I shall deale with Tirlagh, in case he shall refuse to stand to the order that I shall award vpon the examyning of the cause betwene him & Odonell; & surely I feare, constraint must bee the cause, yf it doe take place: on the other syde your Highnes is to waye the great touch to your honour, besyde discoragement to others, yf Odonell bee lefte so to the others ravine & spoile without your protecting & assistaunce, considered that the thwart is happened him, chiefly for that he would neither come to composition with Tirlogh without our assent here, nor yet retayne any Scottes, being by vs forwarned thereof.

My next iorney, & that forthwith, God not letting shalbee to the Mountaynes here, whence I meane not to depart, till I haue broken that nest; whereof, with Gods fauour, I make no doubt, though some liues yt will cost.

I can certefy your Highnes of no great seruice doen by the garrisons there now in myne absence, for that yt hath pleased God, so to visite them with a pestilent feuer, as moe then half of the numbers are layde, & many haue dyed, so that rather to defend then offend they haue bene driuen: yf it bee not the Lords pleasure to stay this his hand, & to giue health to those that are fallen downe, surely Madam I shall not know what to doe without a new supply, or els to fill vp the bandes with Irish here, as continually by these accidents of sicknesse and runninge away of our English soldiers we are enforced to doe, a thing yett I cannot denye but very perillous.

Your Maiesty is to remember the gouernement of Mounster, & to resolue of some meet English man for yt, in the meane season the direction that from my Lords there I haue now receiued, shalbee followed. Iohn Zowtche, I heare, hath agayne donne a good service vpon those Rebelles & slayne about 60 of their kerne & Galloglasse.

I heare of very few & none indeed of accoumpt that make any reckoning of the pardons your Highnes wonted great mercy vnworthely, as it shewes, hath vouchsafed; well I pray god that the errour of this clemency, yf it bee clemency, to spare iustice, bee not too late in this land fownde.

To conclude, I see that the sore of this countrey without force will not bee cured, I see that force is chargeable to your Highnes, I see that charge is grieuous & dislyking, I see, that it pleaseth not God to giue the short successe & end to things, that your Maiesty expecteth, I see that my seruice thus becomes altogether condemned & disfauored, the contrary whereof, God I call to record, hath euer bene the onely proiect of my gayne: am I then to be blamed, if I seeke to bee rid of that, that causeth me my greatest grief, which is your disfauour, & putts me hopelesse of my greatest comfort, which is your Highnes fauour & good grace? I trust not, & therefore with all humblenes & duety I beseech your Highnes to haue consideration of mee, & take me from this place, which I perceaue, doe what I can, wilbee the dayly encrease of my hell & continuall stay of my blisse. And thus as he that desires no greater earthly happines of God, then in all thinges to serue & content your Maiestie I take most humble leaue, beseeching the same God alwayes to defend, direct & prosper your Highnes. Dublin. this x^th of August. 1581./

> Yowr Hyghnes moste humble seruant
> & faythefull subiect,

> Arthur Grey

COMMENTARY

the contention ... Odonell] the attack by Turlough Luineach O'Neill upon Sir Hugh O'Donnell was reported in a letter of 10 July 1581 (No. 17, above, SP 63/84/13); in a related letter to Walsingham (No. 18, above, SP 63/84/14), Grey again refers to the 'bickering betwene Tirlagh and Odonell'.

as formerly I aduertized thether] i.e. in the letters mentioned above, Nos. 17 and 18 (SP 63/84/13 and 63/84/14).

by your Highnes council] by the Irish Council.

to Tirlogh ward] in the direction of Turlough Luineach, i.e. towards his lands. See *OED*, '-ward', 6.

spoile] ruin.

the sayd ... the Pale] Turlough Luineach's agression in Tirconnell (in the north-west of Ireland) might give reason to suppose that he would move south.

which reason ... looked for] which we had good reason to fear, or at least to be wary of.

Liffer ... Tyrone ... Tirconell] the Liffer seems to be the River Mourne, which separates the counties of Tirconnell (the territory of the O'Donnells, roughly equivalent to the modern county of Donegal) and Tyrone, and on opposite sides of which the towns of Lifford and Strabane stand. On the boundary between the lands of Turlough Luineach and O'Donnell, they stand as the **onely keyes** of O'Donnell's country.

warde] keeper or garrison.

the black water] the Blackwater marks the boundary between Co. Tyrone in the north-west, and Armagh and Monaghan in the south and east. Turlough Luineach's approach to the Blackwater in August/September 1580 is recorded in a pair of letters from Dungannon to Grey copied in Spenser's hand (SP 63/76/6 and 63/76/7): the river marked a boundary of Turlough Luineach's territory.

This plott layde] having devised this scheme.

in case . . . weighed] if they were to consider.

behoofes] benefits (perhaps with the sense of 'duties', although *OED*, 2 cites this as a rare usage).

take the traueill] take the trouble.

compownd the cause] settle the matter (*OED*, 'Compound', *v.*, 6).

for the holding . . . with him] to keep him in a state of quietness, of peace.

Dundalk] on the east coast of Ireland, in Co. Louth, approximately 80 km north of Dublin and 30 km away from the Blackwater.

broken & in maner razed] cf. 'yt hath bene thought good and concluded that David Barrie should be sent for to bee talked with, and to vnderstand the cause of the breaking of his castles' (No. 8, above, SP 63/81/36/1).

Beoffe] oxen, or cattle.

(farre against nature I confesse)] a rather oblique remark. Either Grey remarks sardonically, even sarcastically, that a man of Turlough Luineach's nature needs little excuse for a quarrel, or he seems to confess that this temporizing, non-confrontational course of action goes against his own nature.

Galloglasses] see glossary.

creat] see glossary.

but in good . . . you] they pay their allegiance to Turlough Luineach, and not at all to Elizabeth.

his wyfe] Turlough Luineach's wife was Lady Agnes Campbell, daughter of the Earl of Argyll; see biographies. Turlough Luineach regularly employed her as an intermediary.

Parlea] parley.

griefes] grievances.

iniuries . . . Dunganon] Hugh O'Neill, Baron of Dungannon, who had enjoyed a tense, if not outright hostile, relation with Turlough Luineach (in no small part as a conflict over succession to the O'Neill lordship). Dungannon had in the previous year appealed for English help against Turlough Luineach's menacing behaviour (see, for example, No. 2, above, SP 63/75/84).

his Messenger . . . Petitions] this is William Piers (see biographies), who had in 1580 negotiated with Turlough Luineach on behalf of the crown. On the **Petitions** and the general pardon, see headnote.

in this sorte] in this way.

Saufconduct] safe-conduct, a guarantee that he would not be arrested.

carriage] conduct (although *OED*, *n.*, 14 gives the first usage of this (and associated) meaning of the term in the 1590s).

receaver of Traitours messengers] perhaps alluding to the accusations relating to William Nugent (see below).

his peace . . . Essex] Essex's campaign against Turlough Luineach in March and April 1574 ended with no lasting agreement, but after further actions by Essex against his land, Turlough Luineach eventually submitted in late June 1575 (see SP 63/52/48/16–18).

he of late . . . Marschall] the **Knight Marschall** is Sir Nicholas Bagenal; see biographies. He had told Sir Francis Walsingham on 25 April (SP 63/82/52) that he and Grey suspected that Turlough Luineach had been practising with **William Nugent**, the younger brother of Baron Delvin, and went into rebellion when Delvin was arrested with the Earl of Kildare, on suspicion of involvement with Viscount Baltinglass. On Nugent's rebellion, see Walshe, 'The Rebellion of William Nugent'.

invaded & fought with Odonnell] for an account of and commentary upon Turlough Luineach's conflict with O'Donnell, see Nos. 17 and 18, above (SP 63/84/13 and 63/84/14). Grey's accounts there certainly do not describe Turlough Luineach as a villain, or even the aggressor ('a certein bickering which was lately betwene Tirlagh, & ODonell'), even if O'Donnell seems to have come off worse: 'in the which there were certein of Odonelles chief capteins taken & slayne, besides many other of his men'.

Commissioners] crown agents commissioned to investigate and adjudicate.

occasion fell out] things turned out; i.e. Turlough Luineach made the same request that Grey had.

Iustice Dowdhall] James Dowdall, at the time Second Justice of the King's Bench; see biographies.

Lodouick Briskett] see biographies. Bryskett was also present, and involved in military discussions, at Smerwick. See No. 5, above (SP 63/78/29).

the Peaces . . . Essex] see note above.

for performaunce hereof] to ensure that he would perform this.

putt in such Ostages] submit hostages or pledges, persons handed over as guarantees that the undertakings would be fulfilled.

stand to] abide by (*OED*, 'Stand', *v.*, 76).

the conditions . . . same orders] Turlough Luineach's conditions are merely that Dungannon should have to answer charges for injuries against him, at the same time and before the same commissioners to whom he himself has to answer.

temporize] negotiate in order to gain time.

in discourse whereof] in describing the course of action that I took.

fynding hard . . . doings here] seeing that all of my actions in service here are taken badly and misinterpreted.

stand to] see above.

touch] blow, blemish, injury.

ravine] ravin: robbery or rapine.

the thwart is happened him] the injury has been committed to him.

pestilent feuer] complaints about this plague, a common hazard of the Irish service, seem to have been particularly common during 1581. See No. 11, above (HH Cecil Papers 11/91).

layde] cast down.

the gouernement ... English man] Ormond had been dismissed from his position as Lord General of Munster; Grey's call for a suitable 'English man' must surely be an implicit attack upon Ormond, and a call in favour of John Zouche.

the pardons] on the general pardon, see headnote.

I see ... disfauored] an impassioned anaphora, joined to a stirring if highly aggrieved gradatio.

21. *Grey to the Privy Council, 12 August 1581*

TNA: PRO SP 63/85/13

Grey probably returned from his journey into Ulster on 11 August, sending this report to the Privy Council on the following day. For evidence of careful political scheming, there are few letters in this collection to beat it: not only did Grey seize an unprecedented opportunity to catch Turlough Luineach on the back foot, by pinching him between Malby's forces (with O'Donnell) on the west, and his own from the south, thus forcing him to subscribe to a set of articles sent over to him by Grey's commissioners, Dowdall and Bryskett; but Grey perfectly orchestrated his own commission from London, timing his journey carefully in order to be able to claim ignorance, on his return, of the instructions he had meanwhile been sent from Westminster. Turlough Luineach's anxiety and distress at having been outfoxed come palpably through in Grey's account, and the measured, backhanded way in which Grey attributes his lenient course to his respect for the Queen's pacific preferences smacks of the Machiavellian adept. Of course Grey did not expect Turlough Luineach to keep the peace to which he had agreed—as he wrote to Walsingham just before leaving for Ulster (No. 19, above, SP 63/84/26), he knew his course was safe because his negotiations, even if temporarily successful, would eventually prove fruitless—but the aim at the Blackwater was not to secure peace, but to create the defensible pretext for the open war with Turlough Luineach that Grey desired. Grey furthers this agenda later in this letter by underscoring the Dublin government's confidence in Sir Hugh O'Donnell (Turlough Luineach's antagonist), and resisting the Privy Council's incipient plans to divert military resources from Leinster and Connaught to Munster. This letter is also interesting because it provides the first report of the escape of the Baron of Lixnaw's sons from Limerick castle; these two pledges were all that kept Lord Fitzmaurice in obedience, and he rebelled almost instantly. The secretaries handling this letter had before them a masterclass in high politics and the chess-like manipulation of men, ambitions, and commissions.

The text of the letter is in a neat and compact secretary (not Spenser's), familiar from many of the letters in this series. Spenser's own secretary hand appears in the address. Grey has penned the subscription and signature

himself, in his characteristically awkward italic. A later hand has added sub
stantial underlining throughout the text of the letter, probably in order to
emphasize certain points to members of the Privy Council, to whom the
letter would have been circulated upon receipt.

ADDRESS AND ENDORSEMENTS

To the Righte
Honorable the
Lords and otheres of
{h}er Maiesties Privie
{C}ouncell./°

12° Augusti 1581
From the Lord Deputy of Irelande
to the Lordes of the Counsel.

Entred

TEXT

It may please your Lordships. I haue of late receaued 2: lettres from
yow of the 26. and 30 of the laste, whiche came to my handes after
I dispersed my companies in my retorne from my treaty with Turloughe Lennoughe: your Lordships I doubte not do remember what I
aduertised in my last letters, touching the occacion of my late Iorneye
northward, namely how odonnell had praied aide of hir maiestye,
against Turloughe, or els for ever to bee lefte to shifte for him self,
and that in our opinions heere, the losses sustained by him, coulde no
way be repaired, nor Turloughe staied from the totall overthrowe of
him, and his countrey vnlesse I had presently made hedd into those
partes. According to whiche determinacion, I did not only sende
Sir Nicholas Malbey, withe the forces vnder him in Connoughte, to
enter Tierconnell, by the way of Sligo, and prepared victualls, and
municion, to be sente by sea into Loughfoill, for suche services, as I
purposed about Leefer, but martched in person, withe those few
Companies, which I had to the forte vppon the black water, And in
my way thether, I sente to Turloughe, to declare that having hearde
somewhat of the violente manner of dealing betweene him, and
odonnell, I could do no lesse, then deale betweene them, to the stop-
ping of those contrauersies, and to heere and determine the causes,
that had moued so greate outrages, and losse of so many hir maiesties

---

Address] the removal of the sealed bands has obscured some parts of the address, which was
originally written over them.

subiectes° on bothe sides, being sorye that men of theire condicion, and so well hable to serve hir highnes, should so farre exceede them selues as without lycense to enter into warre and to disturbe the state, And therefore I appoincted him a place, and a tyme for conferrence and speache to be had in the matter: To this I was aunswered that he woulde repaier to the place, appoincted, at the time I assigned, For the rumour of my coming had caused him, before this, to retorne from the Chace of odonnell, and heering of a preparacion heere for a battry to be sente, into Loughfoill, he gaue order for the rasing of his owne castle of Strabane, vppon that ryuer, and of the castle of Leefer, belonging to Con odonnell, on Tierconnell side: At the day appoincted he came neere vnto the place withe a minde prepared altogether for warre, (so farre, as I could ghesse) notwithstanding he sente vnto me to know my pleasure, wherevppon I addressed the Iustice Dowdall, and Mr Briskett to treate with him vppon certaine articles, whiche I gaue them by way of Instrvccion, subscribed by me, and by Mr. Threasoror, and Mr Marshall, there withe mee, whiche articles with the aunsweres, or conclucions of the peace I send vnto your Lordships heerewithe, to avoyde tediousnes in my letter, only this I will note, that the Comissioners founde soche passions and alteracions in him, as weare straunge, before he Could bee temperede by them to enny conformity, But in the ende he was so handeled, as he sought withe humility, to come to the entervewe, but in soche mistrustfull manner as the riuer devided vs, So likewise when wee had concluded, sometyme he put of his hatte, and ioyed that he had peace, And by, and by an other difficulty grew, when he, and his followers should swere, and subscribe to the condicions, by whiche stormy manner of dealing, I note his vnsteddy nature, and how lytle truste is to bee hadd, ether to his wordes, or wrytinges, and on the Contrary parte do comend the dealing of those gentlemen, in that they so ouercame his obstinacy, withe perswacon, as the dignety of the state was preserved, and he wrought to seeke whatesoeuer I desired, althoughe the most efficient causes indeade were the forces, by whiche he feared Invasion on bothe sides: And whereas sondry speaches, had bene geven forthe by the rebelles, that he was a princi-pall partie in the rebellion, and had promised ayde, to them from tyme, to tyme, after he had subscribed, he protested, that he had neuer made ennye soche othe, or promisse to enny rebell, thoughe

___

subiectes] as often, this secretary has here joined a terminal 'es' brevigraph to a word already ending in 'e', in effect writing 'subiectees'. As the intention is clear enough, we have chosen to represent this ambiguous usage in the normal way.

sondry had sente vnto him for that purpose which he offred to advow before enny, that would so charge him. The comissioners had in Charge also to deliuer the proclamacion of generall pardon, whiche for all the prouince of Vlster was proclaimed without enny exception, But when yt was made knowne in his Campe yt moued not enny man there, to take the benefyt of yt, for they saied yt concerned offendoures, and offences, whereof there was none in Vlster of that qualety; Turloughes wief seemed ernestly to further this pacificacion, being fearefull of the double force, whiche bothe she saw with me, and hearde to be Coming with odonnell vnder Sir Nicholas Malbey, by whiche I must confesse to your Lordships I might haue taken soche an occacion to haue dishabled Turloughe for euer doing hurte to the pale, as hardely Can be founde soche an oportunitye, but that I know hir maiesties inclinacion so bente, vppon temporising withe a calme, and a peceable cours, as I would not enter into a matter of warre, that afterwarde might lacke dew prosecution, And therefore having sente the Iustice Dowdall, and other comissioners of Turloughes into Tierconnell to attende Sir Nicholas Malbey, for composition to be taken betweene him and odonnell, I accepted the peace before mencioned nothing pleasing to me, thoughe I assure my self, yt will be better thought of at home, then a warre that might haue brought forthe, bothe an honourable and a perpetuall assuraunce against the Northe: After this pacifaccion, and my retorne from the place, I receaued (as I haue formerly sayed) your Lordships letters, withe whiche I finde the articles aggreed vppon by hir maiesty, to Turloughes peticions, and for sondrye respectes am glad, that they came not sooner to my handes, For althoughe the grauntes are very honourable, and more liberall in some thinges, then I Coulde haue perswaded, if I had bene there, yet the condicions, wherevnto he should be tied be such as are verye beneficiall to the state, and suche, as he will neuer accept, For that whiche tendethe to the banishmente of the Scottes, will neuer be yelded vnto by his wief, and hir frendes, neither would he haue consented to yeld anny pledges, And then if he had falne from the condicions, and hir maiesty, not bente to haue maintayned hir purpose by force, yt would presently haue geven an end of all his expectacion from Englande, and made him perhappes desperate in the rest, as by all likelihoode he may be, Neuertheles if Capten Peirs, his messenger (of whome your Lordships wryte) be not verye circumspect how to reveale thes thinges, or to vse warely his message, and soche matter as his master fantasiethe in his platte of Vlster, And in troathe I finde yt very straunge, that enny soche messenger should be sente, without first being directed hether, to acquainte me withe the Cours he purposethe to take, and to enfourme him self by the state heere, what hathe passed, and how farre he may goe in reason, in thes Treaties withe Turloughe For how muche Capten Peers misconceauethe in thes matters, and is abused in his opinion may appeare to your Lordships by the aunswere of euery article of his platte, Whereunto wee haue postilde, whiche I speake not in disgrace of the man, whome indeade I loue, and wishe to be holpen in his particuler, and that he may be vsed in trust in those seruices, wherewithe he is acquainted, ether in the ardes, or Clande-boy, But that he hathe enny Creddyt at all with Turloughe, (but in the way of good fellowship, whiche lastethe no longer then that humour Continuethe) I haue suff{ic}yent proof, and very good cause to iudge, And what golden mountaines soeuer are promised, ether by his messages, or my peace now Concluded, I assure your Lordships I accept yt none otherwise thankeworthye; then as patched stuffe that Cannot longe houlde. For the intollerable pride and insolencye of Turloughe is soche, as Cannot be contynued within the bondes of duetye to hir maiestye, or good neighbourid to hir highnes subiectes This only benifitt I take of the peace now Concluded, and of the time now wonne, that I may, as soone as I Canne fornishe me of a conuenyent proportion of victuall, martche to the mountaines, and breake ether that broode, or retorne withe losse, for vppon tryall of goddes will ether in the one, or the other, I am constauntlye deter-mined.   Your Lordships in your letter wisshed my staye from the borders, in respecte of the trobles of other partes, But I thought yt most convenyent to take this oportunitye, by whiche I suppose the hope, whiche they conceaued in Turloug{he} is cutt of from the confederates in all partes, so as now the occonnours, beginne to make meane vnto mee to bee receaued, and so do some of the obirnes, and the base brother of the Baron of Delvin, all whiche bothe before and in the time of the treaty withe Turloughe, and till the peace was published, had no regard at all to the proclamacion of pardon

And thus muche I thought meete to say aswell in declaracion of my late Iorney northward, as in aunswere of your Lordships lettre of the 30 of Iuly: Your Lordships other letter of the xxvj. of Iuly. concer-nethe the good acceptacion of Iohn Zouches service, the opinion of the reuolte of Odonnelles sonne, and the placing of Sir Warham Sentleger colonell of the forces in Mounster.

To the first I am very glad in the behalf of the gentleman, that hir maiesty and your Lordships do so well conceaue of Mr Zouche, which opinion may be bettered, by a secound service, done since, wherein he hathe had very good Successe, and hathe slaine, & taken of the erle of Desmoundes followers of good accoumpt, and redused Kerrye in manner to depende wholy vppon him, Neuertheles, I feare that an accidente lately happened, will put his service there in some Daunger, for I am enformed, that by the negligence of one Sherif viceconstable in the Castle of Limerick, and by the practise (as yt is thought) of some of the Citizens, the Lord Fitzmorice two sonnes, and two other pledges are escaped, whereby yt is likely that all Fitz-morice his countrey, willbe distempered, I can geue no remedy to this misadventure, but by seueare punishment of the partie to preuente the like negligence, or abuse in men of his sorte heereafter.

Secoundly for Odonnells sonne, supposed by Capten Peirs to haue revolted, and to be supported by his fosterfatheres, there hathe bene no cause of eny soche Conceipt, for nether hathe his sonnes, (who are of age but Childeren) so fallen from theire father, nether hathe eny of the countrey left him, but mainteyned his quarrells with expence of theire bloode, sauing a few followers of Con odonnells, his nephew Whose ambicion, & desire to haue the captency, hathe moued this sturre, and diuers other heeretofore depending euer since the deathe of his father Culloughe odonnell, vppon the Captens of Tirone in the time of Shane oneyll, and euer since vppon Turloughe Lennoughe.

Thirdely for Sir Warham Seintleger, to be Chcif Colloncll in Mounster, I like well of your Lordships Choice of the gentleman, to supply the place for a tyme, till hir maiesty shall resolue farther, for as his profession in the beginning of his lief was to follow the warres, and at his entry into service heere was the firste presidente of that prouince, so hathe his behauiour since this rebellion, deserved well of hir maiesty, And therefore I haue good cause to allow of his nominacion, neuertheles I do not wisshe, that yt should haue long Continuance, because his aucthoritye there must needes be accompanied withe the disliking of therle of ormond, betweene whome there hathe bene some Contrauersies in my tyme And therefore I wishe, that hir maiesty woulde shortely thinke vppon some apt choice of some of hir highnes servauntes in England, and to vse that gentlemans service in some other kinde, And for the present Sir Warham Seintleger, shall haue a comission asosiated withe other of the Colonelles, and Captens, as your Lordships haue well deuised, and his entertainement, assigned with as lytle charg to hir maiesty, as may be, and some smale addicon of horsemen, to his owne retinew already in pay, But that° they should be defalked from other bandes, I do not think conveny-ent, because yt wilbe hinderaunce° to the service, and very offensive to the captens, who if they wante in theire companies had rather aunswere the checques to hir maiesty, then to be abridged in theire numbers for eny private respecte:/

I am aduertised out of the annalye, that while the Cheife baron, and the attorneye, Were holding a sessions there, Orwark was entered the county of Longford with the number of 1000 of all sortes whereof the most parte Scottes, and begann to burne, and spoile the countrey, to the rescew whereof the Cheif baron, assembled suche as Could be gotten vppon the soddaine, and Chardged the Scottes, in whiche there was slaine viij. of them, and xx. or thereaboutes hurte, notwith-standing they weare not hable to rescue the pray, but there was taken from them 1000 Cattell, and vij. or viij. villages burnte: It seemethe by the letter, and informacion whiche I haue receaued, that there is no grea{t} value° in the offarrolles. or that they did any more then they weare enforced vnto by the Cheif Baron, and the attorneye, who bothe weare in daunger, and more forward, then the rest in the Charge geuen, This your Lordships may see, notwithstanding enny peaces, & compotitions, that may be made, how this state is disturbed, withe that nacion of the Scottes, whiche swarme euery where to the annoyance of the Subiectes:/

Lastely I haue humbly to thanke your Lordships for your deter-minacion to sende hether threasure, municion, and victualls, of which kindes, there is not enny of late aryued, but the threasure is staied at Chester, by a post dispatched yesterday, because I heere that 2. pirates, well appoincted with 140 shott, do remaine in the hauen of Beamorice, redye to make a pray of yt, or of some honest mer-chauntes: If the handmaide do retorne from Loughfoill she shall scowre the coast, and fetche the threasure, But in the meane tyme We liue in want and therefore wishe that yt weare well wafted from Chester.° So hauing not farther, whereof to enfourme your Lordships but that Sir William Standley within thes iij. daies, hathe executed

---

that] inserted above the line.   But that . . . hinderaunce] this underscored passage has been flagged in the left margin with a hash mark.   value] a single-character deletion appears at the end of this word.   and therefore . . . Chester] this underscored passage has been flagged in the left margin with a hash mark.

some of the rebelles nccrc Artlow. whose heddes he sendethe me
by water, not yet aryued, & that capten Deeringes company, haue
likewise slaine xiiij. in a glan neere Powerscourte, I comytt your
Lordships to god. At Dublyn the xij[th] of August 1581.

Your Lordships most assured
to Commaund,

Arthur Grey

COMMENTARY

I haue . . . from yow] no record of these letters survives. As Grey mentions further
on in the present letter, they concerned the Queen's instructions for dealing with
Turlough Luineach O'Neill.

after . . . Turloughe Lennoughe] Grey had marched to the Blackwater to confront
and parley with Turlough Luineach, leaving Dublin just after 19 July. He had
returned by 10 August.

my last letters] see Grey to the Privy Council, No. 17, above (SP 63/84/13), and
Grey to Walsingham, No. 18, above (SP 63/84/14).

praied aide] requested assistance; the first of several legalisms in the letter.

shifte for him self] enter into conflicts and negotiations on his own authority; there
is an implied threat here, as well as an appeal, for O'Donnell well understood that
the Queen and her Deputy had an interest in his allegiance as a counterweight to
the O'Neill.

made hedd into those partes] journeyed (with force) into Ulster.

Sir Nicholas Malbey] Malby, governor of Connaught. Grey had dispatched him to
gather his forces and meet the Lord Deputy at Lifford; he had marched from
Athlone at about the same time that Grey had left Dublin.

Tierconnell . . . Sligo] see maps. Turlough Luineach was known to have crossed the
river Mourne at Strabane, and was, as Grey reported in a letter of the previous
month, killing and spoiling at pleasure in O'Donnell's country west of the river.
Grey's plan was for Malby, having marched north-west from Athlone, to gather up
O'Donnell and his men in Sligo, and to press on with their united force towards
Lifford, where O'Donnell had a castle on his bank—now burned—athwart
O'Neill's fortifications at Strabane—also by this point razed. Grey then planned to
meet Malby and O'Donnell at the ford at Lifford, effectively pinching O'Neill and
forcing him back into Ulster. In the end, Grey only got as far as the English fort on
the Blackwater (near Lough Neagh) before Turlough Luineach intercepted him.

Loughfoill] entering by Lough Foyle in the north (see maps), Grey's ships could get
the victual and munitions up the river as far as Lifford.

Leefer] Lifford; see maps.

the forte vppon the black water] the Blackwater runs north-east from Monaghan
into Lough Neagh; the 'new' fort on the Blackwater, completed by the Earl of
Essex in 1575 and destroyed during the war with Hugh O'Neill in 1595, was
situated a few kilometres north-east of Benburb.

to heere and determine] *oyer et terminer* is an ancient (Law French) legal expression in common law use, and in the sixteenth century part of the common parlance of the gentry and aristocratic classes.

causes] matters or issues in contention.

without lycense] Grey's rhetoric emphasized the nominal authority of the Queen in the affairs between O'Neill and O'Donnell.

the rasing . . . Tierconnell side] it was a usual tactic of Irish lords to raze their own castles upon the approach of an English force; the Irish kern with their Scots galloglass were better suited than the English to mobile warfare, and pressed this advantage by destroying the forts and castles which the English might garrison.

Iustice Dowdall, and Mr Briskett] James Dowdall, Justice of the King's Bench since 1565; and Lodowick Bryskett, clerk to the Irish Council and a friend of Spenser's; see biographies.

Mr. Threasoror] Sir Henry Wallopp; see biographies.

Mr Marshall] Sir Nicholas Bagenal; see biographies.

the riuer devided vs] Turlough Luineach was skittish enough about his safety that he parleyed with Grey across the river.

subscribe to the condicions] when Turlough Luineach and his followers were required formally to give their consent to limitations on their activity or power, they balked.

dignety of the state] Grey's chief objective in confronting Turlough Luineach on the Blackwater, and in succouring O'Donnell, was this attempt to uphold the crown's dignity—both by honouring its obligation to O'Donnell, and asserting its authority over Turlough Luineach.

on bothe sides] i.e. from the west (Malby and O'Donnell) and from the south (Grey).

the proclamacion of generall pardon] for the Queen's extension of a general pardon throughout Ireland, see the promulgation in two drafts, one edited in Burghley's hand: SP 63/82/42 and 63/82/43. The order to proclaim the pardon reached Grey on 26 May (see No. 14, above, SP 63/83/43), but this was his first chance to proclaim it himself among O'Neill's men.

Turloughes wief] Agnes Campbell, daughter of Archibald Campbell, fourth Earl of Argyle; see biographies.

hir maiesties inclinacion] Grey was well aware that Elizabeth's preferred policy in Ireland was a parsimonious conciliation.

the articles . . . Turloughes peticions] it is not clear exactly when Turlough Luineach submitted his petition to the Queen, though Captain Piers wrote in January 1581 of his 'requests' (SP 63/80/13); the Queen's answer, contained in letters of 26 and 30 July that do not survive, was overtaken by Grey's journey to the Blackwater. Grey may well, of course, have received the letters from the Queen before he left, and have chosen to march against Turlough Luineach as if he had not, knowing as he did that the Westminster view would never have been viable.

more liberall . . . perswaded] more generous to Turlough Luineach than Grey would have condoned.

to yeld anny pledges] give any hostages for his good behaviour; Turlough Luineach would have considered this a slight to his honour.

falne from the condicions] broken the provisions of the Queen's offer of peace.

an end . . . from Englande] given him the impression that he could do what he liked, without repercussion or hope of reward from England.

Capten Peirs] William Piers, a long-serving soldier in the north of Ireland; see biographies. He mentioned his plot in a letter to Walsingham in 1580 (SP 63/75/58), and Grey had been considering it for some time (see SP 63/80/10 and 63/80/32).

vse warely his message] be cunning and politic in the revealing of his embassy.

his master] unclear.

the aunswere . . . postilde] our detailed response to his plan for Ulster, which we have set down point by point.

holpen in his particuler] furthered in his private affairs.

Creddyt] access or influence.

suff{ic}yent proof] Grey seems to be alluding to some information gathered on his recent journey, perhaps from Turlough Luineach himself.

thankeworthye] meritorious, and deserving of commendation from the Privy Council.

patched stuffe] temporary dealing, which will not last.

vppon tryall of goddes will] Grey alludes to the ancient legal custom of the ordeal, or trial by battle, where God's will was determined by a sweepstakes hazard of one life against another, in a matter of right.

occonnours] a prominent Irish sept of the south-east.

obirnes] with the Tooles, one of the chief septs of Wicklow.

base brother of . . . of Delvin] Edmund Nugent, base brother to Sir Christopher Nugent, ninth Baron Delvin.

Iohn Zouches] Zouche was the Colonel left as effective governor in Munster after the siege at Smerwick.

Odonnelles sonne] see below.

one Sherif . . . of Limerick] Grey pardoned John Shereff for his fault during his Munster journey in October–November 1581; see No. 23, below (SP 63/86/51).

Lord Fitzmorice two sonnes] Patrick and Edmund Fitzmaurice, sons to Thomas Fitzmaurice, sixteenth Lord of Kerry and Baron of Lixnaw.

fosterfatheres] 'fostering' children in other households was a common practice in sixteenth-century Ireland (and not unknown in England); the foster-relations to which this practice gave rise could prove more important and durable than natural kinship.

Conceipt] idea.

the countrey] Tirconnell.

the captency] the leadership of the country; 'captain' was the usual English translation of *taoiseach*.

his father Culloughe odonnell] Con's father, the Calough, who was Sir Hugh O'Donnell's brother.

in the time of Shane oneyll] Turlough Luineach's predecessor as the O'Neill, who was executed by the MacDonnells (a Scottish clan very active in Ireland) in 1567.

for Sir Warham Seintleger . . . Chief Collonell] the replacement of Zouche by Sentleger was a point of rank; as Grey points out, rank also has its inconveniences—here, the Earl of Ormond's dislike of Sentleger.

the disliking . . . ormond] the fact that the Earl of Ormond disliked him; on Ormond, see biographies.

a comission ... Captens] the Privy Council had instructed Grey to appoint Sentleger by means of a commission—a licence within his power—rather than sending out letters of instruction, with a royal warrant, under the Lord Chancellor's seal. This gave Westminster more flexibility in removing Sentleger from office when the time was right.

some smale addicon of horsemen] a few extra mounted soldiers.

defalked from other bandes] deducted (transferred) from other bands of cavalry.

aunswere ... hir maiesty] to answer the check was to comply with instructions on the employment or discharging of servants in the Queen's pay—including soldiers. Grey's point is that it was a matter of honour for the English captains not to have their bands reduced in favour of another captain.

annalye] the county of Longford in Leinster; see maps.

Cheife baron, and the attorneye] Sir Lucas Dillon (see biographies) and Christopher Fleminge, respectively.

Orwark] Brian O'Rourke, the O'Rourke; see biographies.

no great{t} ... offarrolles] Grey's judgement was prescient; though called very dutiful by Sidney in a 1576 account of the Irish septs (SP 63/55/34), the family would come out in rebellion under the Nugents (see SP 63/104/12).

2. pirates ... 140 shott] unidentified.

the hauen of Beamorice] i.e. Beaumaris; see maps.

the handmaide] the Queen's only regular ship of war in the Irish Sea, under the command of George Thornton.

Sir William Standley] an English captain, then based in Wexford; see biographies.

Artlow] i.e. Arklow, in south-east Wicklow; see maps.

capten Deeringes company] Anthony Deering was stationed with a band of horsemen in Connaught, but had perhaps returned east after the confrontation with Turlough Luineach, at which he had certainly assisted.

Powerscourte] the seat of the Tooles or O'Tooles, near Dublin; see maps.

22. *Grey to the Privy Council, September 1581*
TNA: PRO SP 63/85/34

This letter commends the service of Captain William Russell (see biographies), who had gone to Ireland in 1579, where he had been given command of a band of soldiers who were to help to quell the Baltinglass rebellion and the uprising of Feagh MacHugh O'Byrne. In April 1581, he and Sir William Stanley had achieved success against Feagh MacHugh, in reward for which he was granted the lease of Baltinglass Abbey, Co. Wicklow, and was knighted. The production of such letters of commendation was a regular responsibility of Grey's secretariat: they were most frequently carried to England by their commendees, as a kind of official passport giving them access to the court, as well as support in their courting of favour, reimbursement, or reward. Such letters were as important to Grey as they were to their bearers, for his own credit was bound up in the success of his clients, and it was, conversely, a blow to Grey's fortunes that he actively wrote against one Irish captain—Walter Ralegh—whose star would shortly rise to an unusual zenith (see No. 26, below, SP 63/88/12, and 63/92/10).

The text of this letter, including the subscription, is written in the regular secretary hand of Lodowick Bryskett. The signature is Grey's own. The address is in Spenser's characteristic secretary hand, and the endorsements—presumably added upon the filing of the letter in London—are in later, distinct hands. The first addressee note at the foot of the letter's recto ('{Lord}es of the Counsell') is probably also in Bryskett's hand; a second note (reading, 'To the Lordes for Mr Russell:–') is written along the long edge of the verso of the letter, and may also be in Bryskett's Italian hand, though it could, equally, be a later addition.

ADDRESS AND ENDORSEMENTS

To the right Hono
rable the Lords and
otheres of her Highnes
privie Councell

Lords
{..} September 1581
From the Lord Deputy of
Irland.
on the behalfe of mr
William Russell

TEXT

May it please your honorable Lordships This gentleman the bearer hereof Mr William Russell, retourneth now with my lycense, into England for a tyme; partly for dispatche of certein his pryvate affaires and partly to procure a supplye of his band of horsemen, being greatly decayed aswell by service in the field, as by visitacion with sicknes, throughe the contagiousnes of diseases that have reigned muche here of late: by both which he hath lost many of his companie. And as I am to become a sueter vnto your Lordships for him in that behalf, that it might please you to geve direction for suche a convenient supplie as he shall declare vnto you to be nedefull for the filling vp of his number: So can I not but recommend vnto your honours both his painefull and chargeable travell, and his forwardnes and good endevour allwayes in service since his arryvall here; having ben very often in action against the enemies, and chiefly these mounteine Rebells, and in every of them so well discharged his parte, not onely in respect of the sufficiencie of his band, but also for his owne person, as he hath thereby very well deserved the good, and gracious acceptacion of her Maiestie and your honours. Whereof I thinke it my parte to make reporte. And therefore humbly recommending him and his causes as a gentleman deserving very well for his service vnto your Lordships, I take my leave. From Dublin the   of   1581°

> Your honorable Lordships assured to commaund
> Arthur Grey

COMMENTARY

Mr William Russell] Captain and future Lord Deputy; see biographies.

by visitacion . . . his companie] English companies in the more densely populated east of Ireland were indeed decimated by sickness throughout 1581, a frequent topic of dispatches to England. See Grey's lament of 6 April over the 'generall feruent or rather pestilent ague' (No. 11, above, HH Cecil Papers 11/91); his passing report to Walsingham on 23 March that 'It hathe pleazed God this mornyng too make mee powrar by one boye then beefore I was' (SP 63/81/42) may also have been occasioned by the same sickness. The bands of Cecil and Hoorde had also been almost entirely consumed in 1581 by this plague: see No. 15, above (SP 63/83/45).

chargeable travell] costly labours.

these mounteine Rebells] the forces of Feagh MacHugh O'Byrne in Wicklow, whom Russell (along with William Stanley) had been involved in fighting (see also No. 10, above, SP 63/82/6). In *A view*, Spenser claims that the names of the O'Byrnes and O'Tooles reflect the mountainous country that they inhabited, and where Feagh MacHugh had been based, 'for *Brin* in the Brittons language sig-nifyethe woddye, and Toll hillye' (l. 3639), and speaks of the 'strengthe and greate fastenes' (l. 3664) of Glenmalour and Feagh MacHugh's country.

23. *Grey to the Privy Council, 6 November 1581*

TNA: PRO SP 63/86/51

As after his journey to Wexford in May–June (see No. 15, above, SP 63/83/45), and to Ulster in July and August (see No. 20, above, SP 63/85/5, 63/85/6, and No. 21, above, 63/85/13), Grey here sends a formal report of his journey to Munster, 'to place a setled governement' there. Grey recounts

---

From Dublin . . . 1581] Bryskett apparently left these gaps for the date to be completed later.

his interventions in local affairs and actions against the rebels, and also sets out his plans for garrisons in Munster. Given that this report—with its evidence of Spenser's attendance on Grey—was filed after the journey, from Dublin, it is not clear from this evidence whether Spenser accompanied Grey to Munster or not; but the fact that no documents in Spenser's hand survive from the period 12 September to 6 November suggests that he may have. Certainly Grey's reflections here on the decayed state of many of the garrison towns in Leinster and Munster, with his careful reasonings on strategy and supply routes, bespeaks the same experience of the service that informed Spenser's recommendations for the army in *A view of the present state of Ireland* (see especially ll. 4101–286); and it is probable that Spenser's judgements on these matters was informed by such journeys. Grey's record of the military engagements and judicial interventions of this expedition, too—especially his arbitration between the Baron of Upper Ossory, the Earl of Ormond, and Viscount Mountgarrett over their respective borders, and his dealings with the Earl of Clanricard's sons—provides a fascinating context for reading the allegory of justice (e.g. the arbitration between the sons of Milesio, or the reconstitution of Radegone) in Book V of *The Faerie Queene*.

The letter is written in a small, compact secretary hand (not Spenser's). This hand occasionally uses terminal 'e' followed by 'es' brevigraph, which we have throughout recorded simply as '-es'. The subscription and signature are Grey's, while the address is in Spenser's characteristic secretary hand. There is extensive underscoring, and annotation in the left-hand margins; this annotation is in at least two distinct hands, the latter of which is probably that of William Cecil, Lord Burghley (accounting for three of the marginal notes: 'a cedule/', 'Decayes of Maryborogh Dongaruon Phillipstown', and the final annotation, 'vᴗ vᴗ vᴗ').

ADDRESS AND ENDORSEMENTS

To the right Honorable
my very good Lords and
otheres of her Maiesties most
Honorable privie Councell./

Lords
6 Nouember 1581
From the Lord Deputye.

Entred.

TEXT

After the receipt of soche letters, as came from your Lordships in September last, aboute the setling of a gouernement in Mounster, whiche you then wisshed to be comytted to the cariage of Sir Warham Seintleger, I was advertised of his passage into Englande, whereby I founde the necessitye of mine owne repaire into Mounster, And therefore according my former advertisementes, I prepared for yt, And set forewarde from hence with some companies of horssemen and footemen, the xvij^th of the same monethe. The chardg of the pale in myne absence I lefte generally, to the Lord Chauncellour, and counsell, But specially the martiall causes I comytted to Sir Henry Wallopp, and perticulerly Sir Lucas Dillon to haue the care of Meathe, and Westmeathe, and did settle garrisons, aswell vppon the otooles, and Cavenaughes, as vppon the omoores, and occonnoures, Whereof I haue formerly enformed your Lordships: Having thus left the state heere, I founde yt requisyt to take my iourney throughe the Queenes countie, and vpperossery, because vppon the deathe of the late baron, I founde some apparaunce of disorders in those partes{.} The now baron repaired vnto me besides Mariboroughe, and attended me throughe his owne, Countreye, to the countie of Kilkenny, where vppon the meting withe therle of ormounde, and the vicounte Mountgarrett, I made a finall end betweene them, for the infinyte challenges, and contencions, that haue bene, betweene vpperosserye and Kilkenny for thes twenty yeares past. Neuerthe-lesse I finde that for the preservacion of theire quyet heereafter, yt is necessary that vpperossery be lymitted to be sheire grounde, whiche therle, and the vicount desire may be annexed to Kilkenny, The Baron desirous to haue yt of the Queenes countie, The lymitacion whereof, I deferred till I might haue thadvise of the counsell heere:/ At my being in those partes, peticon was made, in the behalf of Iames Meaghe, now called Iames mac Kedaughe omoore, that he might be receaued to pardon, or proteccion, or at lest dispensed withall, till he might do some service wourthie that grace, And for the good behauiour of him self, and those dependauntes vppon him° he would put in pledges, and deale dewtifully as he should be directed, by enny assigned from me, vppon which offerrs knowing hir maiesties dis-potition to Clemencye, I appoincted him to repaire vnto me to Water-ford, To which place he came (according my direccion) and made, an

The generall°
charge of the Pale
in his absence
admitted to the
Lord Chancellor
and Councellor.
{T}he direction
of martial causes
to Sir Henry
Wallop.

hath
compounded the
difference
between the Earl
of Ormond lord
of vpperossery.

necessary that
vpperossery
should be made
shire ground.

Protection
granted to Iames
Meaghe.

Marginal note **generall**] this contracted word inserted above the line.   *after* **vppon him**] 'he' deleted.

humble submission, acknowleging him self to be one, of the Cheif Instrumentes, in thes sturres about the vicount Baltinglas, whome he Long served before the rebellion, but when I entered into the errour of his adoption, to be an omore, wisshing him to renounce the same, and to be accompted Iames Meaghe as he had bene all his Lief, till this yeare past, I found, that the liberty of his loose lief, had setled him in that follye, as he would not acknowledg his owne name, But imputed this exchaung to the ordinaunce god° & laied the synne of his birthe vppon his parentes, neyther did I finde him willing, to redeame his faultes, with enny action thankewourthie from the state, In thende I referred him vppon my letter to Humfrey mac Worthe, who tooke pledges vppon him: Since which time I heere not, but that he hathe contayned him self, within soche bandes, as the Capten

Iames meagh sent for by the° councell for conferement Thomas Meagh in the Towre.

hathe assigned, and is now vppon the councelles Letter, repaired hether for conferrence with mr Secretary Fenton, touching Thomas Meaghe, prisoner in the Tower./ From Waterford I marched to Dongarvan, Lismore, Youghall, and Cork, searching all the woodes, and strengthes, about Dromfinen, and Imokellye, but founde not enny to resist, the rebelles being then scattered in smale companies into remote partes: At my coming to Cork, I setled my campe in Barries countrey for vij dayes, ordering the bandes euery day° to marche abroade, and to visit all the Countrey, betweene Mallow, Youghall, and Cork, where they did some execucion, but to more purpose distroyed the provision which the rebelles had hidden in woodes, and secreate places, whereby the greatest parte of theire releif is taken from them: In the meane season I caused publique proclamacion to be made, that all protectees, and suche as had taken the benefyt of hir maiesties pardon, should resorte vnto me to Cork, at a day appoincted: The bookes delyuered me by Iustice Meaghe, conteyned

500 persons protected by the last pardon not 60 resorted to him vppon proclamacion.

the names of v^C persons, or therabout, but after longe stay cheifly for that purpose there appeared not lx. of the whole number, And those for the most parte, olde men, and freeholders. The yonger, and looser sorte appeared not, but vehement presumption, that they weare revolted, or stood in very doubtfull termes, for they, and theire sewerties, were bothe absent, Neuertheles to make farther tryall of theire entencon I referred them by a secounde proclamacion, to an other day of apparunce, at the cessions in Cork, And till I be enfourmed thereof, I will not absolutelie iudge of the men, But in all apparaunce,

---

ordinaunce god] it seems likely that the word 'of' has been omitted before 'god' here.   *Marginal note after* by the] single-letter deletion.   day] inserted above the line.

I see no likelihoode of good effectes to follow of theire receaving to pardon, when they put in none other assuraunce, but one Kerne to be bounde for an other, which Iustice Meaghe affirmethe is all, that could be gotten, For as they had no pledges to put in so was there no honest, or aunswerable man, that (as he saide) would be bound for a rebbell:/ In my stay about Cork I visited Kinsale, tooke order in all pryvate contrauersies, and setled the countrey of Carbery to beare still the <u>wages of Capten Apsley, and one hundrethe footemen</u>, notwithstanding that I withdrew him to other place of garrison neerer the service: And by Example of Carbery, hope may be conceaved (as soone as eny quyet growethe) to deall with other partes of Mounster, to beare, Convenyent numbers at theire owne Chardges: Lastely at my being there, when Sir George Bourchier, and the rest of the Captens in Mounster weare repaired vnto me, I <u>proponed to them in Consultacon three</u> thinges, whereof I required theire opinions: <u>First what kind of warre might</u> soonest ouerthrow the rebellion, ether continuall Iourneyes of the gouernour, or garrison warre: if garrison warre, what places, and whate numbers weare fyttest for those garrisons, And lastely emonges suche equalitie of Captens, what person, they would most willingly obaye: To the first they concluded vppon garrison warre as indeade in all probability, there is none other way to bring the rebellion to a shorte issue;. To the secounde they aggreed, that those garrisons should be planted at <u>Glanmire</u> neere Cork, at Mallow vppon the passage of the broade water, And at Lismore vppon the same ryver, neere the woodes of Lisfinnen: At Kilmallock and Asketyn in the County of Lymerick, and at Ardert, Dingle, and castle Mange in the county of Kirrye. <u>Thirdely</u> they made eleccon of Iohn Zowche, to be theire cheif Colonell: Theire reasons being herde for euery poinct, I allowed of theire opinions bothe for the manner of the warre, the places of theire residence, and the person of the Cheif collonell, And vniting the Lord Roche, Sir Cormack mac Teige, Sir Donoughe mac Cartye, Sir Thomas of Desmound, and Maurice Roche, to theire asistaunce, espetially for conveyaunce of theire victualles,° I concluded vppon suche numbers in euery garrison, with the captens advises, as ys sett <u>downe in a callender or schedule</u> heere vnto annexed. Neuertheles the wante of victualls was suche, at my being in those partes, as I could not presently, plante those garrisons at Glanmire, and Mallow, But ordered them to remeyne in Cork, and Kilmallock, and from thence to make theire roades and Iourneyes, till

Carbery appointed to beare the Charges of Capten Apsley and 100 footmen

aduise taken with the Capteyns for the seruice in Monster.

1

2

3
Mr Zouche elected corronel of Monster by the Captens

a cedule/

---

of theire victualles] inserted above the line.

the victualles weare aryved, and from thenceforthe to setle them-selues in the places before named./ This done I repaired towerdes the county of Lymerick, visiting Kilmallock, and Asketyn, and ordering my iourneies as I thought might be most convenyent, for the annoyeng of the Traytors, but founde <u>no resistaunce eny</u> where Neuertheles while I was thus employed in the countie of Cork, I was enfourmed (3. dayes after thacte done,) that the traytoures attempting to take a pray <u>from Casshell</u>, weare followed by the Inhabitauntes at the allurement of the archbisshop, and that the Townsemen being nether of corage, or conduicte, weare ouerthrowne, and slaine to the number of Lx: I offred the towne ayde, but that they refused, because they coulde geve no releif towerdes the victeling of the Soldioures, nether to the cariage of the victelles from Waterford or other places, And therefore I ordered the Townes of Fiderte, and Clommell to lende them some competente number of men who with victels of theire owne might remayne for theire assistaunce till other order might be taken: In Lymerick I made some stay, aswell to holde Sessions, as for geving suche necessary aucthorities, and Instruccions to the Colonell, as was conuenyente for the gouernemente: In whiche Sessions some weare arreygned, and executed, namely a notable rebell, nephew to the Bis<u>shop of Limerick</u>, and foster brother to therle of Desmounde, vppon the Bisshoppes accusacion, who likewise

The bishop of
Limerick accused
to be confederate
with the rebels Charged the Bisshop to haue councelled him, and his father to enter into rebellion with desmound, thereby to preserve the proffittes of his Bisshoprick, whiche the Bisshop did not aunswere, because he was visited then with greate infirmyties, an other being a merchaunte of that cyttie, that had yelded releif to the Traytours, A thirde one Warren, that being a victualler in pay, had imbasiled the victualles,

The
viceconstable
fyned for the
escape of Patrick
Fitzmorice and greately abused him self in his Charge: And lastly I caused <u>Iohn Shrief the viceconstable</u> to bee areigned for thescape of Patrick Fitzmorice, and other pledges, but being found not giltye, he was neuertheles put to his fine:/

sendeth for
the Erle of
Clanreckards
sonnes. <u>This done I departed</u> towerdes Galleway, sending Letters to therle of Clanricardes sonnes to repaire vnto me, in my passage throughe Clanricard, allowing the benefyt of theire proteccion, and willing to heere at theire handes suche complayntes as they had against enny person, Cheif officer, or other, within the province, And to know the cause, whie they refused the benefitt of theire pardon, They

their aunsweare. aunswered dilatorily, as thoughe theire weare maniye circumstaunces to be vsed, before they woulde accepte theire pardon, adding that if I would preferre theire sewte to hir maiesty, they woulde acquayncte me with the perticulers, And in the meane season, they desired that they might not appeare before me, I willed them to sende me theire peticions, And if they weare not dishonourable for hir maiesty or inconvenyente for the state, I would not refuse to deall for them, But hetherto, I haue not heard of theire aunswere to that poinct, only this I note in them, That they are men insolente, and full of malice to the state, and moste inconstaunte, and vnfaythfull of theire promisses. And to expresse theire dispotitions to continew thes trobles, they offred violence to a Soldior of my companye, whome they Chaced, and hurte, not farre from the way as I marched: The rest of Connought is quyet, saving that orwarke entertainenethe Scottes, and makethe shew of Assistaunce of <u>William Nugente</u> in soche incursions as he makethe vppon the Countye of Longeford: This is the Substaunce of my late Travell, whereof the purpose was, to place a setled gouernement in Mounster.

It restethe, that I note thus muche to your Lordships that in my iourney by Mariboroughe and Dongarvan, I finde those houses in very greate Ruin, (as Phillipstowne also is,) And hardly defensable by the ordinarie garde of the places, And For as muche as they are of importaunce for the Comaundinge of the countreies about them, I do remember your Lordships to be meanes to hir maiestye, for convenyent reparacions, to be spedely bestowed vppon those three, whiche I suppose cannot be lesse in eache place then v^C li sterling: And so being hastened homeward, aswell by the loose dealing <u>of oreighly</u>, in restoring Shane oneylles sonne to Turloughe Lennoughe, contrary to my expresse comaundement, and his owne faythfull promisse, as by the Causes of the late conspiracy heere in the pale, wherein the most of thenglishe families heere wilbe apparauntly touched, I cease and referre all other matters to the generall letter: At Dublyn this vj^{th} of November. <u>1581</u>

Decayes of
Maryborogh
Dongaruon
Phillipstown

v C
v C
v C

Yowr Lordships most assured
too Commaunde,

Arthur Grey

COMMENTARY

letters . . . Seintleger] after the Earl of Ormond's dismissal as Lord General of Munster, Sir Warham Sentleger was appointed Chief Colonel of the Province. Grey wrote on 12 August to approve of the choice, but to argue that it should be only a temporary appointment: 'I do not wisshe, that yt should haue long Continuance, because his aucthoritye there must needes be accompanied withe the disliking of therle of ormond, betweene whome there hathe bene some Contrauersies in my tyme' (Grey to the Privy Council, 12 August 1581, No. 21, above, SP 63/85/13). He also took the opportunity to commend John Zouche's service (suggesting that he was trying to promote Zouche in this position): 'I am very glad in the behalf of the gentleman, that hir maiesty and your Lordships do so well conceaue of Mr Zouche, which opinion may be bettered, by a secound service, done since, wherein he hathe had very good Successe.' Sentleger, meanwhile, had been recalled to England, presumably in order that he might be personally instructed (or micro-managed) by the Queen and her councillors there; the Privy Council wrote to Grey on 24 August, informing him that Sentleger was 'nowe repaired hether (as we suppose without your Lordships knowledge' (SP 63/85/25). Ormond, meanwhile, was petitioning Burghley to be reinstated (see SP 63/86/3 and 63/86/3/1; and No. 15, above, 63/83/45).

cariage] management, carrying out.

his passage into Englande] in August 1581 (SP 63/85/25 and 63/85/26).

my former advertisementes] such advertisements do not seem to have survived.

Lord Chauncellour] after the death of William Gerrarde earlier in 1581, this position had passed to Adam Loftus; see biographies.

Meathe, and Westmeathe] these counties may have been especially strategically important for the defence of the Pale, standing between Dublin and Ulster.

otooles . . . occonnoures] Irish septs against whom Grey had previously gone on campaign. See No. 15, above (SP 63/83/45), one of the places where I haue formerly enfourmed your Lordships, and which describes the planting of garrisons in Meath and elsewhere.

my iourney] Grey journeyed in a south-westerly direction through the Queen's County (Leix) towards Upper Ossory and Kilkenny; see maps.

vppon . . . baron] Barnaby Fitzpatrick, Baron of Upper Ossory, had died in September 1581.

The now baron] Fitzpatrick was succeeded by his brother, Florence Fitzpatrick.

therle of ormounde . . . vicounte Mountgarrett] Thomas and Edmund Butler.

a finall end] a conclusive agreement.

lymitted to be sheire grounde] i.e. no longer a 'liberty', enjoying a privileged exemption from common law governance. The question of whether Upper Ossory should be shired had gone on for some time; see for example SP 63/75/37 (Waterhouse to Walsingham, 13 August 1580).

lymitacion] determining of the geographical boundaries.

Iames Meaghe . . . omoore] Grey's attention to Meagh's Irish style is deliberate: as he goes on to explain, he asks Meagh to rescind his claim to the O'More lordship.

dispensed withall] granted dispensation.

thes sturres . . . vicount Baltinglas] i.e. the rebellion of James Eustace, Viscount Baltinglass, which had occupied the English administration throughout 1581 (see, for example, No. 7, above, SP 63/81/1, on the committal of the Earl of Kildare). Meagh's confession, dated 17 November, was sent to England in a letter from Fenton to the Earl of Leicester, calling for urgency in the prosecution of Kildare (SP 63/87/48 and 63/87/48/2).

imputed this . . . ordinaunce god] claimed that his adoption of this title was by God's order.

referred him . . . mac Worthe] handed him over to the custody of Captain Humphrey Macworth (see biographies).

contayned him . . . soche bandes] abided by such restrictions.

Thomas Meaghe] James Meagh's brother, suspected of involvement with Kildare in the Baltinglass rebellion, and imprisoned in the Tower of London since March 1581. See No. 37, below, SP 63/93/64).

From Waterford . . . Cork] Grey's journey, through Waterford, Dungarvan, Lismore, Youghal, and Cork, took him westwards along the south coast of Ireland.

Barries countrey] The lands of David Fitzjames Barry, Viscount Barrymore, around Buttevant (north of Cork).

Mallow, Youghall, and Cork] Mallow lies approximately 30 km north of Cork and Youghal approximately 50 km east; see maps.

they did some execucion] *OED* suggests that the more modern meaning of the word, 'destructive effect, infliction of damage or slaughter', came into being in the late 1580s ('Execution', *n.*, 5); it may have that sense here, or merely mean that the soldiers carried out Grey's plan.

distroyed the provision . . . from them] reminiscent of the now notorious description in *A view* of the allegedly strategic starvation of the Munster rebels during the Desmond rebellion: 'yeat thus beinge kepte from manuraunce and theire Cattle from Comminge abroade by this harde restrainte they woulde quicklye Consume themselues and devour one another The profe wheareof I sawe sufficientlye ensampled in Those late warrs of mounster, for notwithstandinge that the same was a moste ritche and plentifull Countrye full of Corne and Cattell that ye woulde haue thoughte they Coulde haue bene able to stande longe yeat ere one yeare and a haulfe they weare broughte to soe wonderfull wretchednes as that anie stone harte would haue rewed the same' (ll. 3248–70).

protectees] those who had accepted the protection of the English government (*OED* gives the first recorded instance of this word as 1602).

Iustice Meaghe] John Myagh, Attorney General, Second Justice, and Commisioner of Munster. These **bookes**, apparently containing the names of approximately 500 protectees of Cork, have not survived.

freeholders] settled yeomen or gentlemen, with estates in land.

but vehement presumption] although the meaning is clear here (that the failure of these men to appear led to a strong presumption that they were in revolt), the syntax seems odd, and suggests a copying error.

sewerties] sureties.

the cessions in Corke] the sessions were seasonal sittings of the county courts (here, of Cork), led by magistrates authorized by commission from the Queen or her Deputy. For a discussion of the rise of commissions for local justice in the late medieval period, see Baker, *Introduction*, 24–6.

but one . . . for another] i.e. one rebellious Irish soldier entered as a guarantee of another's good behaviour.

Kinsale] approximately 25 km south-west of Cork (see maps): Grey continued his journey in a westerly direction.

tooke order . . . contrauersies] adjudicated in private quarrels.

setled . . . Apsley] Apsley was to take charge of 100 footmen at Glanmire (see the note below). See also a letter from Sir George Bourchier to Wallop of 9 September, describing Apsley's warrant (SP 63/86/14/2).

hope . . . Mounster] there is hope that the peace which Apsley's troops have brought to Carbery will provide a model for dealing with the rest of Munster.

George Bourchier] along with John Zouche (see below), one of the two colonels in Munster.

garrison warre] this is not the only place where Grey advocates the planting of garrisons in Munster: see No. 6, above (BL Add. MS 33924). Irenius also promotes this method of war in *A view*.

Lord Roche . . . Maurice Roche] The Roches (a prominent Munster family, with which Spenser himself would come into conflict over land), Cormac MacTeig MacCarthy, formerly Sheriff of Cork, Sir Donogh MacCarthy, MacCarthy Reagh, and Thomas Fitzgerald were prominent Munster lords, on whose assistance Grey depended.

a callender . . . vnto annexed] SP 63/86/51/1, a note on the 'Garrisons now placed in Mounster'. The numbers of soldiers are as follows. In Co. Cork: at Glanmire, 100 footmen under Apsley, 100 footmen under Rawley, and 24 horsemen; at Mallow, 100 footmen under Dowdall, and 100 footmen under Peirs (with a note that 'Sir Cormack and Maurice Roche to asist them with horse'). In Co. Waterford: at Lismore, 150 footmen under Morgan, 50 to defend Youghall, and 50 horsemen. In Co. Limerick: at Killmallock, 200 footmen under Bourchier, and 25 [horsemen?] under the provost marshall; at Askeaton, 200 footmen under Barkeley, and 12 horsemen. In Co. Kerry: at Ardert, 300 footmen under Zouche, 50 horsemen under Acham; at Dingle and Castlemaine, 100 footmen under Case 'to gard the fortificacion there'. In total, 1,400 footmen and 161 horsemen were placed in the garrisons.

make . . . Iourneyes] make expeditions against the rebels.

This done . . . Asketyn] Grey headed northwards, into County Limerick.

Casshell] in Tipperary, east of Kilmallock; see maps.

at the allurement of the archbisshop] encouraged by Meyler (or Miler) Magrath, Archbishop of Cashel.

conduicte] conduct, military skill.

Fiderte] probably Fethard (*Fiodh Ard*), 15 km east of Cashel. **Clommell** (Clonmel) is approximately 25 km south-south-east of Cashel; see maps.

competente] sufficient.

the Colonell] probably John Zouche, Chief Colonel.

a victualler in pay] in English pay as a victualler.

imbasiled] embezzled.

Iohn Shrief] John Shereff would continue as Viceconstable of Limerick. In November 1583, though, Sir Henry Wallop was still accusing him of aiding Fitzmaurice's escape, which, he said, had cost Elizabeth £20,000 (SP 63/105/79). Further accusations of financial corruption were made in 1584 (see SP 63/107/75).

Fitzmorice] Patrick Fitzmaurice and his brother Edmund had escaped from Limerick Castle in August (see SP 63/85/9 and 63/85/14), where they were being held as pledges for the dutiful behaviour of their father Thomas Fitzmaurice, Baron of Lixnaw and Lord of Kerry. Immediately upon their escape (at which their father had certainly connived), the Lord of Kerry abandoned his pretence of support for Zouche and came out in open rebellion with Desmond. Patrick fled to Spain, but returned to Ireland and was recaptured in 1587; he was released in 1591, upon the death of his father, assuming the title of Lord of Kerry.

put to his fine] fined (*OED*, 'Fine', *n*.^{1}, 8c).

therle of Clanricardes sonnes] the brothers Burke, Ulick and John, intermittently in rebellion and under the protection of Nicholas Malby and the English administration in Connaught. See, for example, No. 9, above (SP 63/81/39), and No. 39, below (63/94/15). A third son, William, Malby had been executed in July (see SP 63/84/6).

Cheif officer] not a specific position; rather, any ranking member of the civil or military administration.

dilatorily] delayingly.

as thoughe . . . be vsed] as though there were many circumstances to be considered.

preferre theire sewte] advance, or promote, their causes.

they offred . . . my companye] this incident does not seem to be recorded elsewhere.

orwarke entertainethe Scottes] on O'Rourke and his Scots, see No. 15, above (SP 63/83/45).

houses in very greate Ruin] in No. 25, below (SP 63/88/2), Grey speaks again of the ruinous state of Maryborough and Philipstown, a consequence (he claims) of the financial burdens placed upon them by the soldiers garrisonned there.

they are of importaunce . . . about them] on Spenser's own ideas about the military and civil importance of these stronghold towns, see Woolway Grenfell, 'Significant Spaces'.

24. *Grey to Walsingham, 6 November 1581*

TNA: PRO SP 63/86/53

This letter, a standard report on affairs public and private, has a couple of distinctive features. Grey places the conduct of Irish affairs within the wider framework of European politics: Walsingham's embassy to the Duke of Anjou and to Henri III had been designed to secure Henri's support for his brother's Netherlands campaign against the Spanish there—but at the perilous price (in Grey's eyes) of the Queen's marriage. Walsingham certainly saw a close connection between Spanish aggression in the Low Countries and the possibility (even, the recent reality) of Spanish invasion of Ireland, and French power in Scotland—perceived to be a staging post for a Catholic campaign for Ireland—was a constant threat in these years before the execution of Mary Queen of Scots (widow of François II). It is in this letter, too, that Grey reveals the naivety with which he was manipulated by the cousins Lucas and Robert Dillon, who used the Nugent rebellion in 1581, and the opportunity it afforded to denounce and eject Nicholas Nugent, Chief Justice of the Common Pleas (Ireland), to consolidate their hold on the Irish judiciary (see No. 33, below, SP 63/91/22). Finally, the personal appeal of the final section of the letter, in which Grey challenges Walsingham to fulfil the promises of support staked on their friendship, underscores the degree to which so much of the high politics of this period (like the Dillon–Nugent farce) was based on personal relationships.

The letter is written in Grey's characteristic cursive italic hand, and both subscribed and signed by Grey. The address is written in Spenser's characteristic secretary hand, and the later endorsement in a distinct italic. An addressee note in Grey's hand (reading 'Mr Secretary') appears on the verso of the letter, adjacent to the address and, ultimately, the endorsement.

ADDRESS AND ENDORSEMENT

To the right honorable
my especiall good frend
Sir Fraunces Walsingham
{Knig}ht Chief Secretary
{to} her Maiesty./

6 Nouember 1581
From the lord Deputye.

TEXT

Sir, God bee thancked for yowr saffe returne, truly it was now° more dowghted & sorrowed by yowr freendes heere then in any Ioorney that euer yow made. I perceaue by yowr letters the good lyking that owre auditors booke browght yee there for owre husbandrie heere; well, as for the dowghtes & fawltes therin fownde I wyll referr too the awnsswer of the memorialls which shall not bee long too & then I dowght not but the labour there shall sheowe a greater buzines too fynde faultes, then good iudgement too collect iust matter: In the meane tyme yet, my Lord of Leaster hauyng by this priuat° letters vowtechesaued too gather the chieff poyntes of that bookes dislykes, I could not but particularly seeke too awnsswer & satisfie hym therin which yowrsellf too bee acquaynted with I haue dezyred; yow twoo beeyng they that I chiefflie requyre too bee healld in good opinion with & that I onely wyll seeke patronage of in all good & honest

_____

was now] 'neuer' deleted *after* was, and 'now' inserted above the line.   priuat] inserted above the line.

causies. Yowr reazoons for not impugnyng the cassing of forcies heere, yowr place wayed, I can not but greatly allowe; yet dutie of my place tyed mee, I tooke it, in consscience too delyuer° the thowght & in manner sight of the peryll therof beefore I executed that direction, not vzing yet any perswasion too the contrarie: By the letters therfore of this packett too my Lords there, & too her Maiesties sellf, the Copie wherof heerencloazed° I send (crauyng the same to bee emparted to 30°.) yow shall vnderstande the estate & courss of thynges heere,° with the purpose & effect of my late ioorney intoo Munster.

Yow wryte of a matche toowardes beetwyxt 79° & scot° if it so fall owte lett 60° looke alyttle better too° her° seate in° 70° or ells shee° maye hap too lyze the saddle.

Towttchyng 80° I knowe not what too saye butt euerie waye eyther in league or allyance° I see so iust feare of peryll as, Deus auertat, I doo onely praye.

Wee arre heere now entryng into tryall of sutche of owre pryzoners heere as wee fynde too haue moast matter agaynst, wheruntoo,° beesydes cause of iustice,° & example wee arre the rather stirred by the gallantrie of the fauourares of thiese rebellius sturres, whow murmur° & haue caused too bee guyuen owte that her Maiestie hathe guyuen direction noanc of them too bee tootched for feare of making new sturres & encreazing warre which shee wyll no lenger prosecute, yet heerof woold I saye nothyng too my Lords nor her Maiestie, least it woold haue been taken a perswazion in mee too hoald on chardgies & allter theyr prezent purposies: Neuertheless if lawe cast them heere I wyll God wyll make small staye in guyuyng them theyr dezerts for yowr aduycies thence. I praye yow, sir, lett Sir Lucas Dillon & owre chieff Iustice Dillon bee commended earnestly by yow too her Maiestie; theyr seruice certaynely greatly dezerues it boathe in

---

after **delyuer**] single-letter deletion, possibly 's'.   **heerencloazed**] an oblique pointer in the left margin draws attention to this underscored word.   30] the Earl of Leicester. *after* **thynges heere**] '&' deleted.   79] unknown cipher.   **scot**] in cipher, transliterated above the line.   60] the Queen (as indicated in a note inserted above the line, probably by Walsingham).   *after* **better too**] 'stat' deleted.   **her**] inserted above the line, in cipher, transliterated above the insertion.   **in**] in cipher.   70] Ireland.   **shee**] in cipher, transliterated above the line.   80] possibly Henri III of France.   **league or allyance**] in cipher, partially transliterated above the line.   *after* **whereuntoo,**] 'wee' deleted.   *after* **iustice,**] 'wee arr' deleted.   **whow murmur**] 'haue caus' deleted *after* **whow**, and 'murmur' inserted above the line.

discoouerie of the practizies & apprehending the parties withowte sparyng any how euer neere them in frendshyp, kinred or alliance too theyr owane greate hatred & hazard, procure them therfore sum toaken from her hyghnes that shee knowes it & acceptes of it./

Now Sir for myne owane pryuate, first & chieffliest I commend vnto yow my callyng hoame which beesydes the that yowrsellf° most truly & freendly haue conceaued, waye I beeseetche yow the indisposition of bodie that is coommen on mee by the stoane wherewith I haue been extreemely handled & fynde mysellf greatly subiect vnto it, good sir press therfore this my sute, for thowghe all oother thynges were awnsswerable, my bodie not seruyng I can by no meanes dischardge the place. The next is that yow wyll procure mee a sufficient warrant for my due entertaynement that I maye knowe my estate which since my coomyng yet by want therof I coulld not doo: my Coouenant was this, my dyatt according to the new establisshement, 50. horss. & 100. footmen in paye; and guyue mee all this & wyll I bee, I feare a thowsande pownde loozer: I haue noane to appeale to but yowrsellf; my hastie dispatche yow knowe, & pardon mee to challendge yowr promis, that for all my wrytinges & warrantes I shulld leaue the care to yow; haue consideration of mee I praye yow,° healp mee onely too my due, I wyll God wyllyng,° neuer trooble her Maiestie with any oother sute of benefitt: Lastly Sir I am too acknowledge & render infinite thanckes for yowr greate care & trauayle in° prouyding so well for my niece, god make her lykewyze too her dutie myndefull of this fatherly parte as I trust hee wyll: I haue ij or iij hundrethe powndes of the chylldernes porcioon mooney in my handes, if at this tyme it bee too bee requyred guyue mee knowledge,° I praye yow, &° within one hallf yeare it shall bee readie: I woold bee glad allso too knowe the daye of the mariadge, but gladder° of the newes that I myght bee at it: And thus with my hartyest prayer too the allmyghtie euer too keepe, direct & bless yow in all thynges I take leaue & looue yow deerely. Dublin the vjth of Nouember 1581.

Yowrs most assuredly,

Arthur Grey

---

off *after* **yowrsellf**] '&' deleted.   *after* **praye yow,**] '&' deleted.   *after* **wyllyng,**] 'tr' deleted.   *after* **trauayle in**] 'procu' deleted.   *after* **knowledge,**] '&' deleted.   *after* **yow, &**] 'vp' deleted.   *after* **gladder**] 'y'' deleted.

COMMENTARY

yowr saffe returne] Walsingham was in France between 22 July and 21 September, negotiating with Henri III over the French match, and support for the Duke of Anjou in his campaign against the Spanish in the Netherlands.

owre auditors booke] this may refer to Auditor Jenyson's book of charges for Ireland submitted on 31 March 1581 (SP 63/81/52), though Jenyson was apparently preparing a major statement of accounts closer to this date (see SP 63/83/19, 63/84/39, 63/84/26), which has apparently been lost; see also SP 63/85/68, a summary estimate of the charge for Ireland brought through to September 1581, and 63/85/69, an estimate of Her Majesty's debts in Ireland. On 1 October the Privy Council sent Grey and the Irish Council a memorial to be answered on the Irish charge, a minute and draft of which survive (see SP 63/86/22 and 63/86/22/1); Grey, prepared by Leicester, was ready with a reply as early as 30 September, but it was not formally submitted until 11 December (see SP 63/87/38, with enclosures). In any case, Grey's note of the 'good lyking' that Jenyson's report had found in Westminster is playfully sarcastic: the Queen and Privy Council (and particularly Burghley) were growing intemperately frustrated with the level of expenditure in Ireland.

husbandrie] economy.

awnsswer of the memorialls] sent on 11 December 1581 (see note, above).

yow twoo ... honest causies] an unusually explicit expression of Grey's dependence upon Walsingham's patronage in having his causes pressed upon the Privy Council. It is less usual to see, as here, an acknowledgement of his dependence upon Leicester.

cassing of forcies] disbanding of soldiers.

the Copie wherof heerencloazed I send] see the enclosure to the present letter (SP 63/86/53/1), Grey's copy of his letter to Elizabeth of the same day (SP 63/86/50).

matche ... scot] if '79' is a cipher for Mary Queen of Scots, this obscure comment could possibly refer to her scheme for the 'association', or the joint rule (with her son James, 'Scot') that she proposed for Scotland after October 1581.

lyze the saddle] lose her saddle, be thrown from her horse; that is, lose her position.

Deus auertat] 'may God prevent it' (Lat.).

the gallantrie ... rebellius sturres] there is probably a large degree of sarcasm here, but Grey may also mean that the rebels' bravado, encouraged by their belief that they will not be prosecuted, leaves him all the more determined to see justice upheld.

her Maiestie ... lenger prosecute] as ever, Grey is keen to draw attention to the supposed ill effects of the general pardon he had opposed. Grey's implication is that the Queen has emboldened the traitors to think themselves safe, because she has clearly opted, in the general pardon, for a conciliatory approach.

if lawe cast them heere] another equestrian metaphor: 'if we should manage to make any charges stick'.

owre chieff Iustice Dillon] Sir Robert Dillon, Chief Justice of the Common Pleas (Ireland) since June 1581; see biographies.

in discoouerie ... withowte sparyng any] Grey's comment on Dillon's readiness to act dutifully against his own 'frendshyp' is ironic; it is clear from the historical record that Dillon manipulated Grey's credulity to have his old rival, Chief Justice

Nicholas Nugent, accused of treason and executed so that he could have Nugent's office.

myne owane pryuate] my private affairs.

my callyng hoame] another of Grey's characteristic demands for revocation.

thowghe . . . awnsswerable] even if in other ways I were fit for this post, and it fit for me.

sufficient warrant . . . due entertaynement] Grey seeks Walsingham's support for crown reimbursement of private funds spent during his tenure of the Lord Deputyship.

my dyatt . . . new establisshement] Grey's allowance from the Privy Council was set in the summer of 1580 at a newly agreed rate, more accurately reflecting the expenses of the post. A **dyatt**, or diet, is an allowance for expenses (*OED*, 'Diet', *n.*[1], 6).

in prouyding . . . my niece] Grey is probably referring to the daughter of his sister, Honora, who had married Henry Denny, son and heir of Sir Anthony Denny. Whatever marriage negotiations to which Walsingham had been contributing later fell through (see SP 63/88/10).

chylldernes porcioon mooney] as head of his family, Grey was expected to contribute to the dowry of his sister's children.

25. *Grey to the Privy Council, 3 January 1581/2*
TNA: PRO SP 63/88/2

This letter conveys Grey's growing sense of financial desperation in the wake of the general discharge. It is likely that he had recently received two letters from England dated 29 October 1581 (of which the drafts only now survive): one from the Queen, informing him that the 'debtes and expenses sent from our Auditor of that realme [. . .] are growen farre greater then we looked for', and that in her view 'the seruice don there doth no way Countervayle or aunsweare the charges' (SP 63/86/43). The other letter (63/86/42) came from the Privy Council, who had written that 'wee haue most ernestlie entreated her maiestie that a newe supplie of treisure might be sent ouer'. Elizabeth had granted a warrant for £20,000, they write, but under strict conditions: 'her Maiesties expresse Commaundment is that of the said some of xx^m li xv^m li therof be onelie and none otherwise imployed but in and towardes the full paie and discharge of so manie Bandes of footemen and horsemen and of such pentioners and other ministers as according to our former lettres your Lordship shall theare find.' No part of the £15,000, they write, should without the Queen's special permission be used for any other purpose except payments to discharged bands. The Privy Council's aim was to rid itself of the ongoing financial obligation to soliders currently in pay; the longer Grey forbore discharging them, the more the wages would accrue.

Two problems immediately arose. The Privy Council had selected for its general discharge the leanest, cruellest season of the year, and the discharged soldiers—unable to purchase or get licence for their passage home—began to die in the streets. Grey and Wallop wrote repeatedly into England throughout the winter begging for funds to relieve them, and Grey openly defied the Queen's express order to discharge a further 700 soldiers in Munster, delaying it until March, because of John Zouche's reports of the universal famine there (see SP 63/89/9, 63/89/11, and 63/89/17). Auditor Jenyson related to Burghley in late February (SP 63/89/38) that discharged soldiers were begging in the streets of Dublin, and attempting to trade their clothes and weapons for food. The apparent insolvency of the Dublin administration—and, much more, its failure to care honourably for its own—had immediate repercussions: as John Zouche reported to Walsingham in late March (SP 63/90/28), several of his chief allies among the Irish, who had undertaken to do good service against the rebels, at the discharge in Munster went over to the Earl of Desmond.

If the order for a general discharge, with the financial conditions attached to it, led to misery for the cashiered soldiers, it created even greater problems for the ongoing service, and the desperate situation of those soldiers still in pay. The basic perennial problem was one of credit. It immediately became apparent to Grey, and to his Treasurer, Henry Wallop, that the sum of £5,000 remaining from the discharge would cover almost none of their other debts; and bad debts, in turn, made it impossible to get further credit. Wallop was compelled, as soon as the money arrived, to use a substantial part of the £5,000 remainder to pay off urgent obligations, leaving almost nothing, and throughout November 1581 he sent a series of letters to Burghley, advertising him in pitiful tones that, having been deprived of funds with which to procure basic necessities, he was having to request that victuals be sent from England at much greater expense. In this letter, Grey presents his case for converting some of the reserved £15,000, intended for the discharge, to other more urgent needs; he also takes this opportunity to beg the Privy Council to intercede with Elizabeth, and explain that his disobedience of her restraint should not be interpreted as contempt or neglect. The way this letter and its associated documents present Grey and his ministers caught between obedience, ethical duty, financial constraint, credit, and their mandate to justice and reformation administrative, social, and political, casts an uncompromisingly bleak light on the relationship between friendship (service, credit, faith, trust) and justice (distribution, equity, reform) in *The Faerie Queene*, Books IV and V.

The address and the text of the letter are in Spenser's familiar secretary hand. The signature is in Grey's usual italic hand. The endorsement, in a later hand, was probably added when the letter was filed in London.

ADDRESS AND ENDORSEMENT

To the right Honorable
my very good Lords &
otheres of her Highnes
privie Councell. /

Lords
3 Ianuary 1581
From the Lord Deputye

Entred

TEXT

May yt please your Lordships; In a late lettre written from your Lordships I am expressely required (as by direction from her Maiestie that of the threasure then assigned for this land 15000^{li} should bee converted onely to pay bandes & other companies discharged & to bee cassed & not to other vses without apparaunt necessitie, & the residue being but 5000^{li} to bee imprested to the Souldieres contynuinge still in service and to answere all other growing charges; For my part conferring now with the Councell vpon th'arrivall of the threasure which way her Maiesties said direccion might bee performed and this poore miserable Army somewhatt comforted And fynding by informacion of the Threasurer, how farre his word & creditt is engaged for great Summes, to bee repayed vpon tharrivall of this threasure, of the which the most were borrowed in ready money vpon vrgent necessity of the service, & the rest rysing for provisions bought with the dewes to some poore Townes, that to their vtter vndoing (without payment) haue borne the fynding of the Soldier (in which number especially Maryburgh & Philipstowne may bee reckoned) I see not (without borrowing somewhat of the said direccion° how th'one of these ij extremities might bee avoyded, either the Souldieres to bee lefte to a hazard of mutinie & disorder (which hethervnto hath bene with great difficultie prevented) or elles the Threasureres word & creditt to bee broken, which sure cannot but bring many inconveniences to the service, which is seeldome without necessitie of borrowing, besides his particulare discomfort.

---

direccion] Spenser seems not to have closed this parenthesis because the word 'direccion' abuts the end of its line, providing punctuation enough.

Therefore yf for the preventing of these evilles, & not to make desperate the hope of the Souldieres, that haue so long expected I bee
driven to apply to theis vses some 3000^{li} of the said Sum restreyned,
yt may please° your Lordships in acquainting her Maiestie with our
extremities to bee a meane that her Highnes interprete me not to doe
any thing therein in contempt or neglect of her Maiesties will &
Commaundement, but as compelled by the very force & nature of the
present necessities here. for truly vpon casting downe the money for
the present pay, and dividing the same into shares and portions, wee
fynde that impresting one monethes pay to the garrizons in Leynster
& Vlster, with my self & the other Chief Officeres, without relieving
the other remote partes the whole remayne of the said 5000^{li} will not
suffice the said Allottement, and yett the Souldier neither clothed,
nor his creditt answered, which bee ij Aduersities so great and
daungerous, as how farre they may tempt and provoke men so long
discontented, I leave to your Lordships to discerne & iudg, being for
myne owne part so ouerpestured with the claymoures of the Army,
(which I cannott but confesse to bee iust) & followed still with other
Crosses, which I see this gouernement cannott eschew that I must
more & more importune your Lordships to move her Maiestie for my
revocacion, and to make choyce of some other whome her Highnes
thincketh better hable to menage and weeld so great a burden
and Crosse. And so I Committ your Lordships to the goodnes of
th'Almighty. At Dublin, the third of Ianuary. 1581./

> Your Lordships assured to Commaund,
>
> Arthur Grey

COMMENTARY

a late lettre] by SP 63/88/1, a letter probably drafted after private negotiations
between Grey and Walsingham, the Privy Council granted the Lord Deputy a
limited freedom to dispose of the £15,000: 'We haue thoughte good to let your
Lordship vnderstand that in case there shall any parte of the said somme of fiften
thowsand poundes be left vppon the dischardging of the soudiors, you maye
emplye the same together with the other fyue thowsand in growing chardges as
you shall see cause.' Since Grey is writing here as if the restriction were still in
place, the letter he invokes here is probably an earlier one from the Privy Council,
perhaps even the fair copy of SP 63/86/42 (see headnote).

bandes & other companies discharged] over three thousand soldiers, comprising
bands of footmen and horsemen under captains stationed across Ireland, had been

please] inserted above the line.

discharged from service between November 1581 and January 1581/2 (SP 63/88/ 40/1 provides a complete list of the bands discharged). The general discharge came in the wake of rising discontent in Westminster about the costs of the Irish service (and particularly under the Earl of Ormond in Munster), and after considerable correspondence between Burghley and Auditor Thomas Jenyson on that subject.

cassed] disbanded, discharged.

imprested] loaned, paid in advance.

And fynding . . . great Summes] the **Threasurer**, Sir Henry Wallop, had made frequent pleas to Burghley about the money he had been forced to borrow to furnish the army with basic supplies: 'so much mony is due vppon my billes for ready mony borrowed and Corne bought' (SP 63/87/21, 9 December). In order to maintain his reputation for a reasonable financial probity and trustworthiness ('word and creditt'), Wallop was forced to deduct some of the money due to the soldiers and apply it to his creditors. As he had commented a few weeks earlier in another letter, he considered 'yt very requysyte for the servyce that my poore Credytt should be kept' (SP 63/87/62). On the complicated culture of credit and exchange in early modern England, see Muldrew, *The Economy of Obligation*.

ready money] money available for immediate use. On this issue, Grey's language exactly mirrors Wallop's in his letters to Burghley, suggesting that Grey, Wallop, Waterhouse, and others were drafting their communications after consultation, and attempting to present a united front.

rysyng for] arising from.

bought with the dewes] with the payments due to certain towns. Some Irish towns supported their garrisons at great charge, the cost of which was ultimately borne by the Dublin administration; Grey reveals here that money intended for remunerating these towns had been diverted to the purchase of further provisions.

the fynding of the Soldier] the supply of the garrisons.

Maryburgh & Philipstowne] towns in the central Irish counties of Leix and Offaly, now called Portlaoise and Daingean. On the towns' foundation as part of the plantation of Leix and Offaly, see Dunlop, 'The Plantation of Leix and Offaly'. For an argument that links their development in the mid-sixteenth century to Spenser's own ideas about the civil importance of stronghold towns, see Woolway Grenfell, 'Significant Spaces'.

without borrowing . . . said direccion] 'without relaxing slightly the terms of the Privy Council's prescription (for disbursement of the treasure)'. Grey's wordplay often conveys this sense of cynical world-weariness: Ireland is, he implies, a land of such borrowings, for which the Privy Council must forgive him.

to a hazard of mutinie] the other letters on this subject do not raise the possibility of mutiny, but they do make it clear that the soldiers are in a desperate condition. Wallop and Waterhouse had written to Burghley on 9 December that the lack of money was in danger of causing famine (SP 63/87/20); Wallop adds to Burghley, in another letter of that date, that 'the nakednes of the poore souldiare is so great, as here it is, a thinge lamentable to beholde' (SP 63/87/21).

restreyned] for restricted use. The word is used twice in SP 63/88/1, a draft of a letter which refers back to the letters of 29 October, in which, the Privy Council write, 'youe [i.e. Grey] are restreyned', and then this word is crossed out and replaced with 'dyrected', 'to employ fiften thowsand therof about the dischardging of the souldiors onlye, and not in any other chardges without especiall direction ether from her maiesty or from vs in that behalf'. The letter refers to this later as 'the said restraint'.

casting downe the money] the *OED* does not seem to record this usage, which may be Grey's own metaphor; the sense is surely of laying or placing the money down on the table, to divide into shares and pressing payments.

wee fynde ... said Allottement] cf. Wallop to Burghley, 28 December: 'the remaines of the 5000^li woulde not make an imprest for one moneth to the garrysons in Leinster and Vlster' (SP 63/87/62). This coincidence of expression reinforces the impression that, at the very least, these letters arose from close discussion between Wallop and Grey. On **impresting**, see note above.

the Souldier neither clothed] on the soldiers' 'nakednes', see note above.

his creditt answered] his debts (at least partially) discharged—thus restoring his credit, and enabling him to borrow further for his maintenance.

ouerpestured] over-pestered, i.e. too much called upon.

claymoures] clamours.

other Crosses] vexations or troubles. In the sentence which follows, **that** is to be glossed as 'as a consequence of which'.

revocacion] a now familiar request on Grey's part to be recalled to England. It seems that Wallop himself was asking to be called back at this time of crisis and debt; he wrote to Walsingham on 10 December 1581 that 'my L. Tresorer [i.e. Burghley] delyth hardly with me, and my revocatyon which I hartely desyre my accompte endyd' (SP 63/87/34).

menage] manage. Despite this hendiadys ('menage and weeld'), it seems clear from what follows ('burden and Crosse') that Grey sees the position as needing to be borne, rather than exploited.

third of Ianuary. 1581./] 1582, new style.

26. *Grey to Burghley, 12 January 1581/2*

TNA: PRO SP 63/88/12

The subtleties of patronage and political access define the content and tone of this letter. Having been informed from Westminster of Walter Ralegh's letter to the Queen concerning the Munster service, Grey here takes pains to assure his reputation with Burghley, and to head off what he sees as ill-informed and immature meddling by an inexperienced captain. At the other end of the letter, in a postscript, Grey reports to Burghley on Zouche's apprehension and killing of the leading rebel in Munster, Sir John of Desmond; as a work of one of Burghley's kinsmen, Zouche's good service will elevate Burghley's standing with the Queen, as well as Grey's with Burghley. Grey's complaint of Bland's bad dealing with the victuals was certainly in good faith; as Sir Warham Sentleger reported on 12 April 1582, plague and famine were rife in Cork, with as many as sixty-two dead on a single day (SP 63/91/23/1).

The text of the letter, address, and subscription are in Spenser's characteristic secretary hand; the signature and postscript are in Grey's italic hand. The endorsement, probably added during the filing of the letter in London, is in a distinct hand.

To the right Hono-
rable my very good
Lord the Lord Burghley
Lord High Threasurer
of England yeue
                    this

12. Ianuary 1581.
Lord Deputie of Ireland to my Lord

Mr Rawlies vnskilfulnes in setting
downe a plott to lessen hir
Maiesties expences.

Blandes slacknes in sending of
victels into Munster.

Iohn of Desmondes death.

TEXT

My very good Lord having lately received aduertizement of a Plott
deliuered by Captein Rawley vnto her Maiesty for the lessening of her
charges here in the Province of Mounster & disposing of the Garrizons according to the same, the matter at the first indeed offering a
very plausible shewe of thrifte and Commoditie, might easily occasion
her Maiestie to thinck, that I haue not so carefully as behoved looked
into the state of that cause & the search of her Maiesties proffitt.
Wherefore having with some of the best advised of the Councell here
entred into consideracion thereof, & perceiving many inconveniences
with some impossibilities in the accomplishment thereof, we have (as
by our generall lettre to her Maiestie herewith sent you may perceive)
layd downe owre iudgementes & opinions thereof: which when yt
shall come vnto your Lordships deeper consultacion, I doubt not,
but you will soone discerne a differens betwene the iudgementes of
those, which with grownded experience & approved reason looke
into the condicion of thinges, and those which vpon no grownd but
seeming fancies & affecting creditt with benefitt frame Plottes vpon
impossibilities for otheres to execute. And so trusting that your Lordship with the rest will esteeme of both, for the rest° I will referre you

rest] the letter 'a' has been deleted between 'e' and 's' in this word.

to those reasons, which we haue in our said lettre layd before her Maiestie.

Furthermore, I haue to complayne vnto your Lordship (whose onely redresse I looke for in theise matteres) of the great sclacknes & default of Bland, in sending ouer of the supplies of victelles into Mounster, whereof the proporcions are comenly so sclender, (as I am informed from the Surveyour of the vicetelles there) as that all those garrizons thereby are very miserably distressed, & almost vtterly starved to the very great hinderaunce of the service. And yett I doubt not but he informeth your Lordship farre otherwise: and therefore I earnestly pray your Lordship too looke into the speedy redresse thereof.

Lastely whereas my Lord Chauncellour & your Lordship haue written vnto me touching my payment of the Subsidie I haue accordingly taken order for th'answering thereof. And so for the present committing your Lordship to the goodnes of th'Almighty, I hartely take leave Dublin. the xij^th of Ianuarie 1581

    Your good Lordships assured to commaund

    Arthur Grey

It hathe pleazed God too guyue Ihon Zowtche the kyllyng of Ihon of Desmond that Artche rebell & traytor, I hard of it iij dayes past but this nyght I receaued the certayne confirmation therof, & with hym hathe taken an oother notorius knaue called Iames Fittz Ihon of Strangalie: the newes I trust wyll not dislyke yowr Lordship as well in the pryuate beehallf of yowr powre kinsmans good hap as of the common good, neyther wyll yowr Lordship, I hoape spare, too aduaunce the due commendation of the endeuoure too her Maiestie.

COMMENTARY

a **Plott deliuered by Captein Rawley**] the proposals apparently do not survive. Ralegh had clear ideas about the need for force in the subordination of Munster, and in one letter to Walsingham (SP 63/80/82) spoke approvingly of his half-brother Sir Humphrey Gilbert's brutal pacification of the province; like Grey, he was impatient with the Earl of Ormond's conciliatory policies (see SP 63/80/82 and 63/83/16/1). Grey's disapproval of Ralegh was as much for his person as his policy (see SP 63/92/10); this disapproval may have been the result of Ralegh's liaison at about this time with the daughter of Justice James Goold, which produced a bastard daughter (see *ODNB*).

our generall . . . herewith sent] Grey may be referring to SP 63/88/13, a copy of Grey and Council to the Queen of the same date, which sets out plans for the Munster service.

frame Plottes vpon impossibilities] this phrase, which has echoes of Sidney's account of poetry in the *Defence of Poesy* (composed at about this time), as well as looking forward to Spenser's own plot for reformation in *A View*, seems an oddly Spenserian turn, especially among the frequent alliterations and balanced syntax of this passage—unlike Grey's usual style. This passage provides suggestive evidence that Spenser played more than a scribe's part in the drafting of some of Grey's correspondence.

Bland] John Bland, the Chester-based Deputy Victualler to English forces in Ireland; see biographies.

my payment of the Subsidie] 'An Acte for the grant of one Subsidie, and two Fifteenes, and Tenthes, by the Temporaltie' had been passed by Parliament in the preceding year (23 Eliz. cap. 15).

Ihon Zowtche] Zouche was governor of Munster; see biographies.

the kyllyng . . . of Desmond] see also No. 27, below (SP 63/88/15). The capture or killing of John of Desmond had been a priority of the Munster service since the general revolt in Munster in 1579; a £500 reward was on offer, and the Queen herself acknowledged Zouche's good service in the feat (63/88/42).

Iames Fitz Ihon of Strangalie] nephew to the Earl of Desmond.

yowr powre kinsmans good hap] John Zouche's relation to Burghley is obscure.

27. *Grey to Walsingham, 13 January 1581/2*

TNA: PRO SP 63/88/15

Early in January 1582, Sir John Fitzgerald, also known as John of Desmond (see biographies) was surprised and killed in the woods of Eatharlach, Co. Cork, by John Zouche, governor of Munster; his corpse was hanged over the city gates at Cork, and his head, as this letter describes, sent to Grey in Dublin. Grey takes the opportunity of this letter to Walsingham, in which he recounts these happy events, to remind him of the Dublin government's ongoing financial worries. He had also written to Burghley on 12 January to tell him that 'it hathe pleazed God too guyue Ihon Zowtche the kyllyng of Ihon of Desmond that Artche rebell & traytor, I hard of it iij dayes past but this nyght I receaued the certayne confirmation therof, & with hym hathe taken an oother notorius knaue called Iames Fitz Ihon of Strangalie: the newes I trust wyll not dislyke yowr Lordship' (No. 26, above, SP 63/88/12). Zouche himself had already advertised his deed to Elizabeth and the Privy Council, informing Burghley on 5 January about the killing of Desmond, 'whos end was according too his actiones, for being demandid off the mistchieues which he had done, he answerid iff he myght haue liued longer he wold haue done more'; Zouche further related the 'great Ioye' in Cork at news of Desmond's death (SP 63/88/7). Zouche also celebrated the event in a dispatch to Walsingham, of the same date, in which he reported that he had written to the Queen, and had 'presented the Ring which I found abought the tratour' (SP 63/88/8). The importance of this traffic in corporal proofs should not be underestimated, as it demonstrates the emotional and evidential importance of violent spectacles not only to the Queen, but to the populace whose affections and enormities she and her ministers sought to control. Zouche's (or Grey's?) grim humour ('for a new-yeeres guyft was commended vntoo mee') also speaks to the generally desensitized attitude to violence characteristic of Irish politics and military affairs in this period, an important forcing-ground for the sometimes brutal narratives of *The Faerie Queene*.

The text and subscription of this letter are in Grey's cursive italic hand, and the signature is Grey's. The address is written in Spenser's usual secretary hand, and the endorsement in a distinct, later italic. An addressee note in Grey's hand (reading, '{Mr Sec}retary'), slightly obscured by the binding of the ledger in which the manuscript is now kept, appears at the left foot of the recto of the letter.

ADDRESS AND ENDORSEMENT

To the right Hono-
rable my very
good frend Sir
Fraunces Walsingham
Knight Chief
Secretary to her
Maiesty./

13 Ianuary 1581
The Lord Deputye.

TEXT

I beeseetche yow Sir cause the letter too my Lords heerwith empacketed too bee considered & awnsswered with all conuenient speede for
it emportethe mootche.

This mornyng Ihon of Desmoondes head for a new-yeeres guyft
was commended vntoo mee from the Coronell: The newes I iudge
allreadie too bee with yow there, hyssellf aduertyzing mee that hee
had presently dispatched one from Corck therwith, & therfore I leaue
too declare the manner of the action: onece the seruyce is woorthy of
accounte;° & rewarde in sutche casies & too sutche men is neyther loss

---

after **accounte;**] three- or four-letter deletion, possibly 'lea' (perhaps the beginning of the word 'leas(i)es': see the following lines).

nor expence; her Maiestie myght doo well too beestowe on hym all sutche leasies & landes (yet landes I thynck hee had noane) as the traytor had; If it shall not bee trooblesum too yow I praye yow too mooue it. The proclamation guyues 500^{li}° for his kyllyng, but where is the mooney. Consider owre necessities I beeseetche yow° & so the Lord bee euer with yow: Dublin xiij^{th} of Ianuary 1581.

Yowrs most assuredly

euer,

Arthur Grey

COMMENTARY

the letter too my Lords] it is not immediately clear what letter this is, or what its subject was, and no obvious candidates survive among the Irish State Papers, although Grey's description here is certainly oblique. Letters from Grey to Burghley (No. 26, above, SP 63/88/12) and Grey and the Council to the Queen (SP 63/88/13) survive, both dated 12 January: perhaps a letter to the Privy Council, no longer surviving, was delivered along with them. What is clear, though, is that Grey sees Walsingham as the member of the Privy Council most sympathetic to him, and most willing to see his business expedited.

empacketed] not packed up in this letter, but enclosed in the same package of letters as this.

it emportethe mootche] it matters a great deal, is of great significance, consequence.

new-yeeres guyft] the giving of expensive gifts at New Year was a sixteenth-century courtly tradition. See Starkey, 'The Presence Chamber', 126–30.

commended] given, presented.

the Coronell] John Zouche; see biographies. In October 1581 he had been made chief colonel and director in Munster (SP 63/86/31), and in November, governor of that province (SP 63/86/49).

proclamation] in fact, Zouche seems to have been granted £1,000 for taking the head: 'Mr Zowche the governour of Mounster is here, abowtes his Recckninges, and other affayres of that Province. We allowed him A m^l li mencioned in a proclamacion sent furthe here, for takinge of Sir John of Desmondes heade, besydes other allowaunces' (SP 63/90/62, White to Burghley, 31 March 1582).

owre necessities] Grey's customary plea for money is more urgent than usual: his hardship had been exacerbated by restrictions placed upon money recently sent from England, restrictions which he had flouted. See No. 25, above (SP 63/88/2), in which he describes himself as 'compelled by the very force & nature of the present necessities here'.

500^{li}] Grey seems initially to have written '5000', and then to have deleted the final zero.   yow] inserted above the line.

28. *Grey to Walsingham, 27 January 1581/2*
TNA: PRO SP 63/88/40

This plain-speaking letter from Grey to Walsingham reveals the several fissures within the Dublin administration, and between Ireland and England, that would result in the collapse of Grey's government and his revocation: his betrayal by Fenton, Malby, and Loftus; the growing impatience of Burghley; the animosity of the Countess of Lincoln; Grey's exorbitance in dispensing rewards to his friends and allies in the Irish service; his increasing reliance on private communication with Walsingham to manage his failing relationship with the Queen; and his total opposition to the instructions being sent him from Westminster (particularly in regard to leniency for the Earl of Kildare and Baron of Delvin, and the general discharge of the soldiers). The letter is interesting for the way in which it shows Grey using the vagaries of the post, and the multiple copies and drafts of letters being sent him from London, as a means to anticipate and propitiate the Queen, and of course to lie to her. It is also interesting for the way in which its gossipy tone—complaints about Burghley, hyperbolic deflections of whispered accusations reported against him—conveys his trust in, and reliance on, Walsingham's favour and support.

The text and subscription of this letter are in Grey's characteristic italic hand, and the signature is his customary mark. Spenser's usual secretary hand appears in the address; the endorsement, added upon filing of the letter in London, is in a distinct, later italic. An addressee note in Grey's hand (reading 'Mr Secretary'), appears on the fold below the address, indicating that Grey folded the letter before leaving it for Spenser to address and dispatch.

ADDRESS AND ENDORSEMENT

To right Honorable
my assured good
frend Sir Fraunces
Walsingham Knight
Chief Secretary
to her Maiesty./.

27 Ianuary 1582
The Lord Gray.
Lords

TEXT

Sir, the xxth of this moonethe I receaued yowr letters with a Copie of her Maiesties for reducyng of the whoale garrisoon heere too 3000. the accomplysshyng wherof I presently entered into as a booke heerwith sent shall particularly sheowe the same:° The xxiiijth after Ritch arryued with the originall of the forsaid Copie & oother yowr letters of the xijth of December; by first & last of which I fynde what ientle enformations arre made of mee & how eazely her Maiestie is caryed too conceaue the hardliest of mee, well my God is yet styll where hee was & my rest as euer onely on Hym; yowrsellf I greatly thanck for the warnyng, & yowr aduyce I haue followed in wryghtyng to her Maiestie the Copie wherof I allso send yow, & therfore too yowr sellf wyll no further stande in my cleering for the guyftes I am chardged with; A note therof I thowght necessarie too beetake vnto yow that my faulte at onece, if there bee any, myght appeere & receaue iudgement:° a forme lykewyze of the Custodiams I send wherby it maye appeere whyther the guyftes bee so free & withowte proffitt to her maiestie as the enformation woold affirme; but the best is her maiestie maye chooze whyther the guyftes shall stande or no of the landes & as for the goods, in Gods name, if they shallbee thowght so greate a matter lett them bee turned vppon myne owane head & verifie scripture, hee that hathe lyttle et cetera: and° for the great studderies that I shulld guyue, I woonder wheruppon it is ment, truly Sir I neuer yet hard of any sutche petition, neyther doo I knowe of any of these pale rebells that hathe a stud of vj mares, & for the Irisshe, if it were a stud of 1000: the partie that woold fetche them myght very well dezerue them; but Lord what inuentions ar these, in trowthe they offend mee not so mootche in myne owane beehallf, as that any sutche shulld haue the daryng too abuse so her Hyghnes eares & beeleeff: Further that the Captaynes heere shulld bee in dislyke with mee for my guyuyng to oother & beestowyng nothyng on them, truly myssellf could yet neuer fynde any sutche lykclyhood, too the contrarie, it hathe been heere my chyeffiest coomforte lykyng & wyllyngnes that I haue° tryed in them towardes mee; neyther is there

---

same:] immediately to the left of this word, and on three further occasions on the same page, oblique lines appear in the left margin. These (occasionally accompanied by the word 'wanting', and keyed to underlinings in the text of the letter) appear to be marks added to the manuscript during the extensive Victorian cataloguing process that resulted in the *Calendars*. We have ignored them here.   *after* **iudgement**:] single-character deletion, possibly '&'.   **et cetera: and**] four- or five-letter deletion *after* **et cetera**: (possibly 'next'), and 'and' inserted above the line.   *after* **I haue**] 'ty' deleted.

allmost a Captayne or officer of note heere that hathe not tasted of
rewarde from mee how so euer my masters the enfourmers pleaze too
certifie, well my God I thanck that hoaldes my steps from farther
awrye: But in deede my state is hard, I serued onely for my Princies
fauoure & my Cuntries good, the one I haue lost, the oother lyttle
auayled in; my sellf in pryuate condition hallf vndoon,° add to this
that not one of my assocyats° I can bynde vppon, thowghe cause I
knowe noane, vnless it bee that° so many shrappes° fall not too° thier
shares° as woont was & no small pleazure I am sure it dyd them to
finde° by yowr letters° that 60° was so mootche offended° with mee.°

I perceaue by oothers pryuate letters from hym that 324° is a greate
obseruer° & fawltfynder with thynges heere; I neyther waye it, nor
dowght but too bee fownde euer honester & iuster in dealyng then
hymsellf & so I leaue hym, onely I wysshe of God that hee woold bee
my chardger face too face beefore her Maiestie & the rest of yow. In a
letter to 111° hee fyndes fyrst fawlte with the beestowyng of the
landes, as yf they had been all guyuen awaye in feesymple, next at the
chardge of the penncioners as thowghe the same were alltoogeather
my default, where how lyttle therin I am too bee tootched my late
aduertissement by Sir Nycholas Mallbye declares, & heere fursoothe
a specyall note hee makes of hys seeyng of them there in England, as
thowghe it were an vnwoonted thyng° a Ientleman seruyng heere too
haue lycence for a tyme too repayre ouer, & yet truly Sir I dare auowe
that° by° my passporte there were neuer twoo penncioners seene there
attonece; lastly hee falls into a detestation of this place & termes it a
gullf of consumyng threazure, as in deede truly hee maye, & the more
throwghe hys good meanes & aduyce, for which if repentance & Gods
mercies beefall not the greater hys soale wyll awnsswer in the gullff of
hell.

Amongst these dischardgies Ned Dennie is one; & if now hee bee putt
from the Custodiams that I haue guyuen hym it wyll goe hard with
hym; I wysshed too hym allso an oother thyng if it had stoode in my
guyft, which myght in deede doo hym sum good the oothers beeyng

after **hallf vndoon**] '&', and two or three other illegible letters deleted.   **assocyats**]
in cipher.   **that**] inserted above the line.   **shrappes**] in cipher.   *after* **not too**]
'theyr' deleted.   **thier shares**] in cipher.   **them . . . finde**] in cipher.   **yowr letters**]
in cipher.   **60**] Queen Elizabeth.   **offended**] in cipher.   **mee**] in cipher.   **324**]
William Cecil, Lord Burghley.   **greate obseruer**] 'oberse' deleted *after* **greate**, and
'obseruer' inserted above the line.   **111**] unknown cipher.   *after* **vnwoonted thyng**]
'that' deleted.   *after* **auowe that**] 'I since' deleted.   **by**] inserted above the line.

but very tryffles; it is the abbey of Fowre in westmethe wherof my
Lord of Delluyn hathe by lease onely an estate of° three or xxiiij
yeares: gett it for hym Sir & hee shall haue good cause too thynck yow
freend hym: In the rest if the discreditt bee layed vppon mee that the
grawntes maye not stande; healp yet what yow maye that Ihon Dyue
& Warrham St linger maye haue theyrs & the bonde of the benefitt
too yow shall bee myne.° I long now to heare of the resolution of the
plott yow wrote of: but whyther that fall owte or no, I beeseetche yow
forgett nott my plott° too bee taken from this miserable place; which
obtayned my earthely blyss restored I shall accounte.

The Baron of Dungannon this oother weeke dyd° a seruyce of greate
importance, in takyng one Ihon Cusacke the princypall practizer in
this last consspiracie, the aduyce & perswasion of Sir edward Moore
was no small furtherance therof I praye yow therfore haue mynde of
that that by Ned Denny in hys beehallff I requested; & if miserie
drowned not ryght & pollicie, it were requysite that the Baron had a
fee farme of a hundrethe marckes or powndes of those landes that by
this meanes wyll bee browght too her Maisties handes; hyssellf
meanethe, if God lett not shortly too repayre ouer, & then my
thowghroghe commendation hee shall haue,° thowghe perchaunce
hys speede bee the woorss for it./

Now too the partie apprehended; hee reuealethe mootche & yet is not
hallf sease ouer, the particulares of the matter prezent tyme woolld
not suffre too bee emparted, a note of theyr names that hee hathe
detected allreadie heerwith is sent:

The Lord & Lady of Deluin° hee vtterly confowndes: & whowme
beesydes hee tootchethe the° parable enclozed wyl sheowe° yet too
mee it seemes not of any reguard in 10° behallf, but rather a forgerie
of deluin° too encourage the rest by the hope of° 10.° vnsowght or
vnthowght of it was delyuered & so yow haue it too vze at yowr
owane° best discretion, myne opinion I haue said of it.

after **estate of**] 'xx' deleted.   *after* **myne.**] 'I long' deleted.   *after* **my plott**] five-
or six-letter deletion, beginning 'da'.   **oother weeke dyd**] four-letter deletion *after*
weeke, and 'dyd' inserted above the line.   **haue,**] inserted above the line.   **The Lord &**
Lady of Deluin] in cipher (the actual transliteration would read 'the L and La of
. . .').   **hee tootchethe the**] in cipher.   **enclozed wyl sheowe**] in cipher.   **10**]
unknown cipher.   **deluin**] in cipher.   **the hope of**] in cipher.   **10**] unknown
cipher.   **owane**] inserted above the line.

There arre Sir Lucas & Sir Robart Dillons with Sir Ihon Plunckett that haue & doo styll dischardge the partes of zelus & vpryght seruantes for shame lett them taste of sum rewarde beesydes woordes in the disposition of these esscheated landes.

And lastly Sir I beeseetche yow gett mee warrant for my due enter-taynement, & thowghe no gayne maye bee affourded mee or myne, yet for Gods sake lett not my ryght bee withheald, yet take mee awaye quyckly & guyue mee what yee lyst. The allmyghtie God euer keepe, guyde & bless yow. Dublin xxvijth of Ianuary 1581.

Yowrs most assuredly

euer,

Arthur Grey

I fynde by letters from my lady° of lincolne° that the cause of 76° continuance in this sorte is long of my not aduertising the state of° his cause; wherin as I am wrong conceaued of, so I praye yow that I maye bee cleered by yow as occasion seruethe; all my knowledge & presumption is long since & sundrie tymes delyuered, neyther doo I fynde, if that serue not any thyng of new too tootche hym° neyther doo I thynck it amyss that hee° were called ouer.°

Iames Fittz Christopher there yow arre to see well looked too for greate matter is lyke too fall owte agaynst hym, & if Ihon Cusacke saye trowthe there wyll not one honest Nugent bee fownde heere.

As I was sealyng vp heerof yowr packett of the xxth of this date came vnto mee, wherin I fynde nothyng requyres awnsswer° in these not tootched; & as for the oother entended dischardge, a Gods name, lett it coome, there shall no more any bones bee made at° it, & then Caueat ademptor, is all the care I wyll take: good Sir, stryke hard the iron whyllst I perceaue it is hott now, for my callyng hoame, the lyttle hoape wherof that these yowr letters browght mee, made mee eate my supper with a better appetite then at any meale these twoo moonethes past I had, a thowzande thanckes I render for the newes, only feare

---

my lady] in cipher.   lincolne] in cipher.   76] Gerald Fitzgerald, eleventh Earl of Kildare.   *after* state of] 't' deleted.   hym] in cipher.   that hee] in cipher.   called ouer] in cipher.   awnsswer] 's' deleted at the end of this word.   *after* made at] 'then' deleted.

of a cosnerlyng carde by the next beereaues the full coomfort of the ioye, but perfect it° good Sir, I wyll not bee vnthanckfull./

COMMENTARY

a Copie of her Maiesties] see SP 63/87/45, the Queen to the Lord Deputy on 12 December 1581. Note that Grey claims in a letter to the Queen on 25 January (SP 63/88/39) that he had received her letter on that very day; in this letter he admits to Walsingham that he knew of the order for the reduction of the garrison five days previously.

a booke heerwith sent] the enclosure, listing the names of the soldiers discharged, is extant; see SP 63/88/40/1; 63/88/40/2, a companion book, lists the names of those footmen and horsemen still in service throughout Ireland.

Ritch] Barnaby Rich, the soldier and author; see biographies.

the guyftes I am chardged with] Grey had recently been accused, in letters written by his associates in Dublin, of exorbitant and unlicensed largesse in the rewards shown to his servants (like Spenser) and strategic allies; these charges would contribute substantially to the perceived disfavour attending his ultimate recall. The informations made against him seem to have originated with Thomas Jenyson, the auditor, and with a subset of the Council—Loftus, Fenton, and Malby—who all wrote privately to Burghley and Walsingham (see SP 63/86/71 and 63/86/72, with the enclosure 63/86/72/1, dated 20 November 1581, for Fenton's backstabbing report; and 63/87/42, dated 11 December, for the first of Jenyson's reports to Burghley). Grey informed Walsingham in early January (SP 63/88/9) that he had recently discovered the machinations of some of his most esteemed associates, but by then it was too late. He always maintained that he had shown neither more nor less independence or profligacy than his predecessors in the post.

Custodiams] a term used in Irish law to describe the three-year grant of the benefit (or 'use') of crown land; see glossary. Such grants were commonly made of newly escheated estates, as a short-term benefit made to loyal servitors while the crown's ultimate plans for the land were decided.

hee that hathe lyttle et cetera] Grey is presumably thinking of the parable of the talents, Matthew 25: 14–30. His point is that, if the gifts of goods be found upon consideration excessive, they should be charged upon his own estate, so that he may prove the truth of the scripture, that the poor shall be made poorer.

studderies] Grey had apparently been accused of appropriating the very valuable commodity of an established horse studdery; given his response, it seems that Walsingham's information must have been fairly vague.

awrye] misdoing (a noun).

in pryuate condition hallf vndoon] his personal fortune by this time half spent in the Irish service.

bynde vppon] depend upon.

thowghe cause ... as woont was] 'I don't know why my associates are so unreliable, unless it is because they receive fewer favours and rewards than from

after **perfect it**] 'god' deleted.

former Deputies.' Grey's representation of his 'associates' and clients in the Pale government as dogs, used to scraps ('shrappes') from his table, prepares the way for Spenser's later representation of the recall of Artegall, in *The Faerie Queene* V.xii, from Irena's island.

feesymple] a fee simple was the simplest common law form of the customary inheritable estate in land; it is described in the first chapter of the first book of Sir Thomas Littleton's fifteenth-century *Tenures*, reprinted with annotations as Sir Edward Coke's *The First Part of the Institutes of the Lawes of England* (1625). Grey's point is that he had not made permanent grants of the estates, but only three-year grants of the benefits arising therefrom.

chardge of the pencioners] Burghley had apparently received further complaints about Grey's creation of 'pensioners'—discharged soldiers who were granted permanent livings by the Deputy when cashiered.

my late . . . Mallbye] Grey had written to the Privy Council by Sir Nicholas Malby on 11 December 1581 (SP 63/87/38), accounting for his conduct in respect of pensioners, and enclosing a list of all the new pensioners created during his deputyship (SP 63/87/38/3).

Ned Dennie] Sir Edward Denny; see biographies.

Ihon Dyue] John Dive was one of Grey's 'special favourites', who allegedly profited excessively from the Lord Deputy's grant to him of the lands and goods of the traitor David Sutton; Grey reported the gift in his letter to the Privy Council of 9 December 1581 (SP 63/87/18), and again in the book recording his gifts, SP 63/88/40/3, an enclosure to the present letter.

Warrham St linger] Sir Warham Sentleger; see biographies.

the bonde . . . bee myne] Grey here touches lightly on the complex traffic in benefits and loyalty which the patronage system could quickly generate. Effectively he asks to stand as broker to Walsingham's favour to John Dive and Warham Sentleger.

the resolution . . . yow wrote of] obscure.

Ihon Cusacke] Geoffrey Fenton forwarded to Walsingham and to Burghley the confessions of John Cusack, one of the Baron of Delvin's supporters, on 28 January 1582 (SP 63/88/47, 63/88/47/1, 63/88/47/2, 63/88/48, 63/88/49). In addition to conspiring with Delvin and his wife, he had raised money for the rebellion by mortgaging his estate to a relative.

Sir edward Moore] one of the leading Leinster captains, who commanded a band of horsemen until the discharge reported here, but still kept the ward of Philipstown. He had been knighted, apparently some time in 1579, for his service.

miserie] niggardliness.

fee farme] a fee simple; see note above.

hyssellf meanethe . . . too repayre ouer] O'Neill seems not to have made this journey.

thowghe perchaunce . . . woorss for it.] Grey worries, perhaps slightly histrionic-ally, that Hugh O'Neill will receive less favour from the Queen by bringing Grey's letter of commendation, than if he were to repair to England uncommended.

the partie apprehended] John Cusack; see biographies.

hallf sease] obscure; Grey seems to be saying that the process of examination is not yet half completed.

prezent tyme] the heavy volume of business at the current time.

detected] implicated.

forgerie of deluin] false information supplied about the Baron of Delvin; Cusack seems to have claimed that Delvin had been in contact with the King of Spain.

Sir Lucas & Sir Robart Dillons] Sir Lucas Dillon and Sir Robert Dillon, councillors in Ireland; see biographies.

Sir Ihon Plunckett] Chief Justice of the Queen's Bench in Ireland, he died in September 1582.

the disposition of these esscheated landes] the title to the lands of traitors passed to the crown; these lands were then often redistributed to faithful subjects as rewards.

warrant for my due entertaynement] as usual, Grey closes with a plea for remuneration, and a following plea for recall.

my lady of lincolne] Elizabeth Fiennes de Clinton, sister of Gerald Fitzgerald, eleventh Earl of Kildare; see biographies. As the Queen's second cousin, she had substantial access at court, and Grey understandably feared her after the arrest of the Earl.

the state of his cause] the Countess of Lincoln had obviously alleged that her brother remained imprisoned in Dublin not through his own guilt, but through the Lord Deputy's dilatoriness in proceeding with charges against him. The Countess, along with Kildare's wife Mabel, was at this time pressing for Kildare's removal to England (see e.g. SP 63/80/46), to answer the allegations against him in front of the Privy Council (which she rightly believed he would find much more sympathetic than Grey).

too tootche hym] to bring him into suspicion.

Iames Fittz Christopher] James Fitzchristopher Nugent. Malby and Fenton wrote to Walsingham in 3 October 1581 (SP 63/86/7) requesting that James Nugent, who had got into England with the Lady of Delvin, be apprehended. He was subsequently captured and interrogated by Robert Beale and Sir John Popham (SP 63/89/29).

see well looked too] Grey warns Walsingham to keep James FitzChristopher under surveillance for, as one of the Nugents, he is likely to be named by Cusack as a conspirator.

the oother entended dischardge] the Queen required a further discharge of 700 soldiers, the direction for which (dated either 25 or 28 January) Grey received almost immediately (see SP 63/88/42 for a surviving draft of Elizabeth's letter).

there shall no more any bones bee made at it] it will not be resisted.

Caueat ademptor] let the buyer beware (Lat.).

cosnerlyng carde] a 'cozenerling' (diminutive of 'cozener') is apparently a petty cheater or fraud, and his card the false promise—i.e. of his revocation—that the weary Grey fears Walsingham has sent him.

29. *Copy of John Nugent's confession, 5 February 1581/2*
TNA: PRO SP 63/89/18

Sir Christopher Nugent, ninth Baron Delvin, had been implicated in the winter of 1580–1 in the rebellion of James Eustace, Viscount Baltinglass; he was taken into custody, along with the Earl of Kildare, on 23 December 1580 (see SP 63/79/24, 63/79/25, 63/79/26, and 63/79/30). Delvin's younger brother, William Nugent, seems at the news of Delvin's arrest to have taken himself and his wife, Gennet Marward, into hiding in his castle on Lough Sheelin, thereafter—according to the testimony of John Nugent in this examination—engaging in various combinations with unsavoury and rebellious figures in the Irish political landscape, in an attempt to avoid capture and, perhaps, to foment resistance to a Pale administration increasingly antagonistic to Old English interests in the east of Ireland, and to Catholics. Perhaps the most interesting aspect of this examination is its clearly sophisticated quality: Sir Robert Dillon, then second Justice of the Common Pleas, and Secretary of State Geoffrey Fenton were both eager to see the downfall of Sir Nicholas Nugent, Dillon's longtime enemy and a staunch Catholic defender of Old English interests in the Pale. This examination of Nicholas Nugent's servant John, which implicates Nicholas's wife (and William Nugent's mother-in-law) Ellen Plunkett, has apparently been carefully crafted, and in places distorted, to make connections between William Nugent's rebellion and the far less suspicious—even circumspect—actions of his uncle Nicholas. It is no accident that, upon Nicholas Nugent's trial and execution, Robert Dillon was given his office of Chief Justice. For the secretary copying this examination, the whole affair must have seemed at once tawdry and cunning, consistent with the general Dublin culture of secrecy, self-interest, and hypocrisy (and it is perhaps significant that other copies of this examination include a note before paragraph 20, indicating that all the subsequent statements were added by Fenton himself, in his hand; did Spenser remove this important, and possibly revealing, distinction, before forwarding the copy to Westminster?). Many of the Old English and Irish men named in this examination are not elsewhere recorded, and some of the place names—though undoubtedly in Co. Westmeath, the seat of the Nugents—have resisted identification. For all the rest, see the notes, the biographies contained in the appendix and the maps.

The main text of this document is neatly written in Spenser's characteristic secretary hand, and the annotations, running down the left margin of each page, are in Spenser's mixed hand. That Grey personally checked these annotations is indicated by the second of them, where he has added a final phrase ('hee was my Lord of Delluins steward.') in his distinctive hand. The original endorsement is almost certainly in Spenser's mixed hand, and the others, added later, in distinct italic scripts.

ENDORSEMENTS

Copy of Iohn Nugents
Confession.:/

Iohn Nugents
confession
.Lords.

The coppye of Ihon Nugentes
confession.
5 February 1582.

TEXT

A playne Discourse aswell of William Nugentes rebellious Actes as
also of the search made for his youngest sonne Christofer & also of his
wife Gennett Marwardes behaviour during the tyme of the Rebellion,
where in Ellen Plonkett wife to Nicholas Nugent is touched, made &
declared by Iohn Nugent hereafter particularly ensueth. At the castle
of Dublin the vth of February 1581 ./

The first going out
of William Nugent
vpon the appre-
hension of the Lord
his brother.

1 First vpon thapprehencion of the Lord of Delvin, the said William
Nugent being then in the Clonene, hearing say that Captein Bryan
fitz Williams & McStraunge then Sheriefe was come thether to

Edward Delahyde
sendeth victelles to
William Nugent.
This Edward is taken
but yet not
thoroughly ex-
amyned, hee was my
Lord of Delluins
steward.°

apprehend him he made an escape & tooke his said wife with him to a
Castle that lyeth in Loghsiline in the Breny, which he purposed to
defend against the Princes powre, & had victelles sent to him thether
by Edward Delahide my Lord of Delvins Stuard out of the Clonene &
from the Neighboures therevnto nere adioyning. Whose names I doe
not perfectly know, by reason that I do dwell a farre of. which Edward
& another of the Houshold servauntes of the Clonene called Pieres o

Piers Oconoghan
since taken & his
confession
herewith° sent.
Edmond
Christofer &
Robert Bane
Nugent &
Edmond Faye./

Connoghan are fled & gone out of the Countrey, for the said cause./

2 Item his wyfe being as he thought layed vp safely he sent to his base
brother Edmond Nugent who then was a Horseman. & soone after he
sould his Horses & caused Christofer Nugent, Robert Bane Nugent &
his owne brother Edmond faye to sell their Horses which he gave
them & to become kearne & they & ij of the Fayes viz Robert &

Marginal note hee was my Lord of Delluins steward.] added to Spenser's marginal
annotation in Grey's hand.   Marginal note herewith] a long oblique line, almost certainly
a later addition, pointing to this underscored word appears in the left margin below it.

Edmond, Cahell mac Gillese o Relye & the rest of Sleight° Hee accompanied the said William, where euer he went.

3 Item it was spoken & bruted throughout the Countrey, that the said Captein would have lefte a ward in the Clonene & the said William assembled his people & was lurking about the Clonene afforesaid along while to prevent him: & Richard Nugent of Donnowre was of the company, & as many men as he could make./

Richard Nugent of Donnower./

4 Item about the tyme that Sir Lucas Dillon knight &c & Nicholas Nugent then Iusticer went in Commission into the County of West-meath to appease the warre, the said William Nugent was a Commen procurer of all the Nugentes in generall to Rebellion, except Thomas Nugent of Dardestowne° & Levallen Nugent of Dromcree, that would not bee ledde by him, vntill by the good exhortacion of the said Sir Lucas & Nicholas they were brydeled & stayed./

William Nugent—pro-cureth all the Nugents to breake out.

Iohn Cusack falsefieth this in the Article 36./

5. Item vntill Sir Edward Mores coming into the countrey the said William Nugent & his company were wont to lye at a woodde called killmenekartagh, sometymes at the Bolly Roo, & Levallen Nugent of Dromcree his woodde of the Dirre, where they had great fyres in the night, & victelles was sent to them by the victelleres of Castelton, viz Thomas Bane, Teig o Balrey, Edmond Browne, & William Fernane./

Victellers of Castelton send meat to William Nugent This Castleton is belonging to my Lord of Delvin.

6 Item at which tyme the Oconnoures viz Patrickes sonnes, viz Teig, & Briene, & Lisagh Oconnoures sonnes, Brian Magoghan, his brother Coule & his Cossen Calvagh Magoghan appointed Clonefaddy in Ferrebille as a meeting place for William Nugent to come vnto them, & there they combyned together & it was concluded betwene them, that William Nugent, Brien Magoghan, Sir Nicholas Eustace & a fcw more should goe into the North Edmond Nugent & his company to goe to ORorick his countrey & the Oconnoures to remayne about the great more, of purpose to th'end that they might draw the Irish lordes to come & disturbe the English Pale, where they remayned a long tyme./

The Oconnoures & others combine with William Nugent.

{7.}° Item the said William Nugent procured his base brother Edmond Nugent to come before him into the Countrey, & to make

Purpose fayled, for Proteccion

---

after **of Sleight**] 'he accompanied' deleted.   **Dardestowne**] annotated in the text with a small cross.   {7.}] most of this number, and the '8' that presumably heads the next para-graph, have been subsumed into the binding.

could neuer be graunte{d}

suitt for a Proteccion, vnto th'end that he might have liberty to come into the Countrey, so as he might bee a Procurer of the countrey people to goe with him: at which tyme Edmond Nugent sonne to Gerrott Nugent & as many men as he could make, was perswaded to goe with him; And when soeuer that they had heard of his Coming from the North, to send to the Oconnoures, and they all to meete vpon the great More.

Garrett Nugents sonne.

Iohn Cusack taketh an oth of the Confederates.

{8} Item during which tyme Iohn Cusack now Prisoner wrought with the Gentlemen & Heires of the Pale, that they might bee furtherers of the holy cause now in hand, as they tearmed yt, And his maner was to take a Corporall othe of ech one that made him promise that they would doe & bee ledde by William Nugent their generall in what-soeuer entreprize he would take in hand. and bycause I was neuer required to bee of the number of them, that wrought the Conspiracy against the Prince, I doe not know what they pretended to doe, but what I heard by the Common brute of otheres. And therefore I referre that to the said Iohn Cusack, who knoweth most of all men thereof.

William Nugent doubteth Oneill./

The Rebelles sever them selves.

9 Item when yt was motioned that my Lord Deputy would goe into the North the said William Nugent came vp from thence bycause he stood in doubt of Oneill and he dispersed his People, & went but a fewe in company, whereof Patrick Cusack & another Iohn Cusack were euer two that went with him in his company, & the rest were dispersed as followeth. viz Cahir Beddy oReily, who supplyed Cahill mac Gillese rownie was alwaies succored in Fertullagh; Edmond Nugent, moriertagh mac lysagh & Christofer Nugent remayned in the Countrey & tooke meat & drinck violently wheresoeuer they came./

Piers Boy Nugent telleth th'examin-ate of william Nugent. where-vpon he speaketh with him./

10 Item yt was my vnfortunate Chaunce, that as I had occasion to goe to the Towne of Coilladogherane, I went through the towne of Maxeston, & there it fortuned that I mett Pieres boy Nugent of the same, who told me, that William Nugent & Edmond mac gilleteane Harper lay in his Barne & he would gladly have spoken with me: to whome I made answere & said, that I durst not goe to him; & he said that I should not need to feare. by whose persuasion I went in. And emongst all other Communicacion the said William said, that he was litle beholding to his vncles & kinsmen, which gave him nothing, & was at their owne Ease at Home, & he driven to travell into farre

countreies & that it should not be long so. And said he is it possible, that you should shifte me 20 or 40 Banlavase of rough Canvas to make me a Tent to lye in, in the Night. No indeed, said I, yt is not possible for me to gett so much Canvas, but that yt should bee knowen by mee, but I have a Caliver, and a Flaske which Captein Cruse gave me, and I will bring yt you at Night, and a small bottle to carry some Aqua vite about you, and according to promise I brought the Calliver & the rest the Night following./

11 Item I being in company with the said William & Edmond in the Barne aforesaid, yt fortuned that a litle before supper Iohn Cusack came in, being before in the English pale. and the same William reioysed greatly at his Coming. and as he beganne to tell newes of the Pale, they stood both a litle besyde, & they had long Communicacion together, & what they said, I know not. but Iohn Cusack spake of a Monday, and said William, say not so, keepe that to your self, and by all lykelyhode yt was some meeting day, that was betwene the Conspiratoures./

12 Item when supper was doen, we went all fowre to a litle grove of wood, that lyeth vpon the land of Maxeston, and there we lay vntill yt was towardes day: at which place & tyme the said Iohn Cusack began to tell to the said William that his wife was somewhat crased. and that his vncle Nicholas & his mother Ellen were coming vpon the morrow after into the Countrey to fynd out his sonne Christofer; & tould him, that the said Nicholas was bownd to bring him in by a day, or to submitt his body to the castle, wherevnto the said William answered, that it was lesse force, that he should remayne there awhile, then that he should have iij pledges from him, signifying my Lord of Delvin his brother his wife & his childe. what said Iohn Cusack, will ye seeme to be so vnkynd to your vncle, that ye will suffer him ly in prison for a childe, & cannot tell how long he will live. no doe not so, said Iohn Cusack, for it is the mother of the childes pleasure that the Child bee sent in, in hope to gett her self sett at Liberty: for I saw a lettre written with her owne hand of that effect with her mother to the childes fosterfather. & have not you seene it as yett: no indeed said William I saw yt not, & yf I had seene it, yt shall not be hable to persuade me to putt in the childe. But in this sort yf I can gett my wife inlarged, & at myne owne will, I wilbe contented to send in any of both my sonnes & not otherwise. which argument was mislyked of by the said Cusack & me.

Nicholas Nugent & his wife come vp towards William Nugent.

William Nugent refuseth to deliuer in his child.

William Nugent meeteth with Ellen Plonkett at Richard Crosses house. The said Ellen is wyfe to Nicholas Nugent late Iustice & mother to Iennett of Skryne wyfe to William Nugent. This Crosse is fled.

{13} Item at the breake of the day we removed from that place to another place called Bolly roo, & Iohn Cusack said I promised to mete Ellen Plonkett to day at Killowa, & yf you will I will bring her to some convenient place, where you may have speach together; I wilbe glad thereof said William & there they concluded to mete at Richard Crosses howse in Castelton & thether they came both vpon the said Cusackes draught the night following: & what Company they had, or how they did behave them selues, I doe not know, by reason that I was not present and I referre that to Walter Porter now prisoner, who was then present. But yt fortuned after that I mett the said Crosse° who tould me that yt was through the night, that my Mistris Ellen Plonkett came to his house, & that he was constrayned to flie from the same: how hapned that, said I? yt hapned said he, that she would needes goe to the great Castle, & thether came William Nugent & Tadee Noland in his company; and they had conference together; and I have vndoen my self (quod he) that I followed not Sir Edward mores Counsell when he would have me to goe to Dublin.

Ellen Plonkett deliuereth to thexaminate a lettre from Iennet of Skryne mentioned in the 12th former Article.

{1}4 Item vpon the morrow after her being at Castleton she came as farre as the wodde of Ballinvealle & there lighted, & yt was my fortune to heare of my Master Nicholas Nugentes coming to Dromcree, and thether I went, & being standing with him awhile there he willed me to ryde forward towardes Ballinvealle, & to bidde his wyfe to stay for him; and I did so. And there she deliuered mee the lettre mencioned before by Iohn Cusack and she told me how my Master was vexed for William Nugentes youngest sonne: and therevpon she willed me to goe with the lettre to Hubert Faye, who as she said brought away the childe from kilkarne. & bycause I knew of William Nugentes° mynd before, I said yt was but in vayne for me to goe thether, and that vnlesse it pleased his father that the child would not bee had.

Iohn Plonkett & Oliuer.

Thomas mac Shane Orely./

15 Item soone after my said Master Nicholas Nugent & his brother Oliuer came present, & then they mused what was best to doe therein & in the end they concluded to goe to Iohn Plonkett of Bally Loghcreawe, & he to worke with our Thomas mac Shian Orely who is an alter to William Nugent, to gett the childe, & we lighted on a hill aboue Bally Loghcreaw: & I was sent to the said Iohn Plonkett to

---

Crosse] annotated in the text with a small cross.   *after* **Nugentes**] 'wife' deleted.

require him to come forth, & to speake with his cosen Ellen Plonkett, that staied for him on the hill ouer the towne; & thether came he & fownd her there: & being in communicacion together, Nicholas Nugent came thether, who went a while in the way with his brother Oliuer; & after he had lighted they began to talke of the childe: in somuch that Iohn Plonkett said that° it lay not in Thomas mac Shian to gett the child, vnles yt pleased the father. & when I heard him say so, I said, yf you will keepe counsell of me, I will presume to goe to his father, & I will showe him his wives handwryting, & then I hope he wilbe moved to cause the childe to bee sent in./. *(margin: Nicholas Nugent & Oliuer speake for William Nugents child.)*

16 Item this being doen, I traveiled so farre vntill I came to Fowre, & I fownd William Nugent in Gerrott Nugentes chamber in fower afforesaid, & I shewed him his wives lettre concerning the childe, who answered that he would not assent, that the childe should be deliuered, vnlesse he could gett his wife sett at liberty. which answere I repeated at my retourne./ *(margin: William Nugent at the house of Gerrott Nugent in Fower./)*

17 Item soone after I received another lettre by William Miller of kilkarne, which was subscribed by William Nugentes wife, and directed to Hubert fay concerning the said childe; & I told the said fay of the tenour thereof; who answered that one Robert fay by William Nugentes appointment brought the child from kilkarne & not he, which lettre is forthComing./ *(margin: Another lettre from. Iennett of Skryne for her Childe.)*

18 Item vpon relacion made by me of William Nugentes wantes and lacke of money, Ellen Plonkett deliuered me iij^{li} in money, which I sent to him after by Bryen mac gillhev{e}ike° his footboy./ *(margin: Ellen Plonkett sends money to the traitour william Nugent)*

19 Item when all practizes could not fynd out the child, the said Ellen Plonkett disposed her self to make search for him in the Breny, & went as farre as lough roure. & I went with her & there we learned that the child was sent to a countrey called fearr managh, and there as it is said remayneth./ *(margin: fermanagh is maguyers cuntrie)*

The traiterous Actes giuen me to be° vnderstand and by whome particularly enseweth./

---

that] inserted above the line.   gillhev{e}ike] the unclear letter in this word was apparently smudged in the writing.   be] inserted above the line.

Maguyre promised to ioyne.

20 First William Nugent tould me that Maguire promised to send him iij^{xx} shott & targett men vpon his owne proper charges, when soeuer that he would attempt to doe any harme to the English Pale

The Priour & Art Oneill consented.

21 Item he told me that the Priour Oneill & Art Oneill with as many men as they can make, promised to assist him in this Rebellion, & he told me also that he did send vnto them alredy and that their answere was, that they would not hazard them selues nor their men vntill the said William had begonne the warre & donne some harme of him self.

William Nugent made Generall of the Pale by the Popes authority. which sheweth further that this Rebellion was intended before any apprehencion of matter meantt against the Lord his brother or him self.

22 Item the said William told me that vpon the death of Iames fitz Morish the pope of Rome made Sir Iohn of Desmond Generall & furtherer of the holy cause, so by him termed and the said Sir Iohn gave him the same Authority to bee Generall of the English pale./

23 Item he tould me that yt was partly through his meane that the pray of Breacklure was taken

Practize to intercept Sir Nicholas Malbey.

24 Item the said William tould me that he lay in an Amboishment at killareteary for Captein Malbey, thincking that by taking him he should purchase him self a Pardon

25 He saith that Ellen tould him that she had talked with William Nugent in the great castle at Castleton. He saith further that he thincketh vpon his conscience that Nicholas Nugent knew that Ellen spake with William as is afforesaid

Written by Mr Secretary Fenton./°

26 He confesseth that William Nugent told him, that a litle befo{re} Michaelmas last, the Baron Delvin wrote a lettre to the said William of this tenour: viz lett the poore man enioy his shepe, or elles you doe him great wrong. This lettre William answered in this sort. viz, yf yt had bene a Shepe that had bene scabbed, yt had bene better he should haue perished, then the whole flock.

This lettre was written in the name of fraunces Hamon & directed to Laurence Hamon but meant to the Lord of Delvin./°

27 Another lettre at the same tyme the said William shewed to thexaminate conteyning this matter, viz the worke that I haue taken in hand, I cannot as yett go through with it, for that nether the stones

Marginal note **Written by Mr Secretary Fenton.**/] a bracket connected to this note takes in articles 25, 26, and 27.   *Marginal note* **Delvin.**/] a hand (or index) has been drawn in the left margin, pointing to this note.

nor Masons are ready nor lyme burnt. And therefore we must wayt a tyme. This was written with William his owne hand./.

Signed vnderneath with
Iohn Nugentes owne hand
wherewith all the rest was written

COMMENTARY

William Nugentes] William Nugent was the younger brother of Sir Christopher Nugent, ninth Baron of Delvin; see biographies.

his youngest sonne Christofer] one of the most confusing aspects of historical research in Ireland in this period is the tendency of families to use the same Christian names in successive generations; this Christopher was the younger son of William, the rebel and subject of this examination, whose custody had been granted to his great-uncle, Sir Nicholas Nugent, for close keeping during his father William's rebellion. It is unlikely, as *ODNB* maintains, that Christopher was born in 1582, as this would make the child less than a month old at the time of the events recorded here; probably Christopher was born at some point in 1581.

his wife Gennett Marwardes] the daughter of Walter Marward, Baronet of Skreen and his wife Ellen Plunkett (who later married Sir Nicholas Nugent). Nicholas White records in a letter to Burghley of 12 December 1573 (SP 63/43/14) how William Nugent abducted her from her stepfather's house with 'twenty naked swords'.

Ellen Plonkett] wife to Sir Nicholas Nugent, Chief Justice of the Common Pleas (Ireland), and daughter to Sir John Plunkett, Chief Justice of the Queen's Bench (Ireland).

Nicholas Nugent] Chief Justice of the Common Pleas (Ireland), and, being the fifth son of the seventh Baron Delvin, William Nugent's uncle; see biographies.

Iohn Nugent] the exact relation of John Nugent of Scurlockstown to the main branches of the Nugent family is not clear. Because of the way he refers to Nicholas Nugent as 'my Master', it seems reasonable to conjecture that he was from a client branch of the family, and in some sense in service to the Chief Justice.

v^th of February 1581] 1582, new style.

Lord of Delvin] Sir Christopher Nugent, ninth Baron; see biographies.

the Clonene] Clonyne, the seat of the Nugent family near Castletown Delvin, south-west of Kells in Co. Westmeath; see maps.

Captein Bryan fitz Williams & McStraunge] Captain Brian Fitzwilliam, the brother of sometime and future Lord Deputy Fitzwilliam, had been stationed in Leinster with a band of horsemen for the preceding six or seven years; his band was discharged in early January 1582 (SP 63/88/9, 63/88/40/1). 'McStraunge' may be Nugent's or Spenser's error for Thomas Le Strange, another captain of horse discharged in Leinster in early January 1582, perhaps by this point serving as sheriff of the county.

a Castle . . . in the Breny] the position of the castle is unknown, but was probably on the edge of Lough Sheelin in the Brenny or Breifne (a large area stretching from Cavan westwards towards Fermanagh), just south of Cavan.

Pieres o Connoghan] unidentified.

Edmond Nugent] the base brother of the Baron of Delvin and of William Nugent.

Robert Bane Nugent] unidentified.

Edmond faye] the Fayes were, like the Nugents, an Old English family of Westmeath. It is not clear why William Nugent should have called Edmund Faye his brother, though it is possible that a sister had married into the family.

kearne] or kern; see glossary.

ij of the Fayes viz Robert & Edmond] unidentified.

Cahell mac Gillese o Relye & the rest of Sleight] unidentified.

bruted] noised, reported.

Richard Nugent of Donnowre] little is known of this Richard Nugent (not to be confused with Richard Nugent, eighth Baron Delvin), apart from his participation in resistance to the cess in 1577, which caused several of his cousins and other relations to be imprisoned. He was pardoned for his role in the present rebellion by June (SP 63/93/1).

Sir Lucas Dillon knight &c] Chief Baron of the Exchequer; see biographies.

in Commission] under orders from the Irish Council.

County of Westmeath] north-west of Co. Kildare; see maps.

Thomas Nugent of Dardestowne] Richard Nugent's cousin, and probably William's uncle. Other manuscripts of the examination may have read 'Carlinstone' here (see Public Record Office of Northern Ireland, D/3835/A/5/14, a nineteenth-century transcript of another copy of this examination, now lost). Modern Dardistown is located immediately to the west of Killagh or Killaugh, a few kilometres south-west of the Clonyne; see maps.

Levallen Nugent of Dromcree] considered 'simple witted' and eventually pardoned (see SP 63/93/1), Levallen was probably another of William's uncles. For Drumcree, Co. Westmeath, see maps.

Sir Edward Mores] a captain of horsemen in Leinster, whose band was cassed at the end of 1581 (see SP 63/88/40/1). He remained in command of a band of footmen in the garrison at Philipstown; ultimately he would receive the reward, for his service, of Nicholas Nugent's goods.

killmenekartagh] unidentified.

Bolly Roo] unidentified.

woodde of the Dirre] unidentified

Thomas Bane, Teig o Balrey, Edmond Browne, & William Fernane] unidentified.

Oconnoures … Calvagh Magoghan] the O'Connors were based west of the Annaly (Co. Longford), and north-west of Athlone. These particular men have not been identified.

Clonefaddy in Ferrebille] unidentified.

Sir Nicholas Eustace] in a letter of 18 February 1581, Chancellor William Gerrarde informed Walsingham of the behaviour of Sir Nicholas Eustace, a Roman priest, who would swear Irish gentlemen to confederacy with the rebels while saying mass at their houses (see SP 63/80/61).

ORorick his countrey] Brian O'Rourke, the O'Rourke, was the major Irish lord of Leitrim; see biographies.

the great more] probably the Bog of Allan, south of Lough Ree.

make suitt for a Proteccion] in order to travel freely past the garrison towns, gentlemen required a kind of passport—the protection—from the local governor; in the Pale, protections could be secured by suit to the Lord Deputy or Council.

Edmond Nugent sonne to Gerrott Nugent] unidentified. Gerald Nugent may be another of the seventh Baron's sons.

Iohn Cusack now Prisoner] one of William Nugent's chief co-conspirators, his defection to 'state's evidence' in return for protection made possible the Council's trial and punishment of the other conspirators. It appears that Grey also granted him a pension for his pains (see SP 63/98/64), though this was apparently quickly discontinued after Grey's revocation. His uncle, Edward Cusack of Lismollen, heir to Sir Thomas Cusack, was also pardoned in April (see No. 33, below, SP 63/91/22).

Gentlemen & Heires of the Pale] young gentlemen heirs to Irish noble houses, perhaps influenced by the political practices of the tanists of Irish septs, were notorious for taking on the (often rebellious) political causes that their fathers, bound by their status, could not openly countenance.

holy cause] resistance to the Protestant Elizabeth, who had been excommunicated by a papal bull in 1572. The Pope's influence on the Irish rebellions during this period was a matter of intense speculation in Dublin and Westminster

Corporall othe] an oath of the body; perjurers would suffer execution.

when . . . into the North] Grey journeyed into Ulster against Turlough Luineach O'Neill in the second half of July, returning on or around 9 August (see Nos. 19 and 20, above SP 63/84/26, 63/85/5).

bycause he stood in doubt of Oneill] unsure of O'Neill's chances against the Lord Deputy, and of his faith in the treaty he had negotiated with him, Nugent returned out of Ulster.

Cahir Beddy oReily] unidentified.

Cahill mac Gillese rownie] unidentified.

Fertullagh] unidentified.

moriertagh mac lysagh] unidentified.

Coilladogherane] unidentified.

Maxeston] almost certainly a copyist's (Spenser's?) mistake for 'Mapeston', or modern Mabestown, halfway between Drumcree and the Clonyne in Co. Westmeath; see maps.

Pieres boy Nugent] unidentified.

Edmond mac gilleteane Harper] unidentified.

20 or 40 Banlavase of rough Canvas] possibly 'baulavase'; an obscure measure.

Caliver] light musket.

Captein Cruse] a captain Cruce was discharged in August 1581 (SP 63/85/23), and received the right in a copper mine from John Ussher, at Burghley's and Walsingham's request, in July 1582 (SP 63/94/58).

Aqua vite] unrefined spirits.

the said Iohn Cusack . . . somewhat crased] Gennet Marward's anxiety for the return of her son Christopher is understandable, given his likely age. William

Nugent's reluctance to send the baby in for safe keeping as a 'pledge' clearly derived from his cynical attitude to the Pale government's promises; while his wife believed she would be released upon the commital of the child, William thought they would both be turned over to close keeping.

said Nicholas . . . the castle] Sir Nicholas Nugent had been instructed by legal order to produce Christopher Nugent (William's son) by a given day, or himself be imprisoned in Dublin castle.

Killowa] probably Killagh or Killaugh, Co. Westmeath, 5 km south-west of the Clonyne; see maps.

Richard Crosses howse in Castelton] unidentified. **Castelton** is, again, probably Castletown Delvin; see maps.

draught] horse.

Walter Porter] unidentified.

Tadee Noland] a Nowland Tadee was examined in January 1584 (SP 63/107/46) as to the subsequent flight and conspiracies of William Nugent in Paris and in Rome; he had perhaps returned to Ireland and turned himself in, perhaps in hope of a pardon. His subsequent fate is unrecorded.

wodde of Ballinvealle] probably modern Ballinvally in Co. Westmeath, about 2 km north-west of Castletown Delvin; see maps.

Hubert Faye] unidentified.

kilkarne] Kilcarn in Co. Meath, near Navan; see maps.

his brother Oliuer] little is known of him.

Iohn Plonkett of Bally Loghcreawe] Ellen Plunkett's cousin; Loughcrew is in Co. Meath, about 3 km south of Oldcastle.

Thomas mac Shian Orely] unidentified.

an alter] obscure; a foster-brother?

it lay not in] 'it would not be possible for'.

Fowre] Fore, Co. Westmeath, lies about 6 km north-west of Drumcree, and just over 10 km north-west of the Clonyne; see maps.

William Miller of kilkarne] unidentified.

Robert fay] unidentified.

Bryen mac gillhev{e}ike his footboy] unidentified.

lough roure] possibly Lough Ramor, though this is considerably far east; but Nugent is less likely to have intended Lough Ree, which is perhaps too far west for Ellen Plunkett's journey. It seems likely that there has been some corruption in transmission here.

fearr managh] Fermanagh, north of O'Rourke's country; see maps.

Maguire] chief of the Maguire sept, based in Fermanagh.

iij^{xx} shott . . . proper charges] sixty archers in his own pay.

the Priour Oneill & Art Oneill] Art O'Neill is almost certainly Art MacBaron O'Neill, the younger brother of Hugh O'Neill, Baron of Dungannon and later Earl of Tyrone.

Iames fitz Morish] James Fitzmaurice, son of Sir Maurice Duffe, and grandson of the twelfth Earl of Desmond, and thus first cousin to the fourteenth Earl. He led a revolt, with continental Catholic backing, in Ireland during the late 1570s, and was killed by Tibbot Burke in August 1579.

Sir Iohn of Desmond] Sir John of Desmond, the brother of the Earl of Desmond, was still at this date in open rebellion in Munster.

the pray of Breacklure] on 'pray', see glossary; 'Breacklure' unidentified.

Amboishment at killareteary] the site of this ambush is unidentified.

Captein Malbey] Sir Nicholas Malby; see biographies.

purchase him self a Pardon] William hoped to use a hostage as leverage with the Dublin government, to secure his restoration to obedience.

great castle at Castleton] probably Castletown Delvin, about 20 km south-west of Kells; see maps.

lett the poore man ... whole flock] the Baron of Delvin apparently tried to encourage Nugent to refrain from a rebellion that would disorder the lives and livelihoods of the poor; Nugent replied that it was a price worth paying, for right.

thexaminate] i.e. John Nugent, the author of the present examination.

30. *Grey to the Privy Council, 18 February 1581/2*

TNA: PRO SP 63/89/35

This letter reveals a little of the tensions that must have plagued early modern social life in Ireland, and suggests why Sir John Norris's proposal of March 1585, that the English soldier be left to victual himself in Ireland, could cause more problems than it solved (see No. 42, below, SP 63/115/41). The credit economy so basic to England during this period (see Muldrew, *The Economy of Obligation*) was, as Spenser argued in *A view*, impossible to cultivate—not only because of the frequent wars and the consequent risk of loss, but because of the transient nature of settlement, both for Irish peasants and, as here, English soldiers.

The text of the letter, including the subscription and address, is written in Spenser's usual secretary hand. The endorsement is in a later italic, probably added upon receipt of the letter in London, or at some later stage of the filing process. Grey has added his usual signature.

ADDRESS AND ENDORSEMENTS

To the right Hono-
rable my very good
Lords & otheres of her
Maiesties privie Councell
Yeue this

Lords
February 18-
The Lord Deputye.
on the behalfe of the
Town of Clonmell:

TEXT

Yt may please your Lordships The Towneship of Clonmell hath made peticion vnto mee to bee a meane vnto your Lordships in their behalf for the obteyning of certein Summes of money, which are owing to them by Captein Tanner, Captein George Lower, Captein Thomas Morgan, for the victelling of their Souldieres since their having of chardg here in this Realme, as by their seuerale Billes, which this their Agent will shewe, appeareth. Who for that they are long sithens discharged, & nowe in no paye within this Realme, they haue no meanes to come by their money, but onely by your Lordships. Wherefore I beseeche your Lordships in the poore Townes mens behalf, that yt would please you to call the said Capteins before you, or before whome you shall therevnto appoint, and cause them to make satisfaccion of such Summes, as vnder their owne hand wryting shall appeare due to the said Towneship; whose Agent a right honest Marchaunt and one, who in all such causes of service, as he hath bene vsed in, hath discharged the part of an earnest faithfull Subiect towardes her Maiestie now repaireth to your Lordships to sollicite the same suitt, to whome I beseech your Lordships yield such furtheraunce therein, as to you shall seeme expedient. Even so I committ you to God. Dublin the xviij^{th} of february. 1581

> Your Lordships most assured
> to commaund,
> Arthur Grey

COMMENTARY

Towneship of Clonmell] a garrison town in eastern Munster; see maps.

Captein Tanner, Captein George Lower, Captein Thomas Morgan] a Thomas Morgan is reported in pay in Derry by Edward Sayntloo in 1567 (SP 63/20/28); if he was serving in Ireland at this early date, he had certainly been discharged by 1580, when he petitioned the Privy Council (SP 63/79/68) for £80 he ought to have had by Sir Edward Fitton, as well as a pension or commission to serve abroad. Sir Henry Wallop had written to Burghley on 21 August 1581 for £36 0s. 5¼d. to be paid to Roger Tanner, then discharged (SP 63/85/22); on 18 May 1582 he would certify to Walsingham that this sum had not been defalked (i.e. subtracted, or withheld) from Tanner's final reckoning (SP 63/92/50), meaning that Tanner had left Ireland with almost £40 he owed to the merchants of Clonmel. Of Lower no record survives, but we can probably assume, on Tanner's example, that the townspeople of Clonmel were acting faithfully in their complaint.

this their Agent] this letter was apparently delivered to the agent of the township of Clonmell, Peter Sherlock (see SP 63/92/50), who was travelling to London to present the township's petition.

long sithens discharged] all three men seem to have been discharged by the time of Grey's arrival in 1580.

satisfaccion] restitution.

the xviijth of february. 1581] 1582, new style.

31. *Grey to Walsingham, 1 March 1581/2*

TNA: PRO SP 63/90/1

This letter of direction and request commends Captain Robert Collam to Walsingham, and asks him to write to John Norris, to expedite the plan of allowing Collam to lead a group of soldiers from Ireland to the Low Countries. It demonstrates the military and logistical links between events in Ireland and in the Netherlands, and also an attempt to resolve the consequences of the discharge of soldiers earlier that year (on which see below). It also provides another example of Grey attempting to smooth his way with the Privy Council and the Queen by working through his chief sympathetic contact at court, Sir Francis Walsingham.

Both the text of the letter, including the subscription, and the address are in Spenser's characteristic secretary hand; Grey has added his familiar signature. The endorsement is in a later hand, presumably added during the filing of the letter in London.

ADDRESS AND ENDORSEMENT

To the Honorable my
especiall good frend
Sir Fraunces Walsin-
gham Knight Chief
Secretary to her Maiesty.

1 Marche 1581
The Lord Gray.
To writt to mr Norris
to giue entertainment to
the soldiors that are
sent out of the realm
into Ireland

TEXT

Sir Having bene aduertized from Anthony Brabazon now in the absence of Sir Nicholas Malbey left Gouernour of that Province, that vpon the late discharges here made, he doubted that diverse Soldieres of this countrey birth now out of pay, & stragling to & fro, would enter into some bad Accion, & raise some new broile no lesse daungerous then the first, the which some of them by speaches had also given out, And having in that respect commended vnto me one Robert Colom, who hath here long tyme served as an Officer to diverse Capteins & is knowen to bee a tall Soldier & an honest man the which desyred that he might be licensed to carry ouer with him into the lowe countrey ij or iij^C of those Soldieres as he could levy them; I therevpon tooke advisement with the rest of the Councell here, who very well liked of the mocion, & esteemed yt for very good service to ridde the Countrey of a sort of such daungerous impes which considering the weakenes of her Maiesties forces here now lefte, were hable & like to have attempted some mischievous entreprise. Wherevpon we have consented to license him to transport ij or iij^C or more of them, yf he may, the same being no charge of accoumpt vnto her Maiesty save onely the victelling of ij^C of them for xiij or xiiij daies, vntill they shall arrive there, which cometh not to above l^{li}. the which we thinck well bestowed, to save happily otherwise many fifties. This I have thought good to signify vnto yow, to th'end yt may be made knowen vnto the rest, & withall to desyre you, to write vnto° Mr Iohn Norice favorably in the said Collom & his companies behalf, (like as my self also have already doen) that he will yield them such good countenance & enterteynement as he there° may. The which not doubting but they will deserve, for the present I comitt you to god. Dublin primo Martij. / 1581./

Youres euer most assured,

Arthur Grey

COMMENTARY

the late . . . made] Grey had begun to arouse considerable frustration at the cost of the Irish service (accompanied by accusations that lands and properties obtained from attainted rebels were being bestowed upon his servants and supporters, instead of being used to pay for these costs); between November 1581 and January 1581/2, Elizabeth gave order for numerous bands of soldiers to be discharged

after vnto] 'you' deleted.   there] inserted above the line.

from service, in order to reduce these costs. A letter of Grey's to Elizabeth of 25 January 1581/2 speaks of a letter that he had received from her, dated 12 December 1581, 'touching the reducing of your forces here to 3000, & cassing of the rest': it has been 'entred into', he writes, while rebuffing accusations of financial misconduct, '& order taken for yt, as by a Book herewith sent to your Highnes sayd Secretary in particulare may appeare' (SP 63/88/39; the book, a calendar of the bands discharged, survives as 63/88/40/1). As other letters of the time make clear, though (see No. 26, above, SP 63/88/2), the discharge created problems of its own, not least the need to pay wages to the discharged soldiers; in Galway, as in Dublin, many of the discharged soldiers found themselves stranded, and the Irish Council both feared for their welfare, and worried that their misery might lead to disorder.

some bad Accion] Grey also wrote to the Privy Council on 3 January 1582, to say that unless his Treasurer, Henry Wallop, were to default on money borrowed on credit, the financial restrictions enforced upon him would lead to discontent among the discharged troops and 'a hazard of mutinie & disorder' (No. 26, above, SP 63/88/2).

Robert Colom] Robert Collam, his name also variously spelled Colom and Collom, had been part of the army in Ireland since at least November 1580, when Nicholas Malby reported to Wallop about an action in which he was involved, where various rebels were slain (SP 63/78/80/2). On 27 February 1582, Edward Waterhouse reported to Walsingham that Collum and 200 Irish soldiers had embarked at Galway to assist Norris (SP 63/89/53). On 10 September, Nicholas Malby advised Burghley that a delivery of corn and victual had been made to Collam at Galway (SP 63/95/25). He is mentioned in reports from Ireland in February 1583 (SP 63/99/50 and 63/99/74).

tall] courageous, valiant (*OED*, *a*. 3).

32. *Grey et al. to the Privy Council, 28 March 1582*

TNA: PRO SP 63/90/52

One of the most upsetting aspects of the conflicts between the Irish and English in Ireland during this period was the way both sides seemingly carelessly consumed the lives of men, women, and children. The sympathies of Grey and his Council were regularly extended to English 'pensioners' like this one, whose years of service in Ireland, if they left them alive, left them lame and impoverished. Burghley apparently took offence at Grey's readiness to send such pensioners over to England for alms (see Grey's anger at this offence in No. 28, above (SP 63/88/40); as he complains to Walsingham, 'by my passporte there were neuer twoo penciors seene [in England] attonece'); clearly Grey's sympathy for these wasted soldiers was of a piece with his commitment to a military reformation of Ireland, and his frustration with the lack of committed support from England.

The address and the text of the letter, including the subscription, are in Spenser's characteristic secretary hand. Grey and his council have added their signatures. The endorsement is in a rough mixed hand, and was presumably added later, when the letter was being filed in London.

ADDRESS AND ENDORSEMENT

To the right Honora
ble our very good Lords
and otheres of her
Highnes privy Councell

Lords
28 Marche 1582
The Lord Deputy and Councell
on the behalfe of
Thirst.

TEXT

Yt may please your Lordships this bearer Iohn Thirst late Ensigne
vnto Captein Dowdhall having nowe many yeares served her Maiesty
in this Realme, and alwaies with very good endevour & forwardnes
discharged the partes of a tall Soldier, is now thereby become lame &
gretly° enfeebled in his body. By meanes whereof being altogether
dishabled from service, & otherwise quite vnprovided of living, He
hath bene humble sut{our}° vnto vs to recommend his present
hard estate vnto {your} Lordships wherevpon we humbly beseech
your Lordships tha{t} such favorable Consideracion may be had of
hi{s ex}tremity, as that thereby both otheres may bee e{nco}raged to
contynue their good service, & this {. . .} eternally bownden to pray
for your Lordships long lyf{e &} happines. And so remitting him to
your Lordships {. . .} consideracion, we humbly take leave. D{ublin}
the xxviij^th of March. 1581 . /

Your good Lordships assured to Comm{aund}

Arthur Grey

Adam Dublin cancellarius
Henry Wallop Robert Dillon   Nicholas White
                                              Edward Waterhouse
                                              Geffray Fenton

---

gretly] inserted above the line.   sut{our}] damage to the right edge of the manuscript
has obscured this word, along with several other words in the following passage; the proposed
readings, where they may be ventured, suit the sense and are consistent with Spenser's spelling
in other places.

COMMENTARY

Iohn Thirst] nothing further is known of Thirst.

Captein Dowdhall] Captain John Dowdall is listed in Grey's book of the service, on 27 January 1581/2, as still in service with a band of horse in Munster (SP 63/88/40/2). A letter of August 1581 suggests that Dowdall may have been a Walsingham client (SP 63/85/15).

Adam Dublin cancellarius] Adam Loftus, Chancellor of Ireland; see biographies.

Henry Wallop] Treasurer of Ireland; see biographies.

Robert Dillon] recently elevated to Chief Justice of the Common Pleas (Ireland); see biographies.

Nicholas White] Master of the Rolls in Ireland; see biographies.

Edward Waterhouse] Receiver General of Ireland; see biographies.

Geffray Fenton] Secretary of State for Ireland; see biographies.

33. *Grey to the Privy Council, 12 April 1582*
TNA: PRO SP 63/91/22

On 4 and 5 April 1582, Edward Cusack and Nicholas Nugent, formerly Chief Justice of the Common Pleas in Ireland, were tried and convicted of treason by a jury at the Trim sessions. Grey himself had travelled to Meath, as he said (apparently without irony), 'to see Iustice more equallie mynistred'; sitting as sentencing judge, he pardoned Cusack, but made an example of Nugent, who was hanged on 6 April. The two men had been implicated by the confession of John Cusack in the rebellion of William Nugent (see No. 29, above, SP 63/89/18), but Nugent at least appears to have been the victim of a vicious personal struggle among the Old English families of the Pale. The personal animosity between Nugent and Sir Robert Dillon, who succeeded him as Chief Justice, was well known: ever since a brawl during their student days at the Inns of Court in London, the two men had competed ruthlessly for office in Ireland, and Dillon was said to have been aggrieved by Nugent's promotion to the Chief Justiceship in 1578, claiming Nugent's appointment was the result of a corrupt bribe (see commentary, below). If Nugent's downfall was at least in part engineered by Dillon, neither was Grey himself innocent of a kind of partial justice. Despite his prominent position in Irish legal affairs, Nugent had two years earlier been tried and imprisoned for opposing the levying of the cess, becoming something of a popular partisan for Old English interests—a celebrity that was clearly on Grey's mind. The Lord Deputy had already written to Walsingham (8 April 1582, SP 63/91/17) of his intention to inform the Privy Council of events at the trial, a duty that, as usual, required considerable tact and skill with argument—in this case because Grey had clearly

used Nugent's supposed offence as an opportunity to menace and cow the
Old English families of the Pale, a Machiavellian political tactic that he
rightly guessed would gall some of his antagonists on the Privy Council.
This letter, then, affords us a detailed description of the business of law in
Ireland, and also, in Grey's eyes, of the proper administration of justice; but
it also exposes the very personal nature of that justice, and the importance of
the governor's deputed prerogative role in sentencing, extending mercy
(here, to Cusack), and in managing (or manipulating?) the trial process. The
distinction between an indifferent legal justice and the equitable prerogative
power of the prince and her deputies is, of course, one of the key subjects
of Book V of *The Faerie Queene* (see Zurcher, *Spenser's Legal Language*,
123–82).

The text of the letter is in a compact and regular secretary hand (not
Spenser's). Spenser's familiar, flowing secretary hand appears in the address.
Grey has added the subscription and autograph signature in his distinctive
hand. The endorsement, presumably added during the filing process in
London, is in a different hand.

ADDRESS AND ENDORSEMENT

To the right Honorable
the Lords & otheres of
her Maiesties privye
Councell yeue
          this

Lords
12 April. 1582
From the Lord Deputy

Entred.

TEXT

Maie yt please your Lordshipes Since the comyttinge of Nicholas
Nugent and Edward Cusack I haue bine much labored booth by
theimselues and Frindes that they might be chardged and brought to
tryall, And for that cause the ordinarie Sessions beinge now houlden
at Tryme which is within the Countie where they inhabite and where
their conspiracies and traytarous Councelles were wrought, I thought
it the fyttest tyme for their Arraignementes booth for the Aptnes of
the place and ease of the Countrey being assembled for the other
seruice of the quarter Sessions and gaiole Deliuerie: Besides I
remembred by the experience of the termes before, howe much the

Iurours and apparaunt{. . .}° of the countrey grudged to be so longe
Deteyned and so farr from their hoames {. . .} their owne chardges in
the action of tryalles and Atteindures, and yet for want {of} sufficient
tyme to fynishe all, manie surceassed and were referred to the
ter{me} followinge: For thies reasons principallie with others
materiallie tendinge {to} the same end, after consultacion had with
the Councell, I caused to be made a speciall commission, Naminge
therin as asistauntes and commissioners with the other Iudges,
certe{n} of the privey Councell, and with theim I went in parson and
satt vpon the benche to see Iustice more equallie mynistred and their
tryalles to passe with that sincearitie and integritie as apperteined:
And for that aswell the Propper conscience of the Prisoners might be
satisfied as the myndes of the Iurours throwlie induced and
instructed, and no occacion of skrupull or Dowt left to the generall
multitude of People that thither was resoarted, I caused to be caried
thither Iohn Cusack vpon whose declaracions rested the greatest
matter of evidence and obiections to be handled against theim, who
as at the first simplie and freelie did Disclose what he knewe of
their treasons and consentes thervnto, So now standing to confronte
theim in open Courte, He Did with the same constancye and freed-
ome of mynde as at first, affirme and confirme the whole and full of
his former accusacions without varyenge or alteringe so lytle as might
giue cause to make him suspected of vntruthe or partiallitie: And
albeit there were added to his Declaracions manie other probabilities
and circomestances verie materiall to enforce the treason, yet the
prisoners being obstinat and Willfull occupienge the tyme in
Defendinge and Denyenge, Did all they could by weake and frivolous
presumpcions to falsefie the accusacion, and be Defacinge Iohn
Cusack to insynuat a Discreditt to all his affirmacions Neuertheles
the Iurye being caried with the apparaunt truthe of the evidence
and some of theim knowinge in their privat conscience that the
prisoners were farr from that Innocencye they pretended, after they
were resolued of some particuler Dowtes in lawe by some of the
Iudges and Councell licensed to goe to theim for that purpose, they
founde booth the prisoners guiltie of highe treason and for suche condemned theim by seuerall verdites whervpon the Court proceaded
to giue Iudgement of death of theim booth: But for that {. . .}°

{. . .}] here and in several succeeding lines, damage to the manuscript has obliterated some of
the text.   {. . .}] here and in the line following damage to the manuscript has obliterated
some of the text.

Nugent⁰ being as it seamed vehementlie labored by the spirite and inward sugg{...} of his owne conscience, Did even at the barre the Courte yet syttinge and in the hearinge of so great a multitude standing by, submytt himself to⁰ her Maiesties Mercie confessinge there the Indictment and euery parte therof to be true which he hath also subscribed vnder his hande, And remembringe withall howe vprightlie he had toofore caried himself being retorned foreman of a Iurye and not spared in that seruice those whose offence was non other then his owne I thought not Amiss to pardon his lief not Dowting but by thexperience and fealinge of this affliction, He wilbe hereafter renewed to a better estate and course of lyef, and to doe to her Maiestie some acceptable seruice to repaire this his offence and requite the mercye But for Nicholas Nugent who reteyned still his former obstinacye and yet acknowledged privatlie to Mr Waterhowse and Mr Secretorie Fenton so much of the treason as verified and made good all the other partes of Iohn Cusackes Declaracion, I thought that to a mynde so yll disposed to submytt and confesse his falte at full, the guifte of lief was booth vniust and vnworthie and therfore thought it better to make an example of him to the terrour of others of his sorte, And heare I thought not Amisse to giue to your Lordshipes this specyall note towching his Aptnes to be of the Combynacion with the other Conspiratours, for that being⁰ her Maiesties chief Iustice of the common plees and swornc of hcr privcy Councell heare, And being thrown into a deape Discontentment for being Deposed of two so apparaunt callinges, Adding heareto his wonted Disposicion to repine at and impugne her Maiesties prerogatiue as was not manie yeares past tryed to his punishment, And being withall vncle to William Nugent nowe in Rebellyon, and husband to the mother of the Baroness of Skrene wief to the said William, And seing lastlie howe generallie the whole howse of the Nugentes is blemyshed and spotted with this treason, I Dowt not but your Lordshipes will gather with me howe easilie a man of thies propperties match and kinredd maie be drawen to consent to alteracion of the goverment and to be a partie therin: Thus much I thought good to aduertize your Lordshipes of the proceadinges of the Sessions, And now having formerlie written to Mr Secretorie Walsingham of the generall estate

---

Nugent] 'Cusack' deleted, and 'Nugent' inserted above the line, in a different hand (probably Grey's own). This correction is, of course, incorrect—it was Edward Cusack whom Grey reprieved, and Nugent executed, as the following page, and many other surviving documents, make clear.   to] inserted above the line.   *after* being] a low stroke, perhaps a comma, deleted.

of this Countrey, and particulerlie of Mounster, I Dowt not but he hath informed your Lordshipes of suche thinges as I haue obserued towching that Province, And of the likelihoode of some alteracion which maie be feared will happen yf it be not in good tyme mett withall: For my parte (the same tokens and apparaunces still contynewing) I cannot but Dowt that there wilbe some newe and more breakinge owt then before, whervnto the waie seames made open by the late Cashing of so great a parte of the Armye, and leavinge the mayne bodie of the Province in Manner abandoned to the will and appetyte of thennemye and vnrulie subiecte, which wilbe no smalle opportunytie and encorraidgement to theim to calle in againe forreine Ayde the same being alreadie sollicited by their aduocates abroade as I vnderstand by common aduertisementes from such as haue seane some of their Agentes newlie retorned with lettres and hoapes to feede on the faction till the supplies and preparacions maie be perfected: Neuertheles I thought good notwithstandinge my said privat aduertizementes to Mr Secretorie, to ymparte thus much to your Lordshipes hopinge yt shall not offend to signifie what I heare and finde, though heretofore I haue bine somwhat taxed and reproued as having bine more carefull for privat mens comodities to mainteyne sturres then for lighteninge of her Maiesties costes and chardges to appease the same, howe iustlie the Lord knoweth, and according to desert therin I craue at his handes requytall, Dischardge of myself against anie Crosse event procureth this aduertizementes from me, The Iudgement and resolucion therof is her Maiesties and your Lordshipes whervnto I humblie conforme my self and yt: So humblie beseching your Lordshipes to haue consideracion or rather comisseracion of my privat estate, which yf no other cause weare as manie but for tediousnes might be reckoned, for decaye of health is brought vtterlie vnhable to hould on the toyle of the seruice; and therfore enforced sekes release of the place by your Lordshipes fauorable ayde and mediacion, I take leaue, Prayeng the almightie ever to direct and Defend your Lordshipes Dublin xij° Aprilis 1582: /

Yowr Lordships assured too
Commaunde,
Arthur Grey

COMMENTARY

Since . . . Edward Cusack] since their imprisonment, in Dublin Castle, in January 1581/2.

labored] urged, entreated.

the ordinarie . . . Tryme] the customary sitting of the court at Trim.

the Countie . . . inhabite] Trim is located in Co. Meath, west of Dublin; see maps.

Arraignementes] formal accusations before court.

the other . . . Deliuerie] the **quarter Sessions** was a local judicial sitting, authorized by a royal (or in Ireland a Lord Deputy's) commission of *oyer et terminer* and held four times a year, to handle cases (including some felonies) between the less frequent assizes; see Baker, *Introduction*, 24–5. The **Deliuerie** of the **gaiole** simply meant the emptying out of the cells and the successive trials of any prisoners awaiting judgement.

Iurours and apparaunt{. . .}] the second word has been truncated by damage to the manuscript, and remains obscure: it perhaps refers to those appearing as witnesses at the trials.

tryalles and Atteindures] an **Atteindure** (or attainder) is a formal act of condemnation or indictment. See *OED*, 'Attaindure', for this common misspelling of 'Attainder'.

surceassed] were discontinued.

materiallie tendinge] applying specifically, or pertinently.

asistauntes and commissioners] chief and petty officers of the sessions; because the quarter sessions were authorized by commission, the Lord Deputy could exercise particular control over the composition of the bench at its sittings. Though Grey does not specifically admit as much, his decision to try Nugent at the quarter sessions, rather than leaving the matter to an assize or to the Irish Parliament, was undoubtedly motivated by this opportunity to manipulate the trial process.

I went . . . benche] Grey would not customarily have sat **vpon the benche**, i.e. presided, at the Trim sessions.

the Propper . . . satisfied] perhaps so that they might be convinced of their own guilt, or at least see that justice was being indifferently administered. Grey has an unusual interest in **conscience** in this letter: see below, on the 'privat conscience' of the jurors and the 'inward sugg{. . .}' of Cusack's 'conscience' at the point of his sentence.

induced] prevailed upon.

upon whose declaracions] John Cusack's declarations are laid out in No. 29, above (SP 63/89/18): this document provides a 'playne Discourse [. . .] of William Nugentes rebellious Actes', but seems to implicate Nicholas Nugent only in passing.

caried with] moved by. See *OED*, 'Carry', *v.*, 20, which lists 'Caried with fervent zeale' (*FQ* IV.iv.34) as one of the first instances.

by seuerall verdites] they had been charged with treason on several accounts (see headnote).

at the barre] i.e. before the judges' seat (surrounded by a barrier).

he hath . . . hande] no such subscribed document seems to have survived.

retorned] appointed to serve as.

Mr Waterhowse . . . Fenton] on Edward Waterhouse and Geoffrey Fenton, see biographies. Fenton himself sent a short note to Burghley, in a letter dated 15 April, describing the trial (SP 63/91/35/1).

so yll . . . confesse] Fenton's account of the trial to Burghley makes it appear that Nugent was unsure about whether to confess, and that his decision not to do so was a tactical one, and a grave mistake: 'At the end of which speaches there came one to the shirefe with a secrett messadge from my Lord Deputie, after which he proceeded no further in confession, nether seamed resolued to dye. Some thought he perswaded himselfe that yf he did not confesse he shoulde not be executed: wher in ded the message was contrarie, that yf he had confessed he shoulde haue bene staied' (SP 63/91/35/1). The circulation of secret messages from the judges to the defendants during treason trials is of course not standard procedure; Fenton's record of this curious moment may point to another way in which Grey sought to manipulate this trial, and its outcome, for his own political ends.

this specyall note] Although one cannot be certain of the identity of this note, it may perhaps be SP 63/91/18, a document entitled 'Towchinge Nicholas Nugent', which lays charges very similar to what follow in the present letter: that Nugent resisted the cess and encouraged others to do likewise; that his wife's daughter was married to William Nugent, and that she 'laye at his howse'; that he had intended to bring felony charges against 'two of the Reles notable malefactors', but that since William Nugent's rebellion he had done nothing, because they were thought to be connected to Nugent; and that he had been drawing up documents for the suspcious conveyance of his land—a common preparation of propertied Irish gentlemen about to go openly into rebellion (see *A view*, ll. 818–69; and No. 10, above, SP 63/82/6).

his Aptnes . . . Conspiratours] the likelihood of his having plotted with the other rebels. Grey goes on to make a fairly specious circumstantial case for Nugent's motives for conspiracy.

her Maiesties . . . plees] Nugent had been appointed to this post upon the recall of Lord Deputy Sir Henry Sidney in 1578, and was removed in 1581, after a campaign by Robert Dillon. It was alleged by Henry Wallop that the Irish Chancellor, William Gerrarde, had taken a bribe of £100 to support Nugent's appointment (Wallop to Walsingham, 6 January 1580/1, SP 63/80/1). Wallop was still pressing Dillon's case in a letter to Walsingham over two months later: 'he muche better deservyd the place off Cheffe Iustyce off the comon plees than mr nycolas nugent that nowe hath the same who for his repognancye to the state here to fore hathe byn imprysoned' (28 March 1581, SP 63/81/45).

wonted . . . punishment] i.e. his resistance to the cess, a tax levied by the English government in Ireland on the authority not of the Parliament, but of the Queen's prerogative only. Nugent had stood out against the cess along with his nephew, the Baron of Delvin, and the Lord of Howth, by whose influence he was no doubt in part shielded. It seems likely that the legal-historical arguments against the cess presented to Lord Deputy Sidney by the levy's 'impugners' were drawn up at least in part by Nugent; see the submissions and declarations of January and February 1577/8, SP 63/60/2, 63/60/12 with its two enclosures, and 63/60/17.

William Nugent] on William Nugent and his rebellion, see biographies and Walshe, 'The Rebellion of William Nugent'. Walshe argues that the evidence against Nicholas Nugent's involvement in his nephew's actions was limited, especially since the only recent contact that they appeared to have had was in September

1581, when Nicholas had been sent by the administration to secure William's infant son, Christopher, as surety.

husband . . . Skrene] Nugent's wife, Ellen Plunkett by her first marriage was the mother of Gennet Marward. Marward was styled 'of Skryne' after her father Walter Marward, Baron Skryne; see biographies.

the whole . . . Nugentes] William Nugent was the younger brother of the Baron of Delvin, and was accompanied in his rebellion by other relatives, including his 'base brother' Edmund (SP 63/89/18), and Richard Nugent of Donnowre.

a man of . . . kinredd] a man with such a character, wife, and family.

having formerlie . . . Mounster] in his recent letter to Walsingham dated 8 April (SP 63/91/17), Grey had enclosed a pair of documents providing such news. The first, entitled 'Aduertisements out of Mounster from Iustice Meaghe 23 March 1581' (SP 63/91/17/1), describes the ambush of Captain Fenton and his men, a siege laid by rebels upon the Castle of Bentry, and the arrival of a priest and bishop from Spain. The second is the copy of a pessimistic letter from Sentleger to Grey, giving a critical view on English hopes against the rebellion in Munster: 'yt wilbe vnpossible [. . .] to goe throughe with this service, with so small a nomber of souldours as ys appointed [. . .]: I protest befor god yf the service were to be layd vpon me: I would rather take my Choise to lye in the Towre of London as prysonere duringe my lyfe (so it were not for offendinge her Maiesties lawes) then to take in hand this service vnder .1800. footemen and 300 horssemene, for whosoeuer taketh the matter in hand vnder that nomber will nott end this rebellyone' (SP 63/91/17/2).

some alteracion] a change (for the worse) in the state of Munster.

the same . . . still continyewing] since the same signs of fresh rebellion continue.

some newe . . . then before] a renewed and greater rebellion.

Cashing] discharge. Grey refers to the Queen's insistence that he should discharge 700 soldiers from the Munster service, an order with which he eventually complied at the end of February 1581/2; see SP 63/89/9, Grey's February protest to Walsingham against the discharge. Grey had further written to Walsingham in mid-March (63/90/23) that the discharges had given the rebels new hope, leading to new and threatening combinations between them.

encorraidgement] encouragement.

forreine Ayde] among the news sent by Grey about Munster was information about arrivals from Spain (see above).

my said privat aduertizementes] i.e. 63/91/17 and its two enclosures (see note above).

I haue . . . the same] evidence of this accusation has not survived, but it is easy to see (even on the basis of the present letter) how interested parties might have accused Grey, for example, of taking the Dillons' part against the Nugents or, more generally, of goading the Pale nobility and gentry into rebellion in order to seize their escheated goods and estates.

Dischardge . . . from me] I write this letter to absolve myself of any charge made against me.

decaye of health] Grey makes frequent reference to the plague that has decimated his troops, but his complaint here is probably one of fatigue, bodily and moral.

release of the place] Grey ends with his usual plea for revocation.

34. *Note of letters to Walsingham, 12 April 1582*
TNA: PRO SP 63/91/26

This enclosure to a letter—a fortunate survival—indicates the degree of administrative energy devoted, in the Dublin secretariat, to security. Like most private secretaries of the day, Spenser probably would have kept a letter-book or register of his incoming and outgoing correspondence, and this paper—sent to Walsingham as a sort of check on recent dispatches, would have been extracted from that record. Its existence and survival testify to the seriousness which senior officials in the English and Irish governments attached to the safety of their correspondence. It is also interesting (and dispiriting) to note that only five of the nine letters listed here are now extant: all three of the copies of Edward Butler's letters (SP 63/90/11, 63/90/31, 63/90/46), that of Thomas Arthur to Sir Lucas Dillon (SP 63/90/15), and that of Sir Warham Sentleger to Grey (SP 63/91/17/2); the other four, which were likely more interesting, probably perished precisely because they were read and used so intensively.

The body of the list is in Spenser's secretary hand, here somewhat rushed and loose. The heading and endorsement are both in Spenser's mixed hand, the endorsement somewhat more careful than the other.

ENDORSEMENT

Note of lettres &
Copies to Mr Se-
cretary sent
xij° Aprilis
1582 /

TEXT

A note of lettres & Copies sent to Mr Secretary Walsingham. xij°
Aprilis

Odonelles lettre to the Lord° Deputy.
The Popes lettre to Odonell
The Earle of Desmondes lettre to Odonell
Copy of the Recorder of Limerickes lettre to Sir Lucas Dillon. /
Copy of Sir Warham St Legeres lettre to the Lord Deputy. /
Copy of my Lord of Ormondes lettre

Lord] the 'L' of this word is written over an initial 'll', suggesting that Spenser originally intended to write 'lords'.

Copy of Edward Butleres to mr Waterhouse.
Copy of Edward Butleres to Iohn Zowche.
Copy of Edward Butleres to my Lord of Ormond.

COMMENTARY

Odonelles] Sir Hugh O'Donnell, Lord of Tirconnell; see biographies.

Popes] Gregory XIII.

Earle of Desmondes] Gerald Fitzjames Fitzgerald, fourteenth Earl of Desmond; see biographies.

Recorder of Limerickes] Thomas Arthur, Recorder of Limerick. The recordership was an important legal post in a city, and carried with it certain obligations for the incumbent lawyer.

Sir Warham St Legeres] Sir Warham Sentleger, Provost Marshal of Munster; see biographies.

my Lord of Ormondes] Thomas Butler, eleventh Earl of Ormond; see biographies.

Edward Butleres] the brother of the Earl of Ormond; see biographies.

mr Waterhouse] Edward Waterhouse, Receiver General for Ireland; see biographies.

Iohn Zowche] Captain Zouche, Burghley's kinsman, had been left effective governor of Munster after the November 1580 capture of the fort at Smerwick; see biographies.

35. *Grey to Walsingham, 30 April 1582*
TNA: PRO SP 63/91/53

This short letter illustrates some of the perils and vicissitudes of military service in Elizabethan Ireland, as well as contemporary networks of patronage, commendation, and reward, and the way in which these were supported by epistolary practices. James Vaughan may have been a member of the eminent Vaughan family of Tilleglas, or Talgarth (in Breconshire, or Brecknockshire, Wales). This is one of a series of letters written on his behalf from Ireland to England in 1582, including two others in Spenser's hand: SP 63/91/52, from Grey to Burghley (also dated 30 April), and SP 63/92/30, from Grey and the Council to the Privy Council in England (dated 11 May). The three letters are written with almost identical wordings (the other two mentioning that Vaughan had lost £1,000 at the hands of Turlough Luineach). The production of such similar letters, using similar phrases in a different order, dispatched several weeks apart, suggests the use either of some form of letter-book (containing notes about the soldiers, to be used in such letters, and/or templates of suitable letters of commendation), or of a letter-book containing copies of letters sent. Nicholas White wrote to

Burghley on 9 May, suggesting that Vaughan was Burghley's kinsman (SP 63/92/24), and indeed the majority of the further letters of commendation that pass from various hands in Ireland, either on Vaughan's behalf or referring to him, were sent to Burghley (22 June 1582, from Henry Sidney, SP 63/93/51; 4 December 1582, from Nicholas White, 63/98/11; 5 May 1583, from Nicholas White, 63/102/7; 28 May 1585, from Adam Loftus, 63/116/61; 4 June 1585, from Nicholas Bagenall, 63/117/6). This connection with Burghley seems to have been profitable to Vaughan, who wrote to his patron on 13 September 1583, to thank him for a grant of attainted lands (SP 63/104/74).

The address and text of the letter, including the subscription, are in Spenser's characteristic cursive secretary hand. Grey has added his signature. The endorsement, presumably added when the letter was being filed in London, is in a later hand. An addressee note ('Secretary./') appears at the left foot of the letter's recto, in Spenser's mixed hand.

ADDRESS AND ENDORSEMENT

To the Honorable my
very especiall good frend
Sir Fraunces Walsingham
Knight Chief Secre-
tary to her Maiesty. /

31 April 1582°
From the Lord Deputy
on the behalfe of
Iames Vaughan

TEXT

Sir, this bearer Iames Vaughan late lieutenant vnto Captein Ienkins having by the space of these xx^{ty} yeares very well and painfully serued her Maiesty both here in this Realme & in Fraunce, whereof xv yeares he bare office in the field, and in the same lost both some of his lymmes & the most part of his substaunce being taken Prisoner by Tirlagh Lenagh, and in all that tyme reported to be a tall Soldier & an honest man, is now amongst the rest discharged of her Maiesties pay. Wherevpon intending now to repaire ouer into England he hath earnestly required my favorable lettres vnto you in his behalf to testify his long good service here. Somuch whereof as hath bene performed since my Coming into this land, I can assure you to have

31 April 1582] obviously a secretarial mistake for 30 April.

bene both full of good indevour & valewe. The rest before my tyme
is likewise wittnessed by those which are of very good creditt here,
to have bene no lesse Commendable. And therefore I beseech you to
shewe what favour & good Countenance you may in such reasonable
Causes as he meaneth to sollicitt, the rather to encorage both him &
otheres by his ensample to the like good endevour. And so leaving
him to your favorable Consideracion, I betake you to Almighty god.
Dublin the last of Aprill. 1582. /

Youres most assuredly,

Arthur Grey

Captein Ienkins] William Jenkins is listed in January 1582 as being in charge of one
of the companies of foot discharged in Leinster (see SP 63/88/40/1).

in Fraunce] Vaughan may have been involved in the failed English expedition to
Newhaven (Le Havre) in 1562–3: a report was made to Cecil on 7 January 1563
about one 'young Vaughan', who had just been made lieutenant there (*CSPF 1563*,
p. 30).

lost both . . . substaunce] Vaughan's loss of his **lymmes** may be less serious than it
sounds: the word may refer to any part of the body, and Grey may just mean that
he has sustained bodily injury; his **substaunce** is his wealth, property (*OED*,
n., 16a). See headnote.

tall] courageous, valiant (*OED*, *a.* 3); see No. 31, above (SP 63/90/1).

amongst . . . Maiesties pay] on the discharges and their consequences, see No. 31,
above (SP 63/90/1) and notes

good Countenance] favour, approval, patronage.

36. *Grey to the Privy Council, 7 May 1582*
TNA: PRO SP 63/92/9

This short and perfunctory letter illustrates the traffic in prisoners and
letters between England and Ireland. The post from England to Ireland
came through Bristol and Chester, the latter via Holyhead, for Dublin (On
the post to Ireland, see Feldman and Kane, *Handbook of Irish Postal History*,
4; and Beale, *History of the Post*, 181–3). The 'packet' received by Grey had
travelled immediately and fast (see below), faster than the prisoner described
in the letter.

The address and the text of this letter, including the subscription, are
both in Spenser's characteristic secretary hand; Grey has added his signature. The endorsement is in two distinct hands, the first a mixed hand and

the second a cramped secretary; this suggests that these two parts of the endorsement were added to the letter at different times—probably upon receipt by the Privy Council clerks, and later during filing in the State Paper Office. An addressee note at the left foot of the recto of the letter (reading 'Lords of the Councell') is in an italic hand, probably Spenser's.

ADDRESS AND ENDORSEMENT

To the right Hono-
rable my very good
Lords and otheres of her
Highnes privy Councell.

Lords
7 May 1582
The Lord Deputye.
Iames Fitzedmond{s}

TEXT

Yt may please your Lordships I haue in the last Packett received from your Lordships certein Depositions & Examinations touching one Iames fitz Edmondes taken at Chester, but the Partie him self is not here as yett arrived. But so soone as he Cometh, I will according to your Lordships direccion proceede to his examination and due triall in the which yf any thing shall further fall out, I will accordingly certefy your Lordships. And in the meane season I Committ your Lordships to Almighty god. Dublin, the vijth of May. 1582. /

> Your good Lordships assured to Commaund,
> Arthur Grey

COMMENTARY

Packett] see glossary. The word would come to be taken metonymically for the post-boat, but as *OED* records ('Packet', *n.* 2), this was a later development.

Depositions] statements of record towards an investigation or trial.

Iames fitz Edmondes] nothing further is known of Fitzedmunds; no record of a subsequent examination has survived.

Chester] town in the north-west of England on the River Dee, now silted up and unnavigable, but in the sixteenth century a major port for ships travelling between England and Ireland.

yf any ... certefy your Lordships] if any other substantial information should come to light, I will inform you.

37. *Grey to Walsingham, 29 June 1582*
TNA: PRO SP 63/93/64

This letter amply illustrates the careful anxiety with which Grey and his administration scrutinized the passage of letters in and out of Ireland. Grey reports to Walsingham about a pair of letters that have been intercepted on their way from England to Ireland (the one of which that has survived, No. 38, SP 63/93/64/1, is printed below). Thomas Meagh, or Myagh, was a servant of the Earl and Countess of Kildare, and was suspected of involvement in the rebellion of Kildare and Delvin. He is described by Grey, in a letter to Walsingham of 2 March 1580/1, as 'a mealie mouthed fellowe', who should 'bee apprehended, & strayghtly handlyd', in order to obtain 'the secretts of this combination' (SP 63/81/4). 'Extreemitie must wryng it from hym,' Grey goes on; 'by oother dealyng expect nothyng,' Meagh was indeed arrested, and taken to the Tower of London, where he was tortured.

The address and main text of the letter, including the subscription, are in Spenser's characteristic secretary hand. The postscript and signature, and one supralineal correction, are in Grey's distinctive hand. The addressee note ('Secretary walsingham') added to the left foot of the recto of the letter is in Spenser's Italian hand.

ADDRESS AND ENDORSEMENT

To the right Hono-
rable my very
especiall good frend
Sir Fraunces Walsingham
Knight Chief Secre-
tary to her Maiesty./

29 Iune 1582
The Lord Deputy
letteres intercepted.

TEXT

Sir, having by Chaunce lighted vpon these lettres here inclosed, Coming out of England, I haue thought good to impart them vnto you, to thend yt may appeare, what ill Humoures the already euill disposed state of this countrey draweth from some of those which are there remayning: the one of them being sent from one who is there now kept as close Prisonere, I meane Thomas Meagh, the which for that yt is partly written in some what darke termes and hardly to be construed to the better part, I wish should be examined of him, what is thereby intended: the other Coming from one, who notwithstanding that he walketh there at libertie, yet is very nerely to be touched with treason; by the which you may perceive what great incoragement & hartening these countreymen gather of the smallest favour or countenance which is shewed them there,° which though to the better sort may minister occasion of good desert, yett in the ill affected yt nourisheth cancred stomaches with secrete dislikes, and stirreth them vp to disobedience and Contempt of this gouernement. The deeper Consideracion whereof leaving to their Lordships wisedomes, and your self to Almighty god, for the present I hartely take my leave Dublin the xxix^th of Iune. 1582./

Youres euer most assured

Arthur Grey

I pray yow haue mynde of the contents of my last letters that they maye bee awnsswered & esspecyally for my repayre° ouer./

I haue wrytten to my Lord Threasurer of the extremitie that the Munster Garrisoon is in for want of vittayle & mooney I beeseetche yow sir further the redress or ryd mee of the blame the inconuenience fallyn{g}° that ootherwyze can not bee healped./

COMMENTARY

these lettres here inclosed] only the first of these two letters (from Thomas Meagh to his brother) has survived, and is printed below (No. 38, SP 63/93/64/1).

Humoures] there may be no explicit Galenic metaphor here, and the phrase presumably means 'temperament', 'disposition', though the two meanings are frequently very close in early modern writing.

Thomas Meagh] see biographies. Meagh, or Myagh, had been 'close Prisonere' in the Tower of London since March 1581. A letter from Fenton to Walsingham of 5 November 1581 (SP 63/86/49) asks that he is to have liberty of the Tower, but he was evidently still in custody there.

some what darke termes] not an uncommon phrase, but resonant with the 'darke conceit' of Spenser's 'A Letter of the Authors . . . to Sir Walter Raleigh' (*FQ*). As can be seen from the letter enclosed with this one (No. 38, SP 63/93/64/1), and

---

there,] written above the line, in Grey's hand, indicating that he checked over the work of his secretary, at least on this occasion.   *after* **repayre**] two letters deleted, probably 'of'.   **fallyn{g}**] damage to the edge of the manuscript has cut off the end of this word.

from Grey's annotations upon it, the darkness consists of certain obscure comments, and Meagh's indirect reference to certain English captains through the first letters of their surnames.

Coming from one] unidentifiable; Grey could be referring to the Earl of Kildare or the Baron of Delvin, both of whom had recently arrived in England under the custody of Sir Nicholas Bagenal (see SP 63/93/11). An obligation in £2,000 of 18 June 1583 survives (SP 63/102/91), binding the Earl of Kildare to remain within twenty miles of London, and at least three miles from the court; this kind of arrangement would have given Kildare considerable freedom of movement.

countenance] favour, patronage, support.

cancred stomaches] a cankered stomach was a common sixteenth-century emblem for private malice disguised by seeming friendship.

the contents ... last letters] Grey has frequently asked to be called home from Ireland. On such requests for revocation, see e.g. No. 25, above (SP 63/88/2).

Munster Garrisoon] George Beverley had been installed as controller of the victuals in Ireland in June 1582, and travelled to England with various messages, including one from Grey to Burghley (SP 63/93/46), claiming that Beverley found the 'order and estate' of the office of victualler 'disordered', and 'the accoumpt so imperfect'. He also bore letters from Geoffrey Fenton to Leicester and Burghley (SP 63/63/58 and 59). See biographies.

further the redress] send me money to compensate or make up for this loss.

ryd mee ... healped] an instance of Latinate syntax, characteristic of Grey's style: 'take away that blame which, if this garrison starves, will surely fall to my name.' Grey is clearly anxious not only for the lives of his soldiers in Munster, but for his reputation as a good general; if his men starve, he wants Walsingham to make it clear to the Queen and the Privy Council that it was for lack of supplies from England, over the dispatch of which he had no control. For an important part of Grey's exchange with Burghley over the victualling, see No. 11, above (HH Cecil Papers 11/91).

38. *Copy of Thomas Meagh to James Meagh, 17 May 1582, copied 29 June 1582*

TNA: PRO SP 63/93/64/1

Thomas Meagh, or Myagh, was a servant to the Countess of Kildare, whose apprehension in London in the summer of 1581 led to the detection of the Earl of Kildare in the Pale rebellion of that year. Grey intercepted this letter from Meagh (still in the Tower) to his half-brother James Meagh, alias MacKedagh O'More, in May 1582; it alludes conspiratorially to a change in fortune for O'More, which Grey clearly found disturbing; but, possibly more worryingly, it alludes to further incriminating information Meagh might divulge on Kildare.

The text of the letter, apart from the marginal annotations but including the subscription and (copied) signature, are written in Spenser's characteristic secretary hand. Spenser has also added his signature in the certification appended to the end, and endorsed the letter in his italic hand. Grey has added marginal annotations in his usual hand on the second page of the letter and, it seems, has underlined some of the text.

ENDORSEMENT

Copy of Thomas Meagh
his lettre to Iames Meagh
alias mac Kedagh Omoore.

xvij° Maij 1582

TEXT

IHS Marya.

The Chiefest cause that I send this bearer into Irland {at}° this tyme was to see you and to bring me some money yf he can gett yt; I am assured to be inlarged very shortly after my Lord of Kildares Coming ouer, so that the wan{t} of money to pay, for my fees & other extraordinary Char{ges} wilbe a great lett; I haue written a lettre to Walter Ashpoll to lend me x^{li} sterling vpon my stuffe vpon my stuffe° that he hath in his handes; he promised before my Coming away to lend me somuch, yf I had written to him. I thought he should haue had mo{re} of my corne money in his handes then x^{li} besides the paymentes that I willd him to make. Yf he doe refuse to send yt me, send you for him & be earnes{t} with him to lend the same & charge him with his promis{e} and putt to your helping hand your self. Truly xl^{li} powndes° wilbe the least, that will carry me freely home: yf the money that was due vnto me with Rory Downe before my Coming away, or the frutes of the last Harvest of the Vicarege of Rathangan bee taken out of my handes, be you earnest with my Lord Deputy to cause the same money to bee restored agayne & sent me by this bearer and to tell him of the great neede & pouerty that you vnderstand I am in: truly good brother, farre greater yt would haue bene, were yt not for my wives brother, who hath very eftsones supplied my wantes bee earnest also with the Gouernour to wryte to Mr Secretary Walsingham in my favour. I meane neuer to serve the Earle of Kildare agayne, yf you had knowen how he hath dealt with me both before my Committing and since, you would marveile that I

{at}] this word is slightly obscured by damage to the right margin of the manuscript (also affecting a few subsequent lines of the text), but given the context is undoubtedly 'at'.   **vpon my stuffe**] Spenser's slip here—repeating a phrase in copying—is a common scribal mistake.   *after* **powndes**] a single character has been deleted.

did not requite his vsage of me, having such a tyme as I haue to further any thing that I would say against him. there bee many reportes of me, but the truthe wilbee knowen to you very shortly. I hope to goe ouer with the newe gouernour, and yf you handle the matter well with my Lord Gray to wryte earnestly in my favour, there is no mistrust of my going in creditt. Your case & your name of the Moores is better knowen vnto me, then to your self, such was the care I tooke of you in the tyme of your trouble. I omitt to say any more of the matter, till yt please god wee meete; keepe yt to your self. I haue no mistrust yf god lend you life before the end of three yeares; that your creditt with your presence shalbe such, as you shalbe hable to pleasure all the frendes you haue. I haue written very lately before this vnto you; bee carefull to performe the contentes thereof. keepe your self well from being in the daunger of ij of your neighboures the first lettre of their surname is H. & M. they are accustomed to cary poison & suger together in their mouthes; a sufficient warning to beware of them. I pray you chalenge my brother Pane for dealing so vnfrendly with me. I haue written sondry tymes to him, making choice of him of all other frendes & to this howre I hard nothing from him or any elles in Ireland since my Coming, but our lettre from my mother in law. he will say he durst not wryte vnto me, but he might a written to my wife, whereby I might vnderstand how I am dealt with all in my absence. but I mistrust that the cause is fearing that I should know of the base mynded man Walter Eustace his dealing with me touching the vicaredg of Rathangan. I will say nomore till this beareres retourne, which I looke for in all hast I pray you procure it with as much spede as may bee

Provide a couple of good horses for me against my Coming; I meane to attend daylie on the governour when I come there, which attendaunce I hope will grow to your proffitt & myne. It is not knowen certeinly who shall goe but the eleccion is betwixt Sir Henry Sidney & Sir William fitzWilliam This I take leave with my wives loving Commendation & myne &c./ May xvij° 1582./

Your assured brother during life

Thomas Meagh.

Examinatur Edmund Spenser/

Marginal notes:

Greate care & good disposition too nourrisshe in hys broother glorie of bastardrie & declaring theyr moother a harlott.

the meanyng heerof woold bee learned, for the prezent state of the man is far from any sutche hoape./

Hartpowle & Mackwoorthe, better & truar seruantes too theyr Prince then euer were or wyll bee of the oother surnames./

I haue not yet spoaken with the messenger./

COMMENTARY

Iames Meagh ... Omoore] Meagh, or Myagh, was the bastard son of Kedagh O'More, and was recognized as the chief of the O'Mores. He had submitted to Grey in September 1581 (see SP 63/85/54) and received protection (SP 63/86/10), thereafter surrendering pledges to Captain Mackworth for his good behaviour in October (SP 63/86/19).

IHS Marya] a monogram of the name of Jesus, with that of his mother Mary. 'IHS' was part of the emblem of the Jesuits; there is no doubt that Grey would have regarded with disgust Meagh's superscription of these names at the top of his letter.

this bearer] unidentified.

my Lord of Kildares] Meagh had had a close relationship with the Earl as well as the Countess of Kildare.

for my fees ... Char{ges}] in order to be released from prison, prisoners were required to discharge expenses incurred during their period of their imprisonment.

Walter Ashpoll] unidentified.

vpon my stuffe] a £10 loan, using Meagh's personal possessions, currently in Ashpoll's keeping, as collateral.

my corne money] Meagh is presumably referring to the income from the harvest made from his lands.

Rory Downe] unidentified.

the frutes ... Rathangan] Meagh seems to have had title to the tithes of Rathangan, a small hamlet about 10 km north-west of Kildare; this title had presumably been the gift of his (former) master the Earl.

my wives brother] unidentified.

eftsones] immediately, readily.

Your case ... Moores] as Grey's marginal note makes clear, this comment introduces the passage of intrigue for which this letter was, presumably, copied and forwarded to London. Meagh alludes to his half-brother's bastardy—acknowledging his natural father as Kedagh O'More—and insinuates that his brother will shortly be coming to some influence and power; this is obviously important news for the English governors of Ireland, who were as ever vigilant to glean what information they might about the power relations between 'mere' Irish septs and Old English families.

Hartpowle & Mackwoorthe] on Captain Humphrey Mackworth, a longtime antagonist of the O'Mores, see biographies. In June 1585, Robert Harpoll would be named by Wallop in a letter to Burghley as the constable of Carlow (SP 63/117/55).

my brother Pane] unidentified.

Walter Eustace] possibly the brother of James Eustace, Viscount Baltinglass, the rebel.

39. *Grey et al. to the Privy Council, 10 July 1582*
TNA: PRO SP 63/94/15

This letter was evidently sent to England along with a number of enclosures (five of which survive in the State Papers Ireland, though there could have been more). Together, these documents provide information about two developments in northern and western Irish affairs: the gathering of a large force of Scots under Con O'Donnell, believed by Grey, Nicholas Malby, and others to be under the protection of Turlough Luineach; and the promises of obedience obtained from the Earl of Clanricard, and the English administration's attempts to use him to contain his sons. Taken together, and read alongside other correspondence from the time, they clearly reveal the importance and influence of Malby, governor of Connaught, in regional and national Irish politics (and on this, see Brady, *The Chief Governors*), not only gathering information for Grey and backing up his requests for more troops, but having considerable autonomy to prosecute English affairs in Connaught, and being personally rebuked and restrained by Elizabeth for his supposed expenses.

The letter is written in a neat secretary hand (not Spenser's); Grey and members of the Irish Council have added their autograph signatures. The address is in Spenser's usual secretary hand, and the later endorsement—probably added when the letter was being filed in London—is in a distinct hand.

ADDRESS AND ENDORSEMENTS

To the right Hono-
rable our very good
Lords and otheres of her
Highnes privy Councell/

Lords
10 Iuly 1582
The Lord Deputy and
Councel.

TEXT

It maye please your Lordshipes: Since the departure of Sir Nicholas Malbye with the Erle of Clanricard, whereof wee formerly enformed you: wee have received advertizementes from him of a gathering of a greate force of horsemen, Irishe footemen and Scottes, vnder the leading of Con ODonnell (butt beeing for the more parte of the retynewe of Turlough Lennoughe,) of purpose to invade Connaght and to make theire entrie vppon Oconnour Sligoes Cuntrey, to prevent which and to strengthen Oconnour / Sir Nicholas sent presentlie suche englishe forcies as hee hadd to those partes, and proclaymed an hostinge of that Province to withstand the purpose of those of Vlster, butt the Province beeinge drawen into many partes with pryvat quarrells have not vsed eny dilligence in the rysinge out or fidelitie one to another, whereby the Scottes have entred and spoyled the Countrey, as in the incloased Lettre from the Governour maye appeere. Hee demandeth aide and reliefe from hence, which wee have nott to geve vppon eny soddein, for if wee shoulde remove theis fewe in the Pale which are placed for the prosequution of Th'oConnours wee give open waye to the spoyle of the whole Pale, or if wee shoulde direct the forcies in Mounster, which nowe are imployed vppon Desmond and FitzMorice to resorte to the aide of Mr Malby in Connaght, wee shoulde give scope to the Rebells of Mounster to spoyle all the Countie of Kilkenny, as they have alreadie Tipporarye./

This draught or device of Turloughe Lennoughe tendeth to this (as wee can gather) to withdrawe her Maiesties forcies from the action againste Th'oconnours and dothe make more playne thatt which wee have longe founde in his disposicion and have often advertized, to accepte euery oportunytie thatt hee can finde againste her Maiesty beeing no waye provoked with eny offence or discurtesye to the valewe of a heaire, and therefore if eny bee thatt have perswaded your Lordshipes that the Irishe woulde lyve in quyett, if they weere not provoked maye see his errour by this outrage of Turlough Lennough, which is as wee take it, butt the begynning of the Northern troobles./

Wee perceave also by other privat Lettres, that Sir Nicholas Malbye hathe beene so rebuked in England for layinge charge partelie vppon hir Maiestie butt moste chiefly vppon the Inhabitauntes in his rules vppon suche like extremyties, as hee will not attempte to stoppe this soddein mischief without warraunt, by eny charge to bee layed vppon her Highnes or the Countrey. And therefore as wee have alreadie given him aucthoritie to vse his discrecion for this service: So are wee to crave her Maiesties resolucion from your Lordshipes what shalbee don for the suppressing of thies violencies, and the necessarie defence of the good Subiectes especially of OConnour Sligo, whome wee esteeme one of the soundest of all Connaght, for the streight

wherevnto wee are dryven by the restraynt given by her Maiestie nott
to encrease eny extraordynarie chardge and the necessitie of the
Service dryveth vs to this extremytie, thatt whatsoeuer wee see
convenient, wee dare nott yett resolve vppon eny thinge without her
Maiesties expresse direccion./

Finally, becawse your Lordshipes may also bee informed of the state
of the rest of Connaught, wee sende you the Lettre, which Iohn and
Vlick Burke have sent to Sir Nicholas Malbie, after they had parlee
with theire father beesides Galway, whereby yee maye gesse att theire
insolencies, and howe farre they bee from the Condicion of beeing
Pledgies, and howe farre different from theire fathers opinion of
them, appearing in his Lettre to Sir Nicholas which wee sende your
Lordshipes also incloased./   Whatt your Lordshipes shall
nowe resolve for the Erle, wee wolde gladlie knowe, beeing willing to
followe your direccions therein, butt if hee bee restrayned till his
sonnes or eny of theim shall yeelde them selves to prison, wee thinck
hee shall neuer inioye his Libertie, and therefore have suspended the
revoaking of him to Dublin, notwithstanding your late direccion: Hee
is nowe at Galwaye sicke of the Iandies, and attended by some of the
Governours servauntes, att whose request and by Sir Nicholas advice,
wee have graunted pardon to his sonnes if they will accept it. Whatt
her Maiestie shall resolve in bothe theis cawses, and especially for
the matter of the invasion, wee once agayne praye your Lordshipes
presently to wryte And so committ you to the Lorde. Att Dublin the
x:^{th} of Iulye 1582.

>   Your Lordshipes assured to commaunde./.
>
>   Arthur Grey

Adam Dublin cancellarius
>   Henry Wallop   Lucas Dillon
>   Edward Waterhouse   Geffray Fenton

COMMENTARY

the departure ... enformed you] Clanricard had been committed to Malby's
custody in June (see SP 63/93/35), but had not been committed to imprisonment
in Dublin Castle; it is not certain whether the letter that Grey speaks of has
survived.

advertizementes] perhaps in SP 63/94/15/1, one of the letters that Grey will go
on to mention enclosing (see below).

a gathering . . . greate force] the Privy Council had received, and would continue to receive, copious information about this gathering. Malby's letter to Walsingham of 12 July 1582, for example, speaks of 120 horsemen, 1,200 footmen, and 800 'other loose kernes' (SP 63/94/20). Having passed over Con O'Donnell's country to Sligo, where they committed a number of preys and spoils, and having attacked the Castle of Sligo, they were repulsed. The Earl of Clanricard, evidently anxious to prove his loyalty, had written to Walsingham on 5 July, to warn him likewise: 'I thought good according my bonden duetie to advertise your honor aswell of the Comming of Certaine scottes into the northe of Conaght of whose exploytes I herd nothing as yet' (SP 63/94/10).

Con ODonnell] Hugh O'Donnells's young rival in Tirconnell and, in Malby's words, 'Tirlaghe Lenoghs only fauorit' (SP 63/94/20); see biography of Hugh O'Donnell.

Oconnour Sligoes Cuntrey] in the north of Connaught. The O'Connor Sligo were a branch of the O'Connor family. The accompanying correspondence reveals that they had been especially hurt by this Scottish incursion. Malby spoke of the loyalty of the O'Connor Sligo himself, and urged that he be protected: '[he] is to be cherished, if the state will haue any care of souche a faithfull subiect' (SP 63/94/15/1).

proclaymed an hostinge] called up armed forces in his assistance. *OED* claims that the word **hosting** is particularly applied to armed risings in Ireland. *A view* discusses occasions 'when the Lord deputye hathe raised anie generall hostinges' (ll. 4607–13).

drawen . . . another] local quarrels have prevented the hosting from taking place with any effectiveness or unity.

the Scottes . . . the Countrey] abundantly described in the enclosed correspondence, not just the letter from Malby, e.g. a letter from William Clifford to Malby, which also tells that they have 'burnt slygoe & other townes adiacent, & toke xx hondred cowes' (SP 63/94/15/2).

the incloased . . . Governour] this is SP 63/94/15/1, a letter from Nicholas Malby to Grey, 8 July 1582. As well as describing the invasion of Scots from the north and remarking that 'sondrye of the Scottes wear slayne', Malby asserts the close connections between the Scots and Turlough Luineach: 'what *Ocane* is to Tyrloghe Lenoughe, your honor dothe well knowe.' He goes on to say that if 'Tyrloghe Lenoughe be not bridled in tyme he will pusshe at the best game, for if he may be suffred to bringe *Connought* to his obedience, then halfe the Realme is at his deuotion. This is the mann that is thought in Englande wilbe an honest mann if he wear lett alone.'

wee have . . . eny soddein] we cannot immediately give.

the prosequution of Th'oConnours] 'Thoconors be now assembled all togyther and do mynde to do their wourst. they wander from place to place. The captaines be after them but yet haue not met with them' (Malby to Walsingham, 25 June 1582, SP 63/95/56).

Desmond and FitzMorice] Gerald Fitzgerald, Earl of Desmond, and Thomas Fitzmaurice, sixteenth Lord of Kerry and Baron of Lixnaw, both in rebellion in Munster; see biographies.

Kilkenny . . . Tipporarye] the conflict between Desmond and the O'Connors in Tipperary was described by Grey to Walsingham on 2 July 1582 (SP 63/94/4).

draught or device] both terms mean a plan, plot, or scheme.

and have often advertized] a common claim of Grey's.

Nicholas Malbye . . . rules] see Brady (*The Chief Governors*, 285) on Malby's brief disgrace.

as hee . . . her Highnes] the charge against Malby seems to be that he has no warrant to use his discretion in the suppressing of rebels: a warrant that Grey has hitherto given him, and thinks it necessary to give him.

the restraynt . . . chardge] on this financial restraint, see, for example, No. 25, above SP 63/88/2.

the Lettre] SP 63/94/15/4, from Ulick Burke and his brother, 'Jo. de Burgo', to Malby, in which they write that they are willing to submit, if Malby can obtain assurances of their pardon from Elizabeth.

Pledgies] pledges, or hostages given in assurance of obedient behaviour.

his Lettre . . . also incloased] SP 63/94/15/5. Clanricard writes that his sons are 'redy to searve her Maiestie against the scottes or any other that shall resist her highnes either with their owne Company or in Company with any any other', but that they beseech Elizabeth's 'mercy [. . .] in granting them their pardon'. In his earlier letter to Walsingham (of 5 July), Clanricard himself had said that on 4 July (by virtue of a commission from Malby), he had met his sons, had had 'Certaine conference and speche' with them, and had persuaded them 'to be in redines to searve against the scottes, and they haue aundwered me, that they are bothe willing and redy to do her Maiestie any service they cane' (SP 63/94/10).

have suspended . . . direccion] discussion about the fate of Clanricard had been going on for some time: Grey and the Council wrote to the Privy Council on 22 June 1582: 'Your Lordships seame to hould yt convenyent that for preventing of all badd Attemptes hereafter by the said Earles sonnes against the State They should remaine as pledges by tornes fom three monethes to three monethes in the Castle of Dublin whervnto the Earle promised to procure theim to giue their Consentes' (SP 63/93/45).

Iandies] jaundice (of which Clanricard complains in a letter to Walsingham of 5 July, SP 63/94/10).

40. *Grey to Walsingham, 16 July 1582*
TNA: PRO SP 63/94/28

This terse and slightly vindictive letter from Grey reveals that of which he had been warning all along: the chief Irish lords, he claimed, would use any sign of disagreement between the Queen and her government in Ireland as an opportunity for spoil and conquest. Sir Nicholas Malby, who had received sharp words for his expenditure when last in England, was reluctant to engage Turlough Luineach O'Neill openly; Grey, similarly, was only awaiting the final word for his own revocation in Dublin.

The address and text of this letter, including the subscription, are in Spenser's characteristic secretary hand. Grey has added his own signature, as usual, and the postscript beginning 'I can not forbeare' in his usual hand. The endorsement, added upon receipt and filing of the letter in London, is in a distinct hand.

ADDRESS AND ENDORSEMENT

To the right Hono-
rable my especiall
good frend Sir
Fraunces Walsingham
Knight Chief
Secretary to her Maiesty

16. Iulye 1582
From the Lord Deputy

TEXT

Sir, this day I received aduertizement out of Connagh from the
Gouernour, how that those Scottes, which I lately signified were
entred into that Province vnder the leading of Con Odonell, hearing
that the strength of the Countrey was assembling & making towardes
them, are retired backe, having altogether spoiled the country of
Sligoh and burned the towne yt self. The which I thought good to
aduertize vnto you, to the end yt may bee certified vnto their Lordships. So having no more at this present, I Committ you to the
goodnes of Almighty god. Dublin, the xvjth of Iulie. 1582./

Your very assured loving frend,

Arthur Grey

I can not forbeare too putt yow styll in mynde for my reuocation or
at least for a leaue to repayre ouer, it tootchethe mee neere, but more
the seruyce, bee not therfore forgettfull nor slowe in it I beeseetche
yow. /

COMMENTARY

out of Connagh . . . Gouernour] from Sir Nicholas Malby, the English governor of
    Connaught and Thomond.

those Scottes . . . Con Odonell] in a letter to Grey a few days earlier (SP 63/
    94/20), Sir Nicholas Malby had described Con O'Donnell, Turlough Luineach
    O'Neill's cousin, as the O'Neill's particular favourite.

spoiled] wasted, burned, and pillaged.

Sligoh] Con O'Donnell's campaign had proceeded unusually far west and south;
    Malby was right to be anxious that, if Turlough could bring Connaught under his
    control, he would wield half the kingdom (see SP 63/94/15/1).

at this present] at this present time.

it tootchethe . . . seruyce] 'it is important to me personally, but has even greater consequences for official business here.' As Grey had warned Walsingham on 10 July (SP 63/94/16), the rebels, knowing of his planned revocation, would strike while the New English administration was in disarray.

41. *Grey to Walsingham, 28 July 1582*
TNA: PRO SP 63/94/46

This document functions both as letter of commendation for Nicholas Fitzsimons ('FitzSimon') and as an intervention in an ongoing dispute between the Dublin Corporation and custom officials at Chester and other English ports. The merchants of Dublin had formed a very strong group during the 1570s, refusing to pay custom taxes on their goods (and lobbying for permission to do so), as well as prohibiting foreign merchants from trading in Dublin. There were accusations that they had committed tax offences at Chester, aided by corrupt accomplices among the officials there. Their complaint in July 1582 was that Elizabeth had recently granted them a charter ('a graunt', as this letter has it) allowing 'that we should be fre of Poundage for all kyndes of merchandizes that we should shipp or bringe within your maiesties Portes of Chestir and Leirpole [i.e. Liverpool]', but that the customs officers in England (relying, as it seems from this letter, upon a different interpretation of that charter) 'taketh Custome of wollen cloth Which is the chefist commoditie that we do vse to transport' (SP 63/94/51, John Gaydon, Mayor of Dublin, to Walsingham, 28 July 1582). For more on this dispute, see Woodward, *The Trade of Elizabethan Chester*, 25–30. This is one of a set of letters carried over to England by Fitzsimons (from Grey, Waterhouse, Wallop, Loftus, and John Gaydon, Mayor of Dublin) protesting about this matter and about the customs officers in Chester and Liverpool: many of them include commendation for Fitzsimons himself, and for his 'resonable sutes' (SP 63/94/38, Wallop to Walsingham, 21 July 1582).

The address and text of the letter, including the subscription, are in Spenser's secretary hand. The signature is Grey's, and the endorsement, presumably added later during the filing process in London, is in a distinct hand. The 'addressee note' at the foot of the letter ('{M}r Secretary'), in Spenser's Italian hand, he probably added to remind himself, come time to dispatch the packet, to whom it should be addressed.

ADDRESS AND ENDORSEMENT

To the right Hono-
rable my very especiall
good frend Sir Fraunces

Walsingham Knight
Chief Secretary
to her Maiesty./

28 Iuly 1582
The Lord Deputy
on the behalfe of the
Citie of Dublin

TEXT

Sir whereas there is some Controuersie betwene this Corporacion of
the Cittie of Dublin & the Customeres of westCh{ester}° and Hilbry
touching a graunt by her Maiesty made vnto them, for to bee freed
from Custome & Pondage there, of all such wares and marchandize,
as they are to transport hether from thence, so as now the difference
onely consisteth in the exposicion of the said wordes and her Highnes
meaning therein, for the solliciting whereof they haue presently sent
this Bearer theyr Agent, I beseeche you therein to yield them what
favour & furtheraunce you may, both for the obteyning her Maiesties
said resolucion, and also for their more speedy dispatch; in both
which the willingnes & duetifull mynd, which in the tyme of all these
late troubles they haue carried towardes her Maiesties service hath
well deserved to bee favored. Amongst the which I am in especiall to
Commend vnto you this bearer Nicholas FitzSimon a right honest
marchaunt, & an Alderman of this Cittie of very speciall accoumpt, of
what earnest good will & duetifull zeale to her Maiesties service,
aswell in the tyme of former gouernementes being witnessed &
approved by consent of all the Councell here, (who likewise affirme
his Ancestoures from tyme to tyme to haue bene good servitoures &
faithfull Subiectes;) as also partly fownd true in this tyme of myne
owne experience, so farre forth as I haue had occasion to vse his
service; I could no lesse doe but deliuer vnto you the true report
& acknowledgment praying you both for his owne well deserving &
also the rather for my sake to affoord him your good favour &
Countenance in all such reasonable suittes as he may haue occasion
there to sollicitt. For the which you shall bynd both him with a
perpetuall bond of duety, and my self also to bee thanckfull vnto you
in his behalf. And so leaving him to your favorable consideration for

WestCh{ester}] damage to the manuscript's right margin here and below has partially
obscured the ends of some lines.

the present I betake you to almighty God. Kilmaynham the xxviijth of Iulie. 1582./

Youres euer most assured,

Arthur Grey

COMMENTARY

Customeres . . . Hilbry] the small, uninhabited **Hilbry** (or Hilbre) Island lies off the north-west point of the Wirral peninsula, i.e. on the route between Chester and Dublin. **WestChester** may just mean Chester, although it may refer to the New Haven that had been constructed in the 1560s by the city authorities, about 15 km north-westwards up the River Dee, at Neston, in an attempt to preserve the city's sea-borne trade against the consequences of the silting of the river. See Woodward, *The Trade of Elizabethan Chester* 2–3. A **customer** may merely be a purchaser, but, given the context of the dispute, almost certainly refers here to a customs official.

Custome & Pondage] **Custome**, i.e. custom, is a tax levied upon goods entering a port or country. **Poundage** was a tax of one shilling in the pound, normally paid for all goods sent in trade.

solliciting] petitioning.

Nicholas FitzSimon] i.e. Nicholas Fitzsimons, Agent of the Corporation of Dublin and alderman of the city (as Wallop also notes in his letter of July 1582). On similar commendations for Fitzsimons, see headnote. Fitzsimons wrote to Burghley again in December 1582, arguing that Dublin merchants should not have to pay custom when they ship woollen clothes, 'the chiefest merchandise we carie forth this Realme to serve hir Maiesties garrison resident in that realme', from Chester to Ireland. He begs Burghley to 'be a meane vnto hir Maiestie that wee may have free passage' rather than being 'abused' by the customs officials of Chester and Liverpool, and offers to pay the amount determined by the customs officials directly to Elizabeth for the next four years (SP 63/98/31, 'Humble petitions from Nicholas Fitzsimons', 8 December 1582).

servitoures] servants.

42. *John Norris to Burghley, 30 March 1585*

TNA: PRO SP 63/115/41

This is one of the only surviving letters from Sir John Norris during the period of his Lord Presidency in Munster. Norris hardly made a start in Munster before being called away by Lord Deputy Perrot to serve against Turlough Luineach O'Neill in Ulster, thereafter returning to the Spanish wars in the Netherlands. This letter—expressing his frustration with lack of support for the Lord Presidency, and testifying to the general quiet of the province, perhaps demonstrates why he was so keen to leave.

The address and main text of the letter, including the subscription, are both in Spenser's characteristic secretary hand. Norris has added his own signature. The marginal annotations are in a spidery italic hand, possibly Burghley's. The endorsement is in a compact and regular cursive italic, probably added during the process of filing the letter in London. An addressee note (reading, 'Lord Treasurer') appears on the verso of the final page of the letter, adjacent to the address.

ADDRESS AND ENDORSEMENT

To the right Honorable
his very good Lord the Lord
Burghley Lord Threasorer
{of Engla}nd . /°

Vltimo Martij. 1585
Mr Iohn Norris to
              my Lord

TEXT

Right honorable my very good Lord though no great occasion of Accidentes haue here lately happened to bee aduertized vnto your Lordship yett forsomuch as I purpose from tyme to tyme to acquaint your Lordship with the continuall state of this Province vnder my Charge, I haue thought meete to signifie vnto you, how the same now presently standeth, in reasonable good condicion of peace & quietnes in generall, though otherwise in some places troubled with small stealths & filching by some, which being lately come out of the Rebellion are lefte so bare & needy, that they haue no Waye to keepe life in them, but by that bad occupacion, by meanes whereof some of them wanting good successe therein, being so streightly here prosecuted & restreyned by the scourge of Iustice due to that offence, haue vtterly abandoned the fall to tillage & manuring of the land, seeing great hope of peace likely for the recouery of their decayed estates. But in truthe the wastenes is so huge & vniuersall, Chiefly for want of people, that yt wilbee very long, ere they can bee hable to gett agayne a fore hand or recouer themselues into any habilitie of living.

Address {of Engla}nd] the removal of the sealed bands of the letter has obscured part of the address, which was written over the bands. Four pairs of incisions were made in the paper to accommodate the bands.

Neuerthelesse in peace I doubt not god willing but to keepe them
vnlesse more vehement occasions of trouble doe fall out, then can as
yett bee feared or suspected.   And whereas at my Coming out
of England your Lordship willed me, of such her Maiesties landes
as bee here fallen, to looke out what places I should thinck most
convenient to bee annexed vnto this Presidencie, & that the Lord
Deputie should therevpon hauc ordcr for thc cstablishing of them, I
accordingly named certein places, which I thought fittest, as I signified vnto your Lordship of the which his Lordship hath assigned vnto
me by Custodiam these, videlicet Moally & Tralee But Asketin,
which indeed I named in especiall as fitt both for the convenient
situacion & other Commodities thereof, very answerable to the
service of the Countrey, his Lordship would in no wise yield to lay
forth the same, nor to dispossesse Captein Barcley thereof. One Chief
cause why I nominated that place was for the building & housing
which is therevpon, being almost in present readines to bee vsed,
which in all these other named parcelles is wanting, being vtterly
ruined & requiring great Charges of building & reparacion before
they can bee made serviceable. Whereof I beseche your Lordship to
haue that consideracion that ether such places may bee appointed, as
may bee to some vse & service, or that some Allowaunce may bee sett
downe for the repayring & building of those places, without which
they wilbee to litle purpose. for hardly can I thinck that her Maiesty
will giue away her owne house ready built & builde another newe to
annexe to the Presidencie. Likewise at my coming into this Realme, yt
pleased her Maiesty to promise me some of her landes here for my
self in private, for which I beseech your Lordship also to bee a meane,
that direccion may bee giuen vnto my Lord Deputy to assigne them
vnto me so as I may in due season cast for the inhabiting & framing of
them to some readines, yt being a very hard matter in long tyme to
bring so waste places to any commoditie, nether people nor almost
ought elles being here to bee had in the countrey.

Here haue bene some Quantities of Corne & vittell sent into this
Province for the provision of the garrizon here but nether so good nor
in such quantitie° as perhaps may bee aduertized vnto your Lordship
And now that the forces are with drawen hence, here being this long
while lefte but onely l. footmen, very litle spending of them is made,
so as needes great waste & losse must grow vnto her Maiesty for

Margin notes:
Moally and
Tralee
Asketin

His suite for land

Victualing the
Soldier.

---

quantitie] original 'quait' was overwritten here as 'quan', before completion of the word.

avoyding whereof & the great Accidentes that Comenly follow victelling besides the Charge of Officeres growing to great Summes &
expences to her Maiesty I thinck (vnder correccion of your Lordship)
that yt should not bee amisse to leave the Soldier to victell him selfe,
being as seemeth thereto not vnwilling, incase order might bee giuen
for his payment, or he might haue the xij^s a moneth which (as I heare)
was wont to bee allowed him for his victelling, which in regard of the
great Charge which her Maiesty is otherwise needlesse at, should
very behoofully bee yielded him, to provide himself as he could best,
for his owne best contentment & ease. And yf occasion should happen
that the Soldier should bee drawen forth to service, yt would not bee
hard for him to victell him self for few daies, as the services now lye
variable & vncertein, or from the nigh townes, being now in reasonable good sort & better habilitie° to furnish him then heretofore, of
which I beseech your Lordship accordingly to consider. Here haue of   Pirattes.
late bene many Pirates haunting vpon this coast to the no small hinderaunce of traficque & of her Maiesties impost besides other casualties, of the which there haue bene of late ij by my procurement taken,
& more would I haue enforced my self to restrayne them, but that I
fynd my Lord Deputy vnwilling to grawnt any Allowaunce out of the
commoditie & prizes which might happely arize vnto her Maiesty for
the recompence of private Charges of shipping & men & other
thinges without which yt is impossible to doe any thing to purpose or
to imploy men that way without Consideracion. Therefore yf it might
please your Lordship that commission might bee grawnted me &
some order sett downe for the Allowaunce of private Charges vnto me
for shipping & such like, out of such Pirates & prizes of theires as I
should bring in, & for the ouerplus to bee accoumptable to her
Maiesty which I doubt not but would turne to her farre greater
proffitt & advauntage, I would the rather vse some endevour &
meanes to ridde this coast of many the like, which annoy these her
Maiesties dominions & proffittes greatly. Of all which craving your
Lordships answere, & in the rest being euermore most ready, in all
that I may to your Lordships services & good pleasure I committ you
to the gouernement of Almighty god. Clonmell, the last of
March.   1585 /

   Your Lordships euer most assured to commaund,

   Iohn Norreys:

& better habilitie] inserted above the line.

COMMENTARY

Vltimo Martij. 1585] i.e. 31 March 1585.

at my Coming out of England] Norris had received his commission for the Presidency of Munster in July 1584. His first letter from Munster is dated 7 August 1584 (SP 63/111/51).

by Custodiam] a fixed-term interest in land (in Ireland at this time, usually of three years), the title to which remained in the crown; see glossary.

Moally & Tralee . . . Asketin] Moally, 'comenly Called Mallo' (or Mallow; see SP 63/115/42), is situated about 40 km north-west of Cork; Tralee at the eastern end of the Dingle peninsula; and Askeaton, about 20 km west of Limerick on the south bank of the Shannon estuary; see maps.

Captein Barcley] Captain Edward Barkley, who had served with Bagenal and Norris in Ulster, wrote to Walsingham on 23 October 1584 requesting the grant of attainted lands in Munster (SP 63/112/31); he would eventually make one of the Munster undertakers.

hardly can I thinck] I can hardly believe.

her Maiesty . . . to annexe to the Presidencie] Norris had been given instructions to identify former Desmond lands that could be joined to the office of President of Munster; these lands would then support the office out of their income, and would provide bases for the President's residence. Norris had obviously settled on his three proposals with an eye to strategy: Mallow, Tralee, and Askeaton define a triangle embracing most of Cork.

but onely l. footmen] the garrison at Clonmel had been substantially reduced after the death of the Earl of Desmond and the end of the Munster campaign; most of the military resources of the Dublin government were at this point concentrated in Ulster.

waste & losse must grow] Norris's basic point is that supplying the Munster garrisons out of England is no longer necessary; not only had the number of soldiers serving in the province been considerably reduced, but the local towns, now enjoying their first full year of peace, were better able to provide basic commodities for money.

great Accidentes that Comenly follow victelling] storms and pirates were a serious problem for the English government in its attempt to feed its Irish soldiers out of Chester.

to leave the Soldier to victell him selfe] by paying him an allowance for purchasing food locally.

many Pirates haunting vpon this coast] the danger of pirates to Irish shipping was a frequent preoccupation of Lord Deputies. Regular patrolling of the seas around Ireland was left to Elizabeth's admirals; George Beston was allowed 10s. *per diem* at the end of 1580 for the apprehension of pirates in her Majesty's ship the *Foresight*, and Sir John Perrot 26s. 8d. *per diem*, in the *Revenge* (see *CSPD* 1590, p. 95). The south-west coast of Ireland, with its remote and sheltered bays, seems to have offered an inconspicuous haven for ships coming off the main. For Spenser's implication in privateering and the appropriation of prize spoils, see Zurcher, *Spenser's Legal Language*, 110–15.

her Maiesties impost] a tax levied on custom imported from overseas; the interception of goods by pirates meant fewer goods, and thus a smaller return on the impost; but fear of pirates also contributed to a gradual atrophy in trade over the longer term.

by my procurement] it is not clear whether Norris himself oversaw the boarding and capture of these two pirate vessels, or simply supplied commission and/or funds to a venture undertaken by another. The grant of a Lord President's authority for such a venture would have been a significant boost for adventurers, whose potential gains would thereby have been made secure.

any Allowaunce out of the commoditie & prizes] goods seized from pirates were considered 'prize', and as such by ancient custom were assigned to the royal prerogative. Lord Deputy Perrot, as the Queen's viceroy in Ireland, thus had the privilege of assigning or disposing of any spoil.

without Consideracion] Without recompense for their toil and danger.

commission] a formal licence.

for the ouerplus to bee accoumptable to her Maiesty] Norris proposes that he should by licence be allowed at least the cost of any anti-piratical ventures; that cost subtracted, he proposes that the remainder, or profit, could pass to the Queen.

Clonmell] the easternmost garrison town of Munster, in Tipperary, and traditionally the first, strongest staging post for English ventures in the province; see maps.

43. *Thomas Norris to Walsingham, 1 July 1588*
TNA: PRO SP 63/135/66

The marriage in 1588 of Florence MacCarthy to Ellen (or Eileen), daughter of Donal MacCarthy, first Earl of Clancar and MacCarthy More, was an anxious moment for the English governors of Munster. MacCarthy had spent two years in England (much of it at the court), but remained a Catholic and was suspected of involvement with Spain, especially because of his connections to Sir William Stanley. He was also manoeuvring on two regional domestic political fronts: firstly, to ensure his succession to the title of MacCarthy Reagh, for which he had the complicity of his uncle, Sir Owen MacCarthy (the current MacCarthy Reagh), in quashing the claims of his cousin Donal; and secondly, by marrying Ellen, to acquire the title of MacCarthy More. Fearing the consequences of this consolidation (which, as Norris makes clear in this letter, involved uniting in a single man the heirs and hopes of a number of intermittently disloyal Munster families and lordships), Norris had Florence imprisoned, firstly with his wife in Cork, and then in the Tower of London. For Spenser's own arguments on managing the influence and credit of Irish chiefs and noblemen, see *A view*, ll. 4574–613, and Zurcher, *Spenser's Legal Language*, 183–202. Norris also wrote a letter to Elizabeth (29 June 1588, SP 63/135/55), to inform her of Florence's committal, but one month later (28 July 1588, SP 63/135/93) he was writing to Walsingham, to plead his prisoner's penitence and good will.

The address and the main text of the letter, including the subscription, are in Spenser's regular and flowing secretary hand. The two endorsements are in separate, and distinct hands, probably added during the filing process in London. Norris's autograph signature concludes the letter.

ADDRESS AND ENDORSEMENT

To the right Hono-
rable Sir Fraunces
{W}alsingham Knight
{prin}cipall Secretary
{to} her Maiesty./°

July 1588
From the Vicepresident
of Mounster.

Entred.

TEXT

Right Honorable my most humble dewty remembred; whereas her
Maiesty by her lettres of the third of Iune last past gave me in commaundement to committ the body of florence MacCarthy, and
therevpon to certifye her Highnes of my doinges therein, as also of
the meanes & maner, by which the sayd Florence compassed the
mariage with the Earle of Clancarties daughter; for that the circunstances thereof doe inforce a tædious recitall, I presumed not to
trouble her Highnes with the particularities, but thought them rather
meet to bee aduertized to your Honour (who have also written to me
touching the same) to th'end that by your meanes knowledg thereof
might bee deliuered to her Maiesty at her good pleasure.   Vpon
the first arrivall of the sayd Florence here, coming vnto me he gave
no signe of any such purpose, as sithens fell out, but to give coler (as
seemed) to his intent, and to draw me the further from suspicion
thereof, through his seeming conceived vnkyndnes against the Earle,
he then discouered vnto me some ill dealing of the sayd Earle
towardes him, namely how that being bownd to him in great bandes,
for assuraunce of certein landes, and for performaunce of some other
conditions, emongst which one was, that he should give him his
daughter in mariage, he neuerthelesse had broken with him, and
therefore offred me (yf I should so lyke) the benefitt of the for-
feictures of the sayd bandes: which speaches (as sithens I have
conceived) seeme to have proceded of some further matter in the
secrete of his hart, those his wordes being so contrary to that, which

---

Address] as often, some of the address has been obscured by the removal of the seal upon
receipt/filing of the letter; the missing words can be very safely inferred from other examples.

he eftesoones did attempt. But the very grownd thereof (as I am informed, and as by many strong circunstances may be gathered) proceded from the Earle him self, how euer sithens he would fynd him self grieved therewith and was compacted betwene them in England at the sayd florences there late beeing, & not without the privitie & great furtheraunce of Sir Owen MacCarthy, who by all meanes endevoreth to back & iniuriously to raise vp the sayd Florence against his kinsman Donell MacCarthy, aswell in the succession of the Captenry of his countrey, as also in all other causes, that may advauntage him therevnto; Wherein yt is very certein, that the Earle also hath euer greatly favored him. Besydes yt is here by many reported (the further proofes whereof I have not yett had tyme to sifte out) that the sayd Earle gave to Florence at his coming, his secrete lettres to his wife, to that effect which now hath happened: to whome presently after his arrivall he repayred with the same, and soone after dispatched his hidden intent. And for more lykelyhode that yt was then wrought & concluded in England, I am certeinly given to vnderstand, that at the instant of his departure from thence, Captein Iaques being then in company with him, counseled him very earnestly, whatsoeuer he did, to goe through with the mariage out of hand; assuring him, that for obteyning her Maiesties consent therevnto he would so work with some his frendes there, that yt should bee brought to passe: and to the end to bee more speedily advertized of his procedinges, he sent a servaunt of his owne ouer° hether in company with Florence who vpon conclusion of the matter, was presently dispatched hence back agayne. The further knowledg and intent whereof may there I thinck, best bee boulted out of the sayd Iaques, who thereby seemeth to have beene acquainted with the entreprize from the beginning and to bee privie to any other purpose, that may depend therevpon. For sure yt carrieth great shewe of deepe consequence, considering how strongly the sayd Florence is allyed to such, as euill may bee looked from. first his mother was foster to Iames fitz Morice the Archtraytour, whereby he is nephew to the Lord Roches wife and to the Lord of Muscries mother & coosen german to the Seneschall of Imokhillies wife. All which persons doe hang vpon one weake thred, and have their eyes se{tt} all vpon hope of forreyne helpes. but namely the sayd Lord Roche, who sheweth him self in all his behaveour & also in some open speaches, to bee discontented with this governement, repyning obstinately against all

<hr />

ouer] inserted above the line.

directions of the State here, and supporting him self with the vayne conceipt of his secrete hope, whereof heretofore he hath, and yett dayly doth give apparant demonstrations. So that now the sayd Florence by this his late knott hath given great strength to that syde, and hath combined all the reliques of the house of Iames fitz Morice to the kindred of the Clancarties; which being the greatest name and nacion now in Mounster (all Desmond, all Carbery, all Muscry, all Dowalla being of that line), yt inferreth great importaunce & matter of neare respect to bee prevented, or at the least well eyed; the rather for that the sayd Clancarties have heretofore, before the coming in of the Geraldines vpon them, had all this Province in their subieccion: the continuall memory whereof they yett vse to nourish emongst them, and to deliuer to their posterities by dew succession. And now this new° occasion meeting in a man of the same race being of his quality & sort, who by blood is so nigh allyed to forreyne practizers, by difference of religion devoted to the contrary part, by his owne private disposicion hath alwayes shewed him self dearly well affected and inclined to the Spaniard, being also generally favored of all his countrey, and now in very plausible acceptaunce, the rather for the late gratious favours, which he received of her Maiesty and that by this attempt hath discouered his ambitious desyre to make him self great; yt is greatly to bee regarded, to what end the same may grow. Moreouer now lately (whether for any further intent, or that yt is through his heedlesse vnhappinesse so fallen out) he hath by all meanes laboured to bee interesse° in the old head of Kinsale, which is the Lord Courcies auncient manour house, & a place often heretofore eyed & earnestly motioned, for opinion of great strength to bee fortifyed: the title whereof he hath (as I vnderstand° compassed, and was the same day, that he was apprehended, mynded to ryde thether to take possession thereof. All which concurring so daungerously to the increase of doubt, I would therefore wish (vnder reformacion of better advizement) that though hereafter he shall perhaps work him self grace or pardon of the present dislyke, yett that very good assuraunce bee taken of him before his enlargement, for avoyding of

<hr>

after **new**] 'succ' deleted. It seems that Spenser began accidentally to write 'succession' (as just above; note the similarity of 'dew' and 'new') before realizing his mistake and correcting it to 'occasion'.   **bee interesse**] while this is clearly what Spenser wrote, it seems likely that he miscopied; the sense, however, is clear: Florence MacCarthy sought to be invested in the title of the house and lands of the Old Head of Kinsale.   **(as I vnderstand**] Spenser probably did not close this parenthesis because, in the original, the word 'vnderstand' abuts the end of its line, which to the early modern eye provided punctuation enough.

the euilles which are depending vpon the circunstances of his person and condicion. Him now I have according to her Highnes pleasure committed, as also according to the later direccion in your Honoures lettres of the iiij[th] of the last moneth have caused the Countesse, Mac finin, Teig Merigagh and such others, as I could learne to have bene privy to the practize, to bee apprehended as I could come by them; and doe not doubt but very shortly to come by the rest likewise: of the which I vnderstand that Osullivan More was the greatest forwarder & nearest of councell though indeed all the Chief of that countrey were wrought by Florence to consent therevnto, who (as I am lett to vnderstand) before the mariage gott all their handes to firme that agreement, by a generall combinacion of them, and soone after accomplished the sayd mariage in an old broken church thereby, not in such solemnity & good sort as behoved, & as order of law & her Maiesties iniunctions doe require.   Thus am I carried by large relacion of particulares, into a tædious length of lines, which I beseech your Honour to pardon, in regard of the vrgentnes of the matter, and many occasions meeting with the same. Further I haue thought good to aduertize your Honour of the present good quiett of this Province, in which yt is not vnlikely to continew, yf forreyne invasion doe not occasion the chaunge; which yf any should happen, litle stay (god wote) can here bee hoped for, and lesse meanes of defence, by reason of the great wantes of men, municion, and all other necessaries, which are requisite therevnto: for which I have often importuned my Lord Deputy, but yctt cannott receive any thing to purpose in so great occasion. But I fynd great comfort by your Honours lettres, & lesse cause of feare then wee haue hetherto conceived: which I beseech god to confirme to his good will & pleasure.   To whose gratious proteccion & gouernement recommending your Honour with most humble acknowledgement of my faythfull dewty & devocion to the same, I humbly take leave. from Limerick, the first of Iulie. 1588./

Your Honours most humble at Com-
maundement euer,

Thomas Norreys

COMMENTARY

her lettres . . . last past] these letters do not survive.
committ the body] apprehend and imprison.

the mariage . . . Clancarties daughter] see headnote.

by your meanes] by Walsingham himself (performing the secretarial duty of with-holding information until it can be delivered **at her good pleasure**).

the first . . . Florence here] it may be that Norris is talking about MacCarthy's return to Ireland in 1585 (after having been in London since 1583), but the account seems to be of more recent events.

purpose] intention.

as sithens fell out] as appeared later.

to give coler . . . his intent] see *OED*, 'colour', *n.*[1], 12e: 'to give a specious appear-ance or verisimilitude; to afford ground or pretext' (although the first usage is given as only 1771). MacCarthy made Norris believe in his deceptive tales.

being bownd . . . great bandes] perhaps merely metaphorically, being bound by great compulsions or restraints.

and for . . . conditions] and to do certain other things for him.

the benefitt . . . bandes] the benefits that MacCarthy tells Norris are due to pass to him, on the Earl of Clancarr's breaking of his promise.

to have proceded . . . hart] to have come from a different, secret intention.

compacted . . . in England] Florence MacCarthy was in England between 1583 and 1585.

privitie] private counsel, concealment.

furtheraunce] assistance.

Sir Owen MacCarthy] Florence MacCarthy's uncle, Earl of Carbery, and at the time possessor of the title of MacCarthy Reagh, in the succession to which title he favoured Florence against **his kinsman Donell MacCarthy**: Norris's charge is that Sir Owen has promoted the match in order to increase Florence's power in local politics. See biographies.

the succession . . . countrey] the elective succession to the head of the family, to the title of MacCarthy Reagh. This elective tanist law continued to be seen as a threat to the imposition of English legal and political practices, and as a custom that could create excessively powerful local chieftains beyond the reach of royal control. For Spenser's analysis of the English objections to tanistry, see *A view*, ll. 175–258.

sifte out] scrutinize, or ascertain by scrutiny.

repayred] journeyed.

dispatched . . . intent] carried out his secret intention.

wrought & concluded] arranged, decided upon.

Captein Iaques] or Jaques. He is mentioned as a lieutenant in the service of William Stanley (for his connection to MacCarthy, see headnote) in 1585 (SP 63/118/15) and 1586 (SP 63/140/21/3), and, in August 1591, as having great experience in the Irish wars (SP 63/159/48).

out of hand] immediately (*OED*, 'Hand', *n.*, 33).

intent] purpose, plan, scheme.

boulted out of] found out from, by examination. The metaphor is of sifting, as above (a **boult** is a flour-sieve).

purpose] intended action.

yt carrieth . . . deepe consequence] it appears to be very significant.

such, as . . . looked from] those from whom evil conduct may be expected.

foster] i.e. nurse. See *A view*, ll. 3101–33 on the allegedly dangerous consequences of fostering; and No. 45, below (SP 63/147/16), for another imputation of the connection between fostering and treachery.

Iames fitz . . . Archtraytour] member of the Desmond family, killed while in open rebellion in August 1579. He had actively sought assistance from the Pope and papal armies in France, Spain, and Portugal, and it was his fortification in Smerwick that was occupied by the papal forces in 1580 (see No. 5, above, SP 63/78/29, and notes).

nephew to . . . Roches wife] Maurice Roche, Viscount Fermoy, was married to Eleanor, daughter of Maurice Fitzjohn Fitzgerald and sister of the aforementioned James Fitzmaurice.

Lord of Muscries] Lord of Muskerry was a MacCarthy title.

coosen german] first cousin (or often, by extension, a close relative).

Seneschall of Imokhillies] the Seneschal of Imokilly, John Fitzedmund Fitz-gerald, had been accused in 1586 of dealing with Spain, and was described by Sir Henry Wallop as the most dangerous man in Co. Cork (Wallop to Burghley, 30 May 1586, SP 63/124/47).

All which . . . weake thred] i.e. they depend upon the chance of rebellion.

forreyne helpes] from Spain. See No. 45, below (SP 63/147/16), for the implica-tion that Roche was preparing for a Spanish invasion.

all his behaveour] see No. 45, below (SP 63/147/16), Spenser's bill against Roche, which includes various allegations of Roche's supposedly treacherous behaviour, and more of his **repyning obstinately**.

this his late knott] this marriage.

the reliques . . . fitz Morice] on Fitzmaurice, see above.

all Desmond . . . all Dowalla] Munster lordships. Florence MacCarthy's father had been Lord of Carbery.

the coming . . . upon them] the dominance of the Desmond lordship.

they yett vse] they still tend to.

deliuer . . . posterities] pass on to their children.

a man . . . sort] i.e. Florence MacCarthy.

by blood . . . forreyne practizers] to James Fitzmaurice; see above.

heedlesse vnhappinesse] reckless misfortune.

old head of Kinsale] a headland near to Kinsale, on the south coast of Co. Cork, with its manor house.

Lord Courcies . . . house] Lord Courcy is listed in a report made by certain commissioners in 1586 as one of the Lords of Munster (SP 63/127/75).

motioned] proposed.

compassed] achieved, acquired.

vnder reformacion . . . advizement] unless I am otherwise advised.

assuraunce] pledges or guarantees of his loyalty and good behaviour.

condicion] rank, status.

committed] apprehended, imprisoned.

the Countesse] presumably Florence's mother, wife of the Earl of Carbery.

Mac finin] described as a lord of a lesser country than O'Sullivan More, and married to the Earl of Clancarr's base daughter (SP 63/135/58, Sir William Herbert's 'Description of Munster').

Teig Merigagh] Owen MacTeigh Mergagh.

Osullivan More] Seneschal and marshall of the Earl of Clancar, with one hundred armed men at his command. Married to Florence MacCarthy's sister (SP 63/135/58, Sir William Herbert's 'Description of Munster', where he is mentioned in connection with this incident).

combinacion] conspiracy, plot.

stay] hindrance to such an attack.

I have . . . Lord Deputy] no such letters to the then Lord Deputy, Sir William Fitzwilliam, survive.

your Honours lettres] these letters, having their destination in Ireland, have not survived.

44. *Edmund Spenser's Answer to the Articles for Undertakers, May/June 1589*

TNA: PRO SP 63/144/70

Following the final defeat of the Earl of Desmond in 1583, his escheated lands (i.e. those forfeited to the crown as a result of his treason) in Munster were parcelled and distributed to gentlemen 'undertakers' who promised to settle them with English colonists. The commissioners appointed to oversee the division of the estate were charged in mid-May 1589 with a set of Articles to be put to all undertakers, soliciting their immediate responses. For a copy of the Articles to be answered, dated 11 May, see SP 63/144/14, /17–20. The articles may have been circulating before this date in England, as Sir Edward Denny's answer (SP 63/144/10) is dated 10 May (another reply, SP 63/144/24, is dated 12 May); other extant replies include those of Sir William Herbert (SP 63/144/21), Hugh Cuffe (SP 63/144/26), and Sir Walter Ralegh (SP 63/144/27). Spenser's answer appears among a group of undated replies, all of them from undertakers (or undertakers' agents) based in Ireland.

The text of the document is in Spenser's characteristic secretary hand, here faded and somewhat rough (some text has been lost in the right margin and, apparently, at the bottom of the page). The endorsement appears to be Spenser's own italic hand, somewhat more formal and rounded than in other examples. The signature at the bottom left of the document is in the familiar cursive, abbreviated form. The word 'null' below the endorsement has been added in a secretary hand; it is consistent with the subscriptions appended to the other replies from the undertakers (many, like Spenser's, read 'null'; some indicate rents and chargeable lands).

ENDORSEMENT

Edmund Spenser his aunswere to the comissionne

null.

TEXT

The answere of Edmond Spenser gentleman to the Articles of Instructions given in charge to the Commissioners for examining & inquyring of her Maiesties attainted landes past to the vndertakers

To the first he sayth that he hath vndertaken the peopling of a $\quad$ 1 Segniory of iiij^m acres allotted vnto him by a Particular from the vndertakers, in which the Castle & landes of Kilcolman & Rossack were appointed vnto him, the which want much of the sayd whole Proporcion of iiij^m acres

To the second he sayth that he hath not as yett passed his Patent of $\quad$ 2 the sayd landes for that he covenanted with Mr Rheade who had a former particular graunted him of {the} sayd landes, that incase the sayd Mr Read or any for him came before Whitsontyde last to inhabit the same, that then he should disclame & surrender the Premisses;^{o} & therefore till that tyme expired he was lothe to passe the sayd Patent. But since thexpiracion of the said tyme being willing to have passed yt, he hath not bene permitted for that Iustice Smithes who is onely now lefte of the Quorum hath bene euer absent in England. But so soone as he retourneth he will passe the same.

To the third he sayth that there wanteth of his dew Proporcion m $\quad$ 3 acres as he supposeth at the least

To the iiijth ^{o} fifte & vith ^{o} he knoweth of^o chargeable landes and^o $\quad$ 4/5/6./ chiefrentes within the compas of his Particular but onely^o iiij nobles vpon Ballinegarragh & vi or vij d vpon Ballinfahnigh

---

after **Premisses;**] 'w^c' deleted.   *after* **iiijth**] '&' deleted.   **& vith**] inserted above the line.   *after* **of**] 'noe' deleted   **and**] 'nor' deleted; 'and' inserted above the line.   **but onely . . . Ballinfahnigh**] this line of text inserted in smaller writing, apparently after the next entry was begun. The sense of this addition explains the revisions described in the preceding two notes.

7/8./ To the vijth &° viijth he sayth that as yett he hath not made any division
of his landes to his tenantes, for that his patent is not yett passed vnto
him, nor his landes established.

9/10/11 To the ixth xth ° & xjth he sayth that he hath hetherto but vj° hous-
holdes of English people vpon his land, for the former causes.

12 To the xijth he sayth that so ndry honest persons in Eng{land} have
promised to come ouer to inhabit his land so sone as his pat{ent}
{. . .}°

Edmund Spenser

COMMENTARY

The answere . . . vndertakers] see headnote for general context. Spenser's self-
styling as a 'gentleman' reflects the landed status he acquired from Grey's gifts and
his own canny dealings in Munster.

Segniory] the estates carved out of the Desmond lands were known as seignories,
and varied in size from a few to fifteen thousand acres.

Particular . . . vndertakers] in this sense, not precisely recorded in the *OED*,
'particular' denotes a private rather than a public order, here issued by the council
of the undertakers in Munster (but see *OED*, 'Particular', *n.* 1(c)).

Castle & landes . . . Rossack] Kilcolman Castle and its lands are situated about two
miles north-east of the town of Buttevant in Co. Cork. The lands of Rossack
(modern Rossagh) lie immediately to the south-east of Kilcolman.

passed his Patent] in order officially to establish title to their lands, undertakers
were required to secure a patent from the crown. Although Spenser had been
allotted informal possession of the estate by the undertakers by this date, he had
not yet applied for his patent.

Mr Rheade] Andrew Reade, a Southampton gentleman; little is known of him. As
Ray Heffner argued ('Spenser's Acquisition of Kilcolman'), it is likely that Reade
stayed away from Munster because of Lord Roche's attempts to contest the title of
the Kilcolman lands, which he claimed were his, and not part of the escheated
Desmond estates. As Clerk of the Council in Munster by this time, Spenser would
have been in a much stronger position to fight a bureaucratic battle against the Old
English Lord.

before Whitsontyde last] 22 May 1589.

he should disclame . . . Premisses] Spenser had obviously covenanted with Reade
to hold the premises on his behalf until the end of May, probably in order to keep
Roche and his tenants out of the contested property; in return Reade apparently

---

vijth &] inserted above the line.   xth] inserted above the line.   **but vj**] 'not aboue vij'
deleted; 'but vj' inserted above the line.   **Eng{land} ... pat{ent} {...}**] damage to
the manuscript has obscured the right margin and the foot of the text here, obscuring the
conclusion of Spenser's answer.

gave Spenser the right to declare title in his own right if the situation had not improved sufficiently to Reade's liking. The implication is that Reade and Spenser both assumed that Spenser, with his connections in the local and Dublin governments, would stand a better chance than Reade of fending off Roche.

Iustice Smithes] Jesse or Jessua Smythes, First Justice of Munster and an undertaker, was made a Commissioner of the plantation in the instructions issued to Lord Deputy Perrot in November 1585; see LPL Carew MS 582.

of the Quorum] the small group of judges one of whom was required to be present in order to constitute the Bench (here, of Munster).

chargeable . . . chiefrentes] in the 'Instructions to be annexed to the commission for the inquisition of the state of the tenants and occupiers of the lands and territories escheated to her Majesty by the attainder of the late Earl of Desmond and others', the Privy Council required the commissioners to 'inquire in what sort the escheated lands were chargeable to the Earl of Desmond and to others' (see e.g. LPL Carew MS 606); taxes formerly paid to the Earl of Desmond would, of course, now be due to the crown instead. Similarly, lands that the Earl had held directly from the crown, and on which he (ought to have) paid rent directly to the Queen ('chiefrents'), would now be held on the same conditions by the new tenants. The Queen and Privy Council further elaborated on these rents in their instructions for Sir Valentine Browne of 1587: 'The Lord Deputy is to appoint some person to collect the rents due by certain freeholders to the late Earl of Desmond and others. Part of the said rents have been received by some of the Undertakers, who are to accompt for the same. Certain other rents answered to the said Earl upon certain lands called the chargeable lands, and now in arrear, are to be collected'; see LPL Carew MS 646.

Ballinegarragh . . . Ballinfahnigh] unidentified; presumably these hamlets were associated with chargeable ploughlands.

45. *Bill against Lord Roche, 12 October 1589*

TNA: PRO SP 63/147/16

This document of 1589, one of the last datable documents that we have in Spenser's hand, finds him an undertaker in Co. Cork, involved in local legal business (travelling back from the sessions at Limerick), and involved in a land dispute with Maurice Roche, Viscount Fermoy. Spenser had acquired his title to the lands of Kilcolman and Rossack by special grant from the commissioners of the Munster plantation, following the escheat of all of the Earl of Desmond's properties at his death in 1583. Lord Roche contested Spenser's right to the lands, claiming that he had come into possession 'by making of corrupt bargains with certain persons pretending falsely title to parcel of the Lord Roches lands', and had taken certain castles (presumably both Kilcolman and the bawn at Richardston) and ploughlands that belonged to him (see Heffner, 'Spenser's Aquisition of Kilcolman'). The cause of the dispute is straightforward: while the Queen and the Privy Council had taken careful steps to ensure the fair and accurate appraisal of the Earl of Desmond's lands after the end of the Munster rebellion, inevitably the Earl's title in some parcels of the estates was confused or contested, and in Kilcolman and Rossack Spenser inherited what appears to have been a long-running dispute (on Irish and Old English counter-claims for land in this period, see Sheehan, 'Official Reaction'). In fact, the grant of the land to Spenser was probably a result of this very dispute: Andrew Reade, to whom the estates had at first been assigned, failed ever to take up possession, and the 'corrupt bargains' to which Roche alluded in his complaint—detailed in No. 44, above (SP 63/144/70)—were those between Spenser and Reade, requiring Spenser to inhabit the lands on Reade's behalf (i.e. to keep Roche out) until Whitsuntide 1589, and thereafter, Reade not showing, giving Spenser the right to take possession in his own name. It is clear that neither Reade, nor anyone else in Munster, much desired to drink from the poisoned chalice of the Kilcolman estate, but Spenser—with his administrative and legal experience, access to the Vice-President of Munster, Thomas Norris, and gentlemanly aspirations—seems to have been willing to take the risk. The subsequent volleys on either side (of which this document represents one) were predictably tawdry: Roche wrote directly to Walsingham, detailing how Spenser had threatened and beaten Roche's tenants, stealing their cattle (SP 63/147/15 and 63/147/15/1), while Spenser accused Roche of treasonous and generally antisocial behaviour. The exact recipient of this document must remain uncertain, though it is possible either that Spenser sent it directly to London (perhaps, as in Roche's letter, to Walsingham), or to the Council of Munster, who may have sent it on to England.

The text of the allegations is, for the most part, in Spenser's characteristic secretary hand, here slightly hasty as appropriate for a draft of this kind. The two cursive signatures at the foot of the document may be autograph, while the names appended to each of the items are in a hasty, rounded italic, possibly Spenser's or Cuffe's (with some exceptions, e.g. 'Teig Olyues', which is in Spenser's secretary hand). At least some of the endorsement is in a regular secretary hand, possibly Spenser's (the deletion and 'Kilballye-werye'), while the rest is in a very cursive, broad-nibbed, and fairly illegible italic. The list-like notes to the left of the endorsement, smudged and blotted to illegibility, are in this same rough italic.

ENDORSEMENT

1588
byll against the
Lord Roche°
Kilballyewerye°

Endorsements below **Lord Roche**] 'Kibarr' deleted.   *Endorsements*] against the left side of the endorsement is a long and illegibile list, possibly of names. It appears to be in the same handwriting as the endorsement.

TEXT

Against the Lord Roche.

Imprimis the Lord Roche in Iuly 1586 and at sondry tymes before &
after relieved & maynteyned one Keadagh Okelly a proclaymed Traitour being his fosterbrother & caused the Sessoures man, who had
seized vpon a garran which the sayd Keadagh stole & brought into
the countrey, to bee apprehended And when the sayd Kedagh was
sought for he convayed him away.

   Iames birne

Item the said Lord secretely vpon the first report of the Spaniardes
coming° towardes this countrey caused powder & munition to bee
made in a privy place of his house, from the knowledg of his owne
servauntes

   mr Mc hendry

Item the said Lord vseth in his grace to pray° that god° would take
away this heavy hand from them and speaketh ill of the gouernement,
& hath vttered wordes of contempt of her Maiesties lawes calling
them vniust.

   mr Edmound Spencer°
   Iames byrne

Item the sayd Lord hath imprisoned in his private house sondry
persons videlicit a man of Mr Verdons a man of Mr Spensers ° &
sondry° others of the° freeholders of his countrey

   mr Edmond Spencer
   mr Iohn Vernon

Item the said Lord apprehended one Vllig Okief for stealing of ix
kyne & after vpon° composicion enlarged him, so as the sayd Vllig°

---

after **Spaniardes coming**] 'into' deleted. *after* **to pray**] 'for' deleted. *after* **that
god**] 'may' deleted. *before* **mr Edmound Spencer**] 'Iames burne' deleted. In **Spencer**, 's'
deleted between 'n' and 'c'. Possibly the strangest thing about this document is this deletion:
why Spenser, or this scribe, should have spelled his name 'Spencer' in several instances here,
and in this case taken the trouble to correct the 's' to a 'c', while thereafter signing the document
with the s-form, is at first glance difficult to explain. It may be that he was experimenting with
an affectation—likening the spelling of his own name to that of the courtly Spencers of
Althorp—but he seems not yet, in this document, to have got the hang of it. *after* **Mr
Spensers**] 'V' deleted. **sondry**] inserted above the line. **the**] Spenser has written 'the'
over an original 'his' here; it seems he originally intended to write 'others of his countrey', but
changed it to 'sondry others of the freeholders of his countrey'. **vpon**] a single-stroke
deletion appears at the end of this word. **Vllig**] 'h' deleted at the end of this name.

would make to him a feoffement of his land which he presently did Therevpon the sayd Lord agreed to satisfy the stolen kyne to the parties which ought them which hetherto he hath not doen. Vllig° OKief

Item v kyne being stolen from   were° followed to the Lord Roches house, where they were proved to have bene caten & satisfaccion of the same was by him made accordingly.

Item the sayd Lord made proclamacion in his countrey that none of his people should have any trade or conference with Mr Spenser or Mr Piers or any of their tenantes being english°
     mr Edmond Spencer
     mr peers

Item the said Lord Roche tooke away & killed a fatt beof of Teig Olyues for that Mr Spenser lay in his house one night as he came from the Sessions at Limeric
     Teig Olyues

Item the said Lord Roche killed a beof of his Smithes for mending mr Perces plough yron.
     mr peers

Item the sayd Lord Roche hath concealed from her Maiesty the Manour of Crogh being the freehold of one   who° was a Rebell°
     yt shalbe proved /

Item the sayd Lord Roche hath also lately entred into the sayd Rebelles other land which he gave him in recompence thereof as he alleageth. /

     All this is to bee verified by proofe of the forenamed persons.

     Hugh Cuffe as I am Credeable Informed. Edmund Spenser

---

before **Vllig**] a line has been inserted here to mark the break between item and signature.   **from . . . were**] there is a gap in the text here, presumably left to be completed later.   **being english**] 'being english' apparently added at the same time as the signatures below, as it appears to be in the same fresh, darker ink. It also appears to be in a much hastier secretary script, though probably still Spenser's—suggesting that Spenser signed the claim himself.   **of one . . . who**] there is a gap in the text here, presumably left to be filled in later.   *after* **Rebell**] '&' deleted.

COMMENTARY

Lord Roche] Maurice Roche, Viscount Fermoy; see biographies.

relieved] assisted with food, money or the like.

Keadagh Okelly] this name does not appear in other correspondence from the period, and Roche's precise relationship with him remains unclear. Irenius's account of the Irish custom of 'fosteringe' in *A view* (ll. 2101–33) closely links it with the practice of placing babies from Anglo-Norman families with Irish wet-nurses (one of their 'twoe evill customes'); whatever Roche's exact connection with O'Kelly, the bill seems to allege the same kind of natural corruption in Roche which had occupied Irenius in *A view*.

the Sessoures man] the servant of the cessor, or assessor: the official responsible for determining the cess, a local tax.

garran] small horse bred and used chiefly in Ireland and Scotland (Gael. *gearran*).

Iames birne] another fugitive name: nothing further is known of him, though Byrne's intimate knowledge of Roche's household (even down to the grace Roche said at his own table) suggests that he may have been a servant or local gentleman who turned on his former master or associate.

the Spaniardes . . . countrey] presumably the remnants of the Spanish Armada, many of whom were washed up onto the west coast of Ireland in the Autumn of 1588.

mr Mc hendry] another name that remains a mystery (though see the 'Grant to MacHenry', No. 46, below, BL Add MS 19869).

in his grace] in his prayers (see *OED*, 'Grace', *n.*, 20); here, probably that spoken at his table before a meal.

Mr Verdons] John Verdon. He may have been a merchant, and held a number of titles and lands around Counties Cork and Limerick, including Sovereign of Kilmallock (*c.*1579), member of the Grand Jury of Cork (*c.*1584), Bailiff of Cork (*c.*1588/9), and sheriff in Co. Limerick (*c.*1592). He was granted a commission in 1591 to enquire into lands in Cork belonging to Donogh MacCormock.

freeholders of his countrey] tenants holding land for the term of their lives.

Vllig Okief] another obscure name.

kyne] cattle.

composicion] agreement of terms for a settlement.

enlarged] set free.

make to him a feoffement of his land] effectively to give the title in his land to Roche. Like many of the claims made in this bill, on the face of it this does not appear to be a particularly damning charge. As the pre-eminent lord in his area, Roche would have expected to administer justice between his tenants; appropriating the land of a felon—and then perhaps reassigning it to some favoured relative, or even keeping it—was neither unprecedented or particularly unjust.

Mr Piers] another obscure name. Presumably not the old Captain William Piers, stationed at the time in Carrickfergus. Perhaps the 'Piers Purcell of Croghe' (see Crogh, below) mentioned in a draft report of commissioners, 1586 (SP 63/127/75).

beof] cow.

Teig Olyues] another obscure name.

the Sessions at Limeric] meeting of the provincial court at Limerick.

Manour of Crogh] or Croghe (see note on **Piers**, above).

Hugh Cuffe] an undertaker in the Munster plantation, possibly a merchant (MacCarthy-Morrogh, *The Munster Plantation*, 50), or possibly brother to Henry Cuffe, the Earl of Essex's secretary. His seignory, in Kilmore, Co. Cork, was of 12,000 acres (roughly four times the size of Spenser's), and made him the immediate neighbour of Kilcolman.

as I am Credeable Informed] an obscure note, perhaps suggesting that Cuffe was not present at the signing of the document, but that Spenser was assured that he could vouch for his agreement. If this is the case, it must also remain unclear why Spenser felt that he needed to include Cuffe's name: perhaps Cuffe had contacts at court that Spenser was eager to exploit.

46. *Grant to MacHenry, undated (1589?)*

British Library, Additional MS 19869

This grant of lands cannot be precisely dated, nor do we know the exact identity of MacHenry (though see note, below). It is not clear why Spenser made such a grant, but it may be that, unlike some of the other Munster undertakers, he recognized the claims of at least some of the Irish landowners already living in the area; this grant would thus represent a formal recognition of MacHenry's claim, establishing him as one of Spenser's tenants, and would put its probable composition at about the middle of 1589. Spenser's agreement to repair the castle at Richardstown, in order to provide MacHenry with a place of refuge in trouble, may suggest that the latter had been displaced. Further study of the provenance of this paper—especially some explanation as to how this grant came to reside in the collection from which it was purchased for the British Library (to whom was it addressed, if 'from' MacHenry?)—may suggest additional clues.

The text of the document is in Spenser's characteristic secretary hand, here fairly rushed and the ink much faded. The signature is the usual autograph. The paper is worn at the edges (and repaired), but the seal is intact. The endorsement has been added in an italic hand, not Spenser's.

ENDORSEMENT

from {mac} Henry°

TEXT

Be it knowen to all men by these presentes that I Edmund Spenser of Kilcolman esquire doe giue vnto mac Henry the keeping of all the

from {mac} Henry] there is some damage to the manuscript here, obscuring part of the endorsement; the supplied reading is based on the name/spelling supplied in the main text of the letter. The original size of the document suggests that no further text has been lost.

woodes which I haue in Balliganim & of the rushes & brakes without making any spoyle thereof & also doe covenant with him that he shall haue one house within the bawne of Richardston for him self & his cattell in tyme of warre. And also within the space of vij yeares to repayre the castle of Richardston afore sayd & in all other thinges to vse good neighbour hood to him & his

Edmund Spenser

COMMENTARY

{mac} Henry] the identity of Spenser's associate, like the date of this grant, has not been established. But note that Henry Billingsley, one of Spenser's fellow undertakers, attested in his 1589 answer to the Articles for Undertakers that two or three Irishmen continued to press their claim to certain parts of his seignory; according to his agent, Robert Cooper, one of these was an Edmond MacHenry (see SP 63/145/40 and 63/145/42).

by these presentes] the identity of these other people present (who have not signed the document) is another mystery.

Kilcolman] Spenser's estate, known by the name of its castle, near Buttevant.

esquire] the formal claim to gentlemanly status is typical of a document of this kind, but it also reflects Spenser's rising position in the service and plantation society of Elizabethan Ireland.

Balliganim] unidentified.

rushes & brakes] thickets of brushwood, rough wooded ground. *OED* cites **rush** as synonymous with **brake**, but gives its first usage in that context as 1796 ('Rush', *n.*³).

without ... spoyle thereof] unscrupulous donees occasionally 'spoiled'—or asset-stripped—their lands before making a grant; Spenser here makes a formal commitment to deliver the timber-rich woods in good order.

bawne of Richardston] modern Richardston lies just south of Kilcolman. The castle is said to have been destroyed during a storm in 1865, along with its bawn, or fortified enclosure. Only the mound now remains.

APPENDIX 1

Spenser and Ireland: A Summary Chronology

THIS appendix provides a summary chronology of important events in Ireland in the years between 1507, the accession of King Henry VIII, and 1603, the death of Queen Elizabeth I.[1] It concentrates in particular detail upon events between 1580 and 1589, the period covered by the letters and papers in this book, and it prints in bold the principal events of Spenser's own life and career. Readers may find it helpful to use this chronology in consultation with Willy Maley's *Spenser Chronology*, which provides a more extensive documentary account of Spenser's life.[2]

1507–1508

1509   Accession of Henry VIII.

1534–5 Rebellion of Thomas Fitzgerald, Lord Offaly ('Silken Thomas').

1534   Appointment of Sir William Skeffington, Lord Deputy of Ireland.

1536   Lord Leonard Grey appointed Lord Deputy of Ireland; George Browne consecrated Archbishop of Dublin without papal consent.

1537   High Commissioners under Sir Anthony St Leger dispatched to Ireland 'to ascertain its state'.

1538   Submission of James FitzJohn Fitzgerald, Earl of Desmond; submission of Cahir O'Connor, Lord of Offaly; destruction of images in churches of the Pale.

1540   Appointment of Sir Anthony St Leger, Lord Deputy of Ireland; Lord Leonard Grey committed to the Tower (June); St Leger counsels the King to be called King of Ireland, to quash the appearance of the Pope's title.

1541   Resubmission of James FitzJohn Fitzgerald, Earl of Desmond; Henry VIII proclaimed King of Ireland (33. Hen. 8 c. 1).

1542   Submission of O'Brien at Limerick; submission of Conn O'Neill, the O'Neill, in person to Henry VIII in England; O'Neill created Earl of Tyrone.

[1] For a more extended chronology, see also T. W. Moody, F. X. Martin, and F. J. Byrne, eds. *A New History of Ireland*, 10 vols. (Oxford: Clarendon Press, 1978–2003), viii: *A Chronology of Irish History to 1976* (1982).

[2] Willy Maley, *A Spenser Chronology* (Basingstoke: Macmillan, 1994); for additional remarks and information on payments to Spenser, see also Christopher Burlinson and Andrew Zurcher, '"Secretary to the Lord Deputie here": Edmund Spenser's Irish Papers', *Library*, 7th series, 6 (2005), 30–75.

1543	Submission of O'Brien; O'Brien created Earl of Thomond. Submission of MacWilliam; MacWilliam created Earl of Clanricard.
1547	Death of Henry VIII; accession of Edward VI.
1548	Recall of St Leger; Sir Edward Bellingham appointed Lord Deputy.
1550	Sir Anthony St Leger reappointed Lord Deputy.
1551	Appointment of Sir James Croft, Lord Deputy of Ireland. Flight and deprivation of George Dowdall, Primate of Ireland and Archbishop of Armagh. Orders issued for the division and leasing of Leix and Offaly.
1552	Devaluation of the currency in Ireland causes widespread poverty and disorder. **Edmund Spenser born, probably in London.**
1553	Sir Anthony St Leger reappointed Lord Deputy of Ireland; Henrician Church (including the mass) restored.
1556	Sir Thomas Radcliffe, Lord Fitzwalter (later Earl of Sussex) appointed Lord Deputy.
1557	Irish Parliament confirms reconciliation of Ireland with Rome. Irish Parliament shires Leix (Queen's County) and Offaly (King's County), incorporating the towns of Maryborough and Philipstown; plantations settled.
1558	Death of Mary I; accession of Elizabeth I.
1561–2	Shane O'Neill in England; death of Matthew, Baron of Dungannon. **Spenser enters Merchant Taylors' School.**
1565	Sir Henry Sidney appointed Lord Deputy of Ireland. The Earls of Ormond and Desmond at war against one another at Affane on the Blackwater; both earls summoned to London to settle their dispute.
1567	Shane O'Neill defeated by Hugh O'Donnell at Farsetmore and assassinated by the MacDonnells at Cushendun. Earl of Desmond rearrested and sent to London. Sidney takes Hugh O'Neill to court.
1568	James Fitzmaurice Fitzgerald acknowledged 'captain' in Munster, beginning revolt in support of Catholic defence of Ireland. Hugh O'Donnell marries Fionnuala MacDonnell (Iníon Dubh), daughter of Agnes Campbell.
1569	Turlough Luineach O'Neill marries Agnes Campbell, sister of the Earl of Argyle and widow of James MacDonnell. **Publication of *A theatre for voluptuous worldlings*, containing poems by Spenser; Spenser matriculates at Pembroke College, Cambridge.**
1570	Promulgation of the papal bull *Regnans in excelsis*, excommunicating Elizabeth.
1571	Sir John Perrot appointed President of Munster; Sir Edward Fitton appointed President of Connaught; Sir Henry Sidney recalled; Sir William Fitzwilliam appointed Lord Deputy.

1571–2   Sir Thomas Smith and his son granted possession of the lordship of the O'Neills of Clandeboye.

1572   Earl of Essex granted most of Antrim and made governor of Ulster. Thomas Smith the younger in Strangford Lough (August).

1573   Return of Earl of Desmond to Munster. Thomas Smith assassinated at Comber in the Ards (October).

1574   Brian MacPhelim O'Neill surprised and seized at Belfast by the Earl of Essex, and later executed in Dublin.

1575   John Norris and Sir Francis Drake massacre 500 Scots on Rathlin Island, under the Earl of Essex (July). Recall of Fitzwilliam; reappointment of Sir Henry Sidney as Lord Deputy. James Fitzmaurice flees to the continent.

1576   Sir William Drury appointed President of Munster; Sir Nicholas Malby appointed President of Connaught. Ulick and John Burke, sons of the Earl of Clanricard (*Mac an Iarlas*), brought prisoners to Dublin, then released on their father's assurance.

1577–9   Cess controversy in the Pale.

1578   Recall of Sir Henry Sidney; government of Ireland left to Sir William Drury (1578–9) and Sir William Pelham (1579–80), Lords Justices. **Spenser serves as secretary to Dr John Young, Bishop of Rochester.**

1579   James Fitzmaurice lands at Smerwick (17 July) and constructs a fort; Fitzmaurice killed by Tibbot Burke (18 August); Malby defeats 2,000 men under Sir John of Desmond's papal colours at Monasternenagh near Limerick (3 October); the Earl of Desmond proclaimed traitor by Sir William Pelham (2 November); Earl of Ormond appointed Lord General in Munster. **Spenser living at Leicester House in the Strand. Publication of** *The Shepheardes Calender.*

1580   James Eustace, Viscount Baltinglass, rebels in Leinster (July). **Certain of Spenser's letters with Gabriel Harvey are published (as** *Three proper, wittie, familiar Letters*, **and** *Two other, very commendable letters*).

1580–1589

1580   (August) Arthur, Lord Grey of Wilton, new Lord Deputy of Ireland, arrives in Dublin; **Spenser most likely accompanies him.** Grey defeated by Feagh MacHugh and the O'Byrnes in Glenmalure, Co. Wicklow. Turlough Luineach threatens to invade the Pale with 4,000 footmen and 500 horse; calls for his urraghs.

         (September) Grey sworn in as Lord Deputy. Rebels aided by Baltinglass besiege Maryborough. Spanish and Italian soldiers land at Dingle and fortify Fitzmaurice's defences there. Grey, Pelham, and Hugh O'Neill journey to Drogheda to view the fortifications and treat with Turlough Luineach; Turlough Luineach retires.

(October) Grey marches from Dublin to Dingle with 600 footmen and 200 horse. Earl of Kildare left in command in the Pale. Richard Bingham arrives at Smerwick harbour in the *Swiftsure*.

(November) Grey arrives at Smerwick; joined by Admiral Sir William Winter; attacks the fort; the fort surrenders; all 600 soldiers, reserving 20 or 30 of the captains, killed. Grey returns directly to Dublin.

(December) Grey commended by the Queen. Kildare relieved of command and discharged from the Council. Kildare and the Baron of Delvin committed to Dublin Castle on suspicion of treason.

1581 (January) Commissioners for victualling in Ireland convoked and reprimanded by the Chancellor, Sir William Gerrarde. Grey journeys into Leix and Offaly. Extreme sickness among the soldiers in Munster.

(February) Sir William Morgan's garrisons in Youghal and Cork starving from lack of supplies. David Barry with 600 men rebels in Munster. Queen issues order for Earl of Ormond to be relieved of command in Munster.

(March) Richard Yn Yeren Burke submits to the Queen, agrees to articles with Sir Nicholas Malby, and is recognized as MacWilliam Eighter. Sir Nicholas Malby wars with the sons of the Earl of Clanricard (William, Ulick, and John Burke) in Connaught. Chancellor Sir William Gerrarde returns to England because of infirmity. **Spenser appointed clerk of the faculties in Irish Court of Chancery.**

(April) Adam Loftus and Geoffrey Fenton prefer Robert Dillon to be Chief Justice of the Common Pleas (Ireland); recommend Sir Nicholas Nugent be discredited. Queen drafts a general pardon for the rebels throughout Ireland. Death of Dr Sanders in Munster.

(May) Death of Sir William Gerrarde; warrant to Adam Loftus, Archbishop of Dublin, to be Chancellor of Ireland. Death of John Chaloner, Secretary of State for Ireland; Geoffrey Fenton to be appointed to his office. The Earl of Desmond, David Barry, Patrick Condon, and the Seneschal of Imokilly inflict heavy losses in Munster. Grey journeys into south Leinster; repairs and garrisons Castles Kevan and Comin, reaches Wexford.

(June) Grey returns to Dublin. John Zouche attacks Desmond's camp in Munster.

(July) Turlough Luineach invades Tirconnell and wars with O'Donnell. Grey dispatches Malby via Athlone to Lifford; Grey marches to the fort on the Blackwater, and summons Turlough Luineach. Sir William Russell and Sir William Stanley attack the Cavanaghs under Art Boy, killing two hundred. Lord Fitzmaurice, Baron of Lixnaw and Lord of Kerry submits to John Zouche in Munster, giving his sons as pledges.

(August) Grey treats with Turlough Luineach; after agreeing a peace, returns to Dublin. Escape of the sons of Lord Fitzmaurice from Limerick Castle. Geoffrey Fenton returns to Ireland as Secretary of State. Sir Warham Sentleger called to England to report to the Privy Council and Queen on the Munster rebellion.

(September) Grey departs on journey into Munster.

(October) Submission of James Meagh, alias MacKedagh O'More, to Grey at Waterford. John Zouche made Chief Colonel in Munster. Discovery of the Nugent conspiracy in Westmeath and the Pale.

(November) Grey returns to Dublin. Several gentlemen of the Pale tried and executed for participating in the Nugent conspiracy; Grey distributes their lands and goods to his favourites; Malby, Loftus, and Fenton report secretly to Burghley. Baltinglass leaves Ireland for Spain.

(December) Queen issues order for the discharge of soldiers, with tight constraints on the spending of treasure from England. **Spenser receives lease for Abbey and Manor of Enniscorthy, Co. Wexford. Enniscorthy conveyed to Richard Synnot.**

1582   (January) Zouche surprises and kills Sir John of Desmond. Many soldiers discharged throughout Ireland, and diverted to service in the Low Countries. Grey instructed to send the Earl of Kildare and the Baron of Delvin into England.

(February) John Nugent implicates Nicholas Nugent in the Pale conspiracy. Discharged soldiers stayed by lack of wind starve in the streets of Dublin and Galway. Famine in Munster.

(March) Captain James Fenton and his company ambushed and killed at Bearehaven. Captain Apsley routed and slain by David Barry at Carbery. John Zouche reports general revolt of Irish allies in Munster. Submission of Murrough Ne Doe O'Flaherty to the Queen.

(April) The Queen orders another general pardon, and a further reduction of the garrisons to 2,300 men. Kildare and Delvin to be examined and then sent to England. A valuation and survey ordered of the Earl of Desmond's lands in Munster. Captain Acham and many of his band killed in Munster. Nicholas Nugent tried for treason and executed at Trim. Severe famine in Cork.

(May) Cahil O'Connor surprises and abducts Captain Humphrey Mackworth near Carbery; Mackworth later executed. Earl of Kildare and Baron of Delvin sent into England. Grey journeys to Munster.

(June) Grey returns to Dublin via Philipstown.

(July) Con O'Donnell—Turlough Luineach's 'only favourite'—spoils

Connaught; defence of the county by O'Connor Sligo. The Queen recalls Grey from Ireland.

(August) Grey departs for England. Sir Henry Wallop and Adam Loftus appointed Lords Justices. Death of Richard Oge Burke, second Earl of Clanricard. **Spenser obtains lease of New Abbey, Co. Kildare, one of the escheated estates of Viscount Baltinglass.**

(September) Ulick Burke, son of Clanricard, submits, petitions the Privy Council to succeed his father. Auditor Thomas Jenyson informs Burghley of the great allowances made by Grey.

(October) English ministers repeatedly warned of a deteriorating situation in Munster, Desmond's strength, and the likelihood of a foreign invasion. John Zouche in England, presenting petitions to Elizabeth for continued prosecution of the Munster rebels, and for certainty of entertainment.

(November) The Lords Justices inform the Privy Council of the need to settle Zouche, or some other governor, in Munster. Desmond allegedly sends messengers to Spain to call for troops.

(December) Ormond appointed Governor of Munster.

1583 (January) Death of John Zouche. Desmond narrowly escapes capture in the wood of Kilcoghen. Youghal and Cork are attacked by 600 rebel soldiers, led by Seneschal of Imokilly and others.

(February) Ormond at odds with Dublin government. Garrisons at Kilmallock and Limerick attack the Seneschal of Imokilly in Aherlow. Many rebels slain, hundreds pardoned. Desmond in flight.

(March) Wallop accuses Jenyson of papistry. Turlough Luineach spoils MacQuillin's country for an offence against Sorley Boy MacDonnell. Malby informs Burghley of the Earl of Clanricard's services.

(April) Turlough Luineach, Sorley Boy, and 4,000 men threaten to attack the Pale. William Piers reports that Turlough Luineach would be obedient to Henry Sidney. Knockfergus preyed by Scots. More Scots set to arrive from Scotland with Agnes Campbell. Ormond reports continuing executions and submissions in Munster. Richard Yn Yeren Burke dies; Richard MacOliverus succeeds as MacWilliam. **Spenser appointed commissioner for musters in Kildare.**

(May) Turlough Luineach is reported dead (or fallen into a coma or fit) but survives. Struggles between Hugh O'Neill, Baron of Dungannon, and the sons of Shane O'Neill. Desmond in great extremity.

(June) Seneschal of Imokilly submits. Desmond forsaken by almost all his followers, and by his wife. Walsingham warns Ormond against granting too many protections to rebels, and asks him to expedite capture of Desmond. Negotiations between Dungannon and the Lords

Justices, on the event of Turlough's death. Earl of Kildare cleared of treason.

(July) The Munster rebellion almost suppressed. Death of Cormac MacTeig MacCarthy.

(September) Ormond requests a pardon for the Seneschal of Imokilly. Trial by combat between Conor MacCormac O'Connor and Teig MacGilpatrick O'Connor in Dublin Castle.

(October) Dermot O'Hurley ('Dr Hurley'), nominated by the Pope for the Archbishopric of Cashel, apprehended. Over the coming months, he is tortured and examined, under the commission of Edward Waterhouse and Geoffrey Fenton. Rebellion continues in Muskerry and Carbery.

(November) The Earl of Desmond cornered in the woods of Glanaginty and killed. His head sent to England by Daniel O'Kelly.

(December) Ormond undertakes discharge of bands.

1584   (January) John Perrot appointed Lord Deputy. Issued with various memorials, including proposals to erect a college in Dublin. Sir Thomas of Desmond claims the Desmond earldom. At about this time, William Nugent may return to Ireland.

(February) Warham Sentleger sends accusations of Ormond's treason to England. Nicholas Malby in want of money. His wife makes preparations to go to England.

(March) Death of Malby; Richard Bingham succeeds him as President of Connaught. Valentine Browne said to be ready to survey the escheated lands in Munster. Hugh O'Neill, Baron of Dungannon, made Turlough Luineach's tanist.

(April) Death of Justice Dowdall. Loftus petitions England to be allowed to continue as Lord Chancellor, amid rumours that he is to be replaced. Wallop and Jenyson estimate that the debt in Ireland is £20,000 or more.

(June) Ormond reports to Burghley on the good behaviour of the Seneschal of Imokilly. Commission of survey in Munster appointed; instructions issued. Perrot arrives in Ireland; orders general musters in every county. Feagh MacHugh, the Earl of Clanricard, and others renew their submission to Perrot. Dermot O'Hurley executed. Waterhouse and Bingham knighted. Scots arrive in the north-west.

(July) Henry Bagenal made commissioner for Ulster. Commissions for martial law and military government of Connaught issued to Bingham. John Norris appointed President of Munster. Several thousand Scots land in Ulster, in support of Shane O'Neill.

(August) Continued Scottish incursions in Ulster. Rumours (extracted from a messenger of Turlough Luineach's) that Spanish forces will land in Sligo, and support them and the rebels of Munster and Connaught, in general rebellion. Perrot prepares for a journey north, supported by John Norris. Commission of survey in Munster delayed.

(September) Perrot besieges and captures Dunluce Castle, on the Antrim coast. Perrot agrees to a proposed President of Ulster. Commissioners of the survey enter Munster, passing through Tipperary, Limerick and Kerry. Death of Colin Campbell, Earl of Argyll.

(October) Perrot returns to Dublin from northern journey. Issues plans for the governance of Ulster, asking that Ulster be divided into three lieutenancies held by Turlough Luineach, Dungannon, and Bagenal. King James VI suspected in England of responsibility for recent Scottish incursions. Valentine Browne reports on the ruination of the lands and habitations of Munster. The commissioners return through Limerick.

(November) Commissioners of the Munster survey in Cork city, thence to Waterford, and finally return to Dublin.

(December) William Nugent submits to Perrot.

1585   (January) Further Scottish landings in Ulster. English troops repeatedly bested. Attack by Donnell Gorm on the camp of William Stanley, who is severely wounded. Perrot complains of lack of support from Westminster for the Ulster wars.

(February) After English manoeuvres under Stanley and Bagenal, Sorley Boy MacDonnell offers to enter into negotiation with Perrot.

(March) Sorley Boy flees to Scotland. His and Donnell Gorm's forces are weakened and constrained. John Norris returns to Munster, requesting grants of land from Burghley and Walsingham.

(April) Parliament sits in Dublin. A bill for suspension or repeal of Poyning's Act is put forward, but rejected.

(May) Parliament continues (until 25th). John Norris returns to England, en route to the Netherlands. Ormond travels to England.

(June) Geoffrey Fenton dispatched to England with letters, including requests for money to be diverted from Trinity College. Disputes between Loftus and Perrot.

(July) Loftus sends Burghley a petition on behalf of the Countess of Desmond. Commission for Composition of Connaught, under Bingham. Perrot travels to Ulster.

(August) Four hundred Scots, under Sorley Boy's son, land in Ulster. Increasingly urgent requests for the repeopling of Munster.

(September) Perrot reports on the suspension of Poyning's Act. Captain Thomas Lee, in pursuit of Cahir Owre Cavanagh, is set upon by the Sheriff of Kilkenny; captures him and kills several of his men.

(October) Survey of escheated lands in Munster presented to Perrot. Return of Composition of Connaught (under Bingham), with an account of scores of Irish lords who have surrendered their names and inheritances, and received them as regrants.

(November) Earl of Kildare dies in London. Viscount Baltinglass dies in Madrid. Valentine Browne leaves for England bearing the survey.

(December) Valentine Browne arrives in England; planning begins for the Munster plantation.

1586   (January) A general calm; rumours abound of the preparation of a Spanish army for an invasion of Ireland. Want of victuals in the garrison at Carrickfergus causes starvation.

(February) Further reports of Spanish preparations. Perrot opposes moves to pardon Cahil O'Connor (responsible for the murder of Mackworth). Walsingham communicates Elizabeth's reluctance to appoint a President of Ulster, and her dislike of his actions against the Scots.

(March) Articles issued for the disposing of Munster lands to planters. A skirmish with Scots under Alexander MacSorley in Tirconnell; about sixty Scots slain. MacSorley flees, later found dead. Fenton returns from England, bearing letters rebuking Perrot for unnecessary expense.

(April) Perrot dismayed at the financial restraints placed upon him; requests revocation. Loftus and Perrot reconciled, on orders from England. The heads of Alexander MacSorley and others sent to Dublin. Sorley Boy requests pardon at Perrot's hands. Parliament in session (until May).

(May) Turlough Luineach and Agnes Campbell appeal to Perrot for justice against Tyrone. Submission of Angus MacDonnell (son of Agnes Campbell). Feagh MacHugh O'Byrne enters in submission.

(June) Donnell Gorm MacDonnell, brother to Angus, arrives with 300–400 Scots; spoils MacQuillin's country. Formal submission of Sorley Boy. Division of attainted lands in Munster made by Burghley. Articles for the peopling of those lands issued. Thomas Jenyson returns audited accounts to England.

(July) The Scottish host continues to spoil in the north. Rebellion of 400 under the Burkes in Connaught.

(August) Further septs of the Burkes join the revolt. Bingham demands their submission.

(September) Various commissions for the division of lands in Munster arrive in Ireland. Bingham attacks a large army of Scots at Ardnaree, on the River Moy, on their way to assist the Burkes; up to 1,400 are killed.

(October) Bingham, triumphant, issues detailed accounts of his expenses and charge. Thomas Norris complains of a shortage of men and victuals in Munster. Fenton surveys the coastal defences and garrisons in Munster.

(November) Fenton returns to Cork, to settle a band of footmen there. Formal submission of the Burkes.

(December) Disagreements resurface between Loftus and Perrot, after Perrot's continued intervention in legal cases.

1587 (January) Perrot has Fenton arrested and imprisoned in Dublin on a charge of debt. Bagenal, Loftus, and Bingham protest to England about Perrot's reluctance to take action against Tyrone, who they see as exercising his local authority too boldly.

(February) Queen rebukes Perrot for Fenton's imprisonment; orders his release. Tenants for the Munster lands make preparations to depart from England; Queen and Privy Council express frustration at ongoing surveys, and issue further commissions; arrangements made for bands of soldiers upon these lands. Bingham acquitted of charges brought against him by Theobald Dillon.

(March) Directions issued to Thomas Norris for the apprehension of several former Munster rebels (Seneschal of Imokilly, Patrick Condon, the White Knight, etc.). Tyrone petitions Elizabeth for his hereditary rights.

(April) Formal grants of land made to the undertakers in Munster. Commission of inquest into the extent of Tyrone's lands; formal arbitration between Tyrone and Turlough Luineach.

(May) Bagenal and Perrot fight. Bingham withdrawn from Connaught for temporary service in the Low Countries.

(June) Donnell O'Sullivan protests at the attempts of his uncle, Sir Owen O'Sullivan, to detain his lands.

(July) Challenges by Munster lords of grants to undertakers. Perrot instructed to conduct further surveys of such lands. John Norris, returned from the Low Countries, requests resumption of his office in Munster, with Thomas Norris as his Vice-President. Disputes between Bingham and Perrot. Bingham departs for the Netherlands; replaced by Thomas le Strange.

(August) Extensive reports communicated from Francis Drake about Spanish military preparation.

(September) Complaints among Munster undertakers. George Bingham assumes government of Connaught. Hugh Roe O'Donnell imprisoned in Dublin Castle.

(October) Further preparations in Munster for a possible Spanish invasion. Geoffrey Fenton begins work on fortifications at Doncannon, overlooking Waterford. Teig MacCarthy sues for lands granted to the Munster undertakers.

(November) Extensive memorials on Irish government and administration pass between Sir William Fitzwilliam, Walsingham, and Burghley. Auditor Jenyson dies. Bingham granted possession of Athlone.

(December) Dispute between William Herbert and Denzil Holles about lands in Munster. Appeals from Tyrone for his lands and rights. Further submissions and obediences received from the Countess of Desmond. Sir William Fitzwilliam appointed Lord Deputy; instructions issued.

1588 (January) Reports that the brother of the Earl of Tyrone has raised a force and is in camp, with Tyrone's support. Perrot requests the quick arrival of Fitzwilliam.

(February) Bingham departs London on his journey back to Connaught.

(March) Further instructions issued to Fitzwilliam. Bingham arrives in Ireland. A troop of the O'Cahans suprised by Francis Stafford near to Carrickfergus; many killed.

(April) Tyrone continues to attempt to exert pressure over Turlough Luineach and neighbouring lords.

(May) Spanish Armada sails. Many Connaught lords (such as O'Rourke) submit to Bingham. Florence MacCarthy's marriage to the daughter of the Earl of Clancar.

(June) Fitzwilliam arrives in Ireland, weak and unwell, and is sworn in as Lord Deputy; immediately requests money, and complains at the conditions faced by the soldiery. Florence MacCarthy arrested. News of the Armada reaches Ireland. William Herbert dispatches a number of tracts on the state and government of Munster.

(July) Perrot departs for England. Armada sighted off Cornwall. Council established in Connaught, with Richard Bingham as Chief Commissioner. Feagh MacHugh O'Byrne makes his submission.

(August) Initial encounters between Spanish Armada and English fleet.

(September) Answers made, at a sessions in Munster, to a succession of Irish complaints about the allotting of their lands to English undertakers. Remnants of the Spanish Armada appear off the west coast; many ships wrecked; others make land, and many of their sailors are taken or killed; Bingham is active in this service. Several hundred Scots land in the north, under Callough MacJames MacDonnell.

(October) Further actions in the west against the survivors of the wreck of the Armada, by Richard Bingham, George Bingham, Geoffrey Fenton, and others. Lord Roche complains of harsh treatment after complaints about the allocation of Munster lands.

(November) Fitzwilliam departs on a journey to the north and west, against the Spanish survivors of the Armada; also inspects O'Donnell's country and consults both Turlough Luineach and the Earl of Tyrone over their disagreement. Edward Denny enters into agreement to succeed Bingham as President in Connaught, but no such succession takes place, despite Fitzwilliam's approval.

(December) Perrot issues lengthy descriptions and accounts for his Irish service. Fitzwilliam returns to Dublin.

1589   (January) Florence MacCarthy sent to England. Death of Seneschal of Imokilly.

(February) Lord Roche complains about the undertakers' appropriation of his lands. Earl of Clancar's daughter escapes custody in Cork Castle, apparently at the instigation of Florence MacCarthy. O'Connor Sligo makes appeal for restoration of his lands, along with accusations against Bingham.

(March) Fitzwilliam invades and spoils MacMahon's country, after the expulsion of the Queen's sheriff.

(April) Bingham granted commission against the rebels in Connaught. Official enquiry into the rebellions of the Burkes. O'Rourke in rebellion in Sligo.

(May) Commission inquires into progress of Munster plantation. Articles to the Undertakers. Captain Nicholas Mordant attacks O'Rourke.

(June) Hugh Maguire succeeds on his father's death. Fitzwilliam travels to Galway. Bingham complains to Walsingham that he is being restrained in his efforts against the Connaught rebels, and of the presence of Fitzwilliam there.

(July) Fitzwilliam in Connaught. Walsingham rebukes Fitzwilliam for his treatment of Bingham.

(August) Death of Ross MacMahon.

(September) Disagreements fester between Fitzwilliam and Bingham: both complain to England of the other.

(October) Connaught troubled by the rebellion of the Burkes. O'Rourke makes promises of obedience to Fitzwilliam. Commission of Munster reports to Privy Council. **Accusations between Lord Roche and Spenser.**

(December) Bingham is cleared by Lord Deputy and Council of misgovernment; granted commission to prosecute the Burkes. Fitzwilliam in Connaught.

1590–1603

1590   Bingham campaigns against Brian O'Rourke. O'Rourke flees to Tirconnell, thence to Scotland, but is handed over to Elizabeth. Tyrone spends four months at court in England. Death of Walsingham. Hugh Roe MacMahon is tried and hanged at Monaghan quarter sessions. **Spenser receives grant for Kilcolman. Publication of** *The Faerie Queene*, **Books I–III.**

1591   Brian O'Rourke executed in London. Hugh Roe O'Donnell escapes from Dublin Castle. **Publication of** *Complaints.*

1592   Hugh Roe O'Donnell becomes Lord of Tirconnell. Submits to Fitzwilliam. **Publication of** *Daphnaida* **and** *Axiochus.*

1593   Order is issued for the apprehension of Catholic bishops.

1594   Fitzwilliam recalled, and Sir William Russell becomes Lord Deputy. Enniskillen, unsuccessfully invested in 1592 by Sir Henry Bagenal and Tyrone, is captured by an English force, then besieged by O'Donnell and Maguire, and relieved by Russell.

1595   Russell campaigns against Feagh MacHugh. Tyrone's brother, Art O'Neill, attacks fort on the Blackwater. Tyrone attacks Sir Henry Bagenal's forces and is proclaimed traitor. John Norris returns from France as military commander of Ireland. Death of Turlough Luineach. **Publication of** *Colin Clouts Come Home Again*, *Amoretti*, **and** *Epithalamion.*

1596   Tyrone pardoned after submission; but calls on Munster lords to assist him in rebellion, and receives aid from Spain. Spanish ships gather for an invasion of England; dispersed off Finisterre. Richard Bingham summoned by Irish Council to answer charges. **Publication of** *The Faerie Queene*, **Books IV–VI**, *Prothalamion*, *Fowre Hymnes.*

1597   Russell recalled; Thomas, Lord Burgh, appointed Lord Deputy. Dies in October. Feagh MacHugh killed. A further Spanish fleet intended for England is dispersed.

1598   Tyrone, having agreed a truce with Ormond, attacks Sir Henry Bagenal's army (along with O'Donnell and Maguire) at the Yellow Ford. Munster plantation attacked. Dublin attacked. Death of Burghley. **Spenser nominated as Sheriff of Cork; travels to England, bearing letters from Thomas Norris.**

1599   Death of Richard Bingham. Essex appointed Lord Lieutenant; leaves Ireland without permission in September. Phelim MacFeagh O'Byrne routs English at Deputy's Pass, Co. Wicklow. Conyers Clifford, president of Connaught, killed in Co. Roscommon, in engagement with O'Donnell. Tyrone requests papal support. **Death of Spenser, at Westminster.**

1600   Charles Blount, Lord Mountjoy, appointed Lord Deputy. Campaigns throughout Ireland. George Carew appointed President of Munster.

1601   Essex executed. Spanish ships arrive at Kinsale and along the southern coast. Mountjoy inflicts heavy defeat on Tyrone and O'Donnell at

Kinsale; Spanish forces surrender and permitted to withdraw. O'Donnell travels to Spain.

1602   Mountjoy campaigns across Ulster and Connaught.

1603   Mountjoy offers Tyrone pardon in return for surrender. Tyrone submits on 30 March, six days after Elizabeth's death.

Spenser's Ireland: Short Biographies

THESE brief biographical notes present relevant detail about the lives of those both well-known and obscure figures whose histories crossed that of Spenser, in Ireland, between 1580 and 1589. In composing these accounts, we have not sought to summarize or abstract information from other well-known sources; our focus has been, rather, on collating the documents and events that help to shed light on Spenser's experience, and that will help to enrich a reading of the manuscripts presented in this book. As a consequence, we have only described figures who appear in Spenser's Irish papers, and we have concentrated on those aspects of their lives most germane to the concerns of those papers.

Sir Nicholas Bagenal (d.1591), Knight Marshal of Ireland and member of the Irish Council, served most of his career as a soldier in Ulster, based from 1552 at his house in the Newry. Bagenal first came to prominence in Ireland in the 1540s, when he served Conn Bacach O'Neill in Ulster, but it was his service against the O'Neill (first Shane, and later Turlough Luineach) that made his name, as Knight Marshal under Edward VI and again, from 1565, under Elizabeth; in this post he continued to act as a chief broker for English negotiations with the Ulster lords until his death. At Grey's arrival in the summer of 1580, Bagenal provided information on the intentions of Turlough Luineach, and one of the first surviving documents in Spenser's hand (No. 3, above, SP 63/76/1) is a copy of Bagenal's first dispatch to Grey—a letter conspicuous for its copious and good intelligence. Bagenal's relations with Grey were uniformly good throughout Grey's service in Ireland, apparently because they shared very similar ideas about the service ('force & not elles will salue this'—see No. 3, above, SP 63/76/1), but probably also because Bagenal, like Grey himself, was attached to the Leicester–Sidney patronage network. A good example of Bagenal's importance to the Ulster political and military situation, and of his self-conscious advertisement of that importance, is a letter to Walsingham of January 1582 (SP 63/88/54), in which he attributes the good quiet of the north to his policy in intercepting the Scots, and dealing between Turlough Luineach and Hugh O'Neill. Bagenal continued to serve in Ulster under Lord Deputies Perrot and Fitzwilliam, famously coming to blows with the irascible Perrot at the Lord Deputy's residence in Kilmainham, near Dublin, in 1587. After resigning as Knight Marshal in favour of his son, Henry, he died in February 1591.

George Beverley, victualler of Chester, joined the Irish service in January 1581 (see SP 63/80/18), charged with reforming the supply for Ireland. On 18 July 1582 Beverley filed his report on the Irish victualling (SP 63/94/30/1) with

Burghley, recommending various improvements including a new pier on the Liffey at Dublin. In December of the same year, with Edward Waterhouse he produced a report on how to prevent loss on the Irish victualling (SP 63/98/66). He was still working for the government at Spenser's death in 1599.

Sir Richard Bingham (1528–99) was a career soldier and naval officer originally from Dorset. By the time Bingham arrived in Ireland—at about the same time as Grey—he had served the Queen and various of her allies in engagements all over Europe for over thirty years. As captain of the *Swiftsure*, he supported Grey's assault on the Fort of Gold at Smerwick in November 1580; Grey was immediately impressed with Bingham's knowledge, experience, and industry, describing him to Elizabeth (No. 5, above, SP 63/78/29) as a 'iewell'. Following further naval service, he was appointed to replace Sir Nicholas Malby as President of Connaught upon Malby's death in April 1584. Bingham's severity in Connaught was, in practice, no different from Malby's, but he was quickly given a reputation for rigour and violence—a reputation cemented by the slaughter of over 1,300 Scots, mainly of the Clandonnells, at Ardnaree on the River Moy on 22–3 September 1586 (see SP 63/126/18). He forced through a new composition for land-rents with the Irish and Old English lords of the province in 1585, known as the Composition of Connaught (see SP 63/118/35, a letter to Walsingham outlining Bingham's plans, and 63/120/2, the composition book itself). Bingham had a stormy relationship with Lord Deputy Perrot, who seems to have envied his military successes, and he eventually attracted the opposition, too, of Geoffrey Fenton and Sir John Norris. He was twice tried for, and cleared of, abuses of his office, in 1587 and 1589. During the Nine Years' War, based in Athlone, Bingham was charged with keeping the peace in Connaught, but with scant resources. Frustrated and under increasing pressure from his enemies in the Dublin government, he left Ireland without licence at the end of 1596 and, no longer enjoying the protection of his patron Walsingham (d.1590), narrowly escaped a serious trial. He was appointed Knight Marshal of Ireland at the end of 1598, but died shortly thereafter. His body was buried in Westminster Abbey.

John Bland of Bristol, deputy victualler for Ireland, worked under William Glaseour until the arrival of George Beverley in January 1581. Glaseour had been accused of corruption and incompetence of various kinds; one of Beverley's first acts in the service was to exculpate Bland of wrongdoing (see SP 63/80/42). Bland continued to transport food, supplies, and soldiers into Ireland until at least 1584, but Glaseour reported in May 1588 that Bland had since died in prison (SP 63/135/21).

Sir George Bourchier, captain in Munster and nephew to the Earl of Bath, fought in Munster from at least 1571 (see SP 63/34/33/2). After Smerwick, he served as Colonel of Limerick, and was retained in service after the general discharge of early 1582 (see SP 63/88/40/2), but departed Ireland almost immediately, not to return for almost a year. In 1583 he petitioned the Queen for the presidency of Wexford, to serve against the Cavanaghs; though no new office was forthcoming, Bourchier did receive a commission in the east of Ireland, and was eventually known as Seneschal of Offaly, and master of the fort at Philipstown. In 1587 he was appointed one of a group of commissioners sent into Munster to hear disputes between the undertakers there (see SP 63/129/26); if he actually served, he may well have met Spenser again in that capacity.

Lodowick Bryskett (*c*.1546–1609 × 12) served alongside Spenser as a secretary to the Dublin and Munster governments. The son of an Italian merchant, he matriculated at Cambridge but left without taking a degree. He first went to Ireland in 1565 in the service of Sir Henry Sidney, and briefly acted as temporary clerk to the council in Ireland in 1571. After accompanying Sir Philip Sidney to the continent (1572–4), he served between 1575 and 1582 as clerk to the council in Ireland; in 1577 he became clerk in chancery for the faculties, an office in which he was succeeded by Spenser in 1581. He sought the post of Secretary of State for Ireland in 1581, on the death of Sir John Chaloner, but was rejected in favour of Geoffrey Fenton. In 1583, however, he became clerk to the Council of Munster, employing Spenser as his deputy. He was granted land in Wexford in 1593, and served briefly as sheriff for the county. In 1594, he became clerk of the casualties. In 1595, he contributed two poems (adapted from Tasso) to Spenser's *Astrophel*, and also appears (under the persona of Thestylis) in *Colin Clouts Come Home Againe* and is addressed in the thirty-third sonnet of *Amoretti*. In 1600, he fled the war in Ireland, surrendering the Munster clerkship to Richard Boyle, and in 1604 was deprived, as a non-resident, of the office of clerk of the casualties. In 1606, he published *A Discourse of Civill Life*, translated and heavily adapted from Giambattista Giraldi Cinthio's *Tre dialoghi della vita civile* (perhaps written in the mid-1580s), which includes a long passage on Spenser.

Richard Yn Yeren Burke, from March 1581 known as MacWilliam Eighter (or Eughter, Ewghter, or Iochtar), was the tanist to Sir John Burke (alias Shane MacOliverus), MacWilliam Eighter from 1571 to 1580. Richard Yn Yeren's struggle with John's brother, Richard MacOliverus, for the succession to the name of MacWilliam allowed Sir Nicholas Malby to play the Irish lords off against each other. His submission and recognition as MacWilliam by the English government in the spring of 1581 (see SP 63/81/15 and No. 9, above, 63/81/39) marked a key turning point in the pacification of the Burkes, as it reflected the English government's importance in the legitimation and support of the lords of the 'Irishry'. Richard Yn Yeren's wife was Grace O'Malley (Gráinne Ny Vayle, or Mhaol), who famously sailed to England for an audience with Queen Elizabeth in 1593.

Sir Edward Butler was a younger brother of Thomas Butler, tenth Earl of Ormond. During the Earl's various detentions in England, Edward and his brothers Edmund and Piers developed a strong power base in the Butler lands of

Tipperary; Lord Deputy Sir Henry Sidney relentlessly antagonized the brothers, finally driving them into open revolt in April 1569. Queen Elizabeth permitted Ormond to return to Ireland to deal with this threat to his power in Tipperary— which he did, ruthlessly hunting down and exterminating his brothers' private armies of retainers—and relations with Edward never entirely recovered. By the time of Grey's deputyship, Edward Butler was serving as Sheriff of Tipperary, and even Ormond was reporting positive news of his exploits against the 'rebels' of his country. But Butler also wrote to Edward Waterhouse in March 1582 claiming that his life was in danger, and that he was unable to defend himself because Ormond had stripped him of his retainers and kern; a few days later, he wrote a similar appeal to John Zouche in Munster (see SP 63/90/31 and 63/90/46).

Thomas Butler, tenth Earl of Ormond (1531–1614), exploited the Tudor reconquest of Ireland to transform his family into the pre-eminent Old English house in Ireland. He was sent as a boy to court, to be raised and educated alongside Edward VI; after Mary's accession he returned to Ireland, but, following a feudal battle with the Earl of Desmond at Affane in 1565, was summoned back to England. His years at court proved both a blessing and a curse, for they brought him closer to the Tudors (especially Elizabeth) at the cost of control over his own lordship in Tipperary. By the time Elizabeth permitted Ormond to leave England again, in 1569, his three younger brothers Edmund, Edward, and Piers had plunged into a desperate revolt—largely goaded by the Lord Deputy, Sir Henry Sidney, but eager, too, to test their brother's ability to reclaim his patrimony. Between 1569 and 1571, and with considerable crown support, Ormond violently asserted his legal and military rights in his liberty of Tipperary. Thereafter, he remained conspicuously loyal for the rest of his life, serving Elizabeth as Lord General in Munster between 1579 and 1581, and again from November 1582. Despite his age, he served repeatedly during the Nine Years' War, and died the unquestioned ranking peer of Ireland.

Beneath the veneer of loyalty, Ormond's policies and practices remained self-interested and—at least to some English observers—highly suspect. Lord Grey inherited Sidney's distrust of Ormond, a distrust that probably stemmed originally from Ormond's longstanding rivalry with the Earl of Leicester, but certainly had something to do with Ormond's soft stance on Rome. Grey wrote repeatedly to Walsingham during his deputyship of Ormond's slack service in Munster (see e.g. SP 63/83/6), and Geoffrey Fenton, too, paired Ormond with Kildare as a danger to Ireland who should be recalled to court (SP 63/79/3). It was probably as a result of Grey's and Fenton's informations that Ormond was suspended from his position as Lord General of Munster in 1581 (see SP 63/80/87 and No. 15, above, 63/83/45); but unlike the earls of Kildare and Desmond, Ormond was astute enough to realize that active service to the crown was the only way to avoid marginalization, irrelevance, and accusation, and he quickly argued his way back into favour and the generalship (see SP 63/86/3, 63/86/3/1, and 63/86/4, Ormond's representations to Burghley and Walsingham, detailing over

5,000 Munster rebels he had killed). There is no question that Ormond exploited his position in Munster to wipe out Desmond power there, but as long as his interests continued to reflect those of the crown, he was safe. Spenser raised oblique questions about Ormond's loyalty in *A view of the present state of Ireland*, first by objecting to his 'liberty'—the personal legal and political authority he enjoyed in the county palatine of Tipperary:

for the Countye of Tipperarye which is now the onelye Countye Palatine in Irelande is by abuse of some bad ones made a receptacle to robb the reste of the Countries aboute it by meanes of whose priviledges none will followe theire stealthes, so as it beinge scituate in the verye lapp of all the lande is made now a border which howe inconveniente it is let euerie man iudge.[1]

Spenser could not afford to censure Ormond directly, even in a closed-circulation manuscript dialogue, but Irenius's discussion moves closer to direct censure near the end of the text, where he recommends a new garrison in the Burkes' country:

by which places all the passage of theues dothe lye, which Conveye theire stealthe from all mounster downe wardes towardes Tipperar and the Englishe pale and from the Englishe pale alsoe vp into mounster whereof they vse a Comon trade, Besides that er longe I doubte the Countrye of Tipperary it self will nede suche a strengthe in it which weare good to be theare readie before the evill fall that is dailye of some expected[.][2]

Spenser's comments—likely added to a late draft, possibly after 1596—probably reflect the rebellion of Ormond's cousin Edmund Butler, Viscount Mountgarret, who rebelled while Ormond was campaigning in Ulster; but it was widely thought in New English circles that Ormond would follow the Butler cadets, and certain hardline elements in the English community—of whom, as a Munster planter, Spenser may have been one—probably wished it. But despite Ormond's continuing conciliatory approach to the rebel Hugh O'Neill, Earl of Tyrone, he ruthlessly suppressed the Butler rebellion in south Leinster in 1597, and Elizabeth went on to make him lieutenant-general of the army. In 1604, in recognition of his service to the crown in Ireland over almost fifty years, James VI and I appointed him Vice-Deputy of Ireland.

Agnes Campbell, Lady of Kintire and Dunnavaigh, sister to the fifth Earl of Argyle and widow of James MacDonnell, married Turlough Luineach in August or September 1569—a dynastic alliance that ended years of feuding between the O'Neill and the MacDonnells. The alliance was a strategic one for Turlough Luineach, who could by his wife's means count on the support of thousands of Scots mercenaries, whose numbers critically swelled his forces during the summer campaigns like that of 1580, when he threatened the Pale and finally achieved the

---

[1] *A view*, ll. 920–5.   [2] *A view*, ll. 4280–6.

submission of his Ulster sub-lords, or urraghs. Campbell herself hardly kept quietly in the background: Turlough Luineach frequently employed her on embassies to the English, and the Earl of Essex, Sir Henry Sidney, and Grey all appear to have been impressed with her integrity, articulacy, and courage; see SP 63/42/38/19, a letter from the Earl of Essex describing her wisdom and desire for peace, and 63/65/13, a January 1579 letter from Sir William Gerrarde, Chancellor in Ireland, noting her positive influence on her husband. Her daughter Fionnuala MacDonnell, the Iníon Dubh ('dark daughter'), married Sir Hugh O'Donnell in 1568, strengthening the influence of the Scots in Tyrone and Tirconnell.

John Case, captain, first appeared as soldier in Galway in the summer of 1580. After the siege of Smerwick he was posted with Zouche to Dinglecush, where he weathered the severe sickness of the winter and spring of 1581—apparently not without extreme suffering. He wrote twice to Walsingham in that year with a petition to be returned to Galway (see SP 63/80/66), but eventually left Ireland in September 1581 (see SP 63/85/57).

William Cecil, from 1571 **Baron Burghley** (1521–98), was the Queen's longest-serving councillor. He had been appointed Secretary of State on Elizabeth's first day on the throne, finally relinquishing that post, to become Lord Treasurer, in 1572. Though a committed Protestant, Burghley's policy positions were generally less militant and forward than those of his younger colleague Sir Francis Walsingham, and certainly more bureaucratically minded than those of Robert Dudley, Earl of Leicester. Burghley's participation in the New English govern-ment of Ireland in the late 1570s and 1580s was mainly concerned with the finances; where he had been an active adviser to Sir Henry Sidney on policy and military affairs, Grey tended to consult with him far less frequently and copiously, and to restrict much of their correspondence to matters of victualling, provision of treasure for paying the soldiers, and related administrative issues. Burghley also had a very well-established network of correspondents and intelligencers in Ireland, not all of whom were known to his fellow councillors or to the Lord Deputies (including Grey) on whom he spied. Sir Henry Wallop wrote regularly to him, but Burghley seems to have collected information more clandestinely from Auditor Thomas Jenyson, and possibly from Geoffrey Fenton. At some point during the autumn of 1581, Burghley received information—information that is apparently no longer extant—accusing Grey of matters sufficient to provoke Burghley's 'heavy' displeasure with him. It is generally thought that Grey was recalled in the summer of 1582 because of the Queen's anger at his extravagant award of confiscated lands to his allies and servants, but Elizabeth's displeasure on this score seems to have abated well before his recall, and Grey even speaks of her as 'well satisfied' with his attempts to acquit himself of wrongdoing; more likely is that it was Burghley's ongoing and serious opposition that caused Grey's recall and apparent disgrace. Irenius speaks in *A view of the present state of Ireland* of a 'dissencion' cunningly fomented between Grey and some other 'noble personage', who may well have been Burghley:

> I maye not forgett so memorable a thinge. neither can I be ignorant of that perillous devise and of the wholle meanes by which it was Compassed and verye Cvnninglie Contrived by sowinge firste dissencion betwene him and another noble personage whearein they bothe at lengthe founde how notable they had bene abused, and how theareby vnderhande this vniuersall alteracion of thinges was broughte aboute, But then to late to staye the same[.][3]

Unfortunately, if Burghley had received intelligence against Grey, he seems to have destroyed it. On Grey's side, however, the vagaries of manuscript survival have been kinder, and it is impossible to mistake the tone of genuine anger at Burghley in this letter to Walsingham of 27 January 1582:

> I perceaue by oothers pryuate letters from hym that 324 [Burghley] is a greate obseruer & fawltfynder with thynges heere; I neyther waye it, nor dowght but too bee fownde euer honester & iuster in dealyng then hymsellf & so I leaue hym, onely I wysshe of God that hee woold bee my chardger face too face beefore her Maiestie & the rest of yow . . . hee falls into a detestation of this place & termes it a gullf of consumyng threazure, as in deede truly hee maye, & the more throwghe hys good meanes & aduyce, for which if repentance & Gods mercies beefall not the greater hys soale wyll awnsswer in the gullff of hell.[4]

No evidence exists that this rift was repaired, as Spenser suggests, but Grey does note in a later letter to Walsingham that someone—apparently one of his fellow ministers in Ireland—had sought his forgiveness for a wrong done him:

> 68 hathe sowght reconciliation with mee sum wrong doonne mee is confessed & causers therof that I lyttle woold haue suspected discoouered; the Lord forguyue mee as I forguyue all & so an end.[5]

Hugh Cuffe, one of the original undertakers in Munster, held a vast seignory of 12,000 acres, in the Great Wood, near to Spenser's estate at Kilcolman, Co. Cork. He petitioned Burghley unsuccessfully for the office of Sheriff in Cork in October 1588 (SP 63/137/5). It is not clear whether the appearance of his name as a signatory to the October 1589 'Bill against Lord Roche' (No. 45, above, SP 63/147/16), next to Spenser's at the foot of the paper, indicates his participation in the complaint, or Spenser's expectation of his participation. He may have been the elder brother of Henry Cuffe, secretrary to the Earl of Essex, and thus son of Robert Cuffe, of Donyatt, Somerset. Henry Cuffe at his death (at Tyburn in 1601) was described as a 'Puritan'; Hugh may have had similar associations.

John Cusack, probably of Ellestonreade, a conspirator in the 1581 rebellion of William Nugent, turned state's evidence and was rewarded for giving up his accomplices (see SP 63/88/47/1 and 63/88/47/2). Cusack was named in John Nugent's confession (No. 29, above, SP 63/89/18) as a man of frequent resort and personal access to William Nugent, but the Queen ensured that he was afterward

---

[3] *A view*, ll. 3318–24.   [4] No. 28, above (SP 63/88/40).   [5] SP 63/92/26.

restored to his lands (despite the protest of Sir Henry Wallop—see SP 63/100/5), and even handsomely rewarded following Nugent's escape abroad. In 1586 he was still being described as a 'pensioner' (SP 63/123/21). The care taken over Cusack's reward suggests that a deal may have been struck for his confession; Cusack's uncle Edward was pardoned at the Trim sessions that claimed the life of Nicholas Nugent (see No. 33, above, SP 63/91/22), and it may be that both Cusacks were spared because they made themselves amenable to the fall of the Nugents.

Sir Edward Denny (1547–1600) was the son of Sir Anthony Denny (a privy councillor under Henry VIII), cousin of Walter Ralegh, and close friend and correspondent of Sir Philip Sidney. Denny travelled to Ireland firstly under Essex in 1574, and then again with Lord Grey, in mid-1580, with 200 soldiers under his command. He distinguished himself in the taking of Smerwick (SP 63/78/32) and seems to have conveyed to England Grey's letters describing the siege (No. 5, above, SP 63/78/29). While in England on this errand he apparently surpassed his commission and conveyed a disrespectful report to Burghley: Grey was still apologizing for the indiscretion several months later (No. 11, above, HH Cecil Papers, 11/91; SP 63/80/41). In July 1581, Grey stationed him in Castle Kevan in south Leinster (SP 63/84/2), and made him the gift of a parcel of land (SP 63/88/40/3), but Denny left Ireland shortly thereafter. In 1587, he was awarded an estate near Tralee, Co. Kerry, and by 1588–9 he had returned to Ireland, where he agreed to succeed Richard Bingham as President in Connaught; this plan came to nothing. In April 1589, Denny and his family returned to England. He assisted Admiral Lord Thomas Howard off the Azores in 1591, and fought briefly against Tyrone in 1597 or 1598.

Walter Devereux, first Earl of Essex (1539–76), embarked for Ireland in 1573 (with a loan of some £10,000 from the Queen), intending to colonize and fortify Ulster and Clandeboye, now Co. Antrim. Essex's project was similar to that of Thomas Smith (the younger) in the Ards in 1572, which had ended with Smith's death: and soon he too faced the desertion of his men, a shortage of supplies, plague, and conflict with Lord Deputy Fitzwilliam. He managed to bring Turlough Luineach O'Neill to submission (see SP 52/48/16–18), but his military campaigns stalled amid notorious atrocities, including the murder of Sir Brian MacPhelim O'Neill, his wife, his brother, and 200 men at a Christmas banquet, and the massacre of up to 400 Scots under Sorley Boy MacDonnell, including women and children, on Rathlin Island in July 1575 (see SP 63/52/77–8). Essex died—probably of poison—in Dublin in 1576.

Sir Lucas Dillon (c. 1530–1591) studied at the Middle Temple in the 1550s, then returned to Ireland and settled in Trim, Co. Meath. He was appointed Principal Solicitor in Ireland in 1565, then Attorney General, and after returning to London in 1569 on Council business, was returned Chief Baron of the Exchequer in 1570.

Several documents survive showing his good relationship with Burghley, though he was nominated to the Exchequer position, where he succeeded his father, on Sidney's recommendation. Sidney knighted him in 1575 at Drogheda, and Grey commended him to the Queen as a 'faithfull servaunt a rare iewell of this Countrey birth' (SP 63/79/24/1). Despite participation in the cess controversy of 1577, and an accusation that he had harboured a Catholic priest, he was nominated as Chief Justice of the Queen's Bench in 1583. It was Dillon who arranged the trial by combat of two of the O'Connors in Dublin Castle in 1583. In 1592, Dillon and his cousin Sir Robert were charged with instigating the rebellion of Sir Brian O'Rourke in Connaught (a charge probably confected by their enemies the Nugents), but both were exonerated. After Dillon's death, the Irish were completely excluded from the Dublin government.

Sir Robert Dillon (*c*.1540–1597), son of a prominent Irish judicial family, was named in 1569 second justice of the new presidency and Council of Connaught. He defended Sir Edward Fitton, the first President of Connaught, against the criticism of Lord Deputy Sir William Fitzwilliam, and was appointed Chancellor of the Exchequer in Ireland in June 1572. Sir Henry Sidney regarded Dillon as an ally, and appointed him second Justice of Common Pleas in November 1577. He was passed over for the Chief Justiceship in 1580, but was appointed in July 1581, three months after the fall of Nicholas Nugent. He became a privy councillor and was reputed the wealthiest commoner in the Pale in 1586. In 1588 he was named a commissioner for the new composition of Connaught, but after fresh quarrels with Fitzwilliam and Sir Richard Bingham, he was excluded from the council and in 1591 was accused by William Nugent of encouraging Sir Brian O'Rourke in rebellion. He was removed from office and imprisoned in October 1593, but his supporter, Lord Chancellor Loftus, declared him innocent, and he was restored to the council in 1594. He regained the Chief Justiceship in March 1595.

James Dowdall (d.1584) had a long legal career in Ireland, serving as second Justice of the King's Bench from 15 April 1565. He was granted commission in 1565 and 1566 to negotiate with Shane O'Neill, and then subsequently with Turlough Luineach and, in 1574, with the Earl of Desmond (see SP 63/45/82). On 13 May 1583, a warrant was issued for his appointment as Chief Justice of the King's Bench (SP 63/102/26) on the recommendation of Lucas Dillon. His death was reported in April 1584.

Robert Dudley, Earl of Leicester (1532/3–1588) and one of Elizabeth's chief favourites and ministers throughout her reign, played an important role in Irish affairs during Spenser's secretaryship. Leicester orchestrated Grey's appointment to the deputyship and remained, along with Sir Francis Walsingham, one of Grey's chief correspondents between 1580 and 1582. Only a few of Grey's letters to Leicester survive (e.g. SP 63/81/42), probably as a result of the filing practices in Westminster and the haphazard development of the Paper Office in these years;

but it is clear from Grey's letters to Walsingham, and of surviving letters to Leicester, that the three men shared common assumptions not only on religion and international affairs, but on Irish policy and military strategy (see e.g. No. 24, above, SP 63/86/53, a letter to Walsingham in which Grey directs him to 'empart' an enclosure to Leicester). After Grey's deputyship, Leicester's influence on Irish policy and government appears to have waned, probably in part as a result of Ralegh's ascendancy, and in part because of his own increasing preoccupation with affairs in the Low Countries.

James Eustace, third Viscount Baltinglass (1530–85), was born into a Wicklow dynasty of loyal Old English servitors. His father Roland, second Viscount Baltinglass, had led opposition to the cess in 1577 (see SP 63/57/1 and 63/57/4) and, with several other leading gentlemen of the Pale, was examined in June of 1578 (SP 63/58/56). Upon his father's death, Baltinglass quickly gave rein to his own radical Catholicism, issuing a declaration of rebellion in the summer of 1580 that openly defied Elizabeth's right to rule, on the grounds of her sex as well as her reformed religion. One of the first letters Grey received upon arriving in office in August 1580 was an arrogant brave from Baltinglass and his confederate, Feagh MacHugh O'Byrne (see SP 63/75/40); their taunts had the desired effect, and the deputy marched immediately, and too precipitously, against the Wicklow rebels, suffering a heavy defeat in Glenmalure on 25 August (see SP 63/75/83). Grey's decisive victory at Smerwick in November probably prevented Baltinglass's Wicklow rebellion from catalysing a larger confederacy between the Desmonds in Munster and restive forces in the north; within a few months, he had fled Ireland for the continent (SP 63/80/76/1) and, after several years of fruitless petitions in Lisbon, Rome, and Madrid, he died in 1585.

Geoffrey Fenton (*c*.1539–1608) went to Ireland in 1580 with letters from Burghley, and was quickly joined in John Chaloner's patent as a second Secretary of State under Sir William Pelham (SP 63/74/59). Upon Chaloner's death, Fenton became Principal Secretary of State in Ireland in 1581, serving thereafter under a number of Lord Deputies, though he was at odds with Sir John Perrot, and also quarrelled with Sir Richard Bingham. He was knighted in 1589. He was generally in favour of strong military action against Irish rebellion, but often stressed also that Ireland could not be properly governed without the consent of the Irish, and throughout 1582 and 1583 urged a pardon for the Earl of Desmond, in order to end the war. He was a strong advocate of the Munster plantation, and suggested in 1585 that the English should occupy the rebels' land and the Irish be transported into the interior. Through the 1580s and 1590s, Fenton advocated the assassination of various chieftains, including Florence MacCarthy More, leader of the MacCarthy clan in Desmond, and Hugh O'Neill, Earl of Tyrone. In the Nine Years' War, he acted as Elizabeth's official messenger, conveying letters to Tyrone. Despite his hostility to Scottish involvement in Ulster, and being obliged upon James's accession to share the office of secretary with Sir Richard Coke, he was confirmed in his position for life in 1604. In 1585 Fenton married Alice, daughter of Dr Robert Weston, formerly Lord Chancellor of Ireland, and widow of Dr Hugh Brady, Bishop of Meath; their daughter, Catherine, married Richard Boyle, later first Earl of Cork, in 1603. Before his career in Ireland, Fenton had written a number of literary, philosophical, and religious works, many of them translations from French and Latin, including *Certain Tragicall Discourses of Bandello* (1567), one of the first collections of Italian prose fiction in English; *Monophylo* (1572), a philosophical dialogue on the moral life; *A Forme of Christian Pollicie* (1574); *Golden Epistles Contayning Varietie of Discourse both Morall, Philosophicall, and Divine* (1575); and a translation of Francesco Guicciardini's *Storia d'Italia* from the French version, entitled *The Historie of Guicciardini* (1579), which had a significant influence on the Tacitean English historiography of the late 1590s.

Lady Elizabeth Fiennes de Clinton, Countess of Lincoln (1528?–89), was the second daughter of Gerald Fitzgerald, ninth Earl of Kildare (1487–1534), and Lady Elizabeth Grey, first cousin of King Henry VIII. Following the collapse of Kildare power in Ireland in 1534, she joined the household of Princesses Mary and Elizabeth, and it was here that she was seen by Henry Howard, Earl of Surrey; he wrote a sonnet to her, entitled 'From Tuscan cam my ladies worthi race' (giving her the name 'Geraldine'). In 1542, she married Sir Anthony Browne, Henry VIII's master of the horse; after Browne's death in 1548, she married Edward Fiennes de Clinton, ninth Baron Clinton and Saye, Lord High Admiral. He was created Earl of Lincoln in 1572. Her favour with Elizabeth was instrumental in helping to restore her brother, the eleventh Earl of Kildare, to his title and lands in 1569; it was a power she called on again in 1581 to defend Kildare from conspiracy and treason charges.

Gerald Fitzjames Fitzgerald (*c.*1533–1583), fourteenth Earl of Desmond, inherited the traditional Desmond enmity for the house of Ormond. The two earls clashed repeatedly throughout the early 1560s, and in 1565 engaged in a feudal battle at Affane on the Blackwater, in which Desmond's private army was crushed. Both Ormond and Desmond were summoned to London, where the latter was imprisoned in the Tower with his brother, John, until 1570. Upon elaborate sureties for keeping the peace, he was permitted to return to Munster in 1573, where he found his lordship much changed by the innovations of Lord Deputy Sidney and the new President of Munster, John Perrot. After the departure of the sympathetic Sir Henry Sidney in 1578, Desmond's fortunes crashed: Sir William Drury and Sir William Pelham warred against his family and allies in Munster in their attempt to stamp out Irish customs and the Catholic faith, and eventually Desmond himself faced a stark choice: local control in Munster, or obedience to what appeared to be an interim administration in Dublin. Isolated in the south-west, he chose the former. In 1579 he sacked and burned Youghal and Kinsale; Pelham responded in 1580 by taking the Desmond castles of Carrigafoyle, Askeaton, and Ballyloughan, nearly capturing Desmond and Nicholas Sanders, the papal envoy. While neither Desmond nor his brother made any apparent attempt to relieve the Italian and Spanish troops at Smerwick in 1580, they held out after Grey's victory there, and the Earl repeatedly evaded John Zouche and the Earl of Ormond, if narrowly, for three years. On 11 November 1583, he was surrounded by five soldiers in a cave in the Glanaginty woods and killed; his head was sent to England. His extensive Munster estates—already forfeited by the 1582 act of attainder—were surveyed and distributed by patent to a new generation of English planters.

Gerald Fitzgerald, eleventh Earl of Kildare (1525–85), spent his childhood in hiding and in exile, following the revolt of his uncle, Silken Thomas, in 1534. After finding refuge with Cardinal Pole in Rome, he was welcomed back to England by the Duke of Somerset in 1549, and shortly after married Mabel Browne, daughter of Sir Anthony Browne; by the Brownes' influence, he was restored to his lands, to his earldom, and to favour. Kildare returned to Ireland in 1556, and successfully managed occasional alliances with the Earl of Leicester, Sir Henry Sidney, and Shane O'Neill to recover his rights and territories in Offaly and the Pale. An old antipathy for Lord Deputy Sir William Fitzwilliam resulted in Kildare's apprehension on charges of conspiracy to incite rebellion in 1575, and the Earl was sent to England to endure interrogation and four years of mild imprisonment. By the time he was permitted to return to Ireland, in 1579, his influence in Leinster had dissipated almost entirely, and he was unable to control the outbreak of rebellion and conspiracy during Lord Grey's absence, on campaign, in autumn 1580. Along with the Baron of Delvin, he was accused of slackness and complicity, was again imprisoned, and was sent to London in the spring of 1582; there, by the intervention of sympathetic courtiers—including his sister, the Countess of Lincoln—he was cleared of treason, released from the Tower in 1583, and permitted to return to Ireland in 1584, where he died a year later.

Sir John Fitzgerald, alias John of Desmond (c.1540–1582), was brother and sometime ally of Gerald Fitzgerald, fourteenth Earl of Desmond. Throughout the 1560s, John of Desmond mounted frequent attacks on Butler lands, and even though Ormond insisted in 1565 that he be placed under direct supervision, he maintained his independence, partly because he was generally considered more sensible than his brother. At about this time he conferred secretly with Shane O'Neill, but O'Neill did not succeed in inciting him to rebellion. In March 1567, when his brother was arrested, John of Desmond was knighted and appointed governor of Cork, Limerick, and Kerry by Sir Henry Sidney, an appointment that was rescinded by Queen Elizabeth. He was arrested in December 1567 and detained with his brother in the Tower of London until 1573. During this period, their cousin, James Fitzmaurice Fitzgerald, fomented rebellion in Munster, and both brothers were released in early 1573 in order to fight the rebels. Upon the Earl's rearrest and escape, John of Desmond became marginalized and impoverished and, after a dispute with his brother in early 1579, he allied himself with Fitzmaurice. Upon Fitzmaurice's death on 18 August 1579, he assumed command of the Munster rebellion. In early January 1582, Fitzgerald was surprised and killed in the woods of Eatharlach, in Co. Cork, by John Zouche, governor of Munster. His headless corpse was sent to Cork and hanged in chains over the city gates (see Nos. 26 and 27, above, SP 63/88/12 and 63/88/15); the head travelled to London, via Dublin.

John Fitzedmund Fitzgerald (d.1589), Seneschal of Imokilly, wielded considerable military strength between the 1560s and 1580s. He joined James Fitzmaurice in rebellion in 1569, and spent the next six years alternating between war and submission. After accompanying Fitzmaurice to France in 1575, he remained quiet until the outbreak of a fresh Desmond war. He attacked Youghal in 1579, and participated in a number of subsequent campaigns, closely escaping death on a number of occasions. But the rebellion was gradually defeated, and the Seneschal submitted on 11 June 1583. He was pardoned in May 1585, but trouble arose again over the settling of English planters in Munster, and he was rearrested in March 1587. Imprisoned in Dublin Castle, he died there in January 1589.

Mabel Fitzgerald, Countess of Kildare, daughter of Sir Anthony Browne, married Kildare in 1554. She seems to have been slightly tainted by her husband's supposed involvement in the Baltinglass rebellion: Chancellor Gerrarde accused her in February 1581 of sheltering consorts of Dr Sanders (SP 63/80/61), and Thomas Meagh, her servant, was arrested and tortured in England. But she wrote several letters to Francis Walsingham throughout the 1580s (SP 63/82/4, 63/108/59, 63/112/48) seeking the Queen's presence in a bid to rehabilitate her husband's fortunes.

James Fitzmaurice (d.1579) was the grandson of the twelfth Earl of Desmond and the cousin of the fourteenth earl. In 1568, he was appointed by Desmond— still in the Tower—to govern Munster in his absence (SP 63/23/32/6). This caused immediate anxiety in the English administration, and Fitzmaurice rapidly acquired the status of 'arch-traitor' or 'arch-rebel', suspected of contact with Spain, and notorious for spoiling Ormond's lands, taking the town of Tracton, and spoiling Kilmallock repeatedly in 1570 and 1571. On 18 November 1571, a bizarre combat was arranged between Fitzmaurice and John Perrot, President of Munster, with twenty-four men on each side (SP 63/34/29/3); Fitzmaurice failed to attend. He submitted to Perrot in March 1573, but within two years had sailed for the Catholic continent to gain support for an invasion of Ireland, and possibly England. Rumours abounded of the imminent invasion of a papal force, and in July 1579, Fitzmaurice landed at Dingle, accompanied by friars and bishops. He was killed by Tibbot Burke in a chance encounter in August 1579, but the fort he had begun at Smerwick would, a year later, become the base of the papal troops for which he had lobbied.

Thomas Fitzmaurice, sixteenth Baron of Kerry and Lixnaw (*c*.1502–1590), returned from a military career on mainland Europe in 1551, when he inherited his family's estates. He remained staunchly loyal to the English administration until the mid-1570s, initially rebuffing offers to join the Desmond rebellion after 1579. By 1582, under pressure from the government, marginalized by his sons, and ruined by Desmond, he was pushed into rebellion. This was short-lived, and he surrendered to a sympathetic Ormond in 1583, but he spent the last years of his life poverty-stricken, hedged in by English planters, and under constant suspicion.

Sir William Fitzwilliam (1526–99) was appointed Privy Councillor in Ireland in October 1554, thereafter holding a succession of ministerial posts before appointment as Lord Deputy in January 1572. Fitzwilliam was a conciliator, opposed to the military aggression preferred by Gilbert, Perrot, Fitton, and others; he preferred to work through local Irish political associations and the Old English lords and, with Ormond, opposed Smith's and Essex's ventures in Ulster—which he helped to sabotage. Fitzwilliam was accused of mismanaging funds and, following the Earl of Desmond's escape from Dublin Castle in 1573, he angered the Queen by an aggressive and antagonistic march to Munster. In March 1575, pleading illness and impoverishment, he was recalled and replaced by Sir Henry Sidney. Between 1575 and 1588, Fitzwilliam remained resident at Milton, but in February 1588 he was reappointed as Lord Deputy, to replace Sir John Perrot. At the beginning of November he marched through Ulster, Tirconnell, and Sligo to take in hand the survivors of the Armada. Fitzwilliam returned repeatedly to Connaught to investigate Sir Richard Bingham, the President of the province, between 1589 and 1590, and further undermined his own authority by antagonizing the former deputy Sir John Perrot. In his dealings with the Irish he was no less capricious—he intervened disastrously in these years in the affairs of MacMahon, Maguire, O'Neill, and Tyrone, and was responsible for the much-derided policy of partitioning Monaghan in 1592. After falling seriously (but not mortally) ill in 1594, he secured his release from the deputyship in May, leaving in his wake a wash of recriminations on almost every side.

Arthur Grey, fourteenth Baron Grey of Wilton (1536–93), inherited from his father a tradition of military service and a heavy debt to the crown. A Knight of the Garter from 1572, he was mooted as Lord Deputy of Ireland at least once (in 1571) before he accepted the commission in the spring of 1580. Both Burghley and Leicester supported his appointment, and Grey arrived in Dublin in 1580 with a clear mandate to cut off and quiet the rebellion spreading through Munster, Ulster, and Leinster. His deputyship was marked by two considerable successes: the defeat of the Spanish and Italian force at Smerwick in November 1580, and the successful pacification of Turlough Luineach O'Neill in Ulster. By other measures, though, Grey's deputyship was dogged by failure: his forces failed to capture the Earl of Desmond; his administration failed to reform the Irish victualling, and was hit hard by a horrible famine and sickness throughout Munster and south Leinster in 1581; his council was riven by conspiracy and rebellion in the Pale; and his own relations with the Queen and her two chief ministers quickly deteriorated under the pressure of finances, factionalism, and partisan intelligence. Despite two years of active and by all accounts honest service, driven by Protestant zealotry and an almost chivalric commitment to honour and patronage, Grey succeeded in securing his own recall in July 1582. He served as Marshal under Leicester at Tilbury in 1588, but never again sought active military or political office.

Henry Harrington (d.1613) enjoyed a long and much-commended career of Irish military service. A nephew of Sir Henry Sidney, he followed him to Ireland in 1575, and saw regular service against the O'Byrnes and Tooles in Leinster for forty years. He was granted leases on Baltinglass lands as a reward for his service against Feagh MacHugh O'Byrne, and as late as May 1609 carried to court a letter of commendation from Chichester, noting his long service (SP 63/226/76). He was acting as a member of the Irish Council in January 1610 (SP 63/228/16B), and died in 1613 (*CSPI 1611–14*, pp. 388–9).

Thomas Hoorde, captain, had a short career as a soldier in Ireland under Lord Grey. He may perhaps have had connections to Walsingham, to whom he wrote from Waterford in November 1580, shortly after his arrival (SP 63/78/49). He was soon posted to Wexford, to deal with the Cavanaghs (see SP 63/79/5), but by June 1581, Grey reported on his journey to that part of Ireland that Hoorde's band had been decimated by sickness and discharged (No. 15, above, SP 63/83/45). Hoorde himself was apparently granted a pension (SP 63/83/50), and in July 1581 he was on his way back to England, bearing letters from Edward Denny and Grey (No. 19, above, SP 63/84/26).

Thomas Jenyson (*c.*1525–1587) was appointed in 1551, and for the period of his life, as Auditor-General of Ireland. Shortly after his arrival in Dublin, he was suspended on suspicion of financial misconduct, embezzlement, and poor accounting (accusations that dogged him for the rest of his life). He was dismissed from his post, but in 1560 was made comptroller of the works, keeper of the stores, and clerk of the check at Berwick, and then in 1566, was reappointed as Auditor-General in Ireland. Mutual antagonism with Dublin ministers dogged his undoubtedly corrupt career, and he was finally dismissed in 1587, dying shortly after.

Adam Loftus (*c.*1533–1605), Archbishop of Dublin and Lord Chancellor of Ireland, first went to Ireland as chaplain to Thomas Radcliffe, Earl of Sussex, in 1560, and was appointed chaplain to the Bishop of Kildare by April 1561. He was consecrated Archbishop of Armagh in 1563, made a privy councillor, translated to the archbishopric of Dublin in 1567. Famed as a preacher, he had puritan sympathies, and supported Goodman and Cartwright between 1570 and 1577.

With Robert Garvey he ran a campaign between 1577 and 1579 to seize control of the commission for faculties. His evidence was crucial in implicating the Earl of Kildare in conspiracy in 1580 (see No. 7, above, SP 63/81/1), and in discrediting Nicholas Nugent in 1581—two examples among many of a sometimes politically corrupt factionalism. He served as Lord Justice between 1582 and 1584, again from 1597 to 1599, and from 1599 to 1600.

Florence MacCarthy (1562–c.1640) was son of Sir Donough MacCarthy Reagh, a loyal servant of the English. On his father's death in 1576, he was made a ward of Sir William Drury. *ODNB* claims that in 1578, on coming of age, he fought for Drury against the Desmond rebellion; but letters from Warham Sentleger (SP 63/70/42, 63/80/65), Ormond (No. 8, above, SP 63/81/36/1), and Walter Ralegh (SP 63/83/16/1) suggest that he spent at least some time on the side of the rebels. After the rebellion, MacCarthy went to court, anglicizing his name from Finian to Florence. He had returned to Ireland by 1585, and was supported by his uncle, Sir Owen MacCarthy, in his aspiration for the title of MacCarthy Reagh. But he also hoped to gain the title of MacCarthy More, and in 1588 eloped with Ellen (also known as Eileen), sole daughter of Donal MacCarthy, first Earl of Clancar, the current MacCarthy More. Florence was suspected of having connections with Spain, and his attempt to unite the two lordships panicked the English administration. He was arrested with his wife, imprisoned in Cork and then sent to the Tower of London in February 1589; released in 1591, and with Ormond standing as his guarantor, he returned to Ireland in November 1593. Although the Dublin government supported his attempt to gain control of the Clancar estate, MacCarthy sought support from the Earl of Tyrone and fought with him against the English; after being defeated in April 1600, he was captured in 1601, and spent the next forty years in prison in London.

Sir Owen MacCarthy, or **MacCarthy Reagh** (d.1594), was the Irish Lord of Carbery, on the south coast of Munster about forty miles south-west of Cork. During the last years of Sir Henry Sidney's second deputyship he had offered to submit himself to English tenures and rule, and during Sir William Drury's presidency in Munster converted his cess payments to a fixed rent on the English model (SP 63/58/4); in 1579, along with many other Munster lords, he gave in pledges for his good behaviour (SP 63/70/64). It was Miler Magrath who first reported that MacCarthy Reagh had joined the rebels in 1580 (see SP 63/81/20), but unlike Lord Barry—who 'went out' at about the same time—MacCarthy Reagh was quickly brought to heel by the Earl of Ormond, who satisfied the government that it was only local politics that had occasioned his apparent rebellion. MacCarthy Reagh's two sons were studying in Oxford when, in October 1583, he submitted a petition to the Queen (SP 63/105/2/1) to confer and confirm titles to lands in Munster. In the same document, he also begged relief from the menacings of the government-backed sub-sheriffs, who may have been the same men who drove him into rebellion in 1580. Following his brief implication in the Desmond rebellion in 1580, he remained dutiful until his death during the Nine Years' War.

Humphrey Mackworth (d.1582), captain, first appears in the records of Irish service in September 1575, relieving Carrickfergus (SP 63/53/22), though much of his later service seems to have come during the deputyship of Grey. He fought at Smerwick (No. 5, above, SP 63/78/29), and Grey's later letters speak of his services against the O'Mores, particularly Art Boy's sept: in one controversial encounter, he killed a pledge of the O'Mores, Melaghlen Roe O'Kelly, after an alleged attack (SP 63/92/14). One of Mackworth's Leinster bands was preserved at the general discharge in January 1582 (SP 63/88/40/2), to his cost: in May 1582, he was captured and executed by the O'Connors.

Sir Hugh Magennis, member of a powerful family in Co. Down, was created Baron of Iveagh in 1576. As one of Turlough Luineach's 'urraghs', he was at constant variance with the Ulster lord: in August 1580, he complained of raids and preys taken by Turlough Luineach's men (SP 63/75/75), and a letter from Nicholas Bagenal (No. 3, above, SP 63/76/1) speaks of Turlough Luineach's challenge to Magennis over the death of a person 'so vile as Magneisse could not have in the killing of any such like donne better'. Although traditionally a client of the O'Neills, Magennis had, like several of his neighbours, converted his tenures to the English model and nominally held his lands by yearly rent to the Queen. The maintaining of his allegiance was an important element in the policy of the Dublin government in the 1580s and 1590s.

Sir Nicholas Malby (1530–84) escaped execution for coining in England in 1562 on condition that he fight for the Earl of Warwick in France—a history of criminality and soldiery that perfectly suited him for office in the Elizabethan administration of Ireland. Sir Henry Sidney appointed him sergeant-major of the army in 1567, and he soon won commendation for his wars against Sorley Boy MacDonnell at Carrickfergus. Following injury in Leinster, he convalesced in London before further command with the first Earl of Essex in his Ulster plantation venture, and by 1574 was considered of such experience that he was made councillor in Ireland. Sidney knighted him and dispatched him to Connaught in 1576, where his service against the sons of the Earl of Clanricard, as well as his effective management of the 1577 composition, led to his promotion as President of the province. During Grey's deputyship he largely kept the peace in Connaught, balancing competing claims between the Burkes, and assisting Grey with wars in Tyrone and Tirconnell. He died suddenly in Roscommon in 1584, leaving his son Henry in possession of the second largest estate in Connaught.

Jane (or Gennet) Marward (Marwart, Marwards) (d.1629) was abducted and married in 1573 by William Nugent. She was daughter of Walter Marward, Baron Skryne by Ellen Plunkett, and had three sons with William: Richard, Christopher, and James.

James Meagh or **Myagh**, known from 1580 as **MacKedagh O'More**, was the illegitimate son of Kedagh O'More and brother to Thomas Myagh, servant to the Countess of Kildare. In his youth Meagh had apparently served James Eustace, Viscount Baltinglass, and supported him in the Pale rebellion of 1580–1; he submitted himself to Grey at Waterford in late September or early October 1581 (No. 23, above, SP 63/86/51), and thereafter travelled to Dublin to meet Geoffrey Fenton, on 20 November making confession of the Earl of Kildare's confederacy with Baltinglass (SP 63/87/44/2). He had died by August 1584.

John Meagh (or **Myagh**, or **Meade**), cousin to Richard Myagh, Sovereign of Kinsale, served as second Justice in Munster from at least March 1579 (SP 63/66/1). Based in Cork, he reported regularly to the Lord Deputy and sometimes directly to Burghley on affairs in Munster; his letters during the Munster famine and sickness of 1581 (see e.g. SP 63/92/103), with those of Sir Warham Sentleger, provide an important record of the calamity of the time. He failed to profit by the distribution of escheated Desmond lands in the late 1580s, and died in 1589.

Thomas Meagh (or **Myagh**, **Meade**), brother of James MacKedagh O'More and servant of the Earl and Countess of Kildare, was described by Lord Grey on 2 March 1581 as 'a mealie mouthed fellowe', suspected of involvement in the rebellion of Kildare and Delvin. Grey advised that he 'bee apprehended, & strayghtly handlyd', in order to obtain 'the secretts of this combination': 'extreemitie must wryng it from hym, by oother dealyng expect nothyng' (SP 63/81/4). Meagh was indeed arrested, and taken to the Tower of London, where he was tortured in Skeffington's Irons, and on the rack; Kildare's eventual release suggests that Meagh failed to inculpate him, and he was released on 5 November 1581. On 17 May 1582, Meagh wrote to his brother James (No. 38, above, SP 63/93/64/1, a copy certified by Spenser), telling him that he meant 'neuer to serve the Earle of Kildare agayne', and appearing to warn him about the dishonesty of the captains Harpoll and Mackworth. In 1584 he proposed an ambitious plan—with Ralph Lane and his brother James MacKedagh O'More—to resettle the O'Mores in a depopulated part of Munster, so ridding the Pale of one of its most constant threats (see SP 63/107/61, 63/107/62, and 63/107/63); unsurprisingly, he was ignored.

Richard Mompesson served as a gentleman usher under Lord Grey during the period of his deputyship. It is not entirely clear what Grey's gentlemen attendants did for him; they may well have undertaken minor embassies, carried messages, solicited information and intelligence, and assisted in the duties personal and military that Grey had regularly to perform during his service. Mompesson is the only such gentleman attendant named in the account of Grey's grants of escheated lands and goods in 1582 (SP 63/88/40/3).

Sir John Norris (or **Norreys**) (c.1547–1597), 'Black Jack', brother of Thomas Norris, fought for Admiral Coligny in France, and later in the Low Countries, from 1567. In 1573, he and his brother William accompanied the first Earl of Essex to Ulster. Norris commanded bands of horse and foot in Essex's brutal campaign, massacring over 200 followers of Brian MacPhelim O'Neill in October 1574, and (with Francis Drake) as many as 400 women and children of the MacDonnells on Rathlin Island in July 1575. Between 1577 and 1584 Norris served against the Spanish in the Low Countries, building a reputation for bravery and expedition, but in July 1584 was returned to Ireland, as President of Munster. Lord Deputy Perrot immediately drafted him for service against the Scots, and Norris hardly had time to engage with his Munster duties before receiving a new commission in June 1585—as Colonel-General and Governor of the Queen's forces in the Low Countries. Norris was briefly appointed to Munster in 1590–1, where he directed the rebuilding of fortifications against an expected Spanish invasion. In 1595, despite failing health, he was returned to Ireland to assist William Russell against Hugh O'Neill's rebellion; but quarrels broke out between Norris, Russell, Henry Bagenal, and Richard Bingham, and the Ulster campaign had collapsed by the time Norris's commission expired in 1597. He died later that year.

Sir Thomas Norris, or **Norreys** (1556–99), first served in Ireland in December 1579, as a captain of horse under Sir William Pelham. He warred against Desmond between 1579 and the end of 1583, when Ormond began to discharge the Munster forces after the death of the Earl. Norris returned to Ireland under Lord Deputy Perrot in 1584, sat for Limerick in Perrot's Parliament of 1584–6, and was appointed Vice-President of Munster in his brother's absence. Norris governed Munster effectively, if not without complaint, and secured an estate for the presidency, at Mallow, upon the withdrawal of Sir John Popham from the plantation. In 1589 Norris successfully defused the crisis of Florence MacCarthy's elopement with and marriage to the Earl of Clancar's daughter (see No. 43, above, SP 63/135/66), but within a year he was chasing his own mutinous troops on a march to Dublin. At the outbreak of the Nine Years' War, Norris was called north to fight alongside Lord Deputy Russell and his brother, but was returned to Munster in 1596 and was appointed President there upon John Norris's death in 1597. After the Earl of Tyrone's victory at the Yellow Ford in 1598, Munster descended into chaos, and Norris, lacking soldiers and support from the undertakers, retreated to Cork. He was blamed by many, including the Queen, for cowardice, but upon reinforcement, he regained Kilmallock and Ross Carbery. Wounded in the jaw on his way to meet Essex in 1599, he succumbed to infection and died at Mallow in August.

Christopher Nugent, fifth Baron Delvin (1544–1602), studied in Cambridge before returning in 1565 to Ireland, where he held considerable land, with letters of commendation from Elizabeth to Sir Henry Sidney. In 1566, he fought against Shane O'Neill on behalf of the English, and was knighted by Sidney. But in May 1577 Delvin led the Pale opposition to the cess, and along with Lord Howth, Viscount Baltinglass, and others, he was imprisoned repeatedly in Dublin Castle until he acknowledged the Queen's prerogative. Said to be involved in the preparation of the Baltinglass rebellion in 1580, he was arrested with the Earl of Kildare, and again held in Dublin Castle, but notwithstanding the rebellion of his brother, William Nugent, the charge was not upheld. In 1582 Delvin and Kildare were sent to England in the custody of Sir Nicholas Bagenal, and although no proof of guilt was obtained, Delvin was kept there until 1585. He served the English against the rebels in the Nine Years' War, but in 1599–1600 he was forced to submit to Hugh O'Neill. Again suspected of conspiracy, in 1602 he was once again arrested and lodged in Dublin Castle, where he died.

William Nugent (1550–1625), the younger brother of Christopher Nugent, fifth Baron Delvin, was educated in Oxford. Following his implication in the Pale cess controversy of 1577–9, the rebellion of Viscount Baltinglass, and the arrest of his brother and the Earl of Kildare, he fled inevitable arrest. By March 1581 he had gathered a loose confederation of several hundred men in Co. Meath and, in effect, went into rebellion. Despite support from the O'Connors, by the end of the year his rebellion was broken, and he escaped to mainland Europe in January 1582. He attempted to return in 1584, with a small army of Scots, but the invasion was quickly quashed, and Nugent pleaded for, and was granted, pardon by Lord Deputy Perrot.

Feagh MacHugh O'Byrne (*c.*1544–1597) inherited the political ambitions of his father, Hugh MacShane, for the junior branch of the O'Byrne clan (the Gabhal Raghnaill), left marginalized in their highland fortress of Glenmalure by the surrender and regrant of O'Byrne lands under Henry VIII. Throughout the 1560s Feagh MacHugh and his father harried English interests, then obtained pardons, strengthening their standing among the Gaelic chieftains and with the English. Carefully plotted marriages—Feagh into the Cavanaghs, his sister Margaret to Rory Oge O'More—strengthened the reputation of the family. Feagh MacHugh was, meanwhile, implicated in the murder of Robert Browne, a Wexford gentleman and son-in-law of Nicholas White, then at court. The Seneschal of the O'Byrne country, Francis Agard, drove the Gabhal Raghnaill into rebellion over the affair, cementing by the beginning of 1573 Feagh's position as a leading Gaelic chieftain in the region. Despite his father's submission to Sidney, Feagh MacHugh remained 'out' until 1578, when he submitted at Christ Church to Sir Henry Harrington, the new Seneschal of the O'Byrne country, and called him his 'captain'. When Viscount Baltinglass rebelled, Feagh MacHugh—now chief of his name—ravaged Wexford in revenge against Masterson, another former Seneschal of the O'Byrne country; but Baltinglass crumbled and Feagh MacHugh was isolated. On 25 August 1580, the newly arrived Lord Grey pursued Feagh MacHugh's 600-strong kern army into the Wicklow mountains, and were dealt a heavy defeat in Glenmalure. Feagh MacHugh was ultimately brought to heel by rival O'Byrne interests and a heavily reinforced Grey, and though he was pardoned, remained a serious and unpredictable threat in Wicklow for years to come. Thereafter, Feagh

MacHugh became a great steward of Gaelic culture, though he was also occasionally a harbourer of rebels and a conniver with Spanish interests. In 1594, his peace disintegrated when his son-in-law, Walter Reagh, and two of his sons attacked and killed Sir Pearce Fitzgerald, Sheriff of Kildare, with his family at Ardree. Despite Feagh MacHugh's offer of submission, and his disowning of Reagh and his sons, the English had to take action. Sir William Russell set off suddenly in January 1595 on an expedition to Wicklow, inaugurating a chain of events that would, within two years, destroy the Gabhal Raghnaill and Feagh MacHugh himself.

Sir Donnell O'Connor Sligo (d.1587), an Irish lord in what is now west Donegal, offered the English an important counterweight to the power of the O'Donnells and O'Neills in Ulster. Despite early reservations about his loyalty, Sir Nicholas Malby considered O'Connor Sligo a dutiful subject (see e.g. SP 63/72/38), and by Malby's means he was shortly brought to arbitration with his ancient antagonist, O'Donnell. By July 1582 O'Connor Sligo found himself allied with O'Donnell in resistance to Turlough Luineach O'Neill, and Grey marched to his defence (see No. 39, above, SP 63/94/15, 63/94/15/1, and 63/94/15/2). Richard Bingham, Malby's successor, took a considerably less favourable view of O'Connor Sligo, apparently because he coveted his estates; while the Irish lord participated in Bingham's new composition of Connaught in 1585 (see SP 63/120/2), at his death his estates seem to have been occupied by George Bingham, Sir Richard Bingham's kinsman and agent in Connaught, and his nephew Donogh O'Connor Sligo struggled to take possession of the inheritance (see SP 63/133/64).

Sir Hugh O'Donnell (1535–1600), second son of Manus O'Donnell, succeeded as O'Donnell upon the death of his brother Calvagh in 1566. Hugh O'Donnell was supported in the succession to the Tirconnell lordship by Shane O'Neill, at the expense of his nephew, Calvagh's son Con O'Donnell; it was the official policy of Lords Justice Sir Robert Weston and Sir William Fitzwilliam in 1568 that Con O'Donnell should be maintained against Hugh, to keep the Tirconnell lordship from open and potent rebellion (SP 63/23/16)—a policy that backfired when, in later years, Con O'Donnell became Turlough Luineach O'Neill's proxy in an effort to control Tirconnell. On the other hand, Sir Hugh exploited his position as an O'Neill antagonist during the years of Turlough Luineach's ascendancy in Ulster, a period in which he enjoyed regular English military support from Sir Nicholas Malby and, during Grey's deputyship, from Grey himself (see e.g. No. 20, above, SP 63/85/5). In November 1583, Lords Justices Wallop and Loftus brought O'Donnell, Turlough Luineach, and Hugh O'Neill to articles of peace at an Ulster summit held at Newry (SP 63/105/58 and 63/105/58/1); in the following year, Lord Deputy Perrot again caused Turlough Luineach and O'Donnell to resolve their differences, both Irish lords consenting to regular payments in support of English garrisons in their territories. Complex alliances created by intermarriage united Ulster: O'Donnell had taken as his second wife

Fionnuala (the Iníon Dubh, 'dark daughter'), daughter of Agnes Campbell (Turlough Luineach's wife) by her first husband James MacDonnell; and in 1574 Hugh O'Neill had married Siobhan, O'Donnell's daughter by his first wife. But these alliances proved more costly for the English than peaceful for the Ulster lords, for in addition to the threatening seasonal influx of Scots following both Campbell and her daughter, O'Donnell's son Hugh Roe O'Donnell—after his father's surrender of the headship to him in 1592—continued to menace Turlough Luineach (now the Earl of Clanconnell), and joined with Hugh O'Neill in the Nine Years' War. The now senile Sir Hugh O'Donnell (Lord Deputy Fitzwilliam called him 'simple' in a report of 1592; see SP 63/165/3) played no further part in the tumultuous military politics of the period, and died in 1600.

Conn O'Neill, first Earl of Tyrone (*c*.1482–1559), succeeded to the O'Neill lordship in 1519, but spent considerable time unsuccessfully trying to confirm his supremacy in Ulster, against the family of Art Oge O'Neill and the O'Donnells. He went into rebellion briefly in 1534, and then again in 1539, under pressure from Lord Deputy Leonard Grey, but finally submitted formally in 1542. Henry VIII rewarded him with the title of Earl of Tyrone, and for a while he enjoyed government support (as a member of the Irish council) and power in Ulster. But the contested O'Neill succession created strife in Ulster, which led to Conn O'Neill's arrest in 1552; unable, upon his release, to control his son Shane, he fled to the Pale for shelter in 1558 and died a year later.

Hugh O'Neill, third Baron of Dungannon and second Earl of Tyrone (*c*. 1550–1616), was born into the greatest and most greatly contested lordship in Ireland. His father Matthew, Baron of Dungannon, as eldest son stood to inherit the earldom from Conn Bacach O'Neill, first Earl, but Matthew's legitimacy was undermined by his half-brother Shane, and both the Baron and his first son Brian were killed at Shane's instigation (in 1558 and 1562, respectively). The young Hugh, now first in line to inherit his grandfather's English title, was protected by Sir Henry Sidney, who placed him in his house in Dublin and, later, brought him to England. Back in Ireland from 1569, Hugh O'Neill enjoyed English support as a counterweight to the new Gaelic lord of Ulster, Turlough Luineach O'Neill, and by the time of Lord Grey's arrival in Ireland he was considered the New English government's chief ally in the north. Spenser would have witnessed Hugh O'Neill's close cooperation with Grey during his September 1580 journey to Drogheda with Sir William Pelham, where the three men sent an embassy to treat with the restive Turlough Luineach. Spenser may also have been present when Hugh O'Neill was finally recognized as second Earl of Tyrone, at a Parliament summoned by Lord Deputy Sir John Perrot in 1585–6; this recognition was confirmed by patent in the following year, when Tyrone travelled to London for an audience with the Queen, hoping to agree the limits of his lordship in Ulster.

The subsequent breakdown in the Earl's relationship with the Dublin government—which would lead to rebellion, war, and exile—stemmed from this visit to court. Tyrone achieved a dramatic diplomatic coup, securing the estate of his grandfather's lordship with military and political powers nearly equal to those enjoyed by Thomas Butler, Earl of Ormond, in his Tipperary palatinate. Upon Tyrone's return to Ireland, he found his new status an inevitable source of envy and, soon, strife, as the New English government sought to move forward with its longstanding plans to shire and partition Ulster. Over the succeeding seven to eight years, Tyrone negotiated diplomatically with Sir John Perrot and Sir William Fitzwilliam, Lord Deputies, while fighting off the more aggressive harassment of Sir Henry Bagenal—the new Knight Marshal of Ireland whose political future depended on crown control of Ulster, and who aspired to be the province's first President. Eventually Fitzwilliam's policies and Bagenal's ambitions, having drawn O'Neill's kinsmen into rebellion, forced him down the same road—only confirmed when, following the death in 1595 of Sir Turlough O'Neill (formerly Turlough Luineach), Hugh O'Neill was chosen as O'Neill and captain of Ulster. To the New English who had once supported him, this was the last betrayal, and it was the pressure upon the Queen and Privy Council created by ambitious English captains, administrators, and planters that stalled O'Neill's intermittent overtures for peace between bouts of brutal warfare. In August 1598, at the Yellow Ford on the Blackwater River, Tyrone and his allies defeated 4,000 English soldiers under Sir Henry Bagenal, a victory that immediately raised prospects of general revolt throughout Ireland and the possibility of Spanish military support. Just after Spenser's death in 1599, O'Neill's power and prospects were at their height: almost all of the major Irish, and many Old English, lords had come out in open rebellion behind his banner; the promise of continental support was nearing; and the huge expeditionary force sent to Ireland under the Earl of Essex, through mismanagement and ill fortune, had failed to present a significant threat. Two years later, following O'Neill's defeat to Charles Blount, Lord Mountjoy at the battle of Kinsale, these positions would be completely reversed; and, after mounting isolation and steady attrition, Tyrone was eventually forced, in March 1603, to accept English terms for surrender. That these terms were initially favourable—Mountjoy was anxious to conclude an agreement before Tyrone learned of the Queen's death—only delayed O'Neill's eventual undoing. In 1607, under the relentless pressure for English partition and plantation of his Ulster lordship, along with Rory O'Donnell, Earl of Tirconnell, O'Neill fled to Spain and then to Rome. He died there, in exile, almost ten years later.

Shane O'Neill (*c.*1530–1567), the youngest son of Conn O'Neill, Earl of Tyrone, emerged victorious from the wars of the O'Neill succession in the 1550s; following the assassination of his older brother Matthew, Baron of Dungannon in 1557, he was elected O'Neill upon Tyrone's death in 1559. After military successes against the Lord Deputy Sussex, the Earl of Kildare brokered a truce with the Dublin government, and Shane made his formal submission to Elizabeth herself on 6 January 1562. But negotiations at court subsequently foundered, and he returned to Ireland in May, exercising his military strength once again with attacks upon the

English and the O'Donnells. Through negotiations with councillors Cusack and Kildare, he was promised the rights he had sought in England—especially the traditional O'Neill privileges over their urraghs in Ulster—but Sussex delayed parliamentary confirmation, and Shane returned to fighting. His military strength was at its height in 1565: he attacked the MacDonnells, taking two of their leaders hostage, and destroyed the Scottish occupation of the Antrim coast. He also attacked English garrisons at Newry and Dundrum, Co. Down, and invaded northern Connaught, but in spite of his continued military aggression, he was gradually bested by the new deputy, Sir Henry Sidney. In 1567, he entered Tirconnell in an attempt against O'Donnell, but his army was routed and he lost much of his remaining support. Shane fled to the MacDonnells, hoping to trade Sorley Boy—one of his hostages—for protection. Instead, they cut him to pieces.

Turlough Luineach O'Neill (*c*.1530–1595) held the title of O'Neill between 1567 and 1595. In his early life, he built up a power base around Strabane and western Tyrone through political allegiances and economic development. When Shane O'Neill took control of Tyrone in 1559, Turlough Luineach was designated his tanist; over the succeeding years, he made his own bids for power, assassinating Brian O'Neill, Baron of Dungannon, in April 1562, and in May, during Shane's absence in England, proclaiming himself O'Neill. Shane took no action against Turlough Luineach, and he succeeded quietly to the headship at Shane's death in 1567. He made new political alliances, especially (by means of his marriage to Agnes Campbell in 1569) with the MacDonnells, and attempted to enlist English help to consolidate his power in Ulster; but negotiations with Sidney came to little, and Turlough Luineach was forced to accept the establishment of Hugh O'Neill, third Baron of Dungannon, in a lordship south of the Blackwater River. He negotiated with the crown in 1578 to dismiss his Scottish mercenaries in exchange for the titles of Earl of Clanoneill and Baron of Clogher, but the Dublin administration preferred to keep power firmly divided in Ulster, and supported Hugh O'Neill's manoeuvres across the Blackwater in 1583. Turlough Luineach became increasingly marginalized as Hugh O'Neill—now second Earl of Tyrone—gained power under Sir John Perrot's deputyship, and within a few years found himself the unwonted beneficiary of English support—and a knighthood— as Dublin sought to contain its rampant creature. Old and increasingly feeble, he could not make good his promise to fight Tyrone in 1595 and, shortly after his castle at Strabane was razed, he died.

Brian O'Rourke (d.1591) became chief of his country in 1566, after two of his elder brothers had been killed (possibly at his instigation). He submitted to Lord Deputy Sidney in 1576 and in the following year made composition with the crown, but his loyalty wavered repeatedly during the years of Desmond revolt, and it was not until 1586 that he could be brought—by Richard Bingham—to pay his rents. Despite having sent his son, Brian Oge, to study at Oxford, O'Rourke once again defied the English by succouring surviving Spaniards washed onto western shores after the wreck of the Armada, and in 1589, Bingham's pressure pushed him back into rebellion. When Bingham managed to turn some of his family, O'Rourke was forced to flee to Scotland, where he was captured in March 1591. He was sent to the Tower of London, tried for treason, and was hanged, drawn, and quartered at Tyburn that November.

Sir William Pelham (?1530–1587), a career soldier with experience fighting on the Scottish borders and in France, was appointed to serve in Ireland in the summer of 1579. Though he had been sent over with a specific mandate to renew the fortifications in the Pale, upon Sir William Drury's sudden death in early October Pelham was elected the new Lord Justice (SP 63/69/62). He faced a major revolt in Munster, initially led by James Fitzmaurice, and then by John of Desmond, against which he acted swiftly. Probably under the influence of the Earl of Ormond—Desmond's hereditary enemy—Pelham proclaimed the Earl of Desmond at the beginning of November 1579 (see SP 63/70/4), and in the new year marched to Munster to support Ormond's forces, burning and waging a war of terror against the people of the province. Pelham's goal was not only to break the Desmond rebellion, but to crush the Irish resistance that might welcome a rumoured Spanish invading force. Pelham failed to capture Desmond, but in his Munster journeys he laid the foundations for Grey's early victory at Smerwick (see No. 5, above, SP 63/78/29), and for the slow war of attrition that Ormond would subsequently wage—and win—against the Earl of Desmond. Pelham yielded the sword of state to Grey on 7 September and, despite tentative plans to appoint him new President in Munster, stayed in Ireland only long enough to visit Drogheda with Grey in the middle of September, there to advise on the fortifications. Pelham returned to England; he did not see service again until embarking for the Netherlands with the Earl of Leicester in 1586, where he fought with the Norris brothers and Philip Sidney. He was wounded in the stomach in August 1586, but finally succumbed only in November 1587.

Sir John Perrot (1528–92) was appointed President of Munster in 1571. His approach to the government there, following the outrageous brutality of the previous English governor, Sir Humphrey Gilbert, was consistent with Perrot's own reputation for irascibility and summary violence. He had left Ireland by 1573, but returned for three months in 1579 as commander of a small fleet of ships instructed to harry Spanish and pirate vessels off the south-west coast (see his instructions, SP 12/131/74). In January 1584 Perrot accepted a commission (SP 63/107/29) to become Lord Deputy of Ireland, entering energetically into office in the early summer. His frequent journeys to Ulster, with his commitment to shiring, dividing, and planting the province, made him as unpopular for his great expenses as for his innovative intentions, and Geoffrey Fenton, among others, took the opportunity to write critically of him to Burghley whenever Perrot was absent on campaign (see e.g. SP 63/126/31); in December 1586 Fenton went so far as to suggest that the English councillors in Ireland would be forced to abandon their posts if Perrot were not removed (SP 63/127/6). By the end of his deputyship, in July 1588, Perrot had developed a strong antipathy to Richard Bingham (see SP 65/12, pp. 56–64), to Fenton, and to Sir Nicholas Bagenal. Perrot's attempts to drive legal reform through Parliament, like his efforts to placate and settle Ulster, would prove to have far-reaching effects in the 1590s, as many of the Ulster lords went into open rebellion; but it was his personal style, which earned him many enemies, that caused his downfall. He was tried for treasonous speeches and actions in London in 1592, and found guilty, but died in the Tower before he could be executed.

William Piers (or **Pers/Pierce**), captain, may have come to Ireland in the 1530s. In 1556, as a naval captain, he was recruited to assist in an expedition against the Scots in the North Channel and the Hebrides. He remained in north-east Ireland as constable of Carrickfergus Castle, and took part in further expeditions against the Scots, and, later, in diplomatic contacts with them. In 1567, he may have urged the MacDonnells to kill Shane O'Neill, and was reported, subsequently, to have dug up the body, cut off the head, and sent it to Sir Henry Sidney, who displayed it on the gates of Dublin Castle. In 1569, Sidney appointed him Seneschal of Clandeboye, in recognition of his military service. Throughout the 1560s and early 1570s, he gained the support of local chiefs and established himself economically and politically in the area around Carrickfergus, securing various amenities and offices there. He was a passionate advocate of an English plantation in Ulster, and recommended the expulsion of the Ulster Scots in favour of its Irish lords. It was partly because of Piers's good relations with Brian MacPhelim O'Neill that Essex fell out with him, and had him imprisoned, but after Essex's death in 1577 he was released and once again appointed constable of Carrickfergus. In the summer of 1580, Piers negotiated with Turlough Luineach on behalf of the crown, promising to help him to his urraghs in return for a general expulsion of Scots from the province (No. 3, above, SP 63/76/1), but this proposal was strongly repudiated by Grey, who argued for a much tougher military stance. Marginalized by the death of Brian MacPhelim O'Neill and the ascendancy of Hugh O'Neill, Piers drifted into irrelevance and died in 1603.

Christopher Preston, fourth Viscount Gormanston, succeeded his father Jenico to the Old English lordship, and to a longstanding alliance with the Nugents, sometime in the 1560s or early 1570s. Together with his brother-in-law Christopher Nugent, fifth Baron Delvin, Gormanston resisted Lord Deputy Fitzwilliam's proceedings against the Earl of Desmond in 1574, which were seen by many Old English lords as wantonly antagonistic and driven by the enmity of Desmond's inveterate rival, the Earl of Ormond (see SP 63/48/18, 63/48/18/1, 63/48/22, and 63/48/22/1); Gormanston and Delvin were suspected and questioned for their refusal to subscribe to Fitzwilliam's proclamation of treason against Desmond, though Gormanston, at least, seems to have convinced Fitzwilliam's successor, Sir Henry Sidney, of his good intentions in the matter (see LPL Carew MS 57). Thereafter, Gormanston remained conspicuously loyal, especially in the face of the supposedly treasonous practices of Devlin and the Earl of Kildare in 1580, and provided the Dublin government with information and occasional support in Eastmeath and Monaghan during the 1580s and 1590s (see e.g. No. 4, above, SP 63/76/9 and 63/169/10, 63/169/10/1). He was given command of a band of horsemen under the Earl of Kildare during the Nine Years' War, and in 1595 was stationed at Nobber (SP 63/181/26).

Thomas Pullison, draper and merchant, was Alderman of London, Sheriff in 1573, and Lord Mayor in 1584. He supplied a considerable amount of food and clothing to the English soldiery in Ireland (see No. 6, above, BL Add. MS 33924), and seems to have earned a considerable sum from the trade (see e.g. SP 63/91/19/1).

Sir Walter Ralegh (1554–1618) secured a commission as a captain in Ireland in 1580, where one of his first services was to oversee the massacre at Smerwick. He was sent to London in December 1580, bearing secret papers found among the dead, but returned to Munster early in 1581, and was appointed to the commission governing the province during Sir Warham Sentleger's absence in London. Ralegh's position on colonial policy favoured the brutal style of Humphrey Gilbert (see SP 63/80/82), but his service conspicuously failed to impress Grey (SP 63/92/10). He returned to court later in 1581; catching the Queen's fancy, he soon embarked on the influential life of lyric poems and American voyages for which he became famous. In 1586, he was granted—at 42,000 acres—by far the largest estate in the Munster plantation. He seems to have presented Spenser, bearing *The Faerie Queene*, at court in 1589 or 1590, but he soon disgraced himself by marriage to Bess Throckmorton, one of Elizabeth's maids of honour, and was only returned to favour in 1597, after his colonial adventure to Guiana in 1595. He fought against the Spanish navy at Cadiz in 1596. On the accession of James, he lost many of his privileges, was implicated in treasonable plots, and was imprisoned between 1603 and 1616. After the failure of his second expedition to Guiana in 1617, he was tried and executed for treason in 1618.

Barnaby Rich (1542–1617), a kinsman of Sir Francis Walsingham, arrived in Ireland in July 1573 as part of Walter Devereux's attempted plantation of Ulster. He visited Connaught in 1579 (SP 63/69/17), probably to gather intelligence, and was employed to intercede for the Earl of Kildare in January 1581 (SP 63/80/1). In 1584 he was captain to a band of footmen, fighting the Scots in the north, where he returned under the second Earl of Essex in 1598; he served as a captain in Ireland well into James's reign. He published some twenty-six tracts and treatises—often on Irish military affairs, frequently autobiographical, and typically playful in tone—including *A Right Exelent and Pleasaunt Dialogue, betwene Mercury and an English Souldier* (1574), *Allarme to England* (1578), *Riche his*

Farewell to Militarie Profession (1581), *New Description of Ireland* (1610), *A Short Survey of Ireland* (1609), and *The Irish Hubbub, or, The English Hue and Crie* (1617).

Maurice, sixth Viscount Roche of Fermoy (d.1600), like most of the Old English and Irish lords of Munster, endured throughout Elizabeth's reign the distrust and harassment of the New English government. According to the 1586 report of Sir John Perrot, President in Munster between 1571 and 1573 (see SP 63/122/9), Roche's father David had been a dutiful subject, but his son the sixth Viscount was allied through marriage to the 'arch-traitor' James Fitzmaurice, as well as to the regularly revolting Lord Barry, and as a result his behaviour came under constant suspicion. Two of his sons, Theobald and Redmond, were killed by Patrick Condon and the Seneschal of Imokilly during the Munster famine in April 1582 (SP 63/91/41), leaving Roche with only one legitimate heir, his younger son David. Lord Deputy Perrot seems particularly to have distrusted him (see e.g. SP 63/133/9, 63/133/9/1, and 63/133/9/2), an antagonism apparently exploited by the Munster government and undertakers for their own gain. By the time Spenser compiled his 'Bill against Lord Roche' in October 1589 (No. 45, above, SP 63/147/16), official articles alleging treason and conspiracy to support treason had been on file for over a year (see e.g. SP 63/134/34); while Roche himself was never prosecuted on these charges, there is no doubt that Spenser's contest with him over title to Kilcolman and Rossack was substantially affected by the evil odour in which Roche continued to stand during the 1580s. No doubt frustrated by the apparent greed and antagonism of the Munster undertakers, Roche came out in rebellion during the Nine Years' War and, after being captured, spent most of his final years in Dublin Castle.

Sir William Russell (*c.*1553–1613), fourth son of Francis Russell, second Earl of Bedford, arrived in Ireland in 1579; given charge of a band, he fought in Leinster during the Baltinglass revolt, and Grey knighted him for his successes against Feagh MacHugh O'Byrne in Wicklow. Russell served as lieutenant-general of horse in the Dutch campaign of December 1585, so far distinguishing himself for valour and courage that Philip Sidney bequeathed him both his best suit of armour and, at his death, the governorship of Flushing. On the strength of this experience, Russell was appointed Lord Deputy of Ireland in 1594—a military appointment designed to cow the rebels in Ulster—but his confidence was fatally undermined by the coincident appointment of Sir John Norris as President in Munster, and the two were in open and regular dispute. In January 1595 Russell pursued Feagh MacHugh O'Byrne but, after two years of stalemate, had achieved nothing, and was recalled to London. He is generally considered one of the least effective Lord Deputies of the Elizabethan period, though his ineffectiveness was probably a result of the shared mandate with Norris, his inability to cope with the double-dealing and riven factionalism of the Dublin administration and the Ulster rebels, and the fast pace of a rebellion already well underway.

Dr Nicholas Sanders (or Sander) (*c.*1530–1581) was educated at Winchester College, and in 1548 was elected fellow of New College, Oxford. After refusing the Oath of Supremacy, around 1559 or 1560 he left for Rome and then Louvain, gaining prominence among English exiles. He wrote a number of polemical works, including *The Rocke of the Churche* (1567), which advanced an early version of his theories of resistance to political authority. He took part in the northern uprising of 1569, producing propaganda such as the 1571 *De visibili monarchia*, which reprinted the 1570 papal bull excommunicating Elizabeth, along with a Catholic martyrology. He returned to Rome in 1572, and began to write his attack on the Reformation in England, *De origine ac progressu schismatis anglicani*. Throughout the 1570s, he was involved in papal lobbying of Philip II to support an invasion of England through Ireland; negotiations dragged on, and it was not until June 1579 that Sanders sailed on an expedition under the command of James Fitzmaurice. In Ireland he worked tirelessly to build a Catholic coalition around Fitzmaurice and John of Desmond, but Irish support vacillated and Spanish aid was meagre. He escaped from the Fort of Gold ten days before its fall, and evaded capture; the exact date of his death is not known, but it seems to have come between March and June 1581.

Sir Warham Sentleger, or **St Leger** (1525?–1597), son of Sir Anthony St Leger, former Lord Deputy of Ireland, was appointed governor of Munster in 1565, but his nomination was contested by the Earl of Ormond on the grounds of Sentleger's partiality to Desmond, and withdrawn. He continued to occupy the position of General of the Levies in the Field for the Province of Munster, but his service against Shane O'Neill went unrewarded, and he left Ireland in 1567. He returned in 1568, leasing lands in Kerricurrihy belonging to Desmond's nephew, James Fitzmaurice. He attempted to establish a colony there, with the involvement of Richard Grenville, Sir Humphrey Gilbert, and others, but the project caused revolt, and Sentleger returned again to England. Sentleger and Grenville were given a commission of martial law in March 1569, but the unrest continued, and his attempts to re-establish the Kerricurrihy colony met with persistent financial difficulties. Sentleger fought under Ormond in Munster at the end of the 1570s, and warded Cork and Waterford, but by the time of Lord Grey's arrival the two men had ceased to cooperate. Sentleger accused Ormond of slackness and partiality to the Munster rebels, which no doubt influenced Ormond's suspension from military command in the spring of 1581. Sentleger was appointed colonel in Munster in Ormond's place, but immediately left for England, apparently to secure the presidency of the province, in his absence leaving the government to Captain Zouche. Grey granted Sentleger a custodiam of William Nugent's lands, but his fortunes (including his leases on the Desmond lands) quickly unravelled, and he spent the 1590s in a quiet retirement.

Sir Henry Sidney (1529–86), father of Sir Philip Sidney, served twice as Lord Deputy of Ireland, between 1566 and 1571, and between 1575 and 1578. Like

Ormond, he had been raised alongside the future King Edward VI; in 1551, he married the daughter of John Dudley, Duke of Northumberland, and was knighted. After diplomatic missions to France and Spain, in 1555 he accompanied Lord Deputy Thomas Radcliffe, Lord Fitzwalter (later the Earl of Sussex), to Ireland. Appointments in Wales and France followed. With the support of the Earl of Leicester, he secured the Lord Deputyship of Ireland in 1565, and arrived in January of the following year. His first deputyship was marked by military campaigns against Shane O'Neill and martial law in Munster, but also saw a determined effort to centralize government in Dublin, especially through the creation of presidencies in Munster and Connaught, and through the attempted abolition of traditional Irish levies, or 'cuttings'. Having provoked significant resistance from Old English and Irish lords, Sidney was recalled in 1571, but immediately began campaigning for reinstatement, promising the Queen a new regime for stable and self-supporting finances in Ireland. He was returned in September 1575, but his plans for the cess caused widespread unrest in the Pale and, amid mounting costs, he was again recalled in 1578. He sat on the Privy Council, but played little effective part in government. In 1582, he was again considered for the Lord Deputyship (see No. 38, above, SP 63/93/64/1), but he made it conditional on a number of benefits and the company of his son, Philip, and Elizabeth overruled the plans.

Sir William Stanley (1548–1630) cut his teeth fighting with the Duke of Alva in the late 1560s in the Low Countries; in 1570, upon his return to England, he passed almost immediately into Ireland, where he distinguished himself as a soldier, particularly during the campaign against Desmond in 1579, for which he was knighted. He fought alongside Grey at the defeat in Glenmalure in 1580, and thereafter with William Russell in Wicklow. He returned to Munster in early 1583, and his troops were instrumental in cleaning up the Desmond rebellion. Stanley intended to settle in Munster, and arranged for a plantation around his seat at Lismore. He was not selected for President of Connaught on Malby's death in 1584, but did serve as pro-president for Norris in Munster while Norris was fighting in Ulster. In January 1585 Perrot brought him to Ulster to fight the Scots under Sorley Boy MacDonnell; a serious injury in the Ulster campaign did not prevent him from joining the Earl of Leicester, with a thousand Irish recruits, in the Low Countries. His subsequent defection to the Spanish in early 1587 made him a serious security threat to England, given his skill in soldiery and his intimate knowledge of Ireland; but his threats to support a Spanish invasion never material-ized, and he died a poor exile in 1630.

George Thornton, captain of the *Handmaid*, joined the Irish service in Septem-ber 1576, when Lord Deputy Sir Henry Sidney requested he be given command of a ship and dispatched to guard the treasure between Chester and Dublin (see SP 63/56/24). He quickly rose to become captain of the *Handmaid*, the Queen's foremost ship in the regular Irish service, and Geoffrey Fenton could style him by the end of 1581 'our perpetual admiral' (SP 63/87/11). His regular duties included guarding the shipping between England and Ireland (and particular the dispatch of treasure), providing sea-support for military ventures along the coast, and transporting soldiers. In March 1586 he was also named as Provost Marshal of Munster (SP 63/123/21), and he seems occasionally to have provided intelligence and land-service in that province.

Sir Henry Wallop (*c.*1531–1599) took his first political steps with various local positions in Hampshire, and on the recommendation of Sir Francis Walsingham was appointed Vice-Treasurer of Ireland in 1579, after the death of Sir Edward Fitton. He was immediately struck by illness and poverty, and spent the next several years complaining of a lack of funds. Wallop earned the enmity of Burghley, who accused him of presumptuous complaints, and was forced to cultivate the patronage of Walsingham. He began to ask to be called back to England, but was appointed, jointly with Adam Loftus, as Lord Justice of Ireland between 1582 and 1584. After the end of the Desmond rebellion, he established a settlement at Enniscorthy, Co. Wexford, but continued to be troubled by financial problems. He returned to England between 1589 and 1595, attracting complaints that he was leaving his duties to his deputies. But on returning to Ireland in July 1595, he once again encountered the expense and catastrophe of war, and once again failed to encourage the English administration to send proper funds. He was subject to repeated criticism from home, on charges that he was seeking personal gain and that he had mishandled negotiations with Tyrone, but in spite of his increasingly desperate pleas, he could not secure his revocation. Finally, in March 1599, Elizabeth agreed to have him replaced as Treasurer by Sir George Carey, but Wallop died on 14 April 1599, the very day that Carey reached Ireland.

Sir Francis Walsingham (1532–90) was born into court connections and educated at King's College, Cambridge under Sir John Cheke; he entered Gray's Inn after his father. He studied civil law at Padua during Mary's reign, but upon Elizabeth's accession, returned to England and sat in Parliament in 1559 and in the 1560s, apparently with the patronage of Cecil and Bedford. Walsingham's political career is first recorded in earnest in 1568, when he wrote to Cecil for Nicholas Throckmorton on the subject of a French match (with the Duc d'Anjou). He was thereafter appointed ambassador to France, whither he took his brother-in-law Robert Beale in 1570, and negotiated with Sir Thomas Smith the treaty of Blois. Outdone by Catherine de Medici, he was foiled in France, and returned in late 1573 to be appointed a principal secretary and privy councillor. He was heavily involved in the negotiations for a French match in 1571 and in 1579, and tried to play the French off against the Spanish, though he was well aware that the fate of English religion was hanging in the balance, and was opposed to Cecil's sanguine hopes for a French alliance. On Sir Thomas Smith's death in 1577, Walsingham was knighted and from that point considered principal secretary. His position was particularly strong between 1581 and 1586, when he was the only secretary, and during this period his secretariat expanded dramatically. With Leicester, Beale, and Sir Francis Knollys, Walsingham was considered a key patron for forward Protestants, and this undoubtedly formed the basis of his 'brootherly cariadge' to Grey (No. 14, above, SP 63/83/43), who wrote candidly and copiously to him.

Sir Edward Waterhouse (or **Waterhous**) (1535–91) enjoyed the patronage of Sir Henry Sidney, who employed him as personal secretary when appointed as Lord Deputy of Ireland in 1565. His close association with Sidney resulted in a string of petty and great offices and benefits over a quarter of a century. He served the first Earl of Essex as secretary during his Ulster campaigns, but returned to Sidney's service thereafter, and was sent to England with Philip Sidney between 1576 and 1579 to negotiate over the cess. In October 1579 he was appointed to the Irish Council. In March 1584 he participated, along with Geoffrey Fenton, in the torture of Dermot O'Hurley, Archbishop of Cashel, and was knighted in June 1584. He acted as peacemaker in the quarrel between Perrot and Adam Loftus, Archbishop of Dublin, and in 1586 was appointed Chancellor of the Exchequer and of the green wax in Ireland, with responsibility for recovering debts. He left Ireland in January 1591.

Nicholas White (c.1532–1592) was the son of James White, steward to the Earl of Ormond. He was admitted to Lincoln's Inn in 1552 (where James Dowdall, Nicholas Nugent, and Robert Dillon were all contemporaries), and called to the Bar in 1558. He returned to Ireland and was elected to the Irish Parliament for Kilkenny in 1559, was Justice of the Peace for Kilkenny in 1563, and was made Recorder of Waterford in 1564. In June 1569, he became constable of Wexford Castle. In 1572 he succeeded Draycott as the Master of the Rolls in Ireland. Despite royal favour, he stood out from the New English line, and other Irish privy councillors considered him difficult and partisan. He often came to blows with Loftus, and defended Fitton and the Old English Palesmen over Sidney's cess in 1577. In 1578, when the cess crisis was at its height, White was charged with misfeasance by the Attorney General and suspended from office; only with Sidney's recall, and his own chance to plead his case in London, was he restored. He was now suspected by his fellow privy councillors, particularly after he defended Nicholas Nugent (who was hanged for treason in 1582). White withheld his signature on some Privy Council reports, such as those concerning Malby's actions during the Munster rebellion and Grey's behaviour during the Pale rebellion, sent in 1582, and it was alleged by Henry Wallop in February 1583 that 'there ys not a malytyuser man in this land to owr natyon, nor a greter Ipocrite': White, he said, was not only hindering the prosecution of traitors, but also acting as an informer to Burghley against other ministers. Despite this, the council could not do without his linguistic skills and experience in Irish affairs. Perrot knighted White on his arrival in 1584, and White remained Perrot's consistent supporter throughout his deputyship. In 1586, he was in Connaught with Perrot to look after Bingham's government; Bingham and many others complained of White's influence with the deputy. At Perrot's departure, and Fitzwilliam's arrival, in 1588 the tables were turned, and White was implicated in the charges against Perrot, for which Fitzwilliam had him arrested and deported to England in 1590. He was committed to the Tower in 1591, and died there in 1592.

John Zouche (d.1583), a kinsman of both Lord Burghley and Walter Ralegh and, between 1580 and 1583, captain and Chief Colonel in Munster, served the New English government during the most perilous period of the Desmond revolt. Dispatched to England in the summer of 1580 on an errand to the new Lord Deputy Grey, Zouche seems to have returned to Dublin with him in August; he must have impressed Grey, for the new deputy assigned him a band of footmen (SP 63/75/79) and sent him into Munster, where he distinguished himself at Smerwick. Thereafter he remained in the Munster service until his death in early 1583, harrying and finally defeating Sir John of Desmond, and (barely) surviving the severe fever of the winter of 1581.

APPENDIX 3

Grey's Walsingham Cipher

a		k	
b		l	
c		m	
d		n	
e		o	
f		p	
g		q	
h		r	
i			

s	
t	
u	
v	
w	
x	
y	
z	
&	

Graphs may appear in any orientation. Some graphs are not attested.

Glossary of Irish and Unusual Terms

band, *n*. a company or troop of soldiers, often under the command of a captain.

cash or **cass**, *v*. to cashier, discharge (a soldier); to decommission (a band).

cess, *n*. a prerogative charge levied in Ireland for the maintenance of soldiers; under Elizabeth's deputies, the cess was sometimes commuted to a fixed payment or tax, known by the same name, and justified on the same prerogative (i.e. non-parliamentary) basis.

create or **creaght**, *n*. a herd of cattle or other grazing animals driven nomadically by their owners, e.g. in time of war.

custodiam, *n*. a fixed-term interest (usually of three years) in the benefit from (of the 'use of') crown land.

entertainment, *n*. rate or sum allowed to captains, ministers, or other officers in Ireland to provide for their living and employment; pay, expenses (see *OED*, 'entertainment, *n*.', 2b).

galloglas or galloglass, *n*. mercenary soldiers or retainers, particularly those in the service of Irish chiefs. In *A view of the present state of Ireland*, Irenius describes the galloglas as a footman who wears a quilted coat under a shirt of mail, and says that his name 'dothe discouer him to be allsoe Auncient Englishe ffor *Gallogla* signifies an Englishe servitour or yeoman'.

hosting, *n*. an official gathering of the host (of armed men), a muster.

kern or **kerne**, *n*. an Irish soldier or retainer, less heavily armed then the galloglass, and more likely to be tied to his service by family loyalties. Spenser considers them in *A view of the present state of Ireland* to be 'the proper Irishe soldiour': 'verye valiante and hardye for the moste parte great endurers of Colde Labour honger and all hardnesse verye active and stronge of hande verye swifte of foote verye vigilaunte and circumspecte in theire enterprises verye presente in perills verye great scorners of death'. The term can also refer collectively to a band or company of such soldiers.

kine or **kyne**, *n*. cattle.

packet, *n*. a bundle of letters bound together for expedited carriage by post; esp. the official dispatch between London and Dublin, granted special priority.

Pale, *n*. an area of variable size around Dublin, including parts of Cos. Louth, Meath, Dublin, and Kildare, which until the late sixteenth century was a domain of English families living under English jurisdiction, fortified against Irish incursion.

pledge, *n*. a surety or hostage, given into custody for the assurance of good behaviour.

pray or **prey**, *n*. plunder, often cattle or livestock, taken aggressively or in battle. *v*. To spoil, pillage (a place). **To take the prey of** (a place) was to spoil or ransack it.

protection, *n.* a guarantee of safety and immunity from arrest, prosecution, or attack.

rising out, *n.* the muster or hosting of a feudal lord.

sept, *n.* an Irish family; esp. a sub-division of a clan or country.

tanist, *n.* the designated successor to the headship of an Irish family or sept, elected at the installation of his predecessor and entitled to certain rights and privileges under the *taoiseach* or chief. Spenser suggests in *A view of the present state of Ireland* that the custom of tanistry was adopted to prevent innovation and, upon the death of the chief, to maintain unbroken leadership and order against the threat of incursion from neighbouring Irish or English forces.

urragh, *n.* an Irish subchief, owing military and other services.

Bibliography

Primary Sources

Beacon, Richard, *Solon his follie; or, A Politique Discourse, touching the Reformation of common-weales conquered, declined or corrupted* (Oxford, 1594).

Beale, Robert, 'A Treatise of the Office of a Councellor and Principall Secretarie to her Majestie', in Conyers Read, *Mr Secretary Walsingham and the Policy of Queen Elizabeth*, vol. i (Oxford: Clarendon Press, 1925), 423–43.

Calendar of the Carew Manuscripts Preserved in the Archiepiscopal Library at Lambeth, ed. J. S. Brewer and William Bullen, 6 vols. (London: Longmans, Green & Co. for HMSO, 1867–73).

Calendar of the State Papers Relating to Ireland, 1509–1670, 24 vols. (London: HMSO, 1860–1910).

Calendar of State Papers, Ireland: Tudor Period, 1571–1575, ed. Mary O'Dowd (London: Public Record Office, 2000).

[Church of England], *Articles . . . for the stablyshyng of consent trouchyng true religion* (London: Richard Jugge and John Cawood, 1563).

Churchyard, Thomas, *A generall rehearsall of warres, called Churchyardes Choise* (London: Edward White, 1579).

Day, Angel, *The English Secretorie* (London: Richard Jones, 1592).

Derricke, John, *The Image of Irelande* (London, 1581).

'Dialogue between Peregryne and Sylvanus, c.1598', TNA, State Papers, SP 63/203/119, fos. 283–357.

Faunt, Nicholas, 'Discourse Touching the Office of Principal Secretary of Estate, &c (1592)', ed. Charles Hughes, *English Historical Review*, 20 (1905), 499–508.

Fulwood, William, *The Enimie of Idlenesse: Teaching the Maner and Stile how to Endite, Compose, and Write All Sorts of Epistles and Letters, as well by Answer as Otherwise* (London: Henry Bynneman, 1568).

Gascoigne, George, *A Hundreth Sundrie Flowres* (London: Henry Bynneman and Henry Middleton, 1573).

Herbert, John, 'Duties of a Secretary [1600]', in *Select Statutes and other Constitutional Documents Illustrative of the Reigns of Elizabeth and James I*, ed. G. W. Prothero (Oxford: Clarendon Press, 1894).

Herbert, William, *Croftus, sive de Hibernia Liber*, ed. Arthur Keaveney and John Madden (Dublin: Irish Manuscripts Commission, 1992).

Middleton, Thomas, and William Rowley, *The Changeling*, ed. N. W. Bawcutt (Manchester: Manchester University Press, 1958).

Spenser, Edmund, *The Works of Edmund Spenser: A Variorum Edition*, ed. Edwin Greenlaw et al., 11 vols. (Baltimore: Johns Hopkins University Press, 1932–57).

Strype, John, *Life of the Learned Sr John Cheke, kt.* (London: J. Wyat, 1705).

Webster, John, *The Tragedy of the Dutchesse of Malfy* (London: Nicholas Okes, 1623).

Secondary Sources

Alford, Stephen, *The Early Elizabethan Polity: William Cecil and the British Succession Crisis, 1558–1569* (Cambridge: Cambridge University Press, 1998).

Baker, J. H., *An Introduction to English Legal History*, 4th edn. (London: Butterworth, 2002).

Beal, Peter, ed., *Index of English Literary Manuscripts 1450–1625* (London: Mansell, 1980).

Beale, Philip, *A History of the Post in England from the Romans to the Stuarts* (Aldershot: Ashgate, 1998).

Bradshaw, Brendan, 'Sword, Word and Strategy in the Reformation in Ireland', *Historical Journal*, 21 (1978), 475–502.

—— *The Irish Constitutional Revolution of the Sixteenth Century* (Cambridge: Cambridge University Press, 1979).

—— 'Edmund Spenser on Justice and Mercy', *Historical Studies*, 16 (1987), 76–89.

—— 'Robe and Sword in the Conquest of Ireland', in C. Cross, D. Loades, and J. J. Scarisbrick, eds., *Law and Government under the Tudors: Essays Presented to Sir Geoffrey Elton on his Retirement* (Cambridge: Cambridge University Press, 1988), 139–62.

—— Andrew Hadfield, and Willy Maley, eds., *Representing Ireland, 1534–1660* (Cambridge: Cambridge University Press, 1993).

Brady, Ciarán, 'Faction and the Origins of the Desmond Rebellion', *Irish Historical Studies*, 22 (1981), 289–312.

—— 'Court, Castle and Country: The Framework of Government in Tudor Ireland', in Ciarán Brady and Raymond Gillespie, eds., *Natives and Newcomers: Essays on the Making of Irish Colonial Society 1534–1641* (Dublin: Irish Academical Press, 1986).

—— 'Spenser's Irish Crisis: Humanism and Experience in the 1590s', *Past and Present*, 111 (May 1986), 17–49.

—— *The Chief Governors: The Rise and Fall of Reform Government in Tudor Ireland 1536–1588* (Cambridge: Cambridge University Press, 1994).

—— 'The Captains' Games: Army and Society in Elizabethan Ireland', in Thomas Bartlett and Keith Jeffery, eds., *A Military History of Ireland* (Cambridge: Cambridge University Press, 1996), pp. 136–59.

Burlinson, Christopher, *Allegory, Space and the Material World in the Writings of Edmund Spenser* (Cambridge: Brewer, 2006).

—— and Andrew Zurcher, '"Secretary to the Lord Grey Lord Deputy Here": Edmund Spenser's Irish Papers', *The Library*, 7th series, 6 (2005), 30–69.

Canino, Catherine G., 'Reconstructing Lord Grey's Reputation: A New View of the *View*', *Sixteenth Century Journal*, 29 (1998), 3–18.

Canny, Nicholas, *The Formation of the Old English Elite in Ireland* (Dublin: National University of Ireland, 1975).

—— *The Elizabethan Conquest of Ireland: A Pattern Established, 1565–76* (Hassocks, Sussex: Harvester, 1976).

—— 'Rowland White's "Discors Touching Ireland", c.1569', *Irish Historical Studies*, 20 (1977), 439–63.

—— 'Rowland White's "The Dysorders of the Irisshery", 1571', *Studia Hibernica*, 19 (1979), 147–60.

—— 'Edmund Spenser and the Development of an Anglo-Irish Identity', *Yearbook of English Studies*, 13 (1983), 1–19.

—— 'Protestants, Planters and Apartheid in Early Modern Ireland', *Irish Historical Studies*, 25 (1986), 105–15.

—— 'Identity Formation in Ireland: The Emergence of the Anglo-Irish', in N. Canny and A. Pagden, eds., *Colonial Identity in the Atlantic World, 1500–1800* (Princeton: Princeton University Press, 1987), pp. 159–212.

—— '"Spenser's Irish Crisis": A Comment', *Past and Present*, 120 (August 1988), 201–9.

—— *Making Ireland British: 1580–1650* (Oxford: Oxford University Press, 2001).

Carpenter, Frederic I., *A Reference Guide to Edmund Spenser* (Chicago: Chicago University Press, 1923).

Coughlan, Patricia, ed., *Spenser and Ireland: An Interdisciplinary Perspective* (Cork: Cork University Press, 1989).

Crofts, J., *Packhorse, Waggon and Post: Land Carriage and Communications under the Tudors and Stuarts* (London: Routledge and Kegan Paul; Toronto: University of Toronto Press, 1967).

De Yturriaga, José Antonio, 'Attitudes in Ireland towards the Survivors of the Spanish Armada', *Irish Sword*, 17 (1987–90), 244–54.

Dunlop, Robert, 'The Plantation of Munster, 1584–1589', *English Historical Review*, 3 (1888), 250–69.

—— 'The Plantation of Leix and Offaly', *English Historical Review*, 6 (1891), 61–96.

—— 'Sixteenth-Century Maps of Ireland', *English Historical Review*, 20 (1905), 309–37.

Evans, Florence M. Grier, *The Principal Secretary of State: A Survey of the Office from 1558 to 1680* (Manchester: Manchester University Press, 1923).

Feldman, David, and William Kane, *Handbook of Irish Postal History to 1840* (Dublin: Feldman, 1975).

Fitzgerald, Patrick Desmond, 'Poverty and Vagrancy in Early Modern Ireland 1540–1770' (Unpublished doctoral dissertation, Queen's University of Belfast, 1994).

Fumerton, Patricia, 'Exchanging Gifts: The Elizabethan Currency of Children and Poetry', *ELH*, 53 (1986), 241–78.

Gibson, Jonathan, 'Significant Space in Manuscript Letters', *Seventeenth Century*, 12 (1997), 1–9.

Gillespie, Raymond, *The Transformation of the Irish Economy 1550–1700*, Studies in Irish Economic and Social History, 6 (Dublin: Economic and Social History Society of Ireland, 1991).

Glasgow, Tom, Jr, 'Elizabethan Ships Pictured on Smerwick Map, 1580: Background, Authentication, and Evaluation', *Mariner's Mirror*, 52 (1966), 157–65.

Goldberg, Jonathan, *Writing Matter: From the Hands of the English Renaissance* (Stanford: Stanford University Press, 1990).

Greenlaw, E. A., 'Spenser and the Earl of Leicester', *Publications of the Modern Languages Association of America*, 25 (1910), 535–61.

Grey, M. M., 'The Influence of Spenser's Irish Experiences on *The Faerie Queene*', *Review of English Studies*, 6 (1930), 413–28.

Guiseppi, Montague Spencer, *Guide to the Contents of the Public Record Office*, 3 vols. (London: HMSO, 1963–8).

Hadfield, Andrew, 'The Course of Justice: Spenser, Ireland and Political Discourse', *Studia Neophilologica*, 65 (1993), 187–96.

—— 'Spenser, Ireland, and Sixteenth-Century Political Theory', *Modern Language Review*, 89 (1994), 1–18.

—— *Edmund Spenser's Irish Experience: Wilde Fruit and Salvage Soyl* (Oxford: Clarendon Press, 1997).

Hammer, Paul E. J., 'The Uses of Scholarship: The Secretariat of Robert Devereux, Second Earl of Essex, *c.* 1585–1601', *English Historical Review*, 109 (1994), 16–51.

Hayes-McCoy, Gerard A., *Scots Mercenary Forces in Ireland (1565–1603)* (Dublin: Burns Oates and Washbourne, 1937).

Heffner, Ray, 'Spenser's Acquisition of Kilcolman', *Modern Language Notes*, 46 (1931), 493–8.

Henley, Pauline, *Spenser in Ireland* (Cork: Cork University Press, 1928).

Herron, Thomas, *Spenser's Irish Work: Poetry, Plantation and Colonial Reformation* (Aldershot: Ashgate, 2007).

Highley, Christopher, *Shakespeare, Spenser, and the Crisis in Ireland*, Cambridge Studies in Renaissance Literature and Culture, 23 (Cambridge: Cambridge University Press, 1997).

Jenkins, Raymond, 'Spenser and the Clerkship in Munster', *Publications of the Modern Languages Association of America*, 47 (1932), 109–21.

—— 'Spenser's Hand', *Times Literary Supplement*, 31 (7 January 1932), 12.

—— 'Spenser at Smerwick', *Times Literary Supplement*, 32 (11 May 1933), 331.

—— 'Newes Out of Munster: A Document in Spenser's Hand', *Studies in Philology*, 32 (1935), 125–30.

—— 'Spenser with Lord Grey in Ireland', *Publications of the Modern Languages Association of America*, 52 (1937), 338–53.

—— 'Spenser: The Uncertain Years 1584–1589', *Publications of the Modern Languages Association of America*, 53 (1938), 350–62.

Jones, Frederick M., 'The Plan of the Golden Fort at Smerwick, 1580', *Irish Sword*, 2 (1954–6), 41–2.

Jones, H. S. V., 'Spenser's Defense of Lord Grey', *University of Illinois Studies in Language and Literature*, 5 (1919), 151–219.

Judson, Alexander C., 'Two Spenser Leases', *Modern Language Quarterly*, 50 (1944), 143–7.

Lewis, C. S., *The Allegory of Love* (Oxford: Clarendon Press, 1936).

Lupton, Julia, 'Home-making in Ireland: Virgil's Eclogue I and Book VI of *The Faerie Queene*,' *Spenser Studies*, 8 (1990), 119–45.

McCabe, Richard A., 'Edmund Spenser, Poet of Exile', *Proceedings of the British Academy*, 80 (1993), 73–103.

—— *Spenser's Monstrous Regiment: Elizabethan Ireland and the Poetics of Difference* (Oxford: Oxford University Press, 2002).

MacCarthy-Morrogh, Michael, *The Munster Plantation: English Migration to Southern Ireland, 1583–1641* (Oxford: Clarendon Press, 1986).

McComish, W. A., 'The Survival of the Irish Castle in an Age of Cannon', *Irish Sword*, 9 (1969–70), 16–21.

McCracken, Eileen, *The Irish Woods Since Tudor Times: Distribution and Exploitation* (Newton Abbot: David and Charles, 1971).

McKeon, Michael, *The Secret History of Domesticity: Public, Private, and the Division of Knowledge* (Baltimore: Johns Hopkins University Press, 2005).

Maley, Willy, 'Spenser and Ireland: A Select Bibliography', *Spenser Studies*, 9 (1991), 227–42.

—— *A Spenser Chronology* (London: Macmillan, 1994).

—— 'Spenser and Ireland: An Annotated Bibliography, 1986–96', *Irish University Review*, 26 (1996), 342–53.

—— *Salvaging Spenser: Colonialism, Culture, and Identity* (Basingstoke: Macmillan, 1997).

Moody, T. W., F. X. Martin, and F. J. Byrne, eds., *A New History of Ireland*, 10 vols. (Oxford: Clarendon Press, 1978–2003).

Morgan, Hiram, 'The Colonial Venture of Sir Thomas Smith in Ulster, 1571–5', *Historical Journal*, 28 (1985), 261–78.

Muldrew, Craig, *The Economy of Obligation: The Culture of Credit and Social Relations in Early Modern England* (Basingstoke: Macmillan, 1998).

Nicholls, K. W., *Land, Law and Society in Sixteenth Century Ireland* (Cork: Cork University Press, 1976).

O'Connor, P. J., 'The Munster Plantation Era: Rebellion, Survey and Land Transfer in North County Kerry', *Journal of the Kerry Archaeological and Historical Society*, 15 (1982), 15–36.

O Domhnaill, Seán, 'Warfare in Sixteenth-Century Ireland', *Irish Historical Studies*, 5 (1946–7), 29–54.

O'Dowd, Mary, and R. Dudley Edwards, *Sources for Early Modern Irish History, 1534–1641* (Cambridge: Cambridge University Press, 1985).

Ohlmeyer, Jane H., '"Civilizinge of those Rude Partes": Colonization within Britain and Ireland, 1580s–1640s', in Wm. Roger Louis, ed., *The Oxford History of the British Empire*, 5 vols. (Oxford: Oxford University Press, 1998–9), i: Nicholas Canny, ed., *The Origins of Empire: British Overseas Enterprise to the Close of the Seventeenth Century* (1998), 124–47.

O'Rahilly, Alfred, *The Massacre at Smerwick (1580)*, Historical and Archaeological Papers, 1 (Cork: Cork University Press, 1938).

Palmer, Patricia, *Language and Conquest in Early Modern Ireland: English Renaissance Literature and Elizabethan Imperial Expansion* (Cambridge: Cambridge University Press, 2001).

Parkin-Speer, Diane, 'Allegorical Legal Trials in Spenser's *The Faerie Queene*', *Sixteenth Century Journal*, 23 (1992), 494–505.

Petrie, Charles, 'The Hispano-Papal Landing at Smerwick', *Irish Sword*, 9 (1969–70), 82–94.

Petti, Anthony G., *English Literary Hands from Chaucer to Dryden* (London: Edward Arnold, 1977).

Plomer, H. R., 'Edmund Spenser's Handwriting', *Modern Philology*, 21 (1923), 201–7.

Price, Leah, and Pamela Thurschwell, eds., *Literary Secretaries/Secretarial Culture* (Aldershot: Ashgate, 2005).

Quinn, D. B., '"A Discourse of Ireland" (Circa 1599): A Sidelight on English Colonial Policy', *Proceedings of the Royal Irish Academy*, 47 (1942), 151–66.

—— 'Sir Thomas Smith (1513–1577) and the Beginnings of English Colonial Theory', *Proceedings of the American Philosophical Society*, 89 (1945), 543–60.

Rambuss, Richard, *Spenser's Secret Career*, Cambridge Studies in Renaissance Literature and Culture, 3 (Cambridge: Cambridge University Press, 1993).

Sheehan, Anthony J., 'The Overthrow of the Plantation of Munster in October 1598', *The Irish Sword*, 15 (1982), 11–22.

—— 'Official Reaction to the Native Land Claims in the Plantation of Munster', *Irish Historical Studies*, 23 (1983), 297–318.

—— 'Irish Towns in a Period of Change, 1558–1625', in Ciarán Brady and Raymond Gillespie, eds., *Natives and Newcomers: Essays on the Making of Irish Colonial Society 1534–1641* (Dublin: Irish Academical Press, 1986), 93–119.

Skinner, Quentin, *The Foundations of Modern Political Thought*, 2 vols. (Cambridge: Cambridge University Press, 1978).

Smith, Alan G. R., 'The Secretariats of the Cecils, circa 1580–1612', *English Historical Review*, 83 (1968), 481–504.

Smith, Roland M., 'The Irish Background of Spenser's View', *Journal of English and Germanic Philology*, 42 (1943), 499–515.

—— 'More Irish Words in Spenser', *Modern Language Notes*, 59 (1944), 472–7.

—— 'Spenser's Scholarly Script and "Right Writing"', in D. C. Allen, ed., *Studies in Honor of T. W. Baldwin* (Urbana: University of Illinois Press, 1958), 66–111.

Starkey, David, 'The Presence Chamber: New Year, 1538', in David Starkey, ed., *Henry VIII: A European Court in England* (London: Collins and Brown, 1991), 126–30.

Stewart, Alan, 'The Early Modern Closet Discovered', *Representations*, 50 (Spring 1995), 76–100.

Stewart, Alan, 'Instigating Treason: The Life and Death of Henry Cuffe, Secretary', in Erica Sheen and Lorna Hutson, eds., *Literature, Politics, and Law in Renaissance England* (Basingstoke: Palgrave Macmillan, 2004), 50–70.

—— and Heather Wolfe, *Letterwriting in Renaissance England* (Seattle: University of Washington Press for the Folger Library, 2004).

Tawney, R. H., and Eileen Power, eds., *Tudor Economic Documents: Being Select Documents Illustrating the Economic and Social History of Tudor England*, 3 vols. (London: Longmans, Green, 1951).

Teskey, Gordon, *Allegory and Violence* (Ithaca, NY: Cornell University Press, 1996).

Walshe, Helen Coburn, 'The Rebellion of William Nugent, 1581', in R. V. Comerford and others, eds., *Religion, Conflict and Coexistence in Ireland: Essays Presented to Monsignor Patrick J. Cornish* (Dublin: Gill and Macmillan, 1990), 26–52.

Woodward, D. M., *The Trade of Elizabethan Chester* (Hull: University of Hull Press, 1970).

Woolway Grenfell, Joanne, 'Significant Spaces in Edmund Spenser's *View of the Present State of Ireland*', *Early Modern Literary Studies*, 4.2/Special Issue 3 (September 1998): 6:1–21 <URL:http://purl.oclc.org/emls/04–2/woolsign.htm>.

Yates, Frances, *The Art of Memory* (London: Routledge and Kegan Paul, 1966).

Zurcher, Andrew, *Spenser's Legal Language: Law and Poetry in Early Modern England* (Cambridge: Brewer, 2007).

Index

Nugent, Sir Nicholas, Chief Justice of the Common Pleas xxvii, 132, 135–6, 155–7, 159–64, 166, 173–4, 176, 178–9, 225–6, 243–4, 251, 267

Nugent, Piers Boy 158, 165

Nugent, Richard (of Donnowre) 157, 164, 180

Nugent, Robert Bane 156, 164

Nugent, Thomas (of Dardeston) 157, 164

Nugent, William xxvii, 88, 103, 108, 127, 155–66, 173, 176, 178–80, 228–9, 242, 244, 252, 255, 264

O'Balrey, Teig 157, 164

O'Brien 222–3

O'Byrne, Feagh MacHugh, of Ballinecor xxi, xxvii–xxviii, 9, 13, 46, 49, 70, 78–9, 85–6, 119, 121, 224, 228, 230, 232, 234, 245, 250, 255–56, 263

O'Byrne, James, see Birne, James

O'Byrne, Phelim MacFeagh 234

O'Byrnes of Wicklow xxi, 71–3, 75–80, 84–5, 88, 113, 118, 121, 224, 250, 255

O'Cahan 9, 232

O'Connoghan Piers 156, 164

O'Connors, sept xxviii, xxix, n. 33, 30, 157–8, 164, 193, 195, 244, 252, 255

O'Connor, Brian 157, 164

O'Connor, Cahir, Lord of Offaly 222

O'Connor, Conor MacCormac xxix, 228

O'Connor, Lisagh 157, 164

O'Connor, Patrick 157, 164

O'Connor, Teig 157, 164

O'Connor, Teig MacGillipatrick xxix, 228

O'Connor Sligo, Sir Donnell 193, 195, 227, 233, 256

O'Connor Sligo, Donogh 256

O'Donnell, Conn 111, 114, 192, 195, 197, 226, 256

O'Donnell, Cullough 114, 118

O'Donnell, Sir Hugh 90, 92–3, 95, 99, 106–9, 116–18, 181–2, 195, 223, 225, 232, 241, 256–7, 259

O'Donnell, Hugh Roe 231, 234–235, 257

O'Donnell, Manus 256

O'Donnell, Rory, earl of Tirconnell 258

Offaly, Co. xix, 140, 223, 225, 238, 247

O'Farrells 115, 119

O'Flaherty, Murrough Ne Doe 226

O'Hanlon 9

O'Hurley, Dermot 228

O'Keefe, Ullig 217–19

O'Kelly, Daniel 228

O'Kelly, Kedagh xvii, 217, 219

O'Kelly, Melaghlen Roe 252

O'Kelly, Teigh MacWilliam 42–3

Olive, Teig 216, 218–19

O'Malley, Grace, alias Gráinne Mhaol 238

O'More, James MacKedagh, see Meagh, James

O'Mores, sept xxiv, 46, 124, 128, 191, 252, 253

O'Neill, Art MacBaron 162, 166

O'Neill, Art Oge 257

O'Neill, Brian MacPhelim, lord of Clandeboye xx, 224, 243, 254, 261

O'Neill, Conn, captain of Ulster and first earl of Tyrone xix, xxi, xxv, 7, 10, 222, 236, 257–8

O'Neill, Hugh, Baron of Dungannon, captain of Ulster, and earl of Tyrone xix, xxi, xxv–xxvi, 5–7, 10, 12, 39, 107, 116, 153, 166, 223, 225, 227–8, 234, 236, 240, 245, 254–9, 261

O'Neill, Matthew, Baron of Dungannon xix, xxv, 7, 223, 257–8

O'Neill, the Prior 162, 166

O'Neill, Shane, captain of Ulster and earl of Tyrone xix, xx–xxi n. 7, xxv–xxvi, 7, 12–13, 114, 118, 127, 223, 227–8, 236, 244, 247, 254, 256–9, 261, 264–5

his sons 126

Printed and bound by CPI Group (UK) Ltd, Croydon, CR0 4YY